D1617121

THE TRADITIONAL TEXT

OF THE

HOLY GOSPELS

Πᾶϲι
Τοῖϲ Ἁγίοιϲ ἐν Χριϲτῷ Ἰηϲοῦ

PHIL. i. 1

OXFORD : HORACE HART
PRINTER TO THE UNIVERSITY

THE

TRADITIONAL TEXT

OF THE

HOLY GOSPELS

VINDICATED AND ESTABLISHED

BY THE LATE

JOHN WILLIAM BURGON, B.D.

DEAN OF CHICHESTER

ARRANGED, COMPLETED, AND EDITED

BY

EDWARD MILLER, M.A.

LATE RECTOR OF BUCKNELL, OXON; EDITOR OF THE FOURTH EDITION OF DR. SCRIVENER'S
'PLAIN INTRODUCTION TO THE TEXTUAL CRITICISM OF THE NEW TESTAMENT'; AND
AUTHOR OF 'A GUIDE TO THE TEXTUAL CRITICISM OF THE NEW TESTAMENT'

DEAN BURGON SOCIETY PRESS
Box 354
Collingswood, New Jersey 08108

LONDON
GEORGE BELL AND SONS
CAMBRIDGE: DEIGHTON, BELL AND CO.

1896

ISBN 1-888328-02-9

Published by

**The Dean Burgon Society Press
Box 354
Collingswood, New Jersey 08108
U.S.A.**

January, 1998

ISBN #1-888328-02-9

Foreword

The Publishers. This book, *The Traditional Text of the Holy Gospels*, is published by the Dean Burgon Society, Incorporated (DBS). The Society takes its name from Dean John William Burgon (1813-1888), a conservative Anglican clergyman. The DBS is recognized by the I.R.S. as a non-profit, tax exempt organization. All contributions are tax deductible. The Society's main purpose is stated in its slogan, **"IN DEFENSE OF TRADITIONAL BIBLE TEXTS."** The DBS was founded in 1978, and, since then, has held its annual two-day conference in the United States and Canada. During this time, many excellent messages defending the King James Bible and its underlying Hebrew and Greek texts have been presented. The messages are available in three forms: (1) video cassettes; (2) audio cassettes, and (3) the printed message books. For information on receiving any of the above, plus a copy of the *"THE ARTICLES OF FAITH, AND ORGANIZATION"* of the Dean Burgon Society, please write or phone the office at **609-854-4452**. You may use your CREDIT CARD if you wish, and send your order by **FAX** at **609-854-2464** or by **E-Mail** at **DBSN@Juno.Com**.

The Dean Burgon News. The Society has a paper called *The Dean Burgon News*. It comes out from time to time, as the Lord provides the time and the funds. Within its pages the *News* proclaims:

"The DEAN BURGON SOCIETY, INCORPORATED proudly takes its name in honor of John William Burgon (1813-1888), the Dean of Chichester in England, whose tireless and accurate scholarship and contribution in the area of New Testament Textual Criticism; whose defense of the Traditional Greek Text against its many enemies; and whose firm belief in the verbal inspiration and inerrancy of the Bible, we believe, have all been unsurpassed either before or since his time!"

The Present Reprint. The DEAN BURGON SOCIETY, INCORPORATED is pleased to present, in this form, another of Dean John William Burgon's most convincing books, *The Traditional Text of the Holy Gospels*. This is the third reprint of one of Dean Burgon's books. The first book was *The Last Twelve Verses of Mark*, available as #1139 for a GIFT of **$15** + **$4** for postage and handling. The second book was *The Revision Revised*, available as #611 for a GIFT of **$25** + **$4** for postage and handling. This third book, *The Traditioinal Text*, is page for page like the original book written in 1896 by Dean Burgon, and edited after his death by Rev. Edward Miller. In the **APPENDIX** you will find a 34-page summarization of the main points brought out in the book. It is fully indexed for easy reference. You might want to begin by reading the **APPENDIX** first.

The Importance of *The Traditional Text*. As these pages are being reprinted, there is a battle over the Bible that is raging in liberal, neo-evangelical, and even many fundamental churches, schools, colleges, universities, and seminaries. One of the most recurring falsehoods that is used by the enemies of the Greek Traditional Text or Received Text is the almost unbelievable falsehood that that Greek text was not in existence until 1516 A.D. with Erasmus. This volume thunders out an effective reply to the serious errors of this false position. It proves beyond any reasonable doubt that that Traditional Text was in the hands of the churches in a continuous time line from the original Apostolic times down to the present. The false text of Vatican and Sinai ("B" and "Aleph") cannot make this boast.

Other Books by Dean Burgon. For those wanting to read four other excellent reprints, the following can be ordered from THE DEAN BURGON SOCIETY:

1. *The Last Twelve Verses of Mark*, 400 pages, perfect bound book for a gift of **$15.00**.
2. *The Revision Revised*, 640 pp. hardback for a gift of **$25.00**.
3. *Yhe Causes of Corruption of the Holy Gospels*, 360 pages, hardback for a gift of **$15.00**.
4. *Inspiration and Interpretation*, 567 pages, zeroxed format for a gift of **$25.00**.

Please add **$4.00** or **15%** (whichever is greater) for postage & handling.

Future Reprints. As funds permit, the DEAN BURGON SOCI-ETY hopes to bring into reprint form in book format *Inspiration and Interpretation*and many more books on similar themes.

Sincerely for God's Written Words,

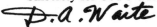

DAW/w`

Rev. D. A. Waite, Th.D., Ph.D.
President, THE DEAN BURGON SOCIETY

**The
Dean Burgon
Society**
In Defense of Traditional Bible Texts
**Box 354
Collingswood, NJ 08108, U.S.A.**

Dean John William Burgon
(1813--1888)

'Tenet ecclesia nostra, tenuitque semper firmam illam et immotam Tertulliani regulam "Id verius quod prius, id prius quod ab initio." Quo propius ad veritatis fontem accedimus, eo purior decurrit Catholicae doctrinae rivus.'

Cave's Proleg. p. xliv.

'Interrogate de semitis antiquis quae sit via bona, et ambulate in eâ.'—Jerem. vi. 16.

' In summa, si constat id verius quod prius, id prius quod ab initio, id ab initio quod ab Apostolis; pariter utique constabit, id esse ab Apostolis traditum, quod apud Ecclesias Apostolorum fuerit sacrosanctum.'—Tertull. adv. Marc. l. iv. c. 5.

PREFACE

—٠—

THE death of Dean Burgon in 1888, lamented
by a large number of people on the other side
of the Atlantic as well as on this, cut him off
in the early part of a task for which he had
made preparations during more than thirty years.
He laid the foundations of his system with
much care and caution, discussing it with his
friends, such as the late Earl of Selborne to whom
he inscribed The Last Twelve Verses, and the
present Earl of Cranbrook to whom he dedicated
The Revision Revised, for the purpose of sounding
the depths of the subject, and of being sure that
he was resting upon firm rock.   In order to enlarge
the general basis of Sacred Textual Criticism,
and to treat of the principles of it scientifically
and comprehensively, he examined manuscripts
widely, making many discoveries at home and
in foreign libraries ; collated some himself and
got many collated by other scholars ; encouraged new and critical editions of some of the
chief Versions ; and above all, he devised and
superintended a collection of quotations from the
New Testament to be found in the works of the
Fathers and in other ecclesiastical writings, going

far beyond ordinary indexes, which may be found
in sixteen thick volumes amongst the treasures of
the British Museum. Various events led him
during his life-time to dip into and publish some
of his stores, such as in his Last Twelve Verses
of St. Mark, his famous Letters to Dr. Scrivener
in the *Guardian* Newspaper, and in The Revision
Revised. But he sedulously amassed materials for
the greater treatise up to the time of his death.

He was then deeply impressed with the incomplete state of his documents; and gave positive
instructions solely for the publication of his Text
of the Gospels as marked in the margin of one
of Scrivener's editions of the New Testament, of
his disquisition on 'honeycomb' which as exhibiting
a specimen of his admirable method of criticism
will be found in Appendix I of this volume, and
perhaps of that on ὄξος in Appendix II, leaving
the entire question as to publishing the rest to
his nephew, the Rev. W. F. Rose, with the help of
myself, if I would undertake the editing required,
and of others.

The separate papers, which were committed to
my charge in February, 1889, were contained in
forty portfolios, and according to my catalogue
amounted to 2,383. They were grouped under
various headings, and some were placed in one
set as 'Introductory Matter' ready for the printer.
Most had been copied out in a clear hand, especially
by 'M. W.' mentioned in the Preface of the Revision
Revised, to whom also I am greatly indebted for
copying others. The papers were of lengths varying
from fourteen pages or more down to a single

sentence or a single reference. Some were almost duplicates, and a very few similarly triplicates.

After cataloguing, I reported to Mr. Rose, suggesting a choice between three plans, viz.,

1. Publishing separately according to the Dean's instructions such papers as were judged to be fit for publication, and leaving the rest :—

2. To put together a Work on the Principles of Textual Criticism out of the MSS., as far as they would go :—

3. To make up what was ready and fit into a Book, supplying from the rest of the materials and from elsewhere what was wanting besides filling up gaps as well as I could, and out of the rest (as well as from the Dean's published works) to construct brief notes on the Text which we had to publish.

This report was sent to Dr. Scrivener, Dean Goulburn, Sir Edward Maunde Thompson, and other distinguished scholars, and the unanimous opinion was expressed that the third of these plans should be adopted.

Not liking to encounter

Tot et tanta negotia solus,

I invited at the opening of 1890 the Rev. G. H. Gwilliam, Fellow of Hertford College, and the Rev. Dr. Waller, Principal of St. John's Hall, Highbury—a man of mathematical accuracy—to read over at my house the first draft of a large portion of Volume I. To my loss, Dr. Waller has been too busy since that time to afford me any help, except what may be found in his valuable

comparison of the texts of the Peshitto and Curetonian printed in Appendix VI : but Mr. Gwilliam
has been ready with advice and help all along
which have been of the greatest advantage to me
especially on the Syriac part of the subject, and
has looked through all the first proofs of this
volume.

It was afterwards forced upon my mind that if
possible the Indexes to the Fathers ought to be
included in the work. Indeed no book could ade-
quately represent Dean Burgon's labours which did
not include his *apparatus criticus* in that province of
Textual Criticism, in which he has shewn himself so
facile princeps, that no one in England, or Germany,
or elsewhere, has been as yet able to come near
him. With Sir E. Maunde Thompson's kind help,
I have been able to get the part of the Indexes
which relates to the Gospels copied in type-writing,
and they will be published in course of time, God
willing, if the learned world evinces sufficient interest
in the publication of them.

Unfortunately, when in 1890 I had completed
a first arrangement of Volume II, my health gave
way ; and after vainly endeavouring for a year to
combine this severe toil with the conduct of a living,
I resigned the latter, and moved into Oxford to
devote myself exclusively to the important work of
turning the unpublished results of the skilful faithfulness and the indefatigable learning of that 'grand
scholar'—to use Dr. Scrivener's phrase—towards
the settlement of the principles that should regulate
the ascertainment of the Divine Words constituting
the New Testament.

The difficulty to be surmounted lay in the fact that after all was gathered out of the Dean's remains that was suitable for the purpose, and when gaps of smaller or greater size were filled, as has been done throughout the series of unfinished and unconnected MSS., there was still a large space to cover without the Master's help in covering it.

Time and research and thought were alike necessary. Consequently, upon advice, I accepted an offer to edit the fourth edition of Scrivener's Plain Introduction, and although that extremely laborious accomplishment occupied far more time than was anticipated, yet in the event it has greatly helped the execution of my task. Never yet, before or since Dean Burgon's death, has there been such an opportunity as the present. The general *apparatus criticus* has been vastly increased; the field of palaeography has been greatly enlarged through the discoveries in Egypt; and there is a feeling abroad that we are on the brink of an improvement in systems and theories recently in vogue.

On returning to the work, I found that the key to the removal of the chief difficulty in the way of such improvement lay in an inflow of light upon what may perhaps be termed as to this subject the Pre-manuscriptal Period,—hitherto the dark age of Sacred Textualism, which precedes what was once 'the year one' of Palaeography. Accordingly, I made a toilsome examination for myself of the quotations occurring in the writings of the Fathers before St. Chrysostom, or as I defined them in order to draw a self-acting line, of those who died before 400 A.D., with the result that the Traditional

Text is found to stand in the general proportion of 3 : 2 against other variations, and in a much higher proportion upon thirty test passages. Afterwards, not being satisfied with resting the basis of my argument upon one scrutiny, I went again through the writings of the seventy-six Fathers concerned (with limitations explained in this book), besides others who yielded no evidence, and I found that although several more instances were consequently entered in my note-book, the general results remained almost the same. I do not flatter myself that even now I have recorded all the instances that could be adduced :—any one who is really acquainted with this work will know that such a feat is absolutely impossible, because such perfection cannot be obtained except after many repeated efforts. But I claim, not only that my attempts have been honest and fair even to self-abnegation, but that the general results which are much more than is required by my argument, as is explained in the body of this work, abundantly establish the antiquity of the Traditional Text, by proving the superior acceptance of it during the period at stake to that of any other.

Indeed, these examinations have seemed to me, not only to carry back the Traditional Text satisfactorily to the first age, but to lead also to solutions of several difficult problems, which are now presented to our readers. The wealth of MSS. to which the Fathers introduce us at second-hand can only be understood by those who may go through the writings of many of them with this view ; and outnumbers over and over again before

the year 1000 all the contemporaneous Greek
MSS. which have come down to us, not to speak of
the years to which no MSS. that are now extant
are in the opinion of all experts found to belong.

It is due both to Dean Burgon and to myself to
say that we came together after having worked on
independent lines, though I am bound to acknowledge my great debt to his writings. At first we
did not agree thoroughly in opinion, but I found
afterwards that he was right and I was wrong.
It is a proof of the unifying power of our principles, that as to our system there is now absolutely
no difference between us, though on minor points,
generally outside of this immediate subject, we do
not always exactly concur. Though I have the
Dean's example for altering his writings largely
even when they were in type, as he never failed
to do, yet in loyalty I have delayed alterations as
long as I could, and have only made them when
I was certain that I was introducing some improvement, and more often than not upon advice
proffered to me by others.

Our coincidence is perhaps explained by our
having been born when Evangelical earnestness
affected all religious life, by our having been trained
under the High Church movement, and at least in
my case mellowed under the more moderate widen-
ing caused by influences which prevailed in Oxford
for some years after 1848. Certainly, the com-
prehensiveness and exhaustiveness — probably in
imitation of German method—which had before
characterized Dr. Pusey's treatment of any subject,
and found an exemplification in Professor Freeman's

historical researches, and which was as I think to
be seen in the action of the best spirits of the
Oxford of 1848–56—to quote my own experience,
—lay at the root and constituted the life of
Burgon's system, and the maintenance of these
principles so far as we could at whatever cost
formed the link between us. To cast away at
least nineteen-twentieths of the evidence on points
and to draw conclusions from the petty remainder,
seems to us to be necessarily not less even than
a crime and a sin, not only by reason of the
sacrilegious destructiveness exercised thereby upon
Holy Writ, but also because such a method is
inconsistent with conscientious exhaustiveness and
logical method. Perfectly familiar with all that
can be and is advanced in favour of such procedure, must we not say that hardly any worse
pattern than this in investigations and conclusions
could be presented before young men at the critical
time when they are entering upon habits of forming
judgements which are to carry them through life?
Has the over-specialism which has been in vogue
of late years promoted the acceptance of the theory
before us, because it may have been under special-
izing influences forgotten, that the really accomplished man should aim at knowing something of
everything else as well as knowing everything
of the thing to which he is devoted, since narrowness in investigation and neglect of all but a favourite theory is likely to result from so exclusive an
attitude?

The importance of the question at stake is often
underrated. Dr. Philip Schaff in his well-known

'Companion' (p. 176),—as Dr. E. Nestle of Ulm in one of his brochures ('Ein ceterum censeo zur neutestamentlichen Textkritik') which he has kindly sent me, has pointed out,—observes that whereas Mill reckoned the variations to amount to 30,000, and Scrivener supposed that they have since increased to four times as much, they 'cannot now fall much short of 150,000.' This amount is appalling, and most of them are of a petty character. But some involve highly important passages, and even Hort has reckoned (Introduction, p. 2) that the disputed instances reach about one-eighth of the whole. Is it too strong therefore to say, that we live over a volcano, with a crust of earth of not too great a thickness lying between?

The first half of our case is now presented in this Volume, which is a complete treatise in itself. A second will I hope follow at an early date, containing a disquisition on the Causes of the Corruption of the Traditional Text; and, I am glad to say, will consist almost exclusively of Dean Burgon's own compositions. I ask from Critics who may not assent to all our conclusions a candid consideration of our case, which is rested solely upon argument and reason throughout. This explanation made by the Dean of his system in calmer times and in a more didactic form cannot, as I think, fail to remove much prejudice. If we seem at first sight anywhere to leap from reasoning to dogmatism, our readers will discover, I believe, upon renewed observation that at least from our point of view that is not so. If we appear to speak too positively, we have done this, not from confidence in any private judgement, but because we are sure, at least in our own minds, that we express the verdict of all the ages and all the countries.

May the great Head of the Church bless our effort on behalf of the integrity of His Holy Word, if not according to our plan and purpose, yet in the way that seemeth Him best!

EDWARD MILLER.

9 BRADMORE ROAD, OXFORD:
Epiphany 1896.

CONTENTS.

—••—

INTRODUCTION.

PAGE

Sacred Textual Criticism—introduced by Origen—settled first in the fourth and before the eighth centuries—fresh rise after the invention of printing — infancy — childhood — youth—incipient maturity — Traditional Text not identical with the Received Text . . . pp. 1-5

CHAPTER I.

PRELIMINARY GROUNDS.

§ 1. Importance of the subject—need of new advance and of candour in investigation. § 2. Sacred Textual Criticism different from Profane — the New Testament assailed from the first. § 3. Overruling Providence—unique conditions, and overwhelming mass of evidence. § 4. Authority of the Church — Hort's admission — existence and descent of the Received Text. § 5. The question one of the many against the few—the plea of antiquity on the side of the few virtually a claim to subtle divination—impossibility of compromise . . pp. 6-18

CHAPTER II.

PRINCIPLES.

§ 1. Two chief branches of inquiry—collection of evidence—employment of evidence. § 2. Providential multiplication of Copies, ordinary and lectionary—of Versions—of Patristic quotations. § 3. Similarity between later Uncials and Cursives—overestimate of the oldest Uncials —Copies the most important class of evidence—but not so old virtually as the earliest Versions and Fathers. § 4. Search for the readings of the autographs—the better attested, the genuine reading—need of tests or notes of truth—seven proposed. § 5. Mere antiquity of an authority not enough—yet antiquity a most important principle. § 6. ' Various readings' a misleading phrase—Corruption patent in B and ℵ—four proofs that their text, not the Traditional, has been fabricated — Scrivener's mistake in supposing that the true texts must be sought in the oldest uncials—their constant disagreement with one another— self-impoverishment of some Critics . . . . . . pp. 19-39

CHAPTER III.

The Seven Notes of Truth.

PAGE

§ 1. Antiquity :—the more ancient, probably the better testimony— but not the sole arbiter. § 2. Number :—much fallacy in ' vitnesses are to be weighed not counted'—used to champion the very few against the very many—number necessarily a powerful, but not the sole note of truth—Heb. iv. 2. § 3. Variety :—a great help to Number— various countries—various ages—no collusion—St. Matt. x. 8. § 4. Weight, or Respectability :—witnesses must be (1) respectable—(2) MSS. must not be transcripts of one another—(3) Patristic evidence must not be copied—(4) MSS. from one archetype = between one and two copies— (5) any collusion impairs weight—(6) a Version outweighs any single MS.—(7) also a Father—weight of single MSS. to be determined by peculiar characteristics. § 5. Continuity :—value of Unbroken Tradition — weakening effects of smaller chasms — fatal consequence of the admitted chasm of fifteen centuries. § 6. Context :—(a) Context of meaning— 1 Cor. xiii. 5—(b) Context of readings—St. Matt. xvii. 21— xi. 2-3 and St. Luke vii. 19—consistency in immediate context . pp. 40–67

CHAPTER IV.

The Vatican and Sinaitic Manuscripts.

§ 1. The seven Old Uncials—some understanding necessary between the two schools— dialogue with a Biblical Student— the superior antiquity of B and א a reasonable presumption that they are the purest— yet nearly 300 years between them and the autographs—no proof that their archetype was much older than they—conflict with the evidence of Versions and Fathers which are virtually much older—any superior excellence in their text merely the opinion of one school balanced by the other—Mai's editions of B—antiquity, number, variety, and continuity against that school—also weight—Traditional Text virtually older— proof that the text of B and א was derived from the Traditional text, not *vice versa*—alleged recensions no proof to the contrary—nor ' con- flation,' proved to be unsound—their disagreement with one another proved by passages. § 2. St. John v. 4—St. Luke xi. 2-4. § 3. The ' Marys' of the Gospels. § 4. Jona and John. § 5. The foregoing instances typical—our appeal only to facts .   .   .   .   . pp. 68–89

CHAPTER V.

The Antiquity of the Traditional Text.

I. *Witness of the Early Fathers.*

§ 1. Involuntary witness of Dr. Hort :—though he denied the antiquity of the Traditional Text—no detailed examination of Dr. Hort's theory intended in this didactic treatise—his admission that we have the period

PAGE

of the Church since St. Chrysostom—driven to label the evidence of those centuries with the unhappy epithet ' Syrian '—foisting into history his ' phantom recensions '—facts, not theory. § 2. Testimony of the Ante-Chrysostom Writers :—two examinations made of all their quotations of the Gospels—trustworthiness of their writings on this point—many of their quotations not capable of use—general list—proportion of 3 : 2 for Traditional Text—verdict of those Writers on thirty test passages—proportion of 3 : 1—validity of these lists—mistakes of Hort and others respecting separate Fathers—antiquity of corruption, though subordinate, also established — list of Early Traditional deponents—Later Traditional—Western or Syrio-Low-Latin—Alexandrian—lessons from these groups . . . . pp. 90–122

CHAPTER VI.

THE ANTIQUITY OF THE TRADITIONAL TEXT.

II. *Witness of the Early Syriac Versions.*

Startling rise of Christianity in Syria — weakness of Cureton's arguments for the superior antiquity of the Curetonian—not helped by the heretical Lewis Codex—the idea of a Vulgate Peshitto founded upon a false parallel—traced to the fifth century by the universal use of the Peshitto by Nestorians, Monophysites, Christians of St. Thomas, and Maronites—very early date proved by numerous MSS. of the same period—attested in the fourth by Ephraem Syrus and Aphraates—must have been in existence before—proved back by its agreement with the Traditional Text—the petty Curetonian an unequal combatant—objection that the Text of the Curetonian and Lewis was the older—inaccurate advocacy of the Lewis—the age of these MSS. to be decided by the known facts — Mepharreshe or distinct Gospels to replace the Mehallete or mixed Gospels of Tatian . . . . pp. 123–134

CHAPTER VII.

THE ANTIQUITY OF THE TRADITIONAL TEXT.

III. *Witness of the Western or Syrio-Low-Latin Text.*

Wiseman wrong in supposing that all Old Latin Texts came from one stem—the *prima facie* inference from similarity of language open to delusion—contrast of other Versions—table of the Old Latin MSS., as

CONTENTS.

used by Tischendorf—no very generic difference—comparison under
the thirty test passages—variety of synonyms denotes variety of
sources—direct evidence of Augustine and Jerome—translations must
have been made by all who wanted them in the bilingual· Roman
Empire—origin of Wiseman's idea in an etymological blunder—Diez's
subsequent teaching—the deflection in the language of the Old Latin
MSS. due to the Low-Latin dialects of the Italian Peninsula, the
'Itala' of St. Augustine being in the most classical of later Latin—
Syriacization of the Codex Bezae, and the teaching of the Ferrar
group—pre-Evangelistic corruption carried to Rome from Antioch, and
afterwards foisted into the Gospels—the Synoptic problem—the
Traditional Text thus attested from the first by Fathers and
Versions.' . . . . pp. 135-147

CHAPTER VIII.

ALEXANDRIA AND CAESAREA.

§ 1. Alexandrian Readings, and the Alexandrian School :—Text, or
Readings?—list of early Alexandrian Fathers—the thirty test passages
in Bohairic—no Alexandrian MSS.· of the period—instability—Origen
the leading figure—elemental and critical—the cradle of criticism.
§ 2. Caesarean School :—dates from 231 A.D., when Origen moved to
Caesarea—his witness to both texts—Pamphilus—Eusebius really
prefers the Traditional—Palestine a central situation—coalition of
readings—Eusebius' fifty MSS. probably included all sorts—Acacius
more probably the scribe of B, and of the six leaves of א—vellum came
into prominent use at Caesarea—an Asiatic product—older MSS.
written on papyrus—papyrus used till the tenth century—cursive hand
on papyrus led to the 'Cursives' . . . . . . pp. 148-158

CHAPTER IX.

THE OLD UNCIALS. THE INFLUENCE OF ORIGEN.

§ 1. Superstitious deference to B—and א— products of the Semi-Arian
or Homoean School—(1) dated from that time—(2) condemned when
Arianism was finally condemned—(3) agree with Origenism—(4) produced at Alexandria—colophons in א under Esther and Ezra, and
agreement with Codex Pamphili — written accordingly at Caesarea.
§ 2. Origen :—his writings much studied by the ancients—of the same
class as B and א, proved from various passages—Gal. iii. 1—St. Matt.
xiv. 19, xv. 35—St. John xiii. 26—St. Luke iv. 8—St. John viii. 38.
§ 3. Sceptical character of all the three . . . . . pp. 159-171

CHAPTER X.

THE OLD UNCIALS. CODEX D.

§ 1. Parallel and connexion between the settlements of the Canon and the Text—end of the controversy after the last General Council—Origenism finally condemned then — no rest in Roman Empire till then—the art of writing on vellum then perfected—existence of better copies than B and ℵ during the early Uncial period—A, Φ, and Σ. § 2. Codex D :—strange character—I. Assimilation on a large scale—St. Mark iii. 26—St. Luke xix. 27—St. Matt. xx. 28—St. Luke xiv. 8–10—II. Extreme licentiousness—St. Mark iv. 1. § 3. St. Luke iii. 23–38. § 4. St. Luke xxii. 20, and St. Mark xv. 43-4. § 5. St. Luke i. 65—St. Mark xiv. 72. &c. § 6. Bad features in D and its family. § 7. Clumsiness and tastelessness in the Old Uncials. § 8. St. John ix. 36, xiv. 22, St. Matt. i. 18, St. Luke xviii. 14, St. John xvii. 2 – delicate points thus rubbed off . . . . pp. 172–195

CHAPTER XI.

THE LATER UNCIALS AND THE CURSIVES.

§ 1. Nature of Tradition — many streams—great period of the two St. Gregories, St. Basil, and St. Chrysostom—Canon of St. Augustine—Uncials and Cursives do not differ in kind—Cursives different enough to be independent witnesses— not copies of Cod. A—a small minority of real dissentients—era of greater perfection from end of seventh century—expression by the majority of later Uncials and the Cursives of the settled judgement of the Church. § 2. The text of the Cursives not debased—(1) the Traditional Text already proved to go back to the first—(2) could not have been formed out of non-existing materials—(3) superior to the text of B and ℵ—proved by the consentience of Copies, Versions, Fathers, and superior under all the Notes of Truth. § 3. St. Luke xix. 42. § 4. St. Matt. xx. 22-23. § 5. St. Matt. iv. 17-22, St. Mark i. 14-20, St. Luke v. 1-11. § 6. St. Mark x. 23-24. § 7. St. Luke xvi. 9. § 8. St. John xvi. 13. § 9. St. Matt. viii. 5-13. § 10. St. Luke xx. 14. § 11. Familiarity through *collation* with the Cursive copies will reveal the general excellence of their text . pp. 196-223

CHAPTER XII.

CONCLUSION.

Recapitulation—*quod semper, quod ubique, quod ab omnibus*, the principle of the Traditional Text—an exhaustive case—and very strong —answers to objections — (1) antiquity of B and ℵ — (2) witnesses must be weighed first — (3) charge of conflation, Eph. v. 30—weak

pleas — (4) Genealogy explained — only true in a limited measure—
reduces some groups of MSS. to one archetype each—advance of this
plea solely as an excuse for B and ℵ—which were founders of an
obscure family dating from Caesarea, with huge gaps in their descent—
perfect genealogy of the Traditional Text through many lines of descent
—attested contemporaneously by numerous Fathers—proved step by
step back to the earliest days—the Traditional Text contrasted with
the Neologian in three ways, viz.—(I) wide and deep against narrowness—(II) founded on facts, not on speculation—(III) increasing now
in strength, instead of daily getting out of date—the verdict of the
Church, and therefore RESTING ON THE ROCK .   .   .   .   pp. 224–239

APPENDIX I.
HONEYCOMB—ἀπὸ μελισσίου κηρίου .   .   .   .   .   pp. 240–252

APPENDIX II.
Ὄξος—VINEGAR   .   .   .   .   pp. 253–258

APPENDIX III.
THE RICH YOUNG MAN   .   .   .   .   .   .   pp. 259–278

APPENDIX IV.
ST. MARK I. I. .   .   .   .   pp. 279–286

APPENDIX V.
THE SCEPTICAL CHARACTER OF B AND ℵ .   .   pp. 287–291

APPENDIX VI.
THE PESHITTO AND CURETONIAN   .   .   .   .   pp. 292–297

APPENDIX VII.
THE LAST TWELVE VERSES OF ST. MARK'S GOSPEL
pp. 298–307

APPENDIX VIII.
NEW EDITIONS OF THE PESHITTO-SYRIAC AND THE
    HARKLEIAN VERSIONS .   .   .   .   .   .   pp. 308–309

GENERAL INDEX .   .   .   .   pp. 311–315

INDEX OF PASSAGES OF THE NEW TESTAMENT
    COMMENTED ON   .   .   .   .   pp. 316–317

THE TRADITIONAL TEXT OF THE NEW TESTAMENT.

INTRODUCTION.

A FEW remarks at the outset of this treatise, which was left imperfect by Dean Burgon at his unexpected death, may make the object and scope of it more intelligible to many readers.

Textual Criticism of the New Testament is a close inquiry into what is the genuine Greek—the true text of the Holy Gospels, of the Acts of the Apostles, of the Pauline and Apostolic Epistles, and the Revelation. Inasmuch as it concerns the text alone, it is confined to the Lower Criticism according to German nomenclature, just as a critical examination of meaning, with all its attendant references and connexions, would constitute the Higher Criticism. It is thus the necessary prelude of any scientific investigation of the language, the purport, and the teaching of the various books of the New Testament, and ought itself to be conducted upon definite and scientific principles. The object of this treatise is to lead to a general settlement of those principles. For this purpose the Dean has stripped the discussion of all adventitious disguise, and has pursued it lucidly into manifold details, in order that no

B

employment of difficult terms or involved sentences may shed any mystification over the questions discussed, and that all intelligent people who are interested in such questions—and who is not?—may understand the issues and the proofs of them.

In the very earliest times much variation in the text of the New Testament, and particularly of the Holy Gospels—for we shall treat mainly of these four books as constituting the most important province, and as affording a smaller area, and so being more convenient for the present inquiry:—much diversity in words and expression, I say, arose in the Church. In consequence, the school of scientific Theology at Alexandria, in the person of Origen, first found it necessary to take cognizance of the matter. When Origen moved to Caesarea, he carried his manuscripts with him, and they appear to have formed the foundation of the celebrated library in that city, which was afterwards amplified by Pamphilus and Eusebius, and also by Acacius and Euzoius[1], who were all successively bishops of the place. During the life of Eusebius, if not under his controlling care, the two oldest Uncial Manuscripts in existence as hitherto discovered, known as B and ℵ, or the Vatican and Sinaitic, were executed in handsome form and exquisite caligraphy. But shortly after, about the middle of the fourth century—as both schools of Textual Critics agree—a text differing from that of B and ℵ advanced in general acceptance ; and, increasing till the eighth century in the predominance won by the end of the fourth, became so prevalent in Christendom, that the small number of MSS. agreeing with B and ℵ forms no sort of comparison with the many which vary from those two. Thus the problem of the fourth century anticipated the problem of the nine-

[1] See Jerome, Epist. 34 (Migne, xxii. p. 448). Cod. V. of Philo has the following inscription :—Εὐζόϊος ἐπίσκοπος ἐν σωματίοις ἀνενεώσατο, i.e. transcribed on vellum from papyrus. Leopold Cohn's edition of Philo, De Opificiis Mundi, Vratislaw, 1889.

teenth. Are we for the genuine text of the New Testament to go to the Vatican and the Sinaitic MSS. and the few others which mainly agree with them, or are we to follow the main body of New Testament MSS., which by the end of the century in which those two were produced entered into possession of the field of contention, and have continued in occupation of it ever since? This is the problem which the following treatise is intended to solve, that is to say, which of these two texts or sets of readings is the better attested, and can be traced back through the stronger evidence to the original autographs.

A few words are now needed to describe and account for the present position of the controversy.

After the discovery of printing in Europe, Textual Criticism began to rise again. The career of it may be divided into four stages, which may be termed respectively, Infancy, Childhood, Youth, and Incipient Maturity[1].

I. Erasmus in 1516 edited the New Testament from a very small number of manuscripts, probably only five, in repute at the time; and six years afterwards appeared the Complutensian edition under Cardinal Ximenes, which had been printed two years before that of Erasmus. Robert Stephen, Theodore Beza, and the Elzevirs, also, as is well known, published editions of their own. In the latter edition of the Elzevirs, issued in 1633, occurred for the first time the widely-used expression 'Textus Receptus.' The sole object in this period was to adhere faithfully to the text received everywhere.

II. In the next, evidence from Manuscripts, Versions, and Fathers was collected, chiefly by Mill and Wetstein. Bentley thought of going back to the fourth century for decisive evidence. Bengel and Griesbach laid stress upon families and recensions of manuscripts, and led the way in departing

---

[1] See my Guide to the Textual Criticism of the New Testament, pp. 7–37. George Bell and Sons, 1886.

from the received standard. Collation of manuscripts was carried on by these two critics and by other able scholars, and largely by Scholz. There was thus an amplification of materials, and a crop of theories. Much that was vague and elemental was intermingled with a promise of a great deal that would prove more satisfactory in the future.

III. The leader in the next advance was Lachmann, who began to discard the readings of the Received Text, supposing it to be only two centuries old. Authorities having already become inconveniently multitudinous, he limited his attention to the few which agreed with the oldest Uncials, namely, L or the Regius at Paris, one or two other fragments of Uncials, a few Cursives, the Old Latin Manuscripts, and a few of the oldest Fathers, making up generally some six or seven in all upon each separate reading. Tischendorf, the discoverer of א, the twin-sister of B, and the collator of a large number of MSS.[1], followed him in the main, as did also Tregelles. And Dr. Hort, who, with Bishop Westcott, began to theorize and work when Lachmann's influence was at the highest, in a most ingenious and elaborate Introduction maintained the cause of the two oldest Uncials—especially B—and their small band of followers. Admitting that the Received Text dates back as far as the middle of the fourth century, Hort argued that it was divided by more than two centuries and a half from the original Autographs, and in fact took its rise at Antioch and should be called 'Syrian,' notwithstanding the predominance which he acknowledged that it has enjoyed since the end of the fourth century. He termed the readings of which B and א are the chief exponents 'the Neutral Text,' and held that that text can be traced back to the genuine Autographs[2].

[1] For an estimate of Tischendorf's great labour, see an article on Tischendorf's Greek Testament in the Quarterly Review for July, 1895.

[2] Dr. Hort's theory, which is generally held to supply the philosophical explanation of the tenets maintained in the school of critics who support B

IV. I have placed the tenets of the opposite school last as exhibiting signs of Incipient Maturity in the Science, not because they are admitted to be so, that being not the case, but because of their intrinsic merits, which will be unfolded in this volume, and because of the immense addition recently made of authorities to our store, as well as on account of the indirect influence exercised of late by discoveries pursued in other quarters [1]. Indeed, it is sought to establish a wider stock of ruling authorities, and a sounder method in the use of them. The leaders in the advocacy of this system have been Dr. Scrivener in a modified degree, and especially Dean Burgon. First, be it understood, that we do not advocate perfection in the Textus Receptus. We allow that here and there it requires revision. In the Text left behind by Dean Burgon [2], about 150 corrections have been suggested by him in St. Matthew's Gospel alone. What we maintain is the TRADITIONAL TEXT. And we trace it back to the earliest ages of which there is any record. We trust to the fullest testimony and the most enlightened view of all the evidence. In humble dependence upon God the Holy Ghost, Who we hold has multiplied witnesses all down the ages of the Church, and Whose cause we believe we plead, we solemnly call upon those many students of the Bible in these days who are earnest after truth to weigh without prejudice what we say, in the prayer that it may contribute something towards the ascertainment of the true expressions employed in the genuine Word of GOD.

and ℵ as pre-eminently the sources of the correct text, may be studied in his Introduction. It is also explained and controverted in my Textual Guide, pp. 38-59; and has been powerfully criticized by Dean Burgon in The Revision Revised, Article III, or in No. 306 of the Quarterly Review, without reply.

[1] Quarterly Review, July 1895, 'Tischendorf's Greek Testament.'
[2] See Preface.

CHAPTER I.

§ 1.

IN the ensuing pages I propose to discuss a problem of the highest dignity and importance [1] : namely, On what principles the true text of the New Testament Scriptures is to be ascertained? My subject is the Greek text of those Scriptures, particularly of the four Gospels; my object, the establishment of that text on an intelligible and trustworthy basis.

That no fixed principles were known to exist before 1880 is proved by the fact that the most famous critics not only differed considerably from one another, but also from themselves. Till then all was empiricism in this department. A section, a chapter, an article, a pamphlet, a tentative essay—all these indeed from time to time appeared : and some were excellent of their kind. But we require something a vast deal more methodical, argumentative, and

---

[1] It is remarkable, that in quarters where we should have looked for more scientific procedure the importance of the Textual Criticism of the New Testament is underrated, upon a plea that theological doctrine may be established upon passages other than those of which the text has been impugned by the destructive school. Yet (a) in all cases consideration of the text of an author must perforce precede consideration of inferences from the text—Lower Criticism must be the groundwork of Higher Criticism ; (b) confirmatory passages cannot be thrown aside in face of attacks upon doctrine of every possible character; (c) Holy Scripture is too unique and precious to admit of the study of the several words of it being interesting rather than important; (d) many of the passages which Modern Criticism would erase or suspect—such as the last Twelve Verses of St. Mark, the first Word from the Cross, and the thrilling description of the depth of the Agony, besides numerous others—are valuable in the extreme ; and, (e) generally speaking, it is impossible to pronounce, especially amidst the thought and life seething everywhere round us, what part of Holy Scripture is not, or may not prove to be, of the highest importance as well as interest.—E. M.

complete, than is compatible with such narrow limits. Even where an account of the facts was extended to greater length and was given with much fullness and accuracy, there was an absence of scientific principle sufficient to guide students to a satisfactory and sound determination of difficult questions. Tischendorf's last two editions differ from one another in no less than 3,572 particulars. He reverses in every page in 1872 what in 1859 he offered as the result of his deliberate judgement. Every one, to speak plainly, whether an expert or a mere beginner, seemed to consider himself competent to pass sentence on any fresh reading which is presented to his notice. We were informed that 'according to all principles of sound criticism' this word is to be retained, that to be rejected: but till the appearance of the dissertation of Dr. Hort no one was so obliging as to tell us what the principles are to which reference is confidently made, and by the loyal application of which we might have arrived at the same result for ourselves. And Hort's theory, as will be shewn further on, involves too much violation of principles generally received, and is too devoid of anything like proof, ever to win universal acceptance. As matters of fact easily verified, it stands in sharp antagonism to the judgement passed by the Church all down the ages, and in many respects does not accord with the teaching of the most celebrated critics of the century who preceded him.

I trust I shall be forgiven, if in the prosecution of the present inquiry I venture to step out of the beaten track, and to lead my reader forward in a somewhat humbler style than has been customary with my predecessors. Whenever they have entered upon the consideration of principles, they have always begun by laying down on their own authority a set of propositions, some of which so far from being axiomatic are repugnant to our judgement and are found as they stand to be even false. True

that I also shall have to begin by claiming assent to a few
fundamental positions : but then I venture to promise that
these shall all be self-evident.   I am very much mistaken
if they do not also conduct us to results differing greatly
from those which have been recently in favour with many
of the most forward writers and teachers.

Beyond all things I claim at every thoughtful reader's
hands that he will endeavour to approach this subject
in an impartial frame of mind.   To expect that he will
succeed in divesting himself of all preconceived notions as
to what is likely, what not, were unreasonable.   But he is
invited at least to wear his prejudices as loose about him
as he can ; to be prepared to cast them off if at any time
he has been shewn that they are founded on misapprehension ; to resolve on taking nothing for granted which
admits of being proved to be either true or false.   And,
to meet an objection which is sure to be urged against
me, by proof of course I do but mean the nearest approach
to demonstration, which in the present subject-matter is
attainable.

Thus, I request that, apart from proof of some sort,
it shall not be taken for granted that a copy of the New
Testament written in the fourth or fifth century will
exhibit a more trustworthy text than one written in the
eleventh or twelfth.   That indeed of two ancient documents
the more ancient might not unreasonably have been expected
to prove the more trustworthy, I am not concerned to
dispute, and will not here discuss such a question ; but the
probabilities of the case at all events are not axiomatic.
Nay, it will be found, as I am bold enough to say, that in
many instances a fourteenth-century copy of the Gospels
may exhibit the truth of Scripture, while the fourth-century
copy in all these instances proves to be the depositary of
a fabricated text.   I have only to request that, until the
subject has been fully investigated, men will suspend their

judgement on this head : taking nothing for granted which admits of proof, and regarding nothing as certainly either true or false which has not been shewn to be so.

§ 2.

That which distinguishes Sacred Science from every other Science which can be named is that it is Divine, and has to do with a Book which is inspired ; that is, whose true Author is God. For we assume that the Bible is to be taken as inspired, and not regarded upon a level with the Books of the East, which are held by their votaries to be sacred. It is chiefly from inattention to this circumstance that misconception prevails in that department of Sacred Science known as ' Textual Criticism.' Aware that the New Testament is like no other book in its origin, its contents, its history, many critics of the present day nevertheless permit themselves to reason concerning its Text, as if they entertained no suspicion that the words and sentences of which it is composed were destined to experience an extraordinary fate also. They make no allowances for the fact that influences of an entirely different kind from any with which profane literature is acquainted have made themselves felt in this department, and therefore that even those principles of Textual Criticism which in the case of profane authors are regarded as fundamental are often out of place here.

It is impossible that all this can be too clearly apprehended. In fact, until those who make the words of the New Testament their study are convinced that they move in a region like no other, where unique phenomena await them at every step, and where seventeen hundred and fifty years ago depraving causes unknown in every other department of learning were actively at work, progress cannot really be made in the present discussion. Men must by all means disabuse their minds of the prejudices which the study of profane literature inspires. Let me explain this matter a little more particularly, and establish the reasonableness of what has gone before by a few plain considerations which must, I think, win assent. I am not about to offer opinions, but only to appeal to certain undeniable facts. What I deprecate, is not any discriminating use of reverent criticism, but a clumsy confusion of points essentially different.

No sooner was the work of Evangelists and Apostles recognized as the necessary counterpart and complement of God's ancient Scriptures and became the ' New Testament,' than a reception was found to be awaiting it in the world closely resembling that which He experienced Who is the subject of its pages. Calumny and misrepresentation, persecution and murderous hate, assailed Him continually. And the Written Word in like manner, in the earliest age of all, was shamefully handled by mankind. Not only was it confused through human infirmity and misapprehension, but it became also the object of restless malice and unsparing assaults. Marcion, Valentinus, Basilides, Heracleon, Menander, Asclepiades, Theodotus, Hermophilus, Apollonides, and other heretics, adapted the Gospels to their own ideas. Tatian, and later on Ammonius, created confusion through attempts to combine the four Gospels either in a diatessaron or upon an intricate arrangement made by sections, under which as a further result the words of one Gospel became assimilated to those of another[1]. Want of familiarity with the sacred words in the first ages, carelessness of scribes, incompetent teaching, and ignorance of Greek in the West, led to further corruption of the Sacred Text. Then out of the fact that there existed a vast number of corrupt copies arose at once the need of Recension, which was carried on by Origen and his school. This was a fatal

---

[1] See below, Vol. II. throughout, and a remarkable passage quoted from Caius or Gaius by Dean Burgon in The Revision Revised (Quarterly Review, No. 306), pp. 323-324.

necessity to have made itself felt in an age when the first principles of the Science were not understood ; for 'to correct' was too often in those days another word for 'to corrupt.' And this is the first thing to be briefly explained and enforced : but more than a counterbalance was provided under the overruling Providence of God.

§ 3.

Before our Lord ascended up to Heaven, He told His disciples that He would send them the Holy Ghost, Who should supply His place and abide with His Church for ever. He added a promise that it should be the office of that inspiring Spirit not only 'to bring to their remembrance all things whatsoever He had told them [1],' but also to 'guide' His Church 'into all the Truth,' or, 'the whole Truth [2]' ($\pi\hat{\alpha}\sigma\alpha\nu$ $\tau\grave{\eta}\nu$ $\grave{\alpha}\lambda\acute{\eta}\theta\epsilon\iota\alpha\nu$). Accordingly, the earliest great achievement of those days was accomplished on giving to the Church the Scriptures of the New Testament, in which authorized teaching was enshrined in written form. And first, out of those many Gospels which incompetent persons had ' taken in hand' to write or to compile out of much floating matter of an oral or written nature, He guided them to discern that four were wholly unlike the rest—were the very Word of God.

There exists no reason for supposing that the Divine Agent, who in the first instance thus gave to mankind the Scriptures of Truth, straightway abdicated His office ; took no further care of His work ; abandoned those precious writings to their fate. That a perpetual miracle was wrought for their preservation—that copyists were protected against the risk of error, or evil men prevented from adulterating shamefully copies of the Deposit—no one, it is presumed, is so weak as to suppose. But it is quite a different thing to claim that all down the ages the sacred

[1] St. John xiv. 26.　　　　[2] St. John xvi. 13.

writings must needs have been God's peculiar care; that the Church under Him has watched over them with intelligence and skill; has recognized which copies exhibit a fabricated, which an honestly transcribed text; has generally sanctioned the one, and generally disallowed the other. I am utterly disinclined to believe—so grossly improbable does it seem—that at the end of 1800 years 995 copies out of every thousand, suppose, will prove untrustworthy; and that the one, two, three, four or five which remain, whose contents were till yesterday as good as unknown, will be found to have retained the secret of what the Holy Spirit originally inspired. I am utterly unable to believe, in short, that God's promise has so entirely failed, that at the end of 1800 years much of the text of the Gospel had in point of fact to be picked by a German critic out of a waste-paper basket in the convent of St. Catherine; and that the entire text had to be remodelled after the pattern set by a couple of copies which had remained in neglect during fifteen centuries, and had probably owed their survival to that neglect; whilst hundreds of others had been thumbed to pieces, and had bequeathed their witness to copies made from them.

I have addressed what goes before to persons who sympathize with me in my belief. To others the argument would require to be put in a different way. Let it then be remembered, that a wealth of copies existed in early times; that the need of zealous care of the Holy Scriptures was always felt in the Church; that it is only from the Church that we have learnt which are the books of the Bible and which are not; that in the age in which the Canon was settled, and which is presumed by many critics to have introduced a corrupted text, most of the intellect of the Roman Empire was found within the Church, and was directed upon disputed questions; that in the succeeding ages the art of transcribing was brought

to a high pitch of perfection ; and that the verdict of all
the several periods since the production of those two
manuscripts has been given till a few years ago in favour
of the Text which has been handed down :—let it be further
borne in mind that the testimony is not only that of all
the ages, but of all the countries : and at the very least so
strong a presumption will ensue on behalf of the Traditional
Text, that a powerful case indeed must be constructed to
upset it. It cannot be vanquished by theories grounded
upon internal considerations—often only another name for
personal tastes—, or for scholarly likes or dislikes, or upon
fictitious recensions, or upon any arbitrary choice of favourite
manuscripts, or upon a strained division of authorities into
families or groups, or upon a warped application of the
principle of genealogy. In the ascertainment of the facts
of the Sacred Text, the laws of evidence must be strictly
followed. In questions relating to the inspired Word, mere
speculation and unreason have no place. In short, the
Traditional Text, founded upon the vast majority of
authorities and upon the Rock of Christ's Church, will, if
I mistake not, be found upon examination to be out of all
comparison superior to a text of the nineteenth century,
whatever skill and ingenuity may have been expended upon
the production or the defence of it.

§ 4.

For due attention has never yet been paid to a circumstance which, rightly apprehended, will be found to go
a great way towards establishing the text of the New
Testament Scriptures on a solid basis. I refer to the fact
that a certain exhibition of the Sacred Text—that exhibition
of it with which we are all most familiar—rests on ecclesiastical authority. Speaking generally, the Traditional Text
of the New Testament Scriptures, equally with the New
Testament Canon, rests on the authority of the Church

Catholic. 'Whether we like it, or dislike it' (remarked a learned writer in the first quarter of the nineteenth century), 'the present New Testament Canon is neither more nor less than the probat of the orthodox Christian bishops, and those not only of the first and second, but of the third and fourth, and even subsequent centuries [1].' In like manner, whether men would or would not have it so, it is a plain fact that the Traditional Greek Text of the New Testament is neither more nor less than the probat of the orthodox Greek Christian bishops, and those, if not as we maintain of the first and second, or the third, yet unquestionably of the fourth and fifth, and even subsequent centuries.

For happily, the matter of fact here is a point on which the disciples of the most advanced of the modern school are entirely at one with us. Dr. Hort declares that 'The fundamental text of late extant Greek MSS. generally is, beyond all question, identical with the dominant Antiochian or Graeco-Syrian text of the second half of the fourth century. ... The bulk of extant MSS. written from about three or four to ten or eleven centuries later must have had in the greater number of extant variations a common original either contemporary with, or older than, our oldest MSS.[2]' And again, 'Before the close of the fourth century, as we have said, a Greek text, not materially differing from the almost universal text of the ninth century and the Middle Ages, was dominant, probably by authority, at Antioch, and exercised much influence elsewhere [3].' The mention of 'Antioch' is, characteristically of the writer, purely arbitrary. One and the same Traditional Text, except in comparatively few particulars, has prevailed in the Church from the beginning till now. Especially deserving of attention is the admission that the Text in

---

[1] Rev. John Oxlee's sermon on Luke xxii. 28–30 (1821), p. 91 (Three Sermons on the power, origin, and succession of the Christian Hierarchy, and especially that of the Church of England).

[2] Westcott and Hort, Introduction, p. 92.   [3] Ibid. p. 142.

question is of the fourth century, to which same century the two oldest of our Sacred Codexes (B and א) belong. There is observed to exist in Church Lectionaries precisely the same phenomenon. They have prevailed in unintermitted agreement in other respects from very early times, probably from the days of St. Chrysostom [1], and have kept in the main without change the form of words in which they were originally cast in the unchangeable East.

And really the problem comes before us (God be praised!) in a singularly convenient, a singularly intelligible form. Since the sixteenth century—we owe this also to the good Providence of God—one and the same text of the New Testament Scriptures has been generally received. I am not defending the 'Textus Receptus'; I am simply stating the fact of its existence. That it is without authority to bind, nay, that it calls for skilful revision in every part, is freely admitted. I do not believe it to be absolutely identical with the true Traditional Text. Its existence, nevertheless, is a fact from which there is no escaping. Happily, Western Christendom has been content to employ one and the same text for upwards of three hundred years. If the objection be made, as it probably will be, 'Do you then mean to rest upon the five manuscripts used by Erasmus?' I reply, that the copies employed were selected because they were known to represent with accuracy the Sacred Word ; that the descent of the text was evidently guarded with jealous care, just as the human genealogy of our Lord was preserved; that it rests mainly upon much the widest testimony; and that where any part of it conflicts with the fullest evidence attainable, there I believe that it calls for correction.

The question therefore which presents itself, and must needs be answered in the affirmative before a single syllable of the actual text is displaced, will always be one

[1] Scrivener, Plain Introduction, ed. 4, Vol. I. pp. 75-76.

and the same, viz. this: Is it certain that the evidence in favour of the proposed new reading is sufficient to warrant the innovation? For I trust we shall all be agreed that in the absence of an affirmative answer to this question, the text may on no account be disturbed. Rightly or wrongly it has had the approval of Western Christendom for three centuries, and is at this hour in possession of the field. Therefore the business before us might be stated somewhat as follows: What considerations ought to determine our acceptance of any reading not found in the Received Text, or, to state it more generally and fundamentally, our preference of one reading before another? For until some sort of understanding has been arrived at on this head, progress is impossible. There can be no Science of Textual Criticism, I repeat—and therefore no security for the inspired Word—so long as the subjective judgement, which may easily degenerate into individual caprice, is allowed ever to determine which readings shall be rejected, which retained.

In the next chapter I shall discuss the principles which must form the groundwork of the Science. Meanwhile a few words are necessary to explain the issue lying between myself and those critics with whom I am unable to agree. I must, if I can, come to some understanding with them ; and I shall use all clearness of speech in order that my meaning and my position may be thoroughly apprehended.

§ 5.

Strange as it may appear, it is undeniably true, that the whole of the controversy may be reduced to the following narrow issue: Does the truth of the Text of Scripture dwell with the vast multitude of copies, uncial and cursive, concerning which nothing is more remarkable than the marvellous agreement which subsists between them? Or is it rather to be supposed that the truth abides exclusively with a very little handful of manuscripts, which at once differ from the great bulk of the witnesses, and—strange to say—also amongst themselves?

The advocates of the Traditional Text urge that the Consent without Concert of so many hundreds of copies, executed by different persons, at diverse times, in widely sundered regions of the Church, is a presumptive proof of their trustworthiness, which nothing can invalidate but some sort of demonstration that they are untrustworthy guides after all.

The advocates of the old uncials—for it is the text exhibited by one or more of five Uncial Codexes known as ABℵCD which is set up with so much confidence— are observed to claim that the truth must needs reside exclusively with the objects of their choice. They seem to base their claim on 'antiquity'; but the real confidence of many of them lies evidently in a claim to subtle divination, which enables them to recognize a true reading or the true text when they see it. Strange, that it does not seem to have struck such critics that they assume the very thing which has to be proved. Be this as it may, as a matter of fact, readings exclusively found in Cod. B, or Cod. ℵ, or Cod. D are sometimes adopted as correct. Neither Cod. A nor Cod. C are ever known to inspire similar confidence. But the accession of both or either as a witness is always acceptable. Now it is remarkable that all the five Codexes just mentioned are never found, unless I am mistaken, exclusively in accord.

This question will be more fully discussed in the following treatise. Here it is only necessary further to insist upon the fact that, generally speaking, compromise upon these issues is impossible. Most people in these days are inclined to remark about any controversy that the truth resides between the two combatants, and most of us would like to meet our opponents half-way. The present contention unfortunately does not admit of such a decision. Real acquaintance with the numerous points at stake must reveal the impossibility of effecting a settlement like that. It depends, not upon the attitude, or the temper, or the intellects of the opposing parties: but upon the stern and incongruous elements of the subject-matter of the struggle. Much as we may regret it, there is positively no other solution.

Indeed there exist but two rival schools of Textual Criticism. And these are irreconcilably opposed. In the end, one of them will have to give way : and, *vae victis !* unconditional surrender will be its only resource. When one has been admitted to be the right, there can no place be found for the other. It will have to be dismissed from attention as a thing utterly, hopelessly in the wrong [1].

---

[1] Of course this trenchant passage refers only to the principles of the school found to fail. A school may leave fruits of research of a most valuable kind, and yet be utterly in error as to the inferences involved in such and other facts. Dean Burgon amply admitted this. The following extract from one of the many detached papers left by the author is appended as possessing both illustrative and personal interest :—

'Familiar as all such details as the present must of necessity prove to those who have made Textual Criticism their study, they may on no account be withheld. I am not addressing learned persons only. I propose, before I lay down my pen, to make educated persons, wherever they may be found, partakers of my own profound conviction that for the most part certainty is attainable on this subject-matter ; but that the decrees of the popular school—at the head of which stand many of the great critics of Christendom—are utterly mistaken. Founded, as I venture to think, on entirely false premisses, their conclusions almost invariably are altogether wrong. And this I hold to be demonstrable ; and I propose in the ensuing pages to establish the fact. If I do not succeed, I shall pay the penalty for my presumption and my folly. But if I succeed— and I wish to have jurists and persons skilled in the law of evidence, or at least thoughtful and unprejudiced persons, wherever they are to be found, and no others, for my judges,—if I establish my position, I say, let my father and my mother's son be kindly remembered by the Church of Christ when he has departed hence.'

CHAPTER II.

§ 1.

THE object of Textual Criticism, when applied to the Scriptures of the New Testament, is to determine what the Apostles and Evangelists of Christ actually wrote—the precise words they employed, and the very order of them. It is therefore one of the most important subjects which can be proposed for examination; and unless handled unskilfully, ought to prove by no means wanting in living interest. Moreover, it clearly takes precedence, in synthetical order of thought, of every other department of Sacred Science, so far as that rests upon the great pillar of Holy Scripture.

Now Textual Criticism occupies itself chiefly with two distinct branches of inquiry. (1) Its first object is to collect, investigate, and arrange the evidence supplied by Manuscripts, Versions, Fathers. And this is an inglorious task, which demands prodigious labour, severe accuracy, unflagging attention, and can never be successfully conducted without a considerable amount of solid learning. (2) Its second object is to draw critical inferences; in other words, to discover the truth of the text—the genuine words of Holy Writ. And this is altogether a loftier function, and calls for the exercise of far higher gifts. Nothing can be successfully accomplished here without large and exact knowledge, freedom from bias and prejudice. Above all, there must be a clear and judicial understanding. The

logical faculty in perfection must energize continually:
or the result can only be mistakes, which may easily
prove calamitous.

My next step is to declare what has been hitherto
effected in either of these departments, and to characterize
the results. In the first-named branch of the subject, till
recently very little has been attempted: but that little
has been exceedingly well done. Many more results have
been added in the last thirteen years : a vast amount of
additional evidence has been discovered, but only a small
portion of it has been thoroughly examined and collated.
In the latter branch, a great deal has been attempted: but
the result proves to be full of disappointment to those who
augured much from it. The critics of this century have
been in too great a hurry. They have rushed to conclusions, trusting to the evidence which was already in their
hands, forgetting that only those conclusions can be
scientifically sound which are drawn from all the materials
that exist. Research of a wider kind ought to have preceded decision. Let me explain and establish what I have
been saying.

§ 2.

It was only to have been anticipated that the Author
of the Everlasting Gospel—that masterpiece of Divine
Wisdom, that miracle of superhuman skill—would shew
Himself supremely careful for the protection and preservation of His own chiefest work. Every fresh discovery of
the beauty and preciousness of the Deposit in its essential
structure does but serve to deepen the conviction that
a marvellous provision must needs have been made in
God's eternal counsels for the effectual conservation of the
inspired Text.

Yet it is not too much to assert that nothing which
man's inventive skill could have devised nearly comes up

to the actual truth of the matter. Let us take a slight but comprehensive view of what is found upon investigation, as I hold, to have been the Divine method in respect of the New Testament Scriptures.

I. From the very necessity of the case, copies of the Gospels and Epistles in the original Greek were multiplied to an extraordinary extent all down the ages and in every part of the Christian Church. The result has been that, although all the earliest have perished, there remains to this day a prodigious number of such transcripts; some of them of very high antiquity. On examining these with care, we discover that they must needs have been (*a*) produced in different countries, (*b*) executed at intervals during the space of one thousand years, (*c*) copied from originals no longer in existence. And thus a body of evidence has been accumulated as to what is the actual text of Scripture, such as is wholly unapproachable with respect to any other writings in the world[1]. More than two thousand manuscript copies are now (1888) known to exist[2].

[1] There are, however, in existence, about 200 MSS. of the Iliad and Odyssey of Homer, and about 150 of Virgil. But in the case of many books the existing authorities are but scanty. Thus there are not many more than thirty of Aeschylus, and they are all said by W. Dindorf to be derived from one of the eleventh century : only a few of Demosthenes, of which the oldest are of the tenth or eleventh century : only one authority for the first six books of the Annals of Tacitus (see also Madvig's Introduction) : only one of the Clementines : only one of the Didachè, &c. See Gow's Companion to School Classics, Macmillan & Co. 1888.

[2] ' I had already assisted my friend Prebendary Scrivener in greatly enlarging Scholz's list. We had, in fact, raised the enumeration of " Evangelia " [copies of Gospels] to 621 : of "Acts and Catholic Epistles " to 239: of " Paul " to 281 : of " Apocalypse " to 108 : of " Evangelistaria " [Lectionary copies of Gospels] to 299 : of the book called " Apostolos" [Lectionary copies of Acts and Epistles] to 81—making a total of 1629. But at the end of a protracted and somewhat laborious correspondence with the custodians of not a few great continental libraries, I am able to state that our available " Evangelia " amount to at least 739 : our " Acts and Cath. Epp." to 261 : our " Paul " to 338 : our " Apoc." to 122 : our " Evst." to 415 : our copies of the " Apostolos " to 128—making a total of 2003. This shews an increase of three hundred and seventy-four.' Revision Revised, p. 521. But since the publication of Dr. Gregory's Prolegomena, and of the fourth edition of Dr. Scrivener's Plain Introduction to the

It should be added that the practice of reading Scripture aloud before the congregation—a practice which is observed to have prevailed from the Apostolic age—has resulted in the increased security of the Deposit: for (1) it has led to the multiplication, by authority, of books containing the Church Lessons ; and (2) it has secured a living witness to the *ipsissima verba* of the Spirit—in all the Churches of Christendom. The ear once thoroughly familiarized with the words of Scripture is observed to resent the slightest departure from the established type. As for its tolerating important changes, that is plainly out of the question.

II. Next, as the Gospel spread from land to land, it became translated into the several languages of the ancient world. For, though Greek was widely understood, the commerce and the intellectual predominance of the Greeks, and the conquests of Alexander having caused it to be spoken nearly all over the Roman Empire, Syriac and Latin Versions were also required for ordinary reading, probably even in the very age of the Apostles. And thus those three languages in which ' the title of His accusation' was written above His cross—not to insist upon any absolute identity between the Syriac of the time with the then ' Hebrew' of Jerusalem—became from the earliest time the depositaries of the Gospel of the World's Redeemer. Syriac was closely related to the vernacular Aramaic of Palestine and was spoken in the adjoining region : whilst Latin was the familiar idiom of all the Churches of the West.

Thus from the first in their public assemblies, orientals

Criticism of the New Testament, after Dean Burgon's death, the list has been largely increased. In the fourth edition of the Introduction (Appendix F, p. 397*) the total number under the six classes of ' Evangelia,' ' Acts and Catholic Epistles,' ' St. Paul,' ' Apocalypse,' ' Evangelistaria,' and ' Apostolos,' has reached (about) 3,829, and may be reckoned when all have come in at over 4,000. The separate MSS. (some in the reckoning just given being counted more than once) are already over 3,000.

and occidentals alike habitually read aloud the writings of the Evangelists and Apostles. Before the fourth and fifth centuries the Gospel had been further translated into the peculiar idioms of Lower and Upper Egypt, in what are now called the Bohairic and the Sahidic Versions,—of Ethiopia and of Armenia,—of Gothland. The text thus embalmed in so many fresh languages was clearly, to a great extent, protected against the risk of further change; and these several translations remain to this day as witnesses of what was found in copies of the New Testament which have long since perished.

III. But the most singular provision for preserving the memory of what was anciently read as inspired Scriptures remains to be described. Sacred Science boasts of a literature without a parallel in any other department of human knowledge. The Fathers of the Church, the Bishops and Doctors of primitive Christendom, were in some instances voluminous writers, whose works have largely come down to our times. These men often comment upon, freely quote, habitually refer to, the words of Inspiration: whereby it comes to pass that a host of unsuspected witnesses to the truth of Scripture are sometimes producible. The quotations of passages by the Fathers are proofs of the readings which they found in the copies used by them. They thus testify in ordinary quotations, though it be at second hand: and sometimes their testimony has more than usual value when they argue or comment upon the passage in question. Indeed, very often the manuscripts in their hands, which so far live in their quotations, are older—perhaps centuries older—than any copies that now survive. In this way, it will be perceived that a threefold security has been provided for the integrity of the Deposit:—Copies,—Versions,—Fathers. On the relation of each of which heads to one another something particular has now to be delivered.

§ 3.

Manuscript copies are commonly divided into Uncial,
i. e. those which are written in capital letters, and Cursive or
'minuscule,' i. e. those which are written in 'running' or
small hand. This division though convenient is misleading.
The earliest of the 'Cursives' are more ancient than the
latest of the 'Uncials' by full one hundred years[1]. The later
body of the Uncials belongs virtually, as will be proved, to
the body of the Cursives. There is no merit, so to speak, in
a MS. being written in the uncial character. The number
of the Uncials is largely inferior to that of the Cursives,
though they usually boast a much higher antiquity. It
will be shewn in a subsequent chapter that there is now, in
the face of recent discoveries of Papyrus MSS. in Egypt,
much reason for inferring that Cursive MSS. were largely
derived from MSS. on Papyrus, just as the Uncials themselves were, and that the prevalence for some centuries of
Uncials took its rise from the local library of Caesarea.
For a full account of these several Codexes, and for many
other particulars in Sacred Textual Criticism, the reader is
referred to Scrivener's Introduction, 1894.

Now it is not so much an exaggerated, as an utterly
mistaken estimate of the importance of the Textual decrees
of the five oldest of these Uncial copies, which lies at the
root of most of the criticism of the last fifty years. We
are constrained in consequence to bestow what will appear
to some a disproportionate amount of attention on
those five Codexes : viz. the Vatican Codex B, and the
Sinaitic Codex ℵ, which are supposed to be both of
the fourth century: the Alexandrian Codex A, and the
fragmentary Parisian Codex C, which are assigned to the
fifth : and lastly D, the Codex Bezae at Cambridge, which
is supposed to have been written in the sixth. To these

---

[1] Evan. 481 is dated A.D. 835 ; Evan. S. is dated A.D. 949.

may now be added, as far as St. Matthew and St. Mark are concerned, the Codex Beratinus Φ, and the Rossanensian Codex Σ, both of which are of the early part of the sixth century or end of the fifth. But these two witness generally against the two oldest, and have not yet received as much attention as they deserve. It will be found in the end that we have been guilty of no exaggeration in characterizing B, ℵ, and D at the outset, as three of the most corrupt copies in existence. Let not any one suppose that the age of these five MSS. places them upon a pedestal higher than all others. They can be proved to be wrong time after time by evidence of an earlier period than that which they can boast.

Indeed, that copies of Scripture, as a class, are the most important instruments of Textual Criticism is what no competent person will be found to deny. The chief reasons of this are their continuous text, their designed embodiment of the written Word, their number, and their variety. But we make also such great account of MSS., because (1) they supply unbroken evidence to the text of Scripture from an early date throughout history until the invention of printing ; (2) they are observed to be dotted over every century of the Church after the first three ; (3) they are the united product of all the patriarchates in Christendom. There can have been no collusion therefore in the preparation of this class of authorities. The risk of erroneous transcription has been reduced to the lowest possible amount. The prevalence of fraud to a universal extent is simply a thing impossible. Conjectural corrections of the text are pretty sure, in the long run, to have become effectually excluded. On the contrary, the testimony of Fathers is fragmentary, undesigned, though often on that account the more valuable, and indeed, as has been already said, is often not to be found ; yet occasionally it is very precious, whether from eminent antiquity or the clearness of their verdict: while Versions, though on larger details they yield a most valuable collateral evidence, yet from their nature are incapable of rendering help upon many important points of detail. Indeed, in respect of the *ipsissima verba* of Scripture, the evidence of Versions in other languages must be precarious in a high degree.

Undeniable it is, that as far as regards Primitiveness, certain of the Versions, and not a few of the Fathers, throw Manuscripts altogether in the shade. We possess no actual copies of the New Testament so old as the Syriac and the Latin Versions by probably more than two hundred years. Something similar is perhaps to be said of the Versions made into the languages of Lower and Upper Egypt, which may be of the third century[1]. Reasonable also it is to assume that in no instance was an ancient Version executed from a single Greek exemplar: consequently, Versions enjoyed both in their origin and in their acceptance more publicity than of necessity attached to any individual copy. And it is undeniable that on countless occasions the evidence of a translation, on account of the clearness of its testimony, is every bit as satisfactory as that of an actual copy of the Greek.

But I would especially remind my readers of Bentley's golden precept, that ' The real text of the sacred writers does not now, since the originals have been so long lost, lie in any MS. or edition, but is dispersed in them all.' This truth, which was evident to the powerful intellect of that great scholar, lies at the root of all sound Textual Criticism. To abide by the verdict of the two, or five, or seven oldest Manuscripts, is at first sight plausible, and is the natural refuge of students who are either superficial, or who wish to make their task as easy and simple as possible. But to put aside inconvenient witnesses is contrary to all principles of justice and of science. The problem is more

---

[1] Or, as some think, at the end of the second century.

complex, and is not to be solved so readily. Evidence of a strong and varied character may not with safety be cast away, as if it were worthless.

§ 4.

We are constrained therefore to proceed to the consideration of the vast mass of testimony which lies ready to our hands. And we must just as evidently seek for principles to guide us in the employment of it. For it is the absence of any true chart of the ocean that has led people to steer to any barren island, which under a guise of superior antiquity might at first sight present the delusive appearance of being the only safe and sure harbour.

1. We are all, I trust, agreed at least in this,—That the thing which we are always in search of is the Text of Scripture as it actually proceeded from the inspired writers themselves. It is never, I mean, ' ancient readings ' which we propose as the ultimate object of our inquiries. It is always the oldest Reading of all which we desire to ascertain ; in other words, the original Text, nothing else or less than the very words of the holy Evangelists and Apostles themselves.

And axiomatic as this is, it requires to be clearly laid down. For sometimes critics appear to be engrossed with the one solicitude to establish concerning the readings for which they contend, that at least they must needs be very ancient. Now, since all readings must needs be very ancient which are found in very ancient documents, nothing has really been achieved by proving that such and such readings existed in the second century of our era :—unless it can also be proved that there are certain other attendant circumstances attaching to those readings, which constitute a fair presumption, that they must needs be regarded as the only genuine wording of the passage in question. The Holy Scriptures are not an arena for the exercise or display of the ingenuity of critics.

2. I trust it may further be laid down as a fundamental principle that of two possible ways of reading the Text, that way which is found on examination to be the better attested and authenticated—by which I mean, the reading which proves on inquiry to be supported by the better evidence—must in every instance be of necessity presumed to be the actual reading, and is to be accepted accordingly by all students.

3. I will venture to make only one more postulate, viz. this: That hitherto we have become acquainted with no single authority which is entitled to dictate absolutely on all occasions, or even on any one occasion, as to what shall or shall not be regarded as the true Text of Scripture. We have here no one infallible witness, I say, whose solitary dictum is competent to settle controversies. The problem now to be investigated, viz. what evidence is to be held to be 'the best,' may doubtless be stated in many ways: but I suppose not more fairly than by proposing the following question,—Can any rules be offered whereby in any case of conflicting testimony it may be certainly ascertained which authorities ought to be followed? The court is full of witnesses who contradict one another. How are we to know which of them to believe? Strange to say, the witnesses are commonly, indeed almost invariably, observed to divide themselves into two camps. Are there no rules discoverable by which it may be probably determined with which camp of the two the truth resides?

I proceed to offer for the reader's consideration seven Tests of Truth, concerning each of which I shall have something to say in the way of explanation by-and-by. In the end I shall ask the reader to allow that where these seven tests are found to conspire, we may confidently assume that the evidence is worthy of all acceptance, and is to be implicitly followed. A reading should be attested then by the seven following

NOTES OF TRUTH.

1. Antiquity, or Primitiveness ;
2. Consent of Witnesses, or Number ;
3. Variety of Evidence, or Catholicity ;
4. Respectability of Witnesses, or Weight ;
5. Continuity, or Unbroken Tradition ;
6. Evidence of the Entire Passage, or Context ;
7. Internal Considerations, or Reasonableness.

§ 5.

The full consideration of these Tests of Truth must be postponed to the next chapter. Meanwhile, three discussions of a more general character demand immediate attention.

I. Antiquity, in and by itself, will be found to avail nothing. A reading is to be adopted not because it is old, but because it is the best attested, and therefore the oldest. There may seem to be paradox on my part: but there is none. I have admitted, and indeed insist upon it, that the oldest reading of all is the very thing we are in search of: for that must of necessity be what proceeded from the pen of the sacred writer himself. But, as a rule, fifty years, more or less, must be assumed to have intervened between the production of the inspired autographs and the earliest written representation of them now extant. And precisely in that first age it was that men evinced themselves least careful or accurate in guarding the Deposit,— least critically exact in their way of quoting it ;—whilst the enemy was most restless, most assiduous in procuring its depravation. Strange as it may sound,—distressing as the discovery must needs prove when it is first distinctly realized,—the earliest shreds and scraps—for they are at first no more—that come into our hands as quotations of the text of the New Testament Scriptures are not only disappointing by reason of their inexactness, their fragmentary character, their vagueness ; but they are often

demonstrably inaccurate.   I proceed to give one example
out of many.

'My God, My God, wherefore hast thou forsaken me?'
μὲ ἐγκατέλιπες;   So it is in St. Matt. xxvii. 46: so in St.
Mark xv. 34.   But because, in the latter place, אB, one
Old Latin, the Vulgate, and the Bohairic Versions, besides
Eusebius, followed by L and a few cursives, reverse the
order of the last two words, the editors are unanimous in
doing the same thing.   They have yet older authority,
however, for what they do.   Justin M. (A.D. 164) and the
Valentinians (A.D. 150) are with them.   As far therefore
as antiquity goes, the evidence for reading ἐγκατέλιπές με
is really wondrous strong.

And yet the evidence on the other side, when it is
considered, is perceived to be overwhelming[1].   Add the
discovery that ἐγκατέλιπές με is the established reading of
the familiar Septuagint, and we have no hesitation whatever in retaining the commonly Received Text, because the
secret is out.   אB were sure to follow the Septuagint,
which was so dear to Origen.   Further discussion of the
point is superfluous.

I shall of course be asked,—Are we then to understand
that you condemn the whole body of ancient authorities as
untrustworthy?   And if you do, to what other authorities
would you have us resort?

I answer:—So far from regarding the whole body of
ancient authorities as untrustworthy, it is precisely 'the
whole body of ancient authorities' to which I insist that
we must invariably make our appeal, and to which we
must eventually defer.   I regard them therefore with more
than reverence.   I submit to their decision unreservedly.
Doubtless I refuse to regard any one of those same
most ancient manuscripts—or even any two or three

---

[1] ACΣ (Φ in St. Matt.) with fourteen other uncials, most cursives, four Old
Latin, Gothic, St. Irenaeus, &c. &c.

of them—as oracular. But why? Because I am able to demonstrate that every one of them singly is in a high degree corrupt, and is condemned upon evidence older than itself. To pin my faith therefore to one, two, or three of those eccentric exemplars, were indeed to insinuate that the whole body of ancient authorities is unworthy of credit.

It is to Antiquity, I repeat, that I make my appeal : and further, I insist that the ascertained verdict of Antiquity shall be accepted. But then, inasmuch as by 'Antiquity' I do not even mean any one single ancient authority, however ancient, to the exclusion of, and in preference to, all the rest, but the whole collective body, it is precisely 'the body of ancient authorities' which I propose as the arbiters. Thus, I do not mean by 'Antiquity' either (1) the Peshitto Syriac : or (2) Cureton's Syriac : or (3) the Old Latin Versions : or (4) the Vulgate : or (5) the Egyptian, or indeed (6) any other of the ancient Versions :—not (7) Origen, nor (8) Eusebius, nor (9) Chrysostom, nor (10) Cyril,—nor indeed (11) any other ancient Father standing alone : neither (12) Cod. A,—nor (13) Cod. B,—nor (14) Cod. C,—nor (15) Cod. D,—nor (16) Cod. ℵ,—nor in fact (17) any other individual Codex that can be named. I should as soon think of confounding the cathedral hard by with one or two of the stones which compose it. By Antiquity I understand the whole body of documents which convey to me the mind of Antiquity,—transport me back to the primitive age, and acquaint me, as far as is now possible, with what was its verdict.

And by parity of reasoning, I altogether decline to accept as decisive the verdict of any two or three of these in defiance of the ascertained authority of all, or a majority of the rest.

In short, I decline to accept a fragment of Antiquity, arbitrarily broken off, in lieu of the entire mass of ancient witnesses. And further than this, I recognize other Notes

of Truth, as I have stated already; and I shall prove this
position in my next chapter.

<h2 style="text-align:center">§ 6.</h2>

II. The term 'various readings' conveys an entirely
incorrect impression of the grave discrepancies discoverable
between a little handful of documents—of which Codexes
B-ℵ of the fourth century, D of the sixth, L of the eighth,
are the most conspicuous samples—and the Traditional
Text of the New Testament. The expression 'various
readings' belongs to secular literature and refers to phenomena essentially different from those exhibited by the
copies just mentioned. Not but what 'various readings,'
properly so called, are as plentiful in sacred as in profane
codexes. One has but to inspect Scrivener's Full and
Exact Collation of about Twenty Greek Manuscripts of the
Gospels (1853) to be convinced of the fact. But when
we study the New Testament by the light of such Codexes
as BℵDL, we find ourselves in an entirely new region of
experience ; confronted by phenomena not only unique
but even portentous. The text has undergone apparently
an habitual, if not systematic, depravation ; has been
manipulated throughout in a wild way. Influences have
been demonstrably at work which altogether perplex the
judgement. The result is simply calamitous. There are
evidences of persistent mutilation, not only of words and
clauses, but of entire sentences. The substitution of one
expression for another, and the arbitrary transposition of
words, are phenomena of such perpetual occurrence, that
it becomes evident at last that what lies before us is not
so much an ancient copy, as an ancient recension of the
Sacred Text. And yet not by any means a recension in
the usual sense of the word as an authoritative revision :
but only as the name may be applied to the product of
individual inaccuracy or caprice, or tasteless assiduity

on the part of one or many, at a particular time or in a long
series of years. There are reasons for inferring, that we
have alighted on five specimens of what the misguided piety
of a primitive age is known to have been fruitful in producing. Of fraud, strictly speaking, there may have been
little or none. We should shrink from imputing an evil
motive where any matter will bear an honourable interpretation. But, as will be seen later on, these Codexes abound
with so much licentiousness or carelessness as to suggest
the inference, that they are in fact indebted for their preservation to their hopeless character. Thus it would
appear that an evil reputation ensured their neglect in
ancient times; and has procured that they should survive
to our own, long after multitudes which were much better
had perished in the Master's service. Let men think of
this matter as they will,—whatever in fact may prove to
be the history of that peculiar Text which finds its chief
exponents in Codd. BℵDL, in some copies of the Old
Latin, and in the Curetonian Version, in Origen, and to
a lesser extent in the Bohairic and Sahidic Translations,—
all must admit, as a matter of fact, that it differs essentially
from the Traditional Text, and is no mere variation of it.

But why, it will be asked, may it not be the genuine
article? Why may not the 'Traditional Text' be the
fabrication?

1. The burden of proof, we reply, rests with our opponents. The consent without concert of (suppose) 990 out
of 1000 copies,—of every date from the fifth to the fourteenth century, and belonging to every region of ancient
Christendom,—is a colossal fact not to be set aside by any
amount of ingenuity. A predilection for two fourth-
century manuscripts closely resembling one another, yet
standing apart in every page so seriously that it is easier
to find two consecutive verses in which they differ than
two consecutive verses in which they entirely agree:—such

a preference, I say, apart from abundant or even definitely clear proof that it is well founded, is surely not entitled to be accepted as conclusive.

2. Next,—Because,—although for convenience we have hitherto spoken of Codexes BאDL as exhibiting a single text,—it is in reality not one text but fragments of many, which are to be met with in the little handful of authorities enumerated above. Their witness does not agree together. The Traditional Text, on the contrary, is unmistakably one.

3. Further,—Because it is extremely improbable, if not impossible, that the Traditional Text was or could have been derived from such a document as the archetype of B-א: whereas the converse operation is at once obvious and easy. There is no difficulty in producing a short text by omission of words, or clauses, or verses, from a fuller text : but the fuller text could not have been produced from the shorter by any development which would be possible under the facts of the case [1]. Glosses would account for changes in the archetype of B-א, but not conversely [2].

4. But the chief reason is,—Because, on making our appeal unreservedly to Antiquity—to Versions and Fathers as well as copies,—the result is unequivocal. The Traditional Text becomes triumphantly established,—the eccentricities of BאD and their colleagues become one and all emphatically condemned.

---

[1] See Vol. II.

[2] All such questions are best understood by observing an illustration. In St. Matt. xiii. 36, the disciples say to our Lord, ' Explain to us (φράσον ἡμῖν) the parable of the tares.' The cursives (and late uncials) are all agreed in this reading. Why then do Lachmann and Tregelles (not Tischendorf) exhibit διασάφησον? Only because they find διασάφησον in B. Had they known that the first reading of א exhibited that reading also, they would have been more confident than ever. But what pretence can there be for assuming that the Traditional reading of all the copies is untrustworthy in this place ? The plea of antiquity at all events cannot be urged, for Origen reads φράσον four times. The Versions do not help us. What else is διασάφησον but a transparent Gloss! Διασάφησον (elucidate) explains φράσον, but φράσον (tell) does not explain διασάφησον.

All these, in the mean time, are points concerning which something has been said already, and more will have to be said in the sequel. Returning now to the phenomenon adverted to at the outset, we desire to explain that whereas 'Various Readings,' properly so called, that is to say, the Readings which possess really strong attestation—for more than nineteen-twentieths of the 'Various Readings' commonly quoted are only the vagaries of scribes, and ought not to be called 'Readings' at all—do not require classification into groups, as Griesbach and Hort have classified them; 'Corrupt Readings,' if they are to be intelligently handled, must by all means be distributed under distinct heads, as will be done in the Second Part of this work.

III. 'It is not at all our design' (remarks Dr. Scrivener) 'to seek our readings from the later uncials, supported as they usually are by the mass of cursive manuscripts; but to employ their confessedly secondary evidence in those numberless instances wherein their elder brethren are hopelessly at variance[1].' From which it is plain that in this excellent writer's opinion, the truth of Scripture is to be sought in the first instance at the hands of the older uncials: that only when these yield conflicting testimony may we resort to the 'confessedly secondary evidence' of the later uncials: and that only so may we proceed to inquire for the testimony of the great mass of the cursive copies. It is not difficult to foresee what would be the result of such a method of procedure.

I venture therefore respectfully but firmly to demur to the spirit of my learned friend's remarks on the present, and on many similar occasions. His language is calculated to countenance the popular belief (1) That the authority of an uncial codex, because it is an uncial, is necessarily greater than that of a codex written in the cursive character: an imagination which upon proof I hold to be groundless.

[1] Plain Introduction, I. 277. 4th edition.

Between the text of the later uncials and the text of the cursive copies, I fail to detect any separative difference : certainly no such difference as would induce me to assign the palm to the former. It will be shewn later on in this treatise, that it is a pure assumption to take for granted, or to infer, that cursive copies were all descended from the uncials. New discoveries in palaeography have ruled that error to be out of court.

But (2) especially do I demur to the popular notion, to which I regret to find that Dr. Scrivener lends his powerful sanction, that the text of Scripture is to be sought in the first instance in the oldest of the uncials. I venture to express my astonishment that so learned and thoughtful a man should not have seen that before certain ' elder brethren ' are erected into a supreme court of judicature, some other token of fitness besides that of age must be produced on their behalf. Whence, I can but ask—, whence is it that no one has yet been at the pains to establish the contradictory of the following proposition, viz. that Codexes BℵCD are the several depositaries of a fabricated and depraved text : and that BℵD, for C is a palimpsest, i. e., has had the works of Ephraem the Syrian written over it as if it were of no use, are probably indebted for their very preservation solely to the fact that they were anciently recognized as untrustworthy documents ? Do men indeed find it impossible to realize the notion that there must have existed such things aᵣ refuse copies in the fourth, fifth, sixth, and seventh cent ιries as well as in the eighth, ninth, tenth, and eleventh ? and that the Codexes which we call BℵCD may possibly, if not as I hold probably, have been of that class [1] ?

Now I submit that it is a sufficient condemnation of

---

[1] It is very remarkable that the sum of Eusebius' own evidence is largely against those uncials. Yet it seems most probable that he had B and ℵ executed from the $ἀκριβῆ$ or ' critical ' copies of Origen. See below, Chapter IX.

Codd. BℵCD as a supreme court of judicature (1) That as a rule they are observed to be discordant in their judgements: (2) That when they thus differ among themselves it is generally demonstrable by an appeal to antiquity that the two principal judges B and ℵ have delivered a mistaken judgement: (3) That when these two differ one from the other, the supreme judge B is often in the wrong: and lastly (4) That it constantly happens that all four agree, and yet all four are in error.

Does any one then inquire,—But why at all events may not resort be had in the first instance to Codd. BℵACD?—I answer,—Because the inquiry is apt to prejudice the question, pretty sure to mislead the judgement, only too likely to narrow the issue and render the Truth hopelessly difficult of attainment. For every reason, I am inclined to propose the directly opposite method of procedure, as at once the safer and the more reasonable method. When I learn that doubt exists, as to the reading of any particular place, instead of inquiring what amount of discord on the subject exists between Codexes ABℵCD (for the chances are that they will be all at loggerheads among themselves), I inquire for the verdict as it is given by the main body of the copies. This is generally unequivocal. But if (which seldom happens) I find this a doubtful question, then indeed I begin to examine the separate witnesses. Yet even then it helps me little, or rather it helps me nothing, to find, as I commonly do, that A is on one side and B on the other,—except by the way that wherever ℵ B are seen together, or when D stands apart with only a few allies, the inferior reading is pretty sure to be found there also.

Suppose however (as commonly happens) there is no serious division,—of course, significance does not attach itself to any handful of eccentric copies,—but that there is a practical unanimity among the cursives and later uncials: I cannot see that a veto can rest with such unstable and

discordant authorities, however much they may singly add
to the weight of the vote already tendered. It is as a
hundred to one that the uncial or uncials which are with
the main body of the cursives are right, because (as will be
shown) in their consentience they embody the virtual decision of the whole Church; and that the dissentients—be
they few or many—are wrong. I inquire however,—What
say the Versions? and last but not least,—What say the
Fathers?

The essential error in the proceeding I object to is best
illustrated by an appeal to elementary facts. Only two of
the 'five old uncials' are complete documents, B and ℵ:
and these being confessedly derived from one and the
same exemplar, cannot be regarded as two. The rest of
the 'old uncials' are lamentably defective.—From the
Alexandrian Codex (A) the first twenty-four chapters of
St. Matthew's Gospel are missing: that is, the MS. lacks
870 verses out of 1,071. The same Codex is also without
126 consecutive verses of St. John's Gospel. More than
one-fourth of the contents of Cod. A are therefore lost[1].—
D is complete only in respect of St. Luke: wanting 119
verses of St. Matthew,—5 verses of St. Mark,—166 verses of
St. John.—On the other hand, Codex C is chiefly defective
in respect of St. Luke's and St. John's Gospel; from the
former of which it omits 643 (out of 1,151) verses; from
the latter, 513 (out of 880), or far more than the half in
either case. Codex C in fact can only be described as
a collection of fragments: for it is also without 260 verses
of St. Matthew, and without 116 of St. Mark.

The disastrous consequence of all this to the Textual
Critic is manifest. He is unable to compare 'the five old
uncials' together except in respect of about one verse in
three. Sometimes he finds himself reduced to the testimony of AℵB: for many pages together of St. John's

----

[1] Viz. 996 verses out of 3,780.

Gospel, he is reduced to the testimony of אBD. Now, when the fatal and peculiar sympathy which subsists between these three documents is considered, it becomes apparent that the Critic has in effect little more than two documents before him. And what is to be said when (as from St. Matt. vi. 20 to vii. 4) he is reduced to the witness of two Codexes,—and those, אB? Evident it is that whereas the Author of Scripture hath bountifully furnished His Church with (speaking roughly) upwards of 2,300 [1] copies of the Gospels, by a voluntary act of self-impoverishment, some Critics reduce themselves to the testimony of little more than one: and that one a witness whom many judges consider to be undeserving of confidence.

[1] Miller's Scrivener (4th edition), Vol. I. Appendix F. p. 397*. 1326 + 73 + 980 = 2379.

CHAPTER III.

THE SEVEN NOTES OF TRUTH.

§ 1. *Antiquity.*

THE more ancient testimony is probably the better testimony. That it is not by any means always so is a familiar fact. To quote the known dictum of a competent judge: ' It is no less true to fact than paradoxical in sound, that the worst corruptions to which the New Testament has ever been subjected, originated within a hundred years after it was composed; that Irenaeus and the African Fathers and the whole Western, with a portion of the Syriac Church, used far inferior manuscripts to those employed by Stunica, or Erasmus, or Stephen, thirteen centuries after, when moulding the Textus Receptus[1].' Therefore Antiquity alone affords no security that the manuscript in our hands is not infected with the corruption which sprang up largely in the first and second centuries. But it remains true, notwithstanding, that until evidence has been produced to the contrary in any particular instance, the more ancient of two witnesses may reasonably be presumed to be the better informed witness. Shew me for example that, whereas a copy of the Gospels (suppose Cod. B) introduces the clause ' Raise the dead ' into our SAVIOUR'S ministerial commission to His Apostles (St. Matt. x. 8),—another Codex, but only of the fourteenth century

---

[1] Scrivener's Introduction, Ed. iv (1894), Vol. II. pp. 264-265.

(suppose Evan. 604 (Hoskier)), omits it ;—am I not bound to assume that our LORD did give this charge to His Apostles ; did say to them, νεκροὺς ἐγείρετε ; and that the words in question have accidentally dropped out of the sacred Text in that later copy? Show me besides that in three other of our oldest Codexes (אCD) the place in St. Matthew is exhibited in the same way as in Cod. B ; and of what possible avail can it be that I should urge in reply that in three more MSS. of the thirteenth or fourteenth century the text is exhibited in the same way as in Evan. 604 ?

There is of course a strong antecedent probability, that the testimony which comes nearest to the original autographs has more claim to be the true record than that which has been produced at a further distance from them. It is most likely that the earlier is separated from the original by fewer links than the later :—though we can affirm this with no absolute certainty, because the present survival of Uncials of various dates of production shews that the existence of copies is measured by no span like that of the life of men. Accordingly as a general rule, and a general rule only, a single early Uncial possesses more authority than a single later Uncial or Cursive, and a still earlier Version or Quotation by a Father must be placed before the reading of the early Uncial.

Only let us clearly understand what principle is to guide us, in order that we may know how we are to proceed. Is it to be assumed, for instance, that Antiquity is to decide this matter? by which is meant only this,—That, of two or more conflicting readings, that shall be deemed the true reading which is observed to occur in the oldest known document. Is that to be our fundamental principle? Are we, in other words, to put up with the transparent fallacy that the oldest reading must of necessity be found in the oldest document? Well, if we have made up our minds that such is to be our method, then let us proceed to construct our text chiefly by the aid of the Old Latin and Peshitto Versions,—the oldest authorities extant of a continuous text: and certainly, wherever these are observed to agree in respect of any given reading, let us hear nothing about the conflicting testimony of ℵ or B, which are of the fourth century; of D, which is of the sixth ; of L, which is of the eighth.

But if our adversaries shift their ground, disliking to be ' hoist with their own petard,' and if such a solution standing alone does not commend itself to our own taste, we must ask, What is meant by Antiquity ?

For myself, if I must assign a definite period, I am disposed to say the first six or seven centuries of our era. But I observe that those who have preceded me in these inquiries draw the line at an earlier period. Lachmann fixes A.D. 400 : Tregelles (ever illogical) gives the beginning of the seventh century : Westcott and Hort, before the close of the fourth century. In this absence of agreement, it is found to be both the safest and the wisest course to avoid drawing any hard and fast line, and in fact any line at all. Antiquity is a comparative term. What is ancient is not only older than what is modern, but when constantly applied to the continuous lapse of ages includes considerations of what is more or less ancient. Codex E is ancient compared with Codex L: Cod. A compared with Cod. E : Cod. ℵ compared with Cod. A : Cod. B though in a much lesser degree compared with Cod. ℵ : the Old Latin and Peshitto Versions compared with Cod. B : Clemens Romanus compared with either. If we had the copy of the Gospels which belonged to Ignatius, I suppose we should by common consent insist on following it almost implicitly. It certainly would be of overwhelming authority. Its decrees would be only not decisive. [This is, I think, too strong : there might be mistakes even in that.—E. M.]

Therefore by Antiquity as a principle involving more or less authority must be meant the greater age of the earlier Copies, Versions, or Fathers. That which is older will possess more authority than that which is more recent : but age will not confer any exclusive, or indeed paramount, power of decision. Antiquity is one Note of Truth : but even if it is divorced from the arbitrary selection of Authorities which has regulated too much the employment of it in Textual Criticism, it cannot be said to cover the whole ground.

§ 2. *Number.*

II. We must proceed now to consider the other Notes, or Tests : and the next is NUMBER.

1. That ' witnesses are to be weighed—not counted,'— is a maxim of which we hear constantly. It may be said to embody much fundamental fallacy.

2. It assumes that the ' witnesses ' we possess,—meaning thereby every single Codex, Version, Father—, (1) are capable of being weighed : and (2) that every individual Critic is competent to weigh them : neither of which propositions is true.

3. In the very form of the maxim,—' *Not* to be counted— *but* to be weighed,'—the undeniable fact is overlooked that ' number' is the most ordinary ingredient of weight, and indeed in matters of human testimony, is an element which even cannot be cast away. Ask one of Her Majesty's Judges if it be not so. Ten witnesses (suppose) are called in to give evidence : of whom one resolutely contradicts what is solemnly deposed to by the other nine. Which of the two parties do we suppose the Judge will be inclined to believe ?

4. But it may be urged—would not the discovery of the one original autograph of the Gospels exceed in ' weight' any ' number' of copies which can be named ? No doubt

it would, I answer. But only because it would be the
original document, and not 'a copy' at all : not 'a witness'
to the fact, but the very fact itself. It would be as if in the
midst of a trial,—turning, suppose, on the history of the
will of some testator—, the dead man himself were to step
into Court, and proclaim what had actually taken place.
Yet the laws of Evidence would remain unchanged : and in
the very next trial which came on, if one or two witnesses
out of as many hundred were to claim that their evidence
should be held to outweigh that of all the rest, they would
be required to establish the reasonableness of their claim to
the satisfaction of the Judge : or they must submit to the
inevitable consequence of being left in an inconsiderable
minority.

5. Number then constitutes Weight, or in other words,—
since I have used 'Weight' here in a more general sense
than usual,—is a Note of Truth.   Not of course absolutely,
as being the sole Test, but *caeteris paribus*, and in its own
place and proportion.   And this, happily, our opponents
freely admit : so freely in fact, that my only wonder is that
they do not discover their own inconsistency.

6. But the axiom in question labours under the far graver
defect of disparaging the Divine method, under which in
the multitude of evidence preserved all down the ages provision has been made as matter of hard fact, not by weight
but by number, for the integrity of the Deposit.   The
prevalent use of the Holy Scriptures in the Church caused
copies of them to abound everywhere.   The demand enforced
the supply.   They were read in the public Services of the
Church.   The constant quotation of them by Ecclesiastical
Writers from the first proves that they were a source to
Christians of continual study, and that they were used as
an ultimate appeal in the decision of knotty questions.
They were cited copiously in Sermons.   They were employed in the conversion of the heathen, and as in the case

of St. Cyprian must have exercised a strong influence in
bringing people to believe.

Such an abundance of early copies must have ensured
perforce the production of a resulting abundance of other
copies made everywhere in continuous succession from them
until the invention of printing.   Accordingly, although
countless numbers must have perished by age, use, destruction in war, and by accident and other causes, nevertheless
63 Uncials, 737 Cursives, and 414 Lectionaries are known
to survive of the Gospels alone[1]. Add the various Versions,
and the mass of quotations by Ecclesiastical Writers, and
it will at once be evident what materials exist to constitute
a Majority which shall outnumber by many times the
Minority, and also that Number has been ordained to be
a factor which cannot be left out of the calculation.

7. Another circumstance however of much significance
has yet to be stated. Practically the Axiom under consideration is discovered to be nothing else but a plausible
proposition of a general character intended to shelter the
following particular application of it :—' We are able '—says
Dr. Tregelles—' to take the *few* documents ... and safely
discard ... the $\frac{89}{90}$ or whatever else their numerical proportion may be[2].' Accordingly in his edition of the Gospels,
the learned writer rejects the evidence of all the cursive
Codexes extant but three. He is mainly followed by the rest
of his school, including Westcott and Hort.

Now again I ask,—Is it likely, is it in any way credible,
that we can be warranted in rejecting the testimony of
(suppose) 1490 ancient witnesses, in favour of the testimony
borne by (suppose) ten? Granting freely that two of these
ten are older by 50 or 100 years than any single MS. of
the 1490 I confidently repeat the question. The respective

[1] But see Miller's edition of Scrivener's Introduction, I. 397*, App. F, where
the numbers as *now* known are given as 73, 1326, 980 respectively.

[2] Account of the Printed Text, p. 138.

dates of the witnesses before us may perhaps be thus stated.
The ten MSS. so confidently relied upon date as follows,
speaking generally :—

2 about A.D. 330–340.
1   „   550.
1   „   7 50.
6 (say) „   950 to A.D. 1350.

The 1490 MSS. which are constantly observed to bear
consentient testimony against the ten, date somewhat thus:—

1 . . A.D. 400.
1 . .   „   450.
2 . .   „   500.
16 (say) „   650 to A.D. 850.
1470 . . „   850 to A.D. 1350.

And the question to which I invite the reader to render an
answer is this:—By what process of reasoning, apart from
an appeal to other authorities, (which we are going to make
by-and-by), can it be thought credible that the few witnesses
shall prove the trustworthy guides,—and the many witnesses
the deceivers ?

Now those many MSS. were executed demonstrably at
different times in different countries. They bear signs in
their many hundreds of representing the entire area of the
Church, except where versions were used instead of copies
in the original Greek. Many of them were written in
monasteries where a special room was set aside for such
copying. Those who were in trust endeavoured with the
utmost pains and jealousy to secure accuracy in the transcription. Copying was a sacred art. And yet, of multitudes
of them that survive, hardly any have been copied from any
of the rest. On the contrary, they are discovered to differ
among themselves in countless unimportant particulars ; and
every here and there single copies exhibit idiosyncrasies
which are altogether startling and extraordinary. There
has therefore demonstrably been no collusion—no assimila-

tion to an arbitrary standard,—no wholesale fraud. It is certain that every one of them represents a MS., or a pedigree of MSS., older than itself; and it is but fair to suppose that it exercises such representation with tolerable accuracy. It can often be proved, when any of them exhibit marked extravagancy, that such extravagancy dates back as far as the second or third century. I venture to think— and shall assume until I find that I am mistaken—that, besides the Uncials, all the cursive copies in existence represent lost Codexes of great antiquity with at least the same general fidelity as Ev. 1, 33, 69, which enjoy so much favour in some quarters only because they represent lost MSS. demonstrably of the same general type as Codd. ℵBD[1].

It will be seen that the proofs in favour of Number being a recognized and powerful Note of Truth are so strong, that nothing but the interests of an absorbing argument can prevent the acknowledgement of this position. It is doubtless inconvenient to find some 1490 witnesses contravening some ten, or if you will, twenty favourites: but Truth is imperative and knows nothing of the inconvenience or convenience of Critics.

8. When therefore the great bulk of the witnesses,—in the proportion suppose of a hundred or even fifty to one,— yield unfaltering testimony to a certain reading; and the remaining little handful of authorities, while advocating a different reading, are yet observed to be unable to agree among themselves as to what that different reading shall precisely be,—then that other reading concerning which all that discrepancy of detail is observed to exist, may be regarded as certainly false.

I will now give an instance of the general need of the testimony of Number being added to Antiquity, in order to establish a Reading.

---

[1] This general position will be elucidated in Chapters IX and XI.

There is an obscure expression in the Epistle to the
Hebrews,—Alford speaks of it as 'almost a *locus desperatus*'
—which illustrates the matter in hand not unaptly. The
received reading of Heb. iv. 2,—'not being mixed [viz.
the word preached] with faith in them that heard it,'—is
supported by the united testimony of the Peshitto and of
the Latin versions [1]. Accordingly, the discovery that א
also exhibits συγκεκερασμένος determined Tischendorf, who
however stands alone with Scholz, to retain in this place
the singular participle. And confessedly the note of
Antiquity it enjoys in perfection; as well as yields a sufficiently intelligible sense. But then unfortunately it proves
to be incredible that St. Paul can have been the author of
the expression [2]. All the known copies but four [3] read not
συγκεκραμένος but -μένους. So do all the Fathers who are
known to quote the place [4]:—Macarius [5], Chrysostom [6],
Theodorus of Mopsuestia [7], Cyril [8], Theodoret [9], Damascene [10], Photius [11], Theophylactus [12], Oecumenius [13]. The
testimony of four of the older of these is even express:
and such an amount of evidence is decisive. But we are

[1] So also the Georgian and Sclavonic versions (the late Dr. Malan).
[2] The Traditional view of the authorship of the Epistle to the Hebrews is
here maintained as superior both in authority and evidence to any other.
[3] א, 31, 41, 114.
[4] Tischendorf wrongly adduces Irenaeus. Read to the end of III. c. 19, § 1.
[5] *Ap.* Galland. vii. 178.
[6] xii. 64 c, 65 b. Καὶ ὅρα τί θαυμαστῶς· οὐκ εἶπεν, οὐ συνεφώνησαν, ἀλλ᾽, οὐ
συνεκράθησαν. See by all means Cramer's Cat. p. 451.
[7] *Ap.* Cramer, Cat. p. 177. Οὐ γὰρ ἦσαν κατὰ τὴν πίστιν τοῖς ἐπαγγελθεῖσι
συνημμένοι· ὅθεν οὕτως ἀναγνωστέον, "μὴ συγκεκερασμένους τῇ πίστει τοῖς
ἀκουσθεῖσι."
[8] vi. 15 d. Ἄρα γὰρ ἔμελλον κατὰ τὸν ἴσον τρόπον συνανακιρνᾶσθαί τε ἀλλήλοις, καθάπερ ἀμέλει καὶ οἶνος ὕδατι, κ.τ.λ. After this, it becomes of little moment
that the same Cyril should elsewhere (i. 394) read συγκεκραμένος ἐν πίστει
τοῖς ἀκούσασι.
[9] iii. 566. After quoting the place, Thdrt. proceeds, Τί γὰρ ὤνησεν ἡ τοῦ
Θεοῦ ἐπαγγελία τοὺς ... μὴ ... οἷον τοῖς τοῦ Θεοῦ λόγοις ἀνακραθέντας;
[10] ii. 234.   [11] *Ap.* Oecum.   [12] ii. 670.
[13] From Dr. Malan, who informs me that the Bohairic and Ethiopic exhibit
'*their heart* was not mixed with': which represents the same reading.

able to add that of the Harkleian, Bohairic, Ethiopic, and Armenian versions. However uncongenial therefore the effort may prove, there can be no doubt at all that we must henceforth read here,—'But the word listened to did not profit them, because they were not united in respect of faith with those who listened [and believed]': or words to that effect [1]. Let this then be remembered as a proof that, besides even the note of Variety to some extent superadded to that of Antiquity, it must further be shewn on behalf of any reading which claims to be authentic, that it enjoys also the support of a multitude of witnesses: in other words that it has the note of Number as well [2].

And let no one cherish a secret suspicion that because the Syriac and the Latin versions are such venerable documents they must be held to outweigh all the rest, and may be right in this matter after all. It will be found explained elsewhere that in places like the present, those famous versions are often observed to interpret rather than to reproduce the inspired verity: to discharge the office of a Targum rather than of a translation. The sympathy thus evinced between ℵ and the Latin should be observed: the significance of it will come under consideration afterwards.

§ 3. *Variety*.

I must point out in the next place, that Evidence on any passage, which exhibits in perfection the first of the two foregoing characteristics—that of Antiquity, may nevertheless so easily fall under suspicion, that it becomes in the highest degree necessary to fortify it by other notes of Truth. And there cannot be a stronger ally than Variety.

---

[1] So Theophylactus (ii. 670), who (with all the more trustworthy authorities) writes συγκεκραμένους. For this sense of the verb, see Liddell and Scott's Lex., and especially the instances in Wetstein.

[2] Yet Tischendorf says, 'Dubitare nequeo quin lectio Sinaitica hujus loci mentem scriptoris recte reddat atque omnium sit verissima.'

No one can doubt, for it stands to reason, that Variety distinguishing witnesses massed together must needs constitute a most powerful argument for believing such Evidence to be true. Witnesses of different kinds ; from different countries ; speaking different tongues :—witnesses who can never have met. and between whom it is incredible that there should exist collusion of any kind :—such witnesses deserve to be listened to most respectfully. Indeed, when witnesses of so varied a sort agree in large numbers, they must needs be accounted worthy of even implicit confidence. Accordingly, the essential feature of the proposed Test will be, that the Evidence of which 'Variety' is to be predicated shall be derived from a variety of sources. Readings which are witnessed to by MSS. only ; or by ancient Versions only : or by one or more of the Fathers only :—whatever else may be urged on their behalf, are at least without the full support of this note of Truth ; unless there be in the case of MSS. a sufficient note of Variety within their own circle. It needs only a slight acquaintance with the principles which regulate the value of evidence, and a comparison with other cases enjoying it of one where there is actually no variety, to see the extreme importance of this third Test. When there is real variety, what may be called hole-and-corner work,—conspiracy,—influence of sect or clique,—are impossible. Variety it is which imparts virtue to mere Number, prevents the witness-box from being filled with packed deponents, ensures genuine testimony. False witness is thus detected and condemned, because it agrees not with the rest. Variety is the consent of independent witnesses, and is therefore eminently Catholic. Origen or the Vatican and the Sinaitic, often stand all but alone, because there are scarce any in the assembly who do not hail from other parts with testimony different from theirs, whilst their own evidence finds little or no verification.

It is precisely this consideration which constrains us to

pay supreme attention to the combined testimony of the Uncials and of the whole body of the Cursive Copies. They are (*a*) dotted over at least 1000 years : (*b*) they evidently belong to so many divers countries,—Greece, Constantinople, Asia Minor, Palestine, Syria, Alexandria, and other parts of Africa, not to say Sicily, Southern Italy, Gaul, England, and Ireland : (*c*) they exhibit so many strange characteristics and peculiar sympathies : (*d*) they so clearly represent countless families of MSS., being in no single instance absolutely identical in their text, and certainly not being copies of any other Codex in existence,—that their unanimous decision I hold to be an absolutely irrefragable evidence of the Truth [1]. If, again, only a few of these copies disagree with the main body of them, I hold that the value of the verdict of the great majority is but slightly disturbed. Even then however the accession of another class of confirmatory evidence is most valuable. Thus, when it is perceived that Codd. אBCD are the only uncials which contain the clause νεκροὺς ἐγείρετε in St. Matt. x. 8, already spoken of, and that the merest fraction of the cursives exhibit the same reading, the main body of the cursives and all the other uncials being for omitting it, it is felt at once that the features of the problem have been very nearly reversed. On such occasions we inquire eagerly for the verdict of the most ancient of the Versions : and when, as on the present occasion, they are divided,—the Latin and the Ethiopic recognizing the clause, the Syriac and the Egyptian disallowing it,—an impartial student will eagerly inquire with one of old time,—'Is there not here a prophet of the LORD besides, that we might inquire of him ? ' He will wish to hear what the old Fathers have to say on this subject. I take the liberty of adding that when he has once perceived that the text employed by Origen

---

[1] See below, Chapter XI, where the character and authority of Cursive Manuscripts are considered.

E 2

corresponds usually to a surprising extent with the text represented by Codex B and some of the Old Latin Versions,
he will learn to lay less stress on every fresh instance of
such correspondence. He will desiderate greater variety
of testimony, — the utmost variety which is attainable.
The verdict of various other Fathers on this passage supplies
what is wanted [1]. Speaking generally, the consentient
testimony of two, four, six, or more witnesses, coming to us
from widely sundered regions is weightier by far than the
same number of witnesses proceeding from one and the same
locality, between whom there probably exists some sort of
sympathy, and possibly some degree of collusion. Thus
when it is found that the scribe of B wrote 'six conjugate
leaves of Cod. ℵ [2],' it is impossible to regard their united
testimony in the same light as we should have done, if one
had been produced in Palestine and the other at Constantinople. So also of primitive Patristic testimony. The
combined testimony of Cyril, patriarch of Alexandria ;—
Isidore of Pelusium, a city at the mouth of the Nile ;—and
Nonnus of Panopolis in the Thebaid, is not nearly so
weighty as the testimony of one of the same three writers
in conjunction with Irenaeus, Bishop of Lyons in Gaul, and
with Chrysostom who passed the greater part of his life at
Antioch. The same remark holds true of Versions. Thus,
the two Egyptian Versions when they conspire in witnessing
to the same singular reading are entitled to far less attention

---

[1] The evidence on the passage is as follows :—
For the insertion :—
  ℵ* etc. BC*ΦΣDPΔ, 1, 13, 33, 108, 157, 346, and about ten more. Old
      Latin (except f), Vulgate, Bohairic, Ethiopic, Hilary, Cyril Alex. (2),
      Chrysostom (2).
Against :—
  EFGKLMSUVXΓΠ.   The rest of the Cursives, Peshitto (Pusey and
      Gwilliam found it in no copies), Sahidic, Eusebius, Basil, Jerome,
      Chrysostom, *in loc.*, Juvencus. Compare Revision Revised, p. 108, note.
  [2] By the Editor. See Miller's Scrivener, Introduction (4th ed.), Vol. I. p. 96,
note 1, and below, Chapter IX.

than one of those same Versions in combination with the Syriac, or with the Latin, or with the Gothic.

§ 4. *Weight, or Respectability.*

We must request our readers to observe, that the term ' weight ' may be taken as regards Textual Evidence in two senses, the one general and the other special. In the general sense, Weight includes all the notes of truth,— it may relate to the entire mass of evidence ;—or else it may be employed as concerning the value of an individual manuscript, or a single Version, or a separate Father. Antiquity confers some amount of Weight : so does Number : and so does Variety also, as well as each of the other notes of truth. This distinction ought not to be allowed to go out of sight in the discussion which is now about to occupy our attention.

We proceed then to consider Weight in the special sense and as attached to single Witnesses.

Undeniable as it is, (*a*) that ancient documents do not admit of being placed in scales and weighed ; and (*b*) that if they did, the man does not exist who is capable of conducting the operation,—there are yet, happily, principles of sound reason,—considerations based on the common sense of mankind, learned and unlearned alike,—by the aid of which something may be effected which is strictly analogous to the process of weighing solid bodies in an ordinary pair of scales. I proceed to explain.

1. In the first place, the witnesses in favour of any given reading should be respectable. ' Respectability ' is of course a relative term ; but its use and applicability in this department of Science will be generally understood and admitted by scholars, although they may not be altogether agreed as to the classification of their authorities. Some critics will claim, not respectability only, but absolute and oracular

authority for a certain set of ancient witnesses,—which others will hold in suspicion. It is clear however that respectability cannot by itself confer pre-eminence, much less the privilege of oracular decision. We listen to any one whose character has won our respect : but dogmatism as to things outside of actual experience or mathematical calculation is the prerogative only of Revelation or inspired utterance; and if assumed by men who have no authority to dogmatize, is only accepted by weak minds who find a relief when they are able

'jurare in verba magistri.'
'To swear whate'er the master says is true.'

And if on the contrary certain witnesses are found to range themselves continually on the side which is condemned by a large majority of others exhibiting other notes of truth entitling them to credence, those few witnesses must inevitably lose in respectability according to the extent and frequency of such eccentric action.

2. If one Codex (z) is demonstrably the mere transcript of another Codex (f), these may no longer be reckoned as two Codexes, but as one Codex. It is hard therefore to understand how Tischendorf constantly adduces the evidence of 'E of Paul' although he was perfectly well aware that E is '*a mere transcript* of the Cod. Claro-montanus[1]' or D of Paul. Or again, how he quotes the cursive Evan. 102 ; because the readings of that unknown seventeenth-century copy of the Gospels are ascertained to have·been derived from Cod. B itself[2].

3. By strict parity of reasoning, when once it has been ascertained that, in any particular instance, Patristic testi-mony is not original but derived, each successive reproduc-tion of the evidence must obviously be held to add nothing at all to the weight of the original statement. Thus, it used to be the fashion to cite (in proof of the spuriousness

[1] Miller's Scrivener, I. p. 176.   [2] Ibid. p. 208.

of 'the last twelve verses' of St. Mark's Gospel) the authority of 'Eusebius, Gregory of Nyssa, Victor of Antioch, Severus of Antioch, Jerome [1],'—to which were added 'Epiphanius and Caesarius [2],'—'Hesychius of Jerusalem and Euthymius [3].' In this enumeration, the names of Gregory, Victor, Severus, Epiphanius and Caesarius were introduced in error. There remains Eusebius,—whose exaggeration (a) Jerome translates, (b) Hesychius (sixth century) copies, and (c) Euthymius (A.D. 1116) refers to [4] and Eusebius himself neutralizes [5]. The evidence therefore (such as it is) collapses hopelessly: being reducible probably to a random statement in the lost treatise of Origen on St. Mark [6], which Eusebius repudiates, even while in his latitudinarian way he reproduces it. The weight of such testimony is obviously slight indeed.

4. Again, if two, three, or four Codexes are discovered by reason of the peculiarities of text which they exhibit to have been derived,—nay, confessedly are derived—from one and the same archetype,—those two, three, or four Codexes may no longer be spoken of as if they were so many. Codexes B and ℵ, for example, being certainly the twin products of a lost exemplar, cannot in fairness be reckoned as = 2. Whether their combined evidence is to be estimated at = 1·75, 1·50, or 1·25, or as only 1·0,—let diviners decide. May I be allowed to suggest that whenever they agree in an extraordinary reading their combined evidence is to be reckoned at about 1·50 : when in an all but unique reading, at 1·25 : when the reading they contain is absolutely unique, as when they exhibit συστρεφομένων δὲ αὐτῶν in St. Matt. xvii. 22, they should be reckoned as a single Codex? Never, at all events, can they be jointly reckoned as absolutely two.

---

[1] Tregelles' Printed Text, &c., p. 247.

[2] Tischendorf, N. T., p. 322.   [3] Tischendorf and Alford.

[4] Burgon's Last Twelve Verses, &c., pp. 38-69 ; also p. 267.

[5] Ad Marinum. Ibid. p. 265.   [6] Ibid. pp. 235-6.

I would have them cited as B-‍א. Similar considerations should be attached to F and G of St. Paul, as being 'independent transcripts of the same venerable archetype [1],' and to Evan. 13, 69, 124, 346, 556, 561, and perhaps 348, 624, 788 [2], as being also the representatives of only one anterior manuscript of uncertain date.

5. It requires further to be pointed out that when once a clear note of affinity has been ascertained to exist between a small set of documents, their exclusive joint consent is henceforward to be regarded with suspicion: in other words, their evidential Weight becomes impaired. For instance, the sympathy between D and some Old Latin copies is so marked, so constant, in fact so extraordinary, that it becomes perfectly evident that D, though only of the sixth century, must represent a Greek or Latin Codex of the inaccurate class which prevailed in the earliest age of all, a class from which some of the Latin translations were made [3].

6. I suppose it may be laid down that an ancient Version outweighs any single Codex, ancient or modern, which can be named : the reason being, that it is scarcely credible that a Version—the Peshitto, for example, an Egyptian, or the Gothic—can have been executed from a single exemplar. But indeed that is not all. The first of the above-named Versions and some of the Latin are older,— perhaps by two centuries—than the oldest known copy. From this it will appear that if the only witnesses producible for a certain reading were the Old Latin Versions and the Syriac Version on the one hand,—Codd. B-‍א on the other,—the united testimony of the first two would

---

[1] Miller's Scrivener, I. p. 181.

[2] Ferrar and Abbott's Collation of Four Important Manuscripts, Abbè Martin, *Quatre MSS. importants,* J. Rendel Harris, On the Origin of the Ferrar Group (C. J. Clay and Sons), 1893. Miller's Scrivener, I. p. 398*, App. F.

[3] See below, Chapter X. Also Mr. Rendel Harris' 'Study of Codex Bezae' in the Cambridge Texts and Studies.

very largely overbalance the combined testimony of the last.
If B or if ℵ stood alone, neither of them singly would be
any match for either the Syriac or the Old Latin Versions,
—still less for the two combined.

7. The cogency of the considerations involved in the
last paragraph becomes even more apparent when Patristic
testimony has to be considered.

It has been pointed out elsewhere [1] that, in and by itself,
the testimony of any first-rate Father, where it can be had,
must be held to outweigh the solitary testimony of any
single Codex which can be named. The circumstance
requires to be again insisted on here. How to represent
the amount of this preponderance by a formula, I know
not : nor as I believe does any one else know. But the
fact that it exists, remains, and is in truth undeniable.
For instance, the origin and history of Codexes ABℵC is
wholly unknown: their dates and the places of their
several production are matters of conjecture only. But
when we are listening to the articulate utterance of any
of the ancient Fathers, we not only know with more or
less of precision the actual date of the testimony before us,
but we even know the very diocese of Christendom in
which we are standing. To such a deponent we can
assign a definite amount of credibility, whereas in the
estimate of the former class of evidence we have only
inferences to guide us.

Individually, therefore, a Father's evidence, where it can be
certainly obtained—*caeteris paribus*, is considerably greater
than that of any single known Codex. Collectively, however,
the Copies, without question, outweigh either the Versions
by themselves, or the Fathers by themselves. I have met
—very rarely I confess—but I have met with cases where
the Versions, as a body, were opposed in their testimony
to the combined witness of Copies and Fathers. Also,

---

[1] Last Twelve Verses of St. Mark, p. 21, &c. ; Revision Revised, p. 297.

but very rarely, I have known the Fathers, as a body, opposed to the evidence of Copies and Versions. But I have never known a case where the Copies stood alone —with the Versions and the Fathers united against them.

I consider that such illustrious Fathers as Irenaeus and Hippolytus,—Athanasius and Didymus,—Epiphanius and Basil,—the two Gregories and Chrysostom,—Cyril and Theodoret, among the Greeks,—Tertullian and Cyprian,— Hilary and Ambrose,—Jerome and Augustine, among the Latins,—are more respectable witnesses by far than the same number of Greek or Latin Codexes. Origen, Clemens Alexandrinus, and Eusebius, though first-rate Authors, were so much addicted to Textual Criticism themselves, or else employed such inconsistent copies, — that their testimony is that of indifferent witnesses or bad judges.

As to the Weight which belongs to separate Copies, that must be determined mainly by watching their evidence. If they go wrong continually, their character must be low. They are governed in this respect by the rules which hold good in life. We shall treat afterwards of the character of Codex D, of ℵ, and of B.

§ 5. *Continuity.*

In proposing Continuous Existence as another note of a genuine reading, I wish to provide against those cases where the Evidence is not only ancient, but being derived from two different sources may seem to have a claim to variety also. I am glad to have the opportunity thus early of pointing out that the note of variety may not fairly be claimed for readings which are not advocated by more than two distinct specimens of ancient evidence. But just now my actual business is to insist that some sort of Continuousness is requisite as well as Antiquity, Number, Variety, and Weight.

We can of course only know the words of Holy Scripture

according as they have been handed down to us ; and in ascertaining what those words actually were, we are driven perforce to the Tradition of them as it has descended to us through the ages of the Church. But if that Tradition is broken in the process of its descent, it cannot but be deprived of much of the credit with which it would otherwise appeal for acceptance. A clear groundwork of reasonableness lay underneath, and a distinct province was assigned, when *quod semper* was added to *quod ubique et quod ab omnibus.* So there is a Catholic of time, as well as of space and of people : and all must be claimed in the ascertainment and support of Holy Writ.

When therefore a reading is observed to leave traces of its existence and of its use all down the ages, it comes with an authority of a peculiarly commanding nature. And on the contrary, when a chasm of greater or less breadth of years yawns in the vast mass of evidence which is ready for employment, or when a tradition is found to have died out, upon such a fact alone suspicion or grave doubt, or rejection must inevitably ensue.

Still more, when upon the admission of the Advocates of the opinions which we are opposing the chasm is no longer restricted but engulfs not less than fifteen centuries in its hungry abyss, or else when the transmission ceased after four centuries, it is evident that according to an essential Note of Truth, those opinions cannot fail to be self-destroyed as well as to labour under condemnation during more than three quarters of the accomplished life of Christendom.

How Churchmen of eminence and ability, who in other respects hold the truths involved in Churchmanship, are able to maintain and propagate such opinions without surrendering their Churchmanship, we are unable to explain. We would only hope and pray that they may be led to see the inconsistencies of their position. And to others who do not accept Church doctrine we would urge that, inasmuch as internal evidence is so uncertain as often to face both ways, they really cannot rest upon anything else than continuous teaching if they would mount above personal likings and dislikings to the possession of definite and unmistakable support. In fact all traditional teaching which is not continuous must be like the detached pieces of a disunited chain.

To put the question in the most moderate form, my meaning is, that although it is possible that no trace may be discoverable in any later document of what is already attested by documents of the fourth century to be the true reading of any given place of Scripture, yet it is a highly improbable circumstance that the evidence should entirely disappear at such a very early period. It is reasonable to expect that if a reading advocated by Codexes א and B, for instance, and the Old Latin Versions, besides one or two of the Fathers, were trustworthy, there ought to be found at least a fair proportion of the later Uncial and the Cursive Copies to reproduce it. If, on the contrary, many of the Fathers knew nothing at all about the matter ; if Jerome reverses the evidence borne by the Old Latin ; if the later Uncials, and if the main body of the Cursives are silent also :—what can be said but that it is altogether unreasonable to demand acceptance for a reading which comes to us upon such a very slender claim to our confidence ?

That is the most important inference : and it is difficult to see how in the nature of the case it can be got over. But in other respects also :—when a smaller break occurs in the transmission, the evidence is proportionally injured. And the remark must be added, that in cases where there is a transmission by several lines of descent which, having in other respects traces of independence, coincide upon a certain point, it is but reasonable to conclude that those lines enjoy, perhaps, a silent, yet a parallel and unbroken tradition all down the ages till they emerge. **This prin-ciple** is often illustrated in the independent yet **consentient** testimony of the whole body of the Cursives and later Uncials [1].

§ 6. *Context.*

A prevailing fallacy with some critical writers on the subject to which the present volume is devoted, may be thus described. In the case of a disputed reading, they seem to think that they do enough if they simply marshal the authorities for and against, and deliver an oracular verdict. In critical editions of the Greek text, such a summary method is perhaps unavoidable. But I take leave to point out that in Sacred Textual Criticism there are several other considerations which absolutely require attention besides, and that those considerations ought to find ex-pression where the space permits. It is to some of these that I proceed now to invite the reader's attention.

A word,—a phrase,—a clause,—or even a sentence or a paragraph,— must have some relation to the rest of the entire passage which precedes or comes after it. There-fore it will often be necessary, in order to reach all the evidence that bears upon a disputed question, to examine both the meaning and the language lying on both sides of the point in dispute. We do not at present lay so much stress upon the contextual meaning, because people are generally not unready to observe it, and it is often open to much difference of opinion : — we refrain espe-cially, because we find from experience that there is in

---

[1] See more upon this point in Chapters V, XI. Compare St. Augustine's Canon: ' Quod universa tenet Ecclesia nec conciliis institutum sed semper retentum est, non nisi auctoritate Apostolica traditum rectissime creditur.' C. Donatist. iv. 24.

the case of the New Testament always enough external evidence of whose existence no doubt can be entertained to settle any textual question that can arise.

Nevertheless, it may be as well to give a single instance. In 1 Cor. xiii. 5, Codex B and Clement of Alexandria read τὸ μὴ ἑαυτῆς instead of τὰ ἑαυτῆς, i.e. ' charity seeketh not what does not belong to her,' instead of ' seeketh not her own.' That is to say, we are invited, in the midst of that magnificent passage which is full of lofty principles, to suppose that a gross violation of the eighth commandment is forbidden, and to insert a commonplace repudiation of gross dishonesty. We are to sink suddenly from a grand atmosphere down to a vulgar level. In fact, the light shed on the words in question from the context on either side of course utterly excludes such a supposition ; consequently, the only result is that we are led to distrust the witnesses that have given evidence which is so palpably absurd.

But as regards the precise form of language employed, it will be found also a salutary safeguard against error in every instance, to inspect with severe critical exactness the entire context of the passage in dispute. If in certain Codexes that context shall prove to be confessedly in a very corrupt state, then it becomes even self-evident that those Codexes can only be admitted as witnesses with considerable suspicion and reserve.

Take as an illustration of what I have been saying the exceedingly precious verse, ' Howbeit, this kind goeth not out but by prayer and fasting' (St. Matt. xvii. 21), which has met with rejection by the recent school of critics. Here the evidence against the verse is confined to B and the first reading of ℵ amongst the Uncials, Evan. 33 alone of the Cursives, e and ff[1] of the Old Latin Versions, as well as the Curetonian and the Lewis, Jerusalem, Sahidic, a few Bohairic copies, a few Ethiopic, and the Greek of Eusebius'

Canons:—evidence of a slight and shifty character, when contrasted with the witness of all the other Uncials and Cursives, the rest of the Versions, and more than thirteen of the Fathers beginning with Tertullian and Origen [1]. It is plain that the stress of the case for rejection, since ℵ being afterwards corrected speaks uncertainly, rests such as it is upon B; and that if the evidence of that MS. is found to be unworthy of credit in the whole passage, weak indeed must be the contention which consists mainly of such support.

Now if we inspect vv. 19, 20, 22, and 23, to go no farther, we shall discover that the entire passage in B is wrapped in a fog of error. It differs from the main body of the witnesses in ten places; in four of which its evidence is rejected by Lachmann, Tischendorf, Tregelles, Westcott and Hort, and the Revisers [2]; in two more by the Revisers [3]; and of the remaining four, it is supported in two by only ℵ and severally by one or six Cursives, and in the other two by only ℵ and D with severally four or five Cursive copies [4].

Inspection of the Context therefore adds here strong confirmation:—though indeed in this instance to have recourse to such a weapon is to slay the already slain.

St. Matthew (xi. 2, 3) relates that John Baptist 'having heard in the prison the works of CHRIST, sent two of his Disciples' (δύο τῶν μαθητῶν αὐτοῦ) with the inquiry, 'Art Thou He that should come [5], or are we to look for another (ἕτερον)?' So all the known copies but nine. So the Vulgate, Bohairic, Ethiopic. So Origen. So Chrysostom. It is interesting to note with what differences

---

[1] See Revision Revised, pp. 91, 206, and below, Chapter V.
[2] καθ' ἰδίαν, ἐδυνήθημεν, τριημέρᾳ, ἀναστήσεται.
[3] μετάβα, ἔνθεν.
[4] συστρεφομένων, ὀλιγοπιστίαν; omission of Ἰησοῦς, λέγει.
[5] ὁ ἐρχόμενος, for which D absurdly substitutes ὁ ἐργαζόμενος, 'he that worketh.'

of expression St. Luke reproduces this statement. Having
explained in ver. 18 that it was the Forerunner's disciples
who brought him tidings concerning CHRIST, St. Luke
(vii. 19) adds that John 'called for certain two' (δύο τινάς)
of them, and 'sent them to JESUS': thus emphasizing,
while he repeats, the record of the earlier Evangelist.
Inasmuch however as ἕτερον means, in strictness, 'the other
of two,' in order not to repeat himself, he substitutes ἄλλον
for it. Now all this is hopelessly obscured by the oldest
amongst our manuscript authorities. It in no wise sur-
prises us to find that τινάς has disappeared from D, the
Peshitto, Latin, Bohairic, Gothic, and Ethiopic. The word
has disappeared from our English version also. But it
offends us greatly to discover that (1) אBLRXℲ (with
Cyril) obliterate ἄλλον from St. Luke vii. 19, and thrust
ἕτερον into its place,—as clear an instance of vicious assimilation as could anywhere be found : while (2) for δύο (in
St. Matt. xi. 3) אBCDPZΔ write διά: which is acquiesced
in by the Peshitto, Harkleian, Gothic and Armenian Versions. The Old Latin Versions prevaricate as usual: two
read, *mittens duos ex discipulis suis* : all the rest,—*mittens
discipulos suos,*—which is the reading of Cureton's Syriac
and the Dialogus (p. 819), but of no known Greek MS.[1]
Lastly (3) for Ἰησοῦν in St. Luke, BLRℲ substitute κύριον.
What would be thought of us if we were freely imposed
upon by readings so plainly corrupt as these three ?

But light is thrown upon them by the context in
St. Luke. In the thirteen verses which immediately
follow, Tischendorf himself being the judge, the text has
experienced depravation in at least fourteen particulars[2].

---

[1] So, as it seems, the Lewis, but the column is defective.

[2] Viz. Ver. 20, ἀπέστειλεν for ἀπέσταλκεν, אB ; ἕτερον for ἄλλον, אDLXℲ.
Ver. 22, omit ὅτι, אBLXℲ ; insert καὶ before κωφοί, אBDFΓΔ*∴ ; insert καὶ
before πτωχοί, אFX. Ver. 23, ὃς ἂν for ὃς ἐάν, אD. Ver. 24, τοῖς ὄχλοις for πρὸς
τοὺς ὄχλους, אD and eight others ; ἐξήλθατε for ἐξεληλύθατε, אABDLℲ. Ver. 25,
ἐξήλθατε for ἐξεληλύθατε, אABDLℲ. Ver. 26, ἐξήλθατε for ἐξεληλύθατε, אBDLℲ.
Ver. 28, insert ἀμὴν before λέγω, אLX ; omit προφήτης, אBKLMX. Ver. 30,

With what reason can the same critic straightway insist on other readings which rest exclusively upon the same authorities which the fourteen readings just mentioned claim for their support?

This Note of Truth has for its foundation the well-known law that mistakes have a tendency to repeat themselves in the same or in other shapes. The carelessness, or the vitiated atmosphere, that leads a copyist to misrepresent one word is sure to lead him into error about another. The ill-ordered assiduity which prompted one bad correction most probably did not rest there. And the errors committed by a witness just before or just after the testimony which is being sifted was given cannot but be held to be closely germane to the inquiry.

So too on the other side. Clearness, correctness, self-collectedness, near to the moment in question, add to the authority of the evidence. Consequently, the witness of the Context cannot but be held to be positively or negatively, though perhaps more often negatively than positively, a very apposite Note of Truth.

§ 7. *Internal Evidence.*

It would be a serious omission indeed to close this enumeration of Tests of Truth without adverting to those Internal Considerations which will make themselves heard, and are sometimes unanswerable.

Thus the reading of πάντων (masculine or neuter) which is found in Cod. B (St. Luke xix. 37) we reject at once because of its grammatical impossibility as agreeing with δυνάμεων (feminine); and that of καρδίαις (2 Cor. iii. 3) according to the witness of AℵBCDEGLP on the score of its utter impossibility[1]. Geographical reasons are suffi-

omit εἰς ἑαυτούς, ℵD. Ver. 32, ἃ λέγει for λέγοντες, ℵ*B. See Tischendorf, eighth edition, *in loco*. The *Concordia discors* will be noticed.

[1] The explanation given by the majority of the Revisers has only their English Translation to recommend it, 'in tables that are hearts of flesh' for

ciently strong against reading with Codd. אIKNΠ ἑκατὸν καὶ ἑξήκοντα in St. Luke xxiv. 13 (i. e. a hundred and threescore furlongs), to make it of no manner of importance that a few additional authorities, as Origen, Eusebius, and Jerome, can be produced in support of the same manifestly corrupt reading. On grounds of ordinary reasonableness we cannot hear of the sun being eclipsed when the moon was full, or of our Lord being pierced before death. The truth of history, otherwise sufficiently attested both by St. Matthew and Josephus, absolutely forbids αὐτοῦ (אBDLΔ) to be read for αὐτῆς (St. Mark vi. 22), and in consequence the wretched daughter of Herodias to be taken to have been the daughter of Herod.

In these and such-like instances, the Internal reasons are plain and strong. But there is a manifest danger, when critics forsake those considerations which depend upon clear and definite points, and build their own inventions and theories into a system of strict canons which they apply in the teeth of manifold evidence that has really everything to recommend it. The extent to which some critics are ready to go may be seen in the monstrous Canon proposed by Griesbach, that where there are more readings than one of any place, that reading which favours orthodoxy is an object of suspicion[1]. There is doubtless some reason in the Canon which asserts that 'The harder the reading, the less likely it is to have been invented, and the more likely it is to be genuine,' under which δευτεροπρώτῳ

ἐν πλαξὶ καρδίαις σαρκίναις. In the Traditional reading (a) πλαξὶ σαρκίναις answers to πλαξὶ λιθίναις ; and therefore σαρκίναις would agree with πλαξί, not with καρδίαις. (b) The opposition between λιθίναις and καρδίαις σαρκίναις would be weak indeed, the latter being a mere appendage in apposition to πλαξί, and would therefore be a blot in St. Paul's nervous passage. (c) The apposition is harsh, ill-balanced (contrast St. Mark viii. 8), and unlike Greek: Dr. Hort is driven to suppose πλαξί to be a 'primitive interpolation.' The faultiness of a majority of the Uncials is corrected by Cursives, Versions, Fathers.

[1] 'Inter plures unius loci lectiones ea pro suspecta merito habetur, quae orthodoxorum dogmatibus manifeste prae ceteris favet.' N. T. Prolegomena, I. p. lxvi.

(St. Luke vi. 1) must receive additional justification. But people are ordinarily so constituted, that when they have once constructed a system of Canons they place no limits to their operation, and become slaves to them.

Accordingly, the true reading of passages must be ascertained, with very slight exception indeed, from the preponderating weight of external evidence, judged according to its antiquity, to number, variety, relative value, continuousness, and with the help of the context. Internal considerations, unless in exceptional cases they are found in strong opposition to evident error, have only a subsidiary force. Often they are the product of personal bias, or limited observation : and where one scholar approves, another dogmatically condemns. Circumstantial evidence is deservedly rated low in the courts of justice : and lawyers always produce witnesses when they can. The Text of Holy Scripture does not vary with the weathercock according to changing winds of individual or general opinion or caprice : it is decided by the Tradition of the Church as testified by eye-witnesses and written in black and white and gold in all countries of Christendom, and all down the ages since the New Testament was composed.

I desire to point out concerning the foregoing seven Notes of Truth in Textual Evidence that the student can never afford entirely to lose sight of any of them. The reason is because although no doubt it is conceivable that any one of the seven might possibly in itself suffice to establish almost any reading which can be named, practically this is never the case. And why? Because we never meet with any one of these Tests in the fullest possible measure. No Test ever attains to perfection, or indeed can attain. An approximation to the Test is all that can be expected, or even desired. And sometimes we are obliged to put up with a very slight approximation indeed. Their strength resides in their co-operation.

CHAPTER IV.

§ 1.

NO progress is possible in the department of 'Textual Criticism' until the superstition—for we are persuaded that it is nothing less—which at present prevails concerning certain of 'the old uncials' (as they are called) has been abandoned. By 'the old uncials' are generally meant, [1] The *Vatican* Codex (B),—and [2] the *Sinaitic* Codex (ℵ),—which by common consent are assigned to the fourth century: [3] the *Alexandrian* (A), and [4] the *Cod. Ephraemi rescriptus* (C),—which are given to the fifth century: and [5] the *Codex Bezae* (D),—which is claimed for the sixth century: to which must now be added [6] the *Codex Beratinus* (Φ), at the end of the fifth, and [7] the *Codex Rossanensis* (Σ), at the beginning of the sixth century. Five of these seven Codexes for some unexplained reason, although the latest of them (D) is sundered from the great bulk of the copies, uncial and cursive, by about as many centuries as the earliest of them (Bℵ) are sundered from the last of their group, have been invested with oracular authority and are supposed to be the vehicles of imperial decrees. It is pretended that what is found in either B or in ℵ or in D, although unsupported by any other manuscript, may reasonably be claimed to exhibit the truth of scripture, in defiance of the combined evidence of all other documents to the contrary. Let a reading be advocated by B and ℵ in conjunction, and it is assumed as a matter of course that such evidence must needs outweigh the combined evidence of all other MSS. which can be named. But when (as often happens) three or four of these 'old uncials' are in accord,—especially if (as is not unfrequently the case) they have the support of a single ancient version (as the Bohairic),—or a solitary early Father (as Origen), it seems to be deemed axiomatic that such evidence must needs carry all before it [1].

I maintain the contradictory proposition, and am prepared to prove it. I insist that readings so supported are clearly untrustworthy and may be dismissed as certainly unauthentic.

But let us in this chapter seek to come to some understanding with one another. My method shall be to ask a plain question which shall bring the matter to a clear issue. I will then (1) invent the best answers I am able to that question: and then (2) to the best of my ability— I will dispose of these answers one by one. If the reader (1) is able to assign a better answer,—or (2) does not deem my refutation satisfactory,—he has but to call me publicly to account: and by the rejoinder I shall publicly render either he, or I, must be content to stand publicly discredited. If I knew of a fairer way of bringing this by no means recondite matter to a definite issue, the reader may be well assured I should now adopt it [2].—My general question is,—Why throughout the Gospels are B and ℵ accounted so trustworthy, that all but the absolute disposal of every disputed question about the Text is held to depend upon their evidence?

And I begin by asking of a supposed Biblical Student,— Why throughout the Gospels should Codex B and ℵ be deemed more deserving of our confidence than the other Codexes?

---

[1] See Hort's Introduction, pp. 210–270.

[2] I have retained this challenge though it has been rendered nugatory by the Dean's lamented death, in order to exhibit his absolute sincerity and fearlessness.—E. M.

Biblical Student. Because they are the most ancient of our Codexes.

Dean Burgon. This answer evidently seems to you to convey an axiomatic truth : but not to me. I must trouble you to explain to me why ' the most ancient of our Codexes' must needs be the purest ?

B. S. I have not said that they ' must needs be the purest' : and I request you will not impute to me anything which I do not actually say.

The Dean. Thank you for a most just reproof. Let us only proceed in the same spirit to the end, and we shall arrive at important results. Kindly explain yourself therefore in your own way.

B. S. I meant to say that because it is a reasonable presumption that the oldest Codexes will prove the purest, therefore Bℵ—being the oldest Codexes of the Gospels— may reasonably be expected to be the best.

The Dean. So far happily we are agreed. You mean, I presume, that inasmuch as it is an admitted principle that the stream is purest at its source, the antiquity of B and ℵ creates a reasonable presumption in their favour. Is that what you mean ?

B. S. Something of the kind, no doubt. You may go on.

The Dean. Yes, but it would be a great satisfaction to me to know for certain, whether you actually do, or actually do not mean what I suppose :—viz., to apply the principle, *id verum esse quod primum*, I take you to mean that in B and ℵ we have the nearest approach to the autographs of the Evangelists, and that therefore in them we have the best evidence that is at present within reach of what those autographs actually were. I will now go on as you bid me. And I take leave to point out to you, that it is high time that we should have the facts of the case definitely before us, and that we should keep them steadily in view throughout our subsequent discussion. Now all critics are agreed, that B and ℵ were not written earlier than about 340, or say before 330 A. D. You will admit that, I suppose?

B. S. I have no reason to doubt it.

The Dean. There was therefore an interval of not far short of three hundred years between the writing of the original autographs and the copying of the Gospels in B and ℵ [1]. Those two oldest Codexes, or the earliest of them, are thus found to be separated by nearly three centuries from the original writings,—or to speak more accurately,—by about two centuries and three-quarters from three of the great autographs, and by about 250 years from the fourth. Therefore these MSS. cannot be said to be so closely connected with the original autographs as to be entitled to decide about disputed passages what they were or were not. Corruption largely infected the several writings [2], as I shall shew at some length in some subsequent chapters, during the great interval to which I have alluded.

B. S. But I am surprised to hear you say this. You must surely recollect that B and ℵ were derived from one and the same archetype, and that that archetype was produced 'in the early part of the second century if not earlier [3],' and was very close to the autographs, and that they must be accordingly accurate transcripts of the autographs, and—

The Dean. I must really pray you to pause :—you have left facts far behind, and have mounted into cloud-land. I must beg you not to let slip from your mind, that we start with a fact, so far as it can be ascertained, viz. the production of B and ℵ, about the middle of the fourth

---

[1] Here the Dean's MS. ceases, and the Editor is responsible for what follows. The MS. was marked in pencil, 'Very rough —but worth carrying on.'

[2] See a passage from Caius quoted in The Revision Revised, p. 323. Eusebius, Hist. Eccles. v. 28.   [3] Hort, Introduction, p. 223.

century. You have advanced from that fact to what is only a probable opinion, in which however I am agreed with you, viz. that B and ℵ are derived from one and the same older manuscript. Together therefore, I pray you will not forget, they only count nearly as one. But as to the age of that archetype—forgive me for saying, that—unintentionally no doubt but none the less really—you have taken a most audacious leap. May I ask, however, whether you can quote any ancient authority for the date which you have affixed?

B. S. I cannot recollect one at the present moment.

The Dean. No, nor Dr. Hort either,—for I perceive that you adopt his speculation. And I utterly deny that there is any probability at all for such a suggestion :—nay, the chances are greatly, if not decisively, against the original from which the lines of B and ℵ diverged, being anything like so old as the second century. These MSS. bear traces of the Origenistic school, as I shall afterwards shew [1]. They have too much method in their error for it to have arisen in the earliest age : its systematic character proves it to have been the growth of time. They evince effects, as I shall demonstrate in due course, of heretical teaching, Lectionary practice, and regular editing, which no manuscript could have contracted in the first ages of the Church.

B. S. But surely the differences between B and ℵ, which are many, prove that they were not derived immediately from their common ancestor, but that some generations elapsed between them. Do you deny that?

The Dean. I grant you entirely that there are many differences between them,—so much the worse for the value of their evidence. But you must not suffer yourself to be misled by the figure of genealogy upon points where it presents no parallel. There were in manuscripts no

[1] See Appendix V, and below, Chapter IX.

periods of infancy, childhood, and youth, which must elapse before they could have a progeny. As soon as a manuscript was completed, and was examined and passed, it could be copied : and it could be copied, not only once a year, but as often as copyists could find time to write and complete their copies [1]. You must take also another circumstance into consideration. After the destruction of manuscripts in the persecution of Diocletian, and when the learned were pressing from all quarters into the Church, copies must have been multiplied with great rapidity. There was all the more room for carelessness, inaccuracy, incompetency, and capricious recension. Several generations of manuscripts might have been given off in two or three years.—But indeed all this idea of fixing the date of the common ancestor of B and ℵ is based upon pure speculation :—Textual Science cannot rest her conclusions upon foundations of sand like that. I must bring you back to the Rock : I must recall you to facts. B and ℵ were produced in the early middle, so to speak, of the fourth century. Further than this, we cannot go, except to say— and this especially is the point to which I must now request your attention,—that we are in the possession of evidence older than they are.

B. S. But you do not surely mean to tell me that other Uncials have been discovered which are earlier than these ?

The Dean. No : not yet : though it is possible, and perhaps probable, that such MSS. may come to light, not in vellum but in papyrus ; for as far as we know,

---

[1] As a specimen of how quickly a Cursive copy could be written by an accomplished copyist, we may note the following entry from Dean Burgon's Letters in the Guardian to Dr. Scrivener, in a letter dated Jan. 29, 1873. ' Note further, that there is . . . another copy of the O. T. in one volume . . . at the end of which is stated that Nicodemus ὁ ξένος, the scribe, began his task on the 8th of June and finished it on the 15th of July, A. D. 1334, working very hard—as he must have done indeed.'

B and ℵ mark the emergence into prominence of the 'Uncial' class of great manuscripts[1]. But though there are in our hands as yet no older manuscripts, yet we have in the first place various Versions, viz., the Peshitto of the second century[2], the group of Latin Versions[3] which begin from about the same time, the Bohairic and the Thebaic of the third century, not to speak of the Gothic which was about contemporary with your friends the Vatican and Sinaitic MSS. Next, there are the numerous Fathers who quoted passages in the earliest ages, and thus witnessed to the MSS. which they used. To take an illustration, I have cited upon the last twelve verses of St. Mark's Gospel no less than twelve authorities before the end of the third century, that is down to a date which is nearly half a century before B and ℵ appeared. The general mass of quotations found in the books of the early Fathers witnesses to what I say[4]. So that there is absolutely no reason to place these two MSS. upon a pedestal by themselves on the score of supreme antiquity. They are eclipsed in this respect by many other authorities older than they are. Such, I must beg you to observe, is the verdict, not of uncertain speculation, but of stubborn facts.

B. S. But if I am not permitted to plead the highest antiquity on behalf of the evidence of the two oldest Uncials,—

The Dean. Stop, I pray you. Do not imagine for a single instant that I wish to prevent your pleading anything at all that you may fairly plead. Facts, which refuse to be explained out of existence, not myself, bar your way. Forgive me, but you must not run your head against a brick wall.

B. S. Well then[5], I will meet you at once by asking

---

[1] See below, Chapter VIII. § 2.   [2] See Chapter VI.
[3] See Chapter VII.   [4] See next Chapter.
[5] Another fragment found in the Dean's papers is introduced here.

a question of my own. Do you deny that B and א are the most precious monuments of their class in existence?

The Dean. So far from denying, I eagerly assert that they are. Were they offered for sale to-morrow, they would command a fabulous sum. They might fetch perhaps £100,000. For aught I know or care they may be worth it. More than one cotton-spinner is worth—or possibly several times as much.

B. S. But I did not mean that. I spoke of their importance as instruments of criticism.

The Dean. Again we are happily agreed. Their importance is unquestionably first-rate. But to come to the point, will you state plainly, whether you mean to assert that their text is in your judgement of exceptional purity?

B. S. I do.

The Dean. At last there we understand one another. I on the contrary insist, and am prepared to prove, that the text of these two Codexes is very nearly the foulest in existence. On what, pray, do you rely for your opinion which proves to be diametrically the reverse of mine [1]?

B. S. The best scholars tell me that their text, and especially the text of B, is of a purer character than any other: and indeed I myself, after reading B in Mai's edition, think that it deserves the high praise given to it.

The Dean. My dear friend, I see that you have been taken in by Mai's edition, printed at Leipzig, and published in England by Williams & Norgate and D. Nutt. Let me tell you that it is a most faulty representation of B. It mixes later hands with the first hand. It abounds in mistakes. It inserts perpetually passages which are nowhere found in the copy. In short, people at the time fancied that in the text of the mysterious manuscript in

[1] Here the fragment ends.

the Vatican they would find the *verba ipsissima* of the Gospels: but when Cardinal Mai was set to gratify them, he found that B would be unreadable unless it were edited with a plentiful correction of errors. So the world then received at least two recensions of B mixed up in this edition, whilst B itself remained behind. The world was generally satisfied, and taken in. But I am sorry that you have shared in the delusion.

B. S. Well, of course I may be wrong: but surely you will respect the opinion of the great scholars.

The Dean. Of course I respect deeply the opinion of any great scholars: but before I adopt it, I must know and approve the grounds of their opinion. Pray, what in this instance are they?

B. S. They say that the text is better and purer than any other.

The Dean. And I say that it is nearly the most corrupt known. If they give no special grounds except the fact that they think so, it is a conflict of opinion. There is a balance between us. But from this deadlock I proceed to facts. Take for example, as before, the last twelve verses of St. Mark. On the one side are alleged B and ℵ,— of which B by the exhibition of a blank space mutely confesses its omission, and ℵ betrays that it is double-minded [1]; one Old Latin MS. (*k*), two Armenian MSS., two Ethiopic, and an Arabic Lectionary; an expression of Eusebius, who elsewhere quotes the passage, which was copied by Jerome and Severus of Antioch, saying that the verses were omitted in some copies. L of the eighth century, and a few Cursives, give a brief, but impossible, termination. On the other side I have referred to [2] six witnesses of the second century, six of the third, fifteen of the fourth, nine of the fifth, eight of the sixth and seventh,

---

[1] See Dr. Gwynn's remarks which are quoted below, Appendix VII.
[2] The Revision Revised, p. 423. Add a few more; see Appendix VII.

all the other Uncials, and all the other Cursives, including the universal and immemorial Liturgical use. Here, as you must see, B and ℵ, in faltering tones, and with only an insignificant following, are met by an array of authorities, which is triumphantly superior, not only in antiquity, but also in number, variety, and continuousness. I claim also the superiority as to context, internal considerations, and in weight too.

B. S. But surely weight is the ground of contention between us.

The Dean. Certainly, and therefore I do not assume my claim till I substantiate it. But before I go on to do so, may I ask whether you can dispute the fact of the four first Notes of Truth being on my side?

B. S. No: you are entitled to so much allowance.

The Dean. That is a very candid admission, and just what I expected from you. Now as to Weight. The passage just quoted is only one instance out of many. More will abound later on in this book: and even then many more must of necessity remain behind. In point of hard and unmistakable fact, there is a continual conflict going on all through the Gospels between B and ℵ and a few adherents of theirs on the one side, and the bulk of the Authorities on the other, and the nature and weight of these two Codexes may be inferred from it. They will be found to have been proved over and over again to be bad witnesses, who were left to survive in their handsome dresses whilst attention was hardly ever accorded to any services of theirs. Fifteen centuries, in which the art of copying the Bible was brought to perfection, and printing invented, have by unceasing rejection of their claims sealed for ever the condemnation of their character, and so detracted from their weight.

B. S. Still, whilst I acknowledge the justice of much that you have said, I cannot quite understand how the text of later copies can be really older than the text of earlier ones.

The Dean. You should know that such a thing is quite possible. Copies much more numerous and much older than B and ℵ live in their surviving descendants. The pedigree of the Queen is in no wise discredited because William the Conqueror is not alive. But then further than this. The difference between the text of B and ℵ on the one side and that which is generally represented by A and Φ and Σ on the other is not of a kind depending upon date, but upon recension or dissemination of readings. No amplification of B and ℵ could by any process of natural development have issued in the last twelve verses of St. Mark. But it was easy enough for the scribe of B not to write, and the scribe of ℵ consciously[1] and deliberately to omit, verses found in the copy before him, if it were determined that they should severally do so. So with respect to the 2,556 omissions of B. The original text could without any difficulty have been spoilt by leaving out the words, clauses, and sentences thus omitted : but something much more than the shortened text of B was absolutely essential for the production of the longer manuscripts. This is an important point, and I must say something more upon it.

First then[2], Cod. B is discovered not to contain in the Gospels alone 237 words, 452 clauses, 748 whole sentences, which the later copies are observed to exhibit in the same places and in the same words. By what possible hypothesis will such a correspondence of the Copies be accounted for, if these words, clauses, and sentences are indeed, as is pretended, nothing else but spurious accretions to the text ?

Secondly, the same Codex throughout the Gospels

---

[1] Dr. Gwynn, Appendix VII.
[2] Another MS. comes in here.

exhibits 394 times words in a certain order, which however is not the order advocated by the great bulk of the Copies. In consequence of what subtle influence will it be pretended, that all over the world for a thousand years the scribes were universally induced to deflect from the authentic collocation of the same inspired words, and always to deflect in precisely the same way?

But Cod. B also contains 937 Gospel words, of which by common consent the great bulk of the Cursive Copies know nothing. Will it be pretended that in any part of the Church for seven hundred years copyists of Evangelia entered into a grand conspiracy to thrust out of every fresh copy of the Gospel self-same words in the self-same places [1]?

You will see therefore that B, and so ℵ, since the same arguments concern one as the other, must have been derived from the Traditional Text, and not the Traditional Text from those two Codexes.

B. S. You forget that Recensions were made at Edessa or Nisibis and Antioch which issued in the Syrian Texts, and that that was the manner in which the change which you find so difficult to understand was brought about.

The Dean. Excuse me, I forget no such thing; and for a very good reason, because such Recensions never occurred. Why, there is not a trace of them in history: it is a mere dream of Dr. Hort: they must be 'phantom recensions,' as Dr. Scrivener terms them. The Church of the time was not so unconscious of such matters as Dr. Hort imagines. Supposing for a moment that such Recensions took place, they must have been either merely local occurrences, in which case after a controversy on which history is silent they would have been inevitably rejected by the other Churches in Christendom; or they must have been general operations of the Universal Church, and then inasmuch as

[1] The MS. ceases.

they would have been sealed with the concurrence of fifteen centuries, I can hardly conceive greater condemnations of B and ℵ. Besides, how could a text which has been in fact Universal be ' Syrian'? We are on *terra firma*, let me remind you, not in the clouds. The undisputed action of fifteen centuries is not to be set aside by a nickname.

B. S. But there is another way of describing the process of change which may have occurred in the reverse direction to that which you advocate. Expressions which had been introduced in different groups of readings were combined by ' Conflation ' into a more diffuse and weaker passage. Thus in St. Mark vi. 33, the two clauses καὶ προῆλθον αὐτούς, καὶ συνῆλθον αὐτοῦ, are made into one conflate passage, of which the last clause is 'otiose' after συνέδραμον ἐκεῖ occurring immediately before [1].

The Dean. Excuse me, but I entirely disagree with you. The whole passage appears to me to savour of the simplicity of early narratives. Take for example the well-known words in Gen. xii. 5, 'and they went forth to go into the land of Canaan ; and into the land of Canaan they came [2].' A clumsy criticism, bereft of any fine appreciation of times and habits unlike the present, might I suppose attempt to remove the latter clause from that place as being ' otiose.' But besides, your explanation entirely breaks down when it is applied to other instances. How could conflation, or mixture, account for occurrence of the last cry in St. Mark xv. 39, or of vv. 43–44 in St. Luke xxii describing the Agony and Bloody Sweat, or of the first Word from the Cross in St. Luke xxiii. 34, or of the descending angel and the working of the cure in St. John v. 3–4, or of St. Peter's visit to the sepulchre in St. Luke xxiv. 12, or what would be the foisting of verses or passages of different lengths into

---

[1] Hort, Introduction, pp. 95–99.
[2] וַיֵּצְאוּ לָלֶכֶת אַרְצָה כְּנַעַן וַיָּבֹאוּ אַרְצָה כְּנָעַן :

the numerous and similar places that I might easily adduce? If these were all transcribed from some previous text into which they had been interpolated, they would only thrust the difficulty further back. How did they come there? The clipped text of B and ℵ—so to call it —could not have been the source of them. If they were interpolated by scribes or revisers, the interpolations are so good that, at least in many cases, they must have shared inspiration with the Evangelists. Contrast, for example, the real interpolations of D and the Curetonian. It is at the least demonstrated that that hypothesis requires another source of the Traditional Text, and this is the argument now insisted on. On the contrary, if you will discard your reverse process, and for ' Conflation' will substitute ' Omission' through carelessness, or ignorance of Greek, or misplaced assiduity, or heretical bias, or through some of the other causes which I shall explain later on, all will be as plain and easy as possible. Do you not see that? No explanation can stand which does not account for all the instances existing. Conflation or mixture is utterly incapable of meeting the larger number of cases. But you will find before this treatise is ended that various methods will be described herein with care, and traced in their actual operation, under which debased texts of various kinds were produced from the Traditional Text.

B. S. I see that there is much probability in what you say : but I retain still some lingering doubt.

The Dean. That doubt, I think, will be removed by the next point which I will now endeavour to elucidate. You must know that there is no agreement amongst the allies, except so far as the denial of truth is concerned. As soon as the battle is over, they at once turn their arms against one another. Now it is a phenomenon full of suggestion, that such a *Concordia discors* is conspicuous amongst B and ℵ and their associates. Indeed these two Codexes are individually at variance with themselves, since each of them has undergone later correction, and in fact no less than eleven hands from first to last have been at work on ℵ, which has been corrected and re-corrected backwards and forwards like the faulty document that it is. This by the way, but as to the continual quarrels of these dissentients[1], which are patent when an attempt is made to ascertain how far they agree amongst themselves, I must request your attention to a few points and passages[2].

§ 2. *St. John* v. 4.

When it is abruptly stated that ℵBCD—four out of 'the five old uncials'—omit from the text of St. John's Gospel the account of the angel descending into the pool and troubling the water,—it is straightway supposed that the genuineness of St. John v. 4 must be surrendered. But this is not at all the way to settle questions of this kind. Let the witnesses be called in afresh and examined.

Now I submit that since these four witnesses omitting A, (besides a multitude of lesser discrepancies,) are unable to agree among themselves whether 'there was at Jerusalem a sheep-*pool*' (ℵ), or 'a pool at the sheep-*gate*': whether it was 'surnamed' (BC), or 'named' (D), or neither (ℵ):—which appellation, out of thirty which have been proposed for this pool, they will adopt,—seeing that

[1] An instance is afforded in St. Mark viii. 7, where 'the Five Old Uncials' exhibit the passage thus :

A. και ταυτα ευλογησας ειπεν παρατεθηναι και αυτα.

ℵ*. και ευλογησας αυτα παρεθηκεν.

ℵ¹. και ευλογησας ειπεν και ταυτα παρατιθεναι.

B. και ευλογησας αυτα ειπεν και ταυτα παρατιθεναι.

C. και ευλογησας αυτα ειπεν και ταυτα παραθετε.

D. και ευχαριστησας ειπεν και αυτους εκελευσεν παρατιθεναι.

Lachmann, and Tischendorf (1859) follow A ; Alford, and Tischendorf (1869) follow ℵ ; Tregelles and Westcott, and Hort adopt B. They happen to be all wrong, and the Textus Receptus right. The only word they all agree in is the initial καί.

[2] After this the MSS. recommence.

C is for '*Bethesda*'; B for '*Bethsaida*'; ℵ for '*Bethzatha*'; D for '*Belzetha*':—whether or no the crowd was great, of which they all know nothing,—and whether some were 'paralytics,'—a fact which was evidently revealed only to D:—to say nothing of the vagaries of construction discoverable in verses 11 and 12:—when, you see, at last these four witnesses conspire to suppress the fact that an Angel went down into the pool to trouble the water;— this concord of theirs derives suggestive illustration from their conspicuous discord. Since, I say, there is so much discrepancy hereabouts in B and ℵ and their two associates on this occasion, nothing short of unanimity in respect of the thirty-two contested words—five in verse 3, and twenty-seven in verse 4 — would free their evidence from suspicion. But here we make the notable discovery that only three of them omit all the words in question, and that the second Corrector of C replaces them in that manuscript. D retains the first five, and surrenders the last twenty-seven : in this step D is contradicted by another of the ' Old Uncials,' A, whose first reading retains the last twenty-seven, and surrenders the first five. Even their satellite L forsakes them, except so far as to follow the first hand of A. Only five Cursives have been led astray, and they exhibit strikingly this *Concordia discors.* One (157) follows the extreme members of the loving company throughout. Two (18, 314) imitate A and L : and two more (33, 134) have the advantage of D for their leader. When witnesses prevaricate so hopelessly, how far can you believe them ?

Now—to turn for a moment to the other side—this is a matter on which the translations and such Fathers as quote the passage are able to render just as good evidence as the Greek copies : and it is found that the Peshitto, most of the Old Latin, as well as the Vulgate and the Jerusalem, with Tertullian, Ammonius, Hilary, Ephraem the Syrian, Ambrose (two), Didymus, Chrysostom (eight), Nilus (four), Jerome, Cyril of Alexandria (five), Augustine (two), and Theodorus Studita, besides the rest of the Uncials[1], and the Cursives[2], with the slight exception already mentioned, are opposed to the Old Uncials[3].

Let me next remind you of a remarkable instance of this inconsistency which I have already described in my book on The Revision Revised (pp. 34–36). 'The five Old Uncials' (אABCD) falsify the Lord's Prayer as given by St. Luke in no less than forty-five words. But so little do they agree among themselves, that they throw themselves into six different combinations in their departures from the Traditional Text; and yet they are never able to agree among themselves as to one single various reading : while only once are more than two of them observed to stand together, and their grand point of union is no less than an omission of the article. Such is their eccentric tendency, that in respect of thirty-two out of the whole forty-five words they bear in turn solitary evidence.

§ 3.

I should weary you, my dear student, if I were to take you through all the evidence which I could amass upon this disagreement with one another,—this *Concordia discors*. But I would invite your attention for a moment to a few points which being specimens may indicate the continued divisions upon Orthography which subsist between the Old Uncials and their frequent errors. And first[4], how

---

[1] SΠ mark the place with asterisks, and Λ with an obelus.

[2] In twelve, asterisks : in two, obeli.

[3] The MS., which has not been perfect, here ceases.

[4] In the Syriac *one* form appears to be used for *all* the *Marys* (ܡܰܪܝܰܡ = Mar-yam, also sometimes, but not always, spelt in the *Jerusalem Syriac* ܡܰܪܝܳܡ = Mar-yām), also for *Miriam* in the O. T., for *Mariamne* the wife of Herod, and others; in fact, wherever it is intended to represent a Hebrew female name. At Rom. xvi. 6, the Peshitto has ܡܰܪܺܝܰܐ = Μαρία, obviously as

do they write the 'Mary's' of the Gospels, of whom in strictness there are but three?

'The Mother of JESUS [1],' as most of us are aware, was not 'Mary' (Μαρία) at all; but '*Mariam*' (Μαριάμ),— a name strictly identical with that of the sister of Moses [2]. We call her ' Mary' only because the Latins *invariably* write her name 'Maria.' So complete an obliteration of the distinction between the name of the blessed Virgin—and *that* of (1) her sister, Mary the wife of Clopas [3], of (2) Mary Magdalene, and of (3) Mary the sister of Lazarus, may be deplored, but it is too late to remedy the mischief by full 1800 years. The question before us is not that ; but only — how far the distinction between '*Mariam*' and '*Maria*' has been maintained by the Greek copies?

Now, as for the cursives, with the memorable exception of Evann. 1 and 33,—which latter, because it is disfigured by more serious blunders than any other copy written in the cursive character, Tregelles by a *mauvaise plaisanterie* designates as ' the queen of the cursives,'—it may be said at once that they are admirably faithful. Judging from the practice of fifty or sixty which have been minutely

a translation of the Greek form in the text which was followed. (See Thesaurus Syriacus, Payne Smith, coll. 2225, 2226.)

In Syriac literature ܡܪܝܐ = Maria occurs from time to time as the name of some Saint or Martyr—e. g. in a volume of Acta Mart. described by Wright in Cat. Syr. MSS. in B. M. p. 1081, and which appears to be a fifth-century MS.

On the hypothesis that Hebrew-Aramaic was spoken in Palestine (*pace* Drs. Abbot and Roberts), I do not doubt that *only one* form (cf. Pearson, Creed, Art. iii. and notes) of the name was in use, 'Maryam,' a vulgarized form of ' Miriam '; but it may well be that Greek Christians kept the Hebrew form Μαριαμ for the Virgin, while they adopted a more Greek-looking word for the other women. This fine distinction has been lost in the *corrupt* Uncials, while observed in the *correct* Uncials and Cursives, which is all that the Dean's argument requires.—(G. H. G.)

[1] The MSS. continue here.　　　　　　　　　[2] LXX.

[3] St. John xix. 25. As the passage is *syndeton*, the omission of the καί which would be necessary if Μαρία ἡ τοῦ Κλωπᾶ were different from ἡ ἀδελφὴ τῆς μητρὸς αὐτοῦ could not be justified. Compare, e. g., the construction in the mention of four in St. Mark xiii. 3. In disregarding the usage requiring exclusively either *syndeton* or *asyndeton*, even scholars are guided unconsciously by their *English* experience.—(ED.)

examined with this view, the traces of irregularity are so
rare that the phenomenon scarcely deserves notice. Not
so the old uncials. Cod. B, on the first occasion where
a blunder is possible [1] (viz. in St. Matt. i. 20), exhibits Μαρία
instead of Μαριάμ :—so does Cod. C in xiii. 55,—Cod. D in
St. Luke i. 30, 39, 56 : ii. 5, 16, 34,—Codd. CD in St. Luke
by אBC, in St. Matt. i. 34, 38, 46,—Codd. אD, in ii. 19.

On the other hand, the Virgin's sister (Μαρία), is twice
written Μαριάμ : viz. by C, in St. Matt xxvii. 56 ; and by א,
in St. John xix. 25:—while Mary Magdalene is written
Μαριάμ by 'the five old uncials' no less than eleven times :
viz. by C, in St. Matt. xxvii. 56,—by א, in St. Luke xxiv. 10,
St. John xix. 25, xx. 11,—by A, in St. Luke viii. 2,—by אA,
in St. John xx. 1,—by אC, in St. Matt. xxviii. 1,—by אB,
in St. John xx. 16 and 18,—by BC, in St. Mark xv. 40,—
by אBC, in St. Matt. xxvii. 61.

Lastly, Mary (Μαρία) the sister of Lazarus, is called
Μαριάμ by Cod. B in St. Luke x. 42 : St. John xi. 2 : xii.
3 ;—by BC, in St. Luke xi. 32 ;—by אC, in St. Luke x.
39.—I submit that such specimens of licentiousness or
inattention are little calculated to conciliate confidence in
Codd. אBCD. It is found that B goes wrong nine times :
D, ten (exclusively in respect of the Virgin Mary) : C,
eleven : א, twelve.—Evan. 33 goes wrong thirteen times : 1,
nineteen times.—A, the least corrupt, goes wrong only twice.

§ 4.

Another specimen of a blunder in Codexes אL33 is
afforded by their handling of our LORD'S words,—'Thou
art Simon the son of Jona.' That this is the true reading
of St. John i. 43 is sufficiently established by the fact that

[1] The genitive Μαρ'ας is used in the Textus Receptus in Matt. i. 16, 18 ; ii.
11 ; Mark vi. 3 ; Luke i. 41. Μαριάμ is used in the Nominative, Matt. xiii. 55 ;
Luke i. 27, 34, 39, 46, 56 ; ii. 5, 19. In the Vocative, Luke i. 30. The
Accusative, Matt. i. 20 ; Luke ii. 16. Dative, Luke ii. 5 ; Acts i. 14.
Μαριάμ occurs for another Mary in the Textus Receptus, Rom. xvi. 6.

it is the reading of all the Codexes, uncial and cursive alike,—excepting always the four vicious specimens specified above. Add to the main body of the Codexes the Vulgate, Peshitto and Harkleian Syriac, the Armenian, Ethiopic, Georgian, and Slavonic versions :—besides several of the Fathers, such as Serapion[1],—Basil[2],—Epiphanius[3],—Chrysostom[4],—Asterius[5],—and another (unknown) writer of the fourth century[6] :—with Cyril[7] of the fifth,—and a body of evidence has been adduced, which alike in respect of its antiquity, its number, its variety, and its respectability, casts such witnesses as B-ℵ entirely into the shade. When it is further remembered that we have preserved to us in St. Matt. xvi. 17 our Saviour's designation of Simon's patronymic in the vernacular of Palestine, 'Simon Bar-jona,' which no manuscript has ventured to disturb, what else but irrational is the contention of the modern School that for 'Jona' in St. John i. 42, we are to read 'John'? The plain fact evidently is that some second-century critic supposed that 'Jonah' and 'John' are identical: and of his weak imagination the only surviving witnesses at the end of 1700 years are three uncials and one cursive copy,—a few copies of the Old Latin (which fluctuate between 'Johannis,' 'Johanna,' and 'Johna'),—the Bohairic Version, and Nonnus. And yet, on the strength of this slender minority, the Revisers exhibit in their text, 'Simon the son of John,'—and in their margin volunteer the information that the Greek word is 'Joanes,' —which is simply not the fact : Ιωανης being the reading of *no* Greek manuscript in the world except Cod. B[8].

---

[1] Serapion, Bp. of Thmuis (on a mouth of the Nile) A.D. 340 (*ap.* Galland. v. 60 a).
[2] Basil, i. 240 d.   [3] Epiphanius, i. 435 c.
[4] Chrysostom, iii. 120 d e ; vii. 180 a, 547 e *quat.*; viii. 112 a c (nine times).
[5] Asterius, p. 128 b.
[6] Basil Opp. (i. Append.) i. 500 e (cf. p. 377 Monitum).
[7] Cyril, iv. 131 c.
[8] A gives Ιωνα; ℵ, Ιωαννης; C and D are silent. Obvious it is that the

Again, in the margin of St. John i. 28 we are informed that instead of Bethany—the undoubted reading of the place,—some ancient authorities read 'Betharabah.' Why, there is not a single ancient Codex,—not a single ancient Father,—not a single ancient Version,—which so reads the place[1].

§ 5.

B. S. But[2], while I grant you that this general disagreement between B and ℵ and the other old Uncials which for a time join in their dissent from the Traditional Text causes the gravest suspicion that they are in error, yet it appears to me that these points of orthography are too small to be of any real importance.

The Dean. If the instances just given were only exceptions, I should agree with you. On the contrary, they indicate the prevailing character of the MSS. B and ℵ are covered all over with blots[3],—ℵ even more so than B. How they could ever have gained the characters which have been given them, is passing strange. But even great scholars are human, and have their prejudices and other weaknesses; and their disciples follow them everywhere as submissively as sheep. To say nothing of many great scholars who have never explored this field, if men of ordinary acquirements in scholarship would only emancipate themselves and judge with their own eyes, they would soon see the truth of what I say.

revised text of St. John i. 43 and of xxi. 15, 16, 17,—must stand or fall together. In this latter place the Vulgate forsakes us, and ℵB are joined by C and D. On the other hand, Cyril (iv. 1117),—Basil (ii. 298),—Chrysostom (viii. 525 c d),—Theodoret (ii. 426),—Jo. Damascene (ii. 510 e),—and Eulogius ([A. D. 580] *ap.* Photium, p. 1612), come to our aid. Not that we require it.

[1] '*Araba*' (instead of '*abara*') is a word which must have exercised so powerful and seductive an influence over ancient Eastern scribes,—(having been for *thirty-four centuries* the established designation of the sterile Wady, which extends from the Southern extremity of the Dead Sea to the North of the Arabian Gulf)—that the only wonder is it did not find its way into Evangelia. See Gesenius on עֲרָבָה ('Αραβα in the LXX of Deut. ii. 8, &c. So in the Revised O. T.).

[2] The MSS. have ceased.   [3] See Appendix V.

B. S. I should assent to all that you have told me, if I could only have before me a sufficient number of instances to form a sound induction, always provided that they agree with these which you have quoted Those which you have just given are enough as specimens : but forgive me when I say that, as a Biblical Student, I think I ought to form my opinions upon strong, deep, and wide foundations of facts.

The Dean. So far from requiring forgiveness from me, you deserve all praise. My leading principle is to build solely upon facts,—upon real, not fancied facts,—not upon a few favourite facts, but upon all that are connected with the question under consideration. And if it had been permitted me to carry out in its integrity the plan which I laid down for myself[1],—that however has been withheld under the good Providence of Almighty GOD.—Nevertheless I think that you will discover in the sequel enough to justify amply all the words that I have used. You will, I perceive, agree with me in this,—That whichever side of the contention is the most comprehensive, and rests upon the soundest and widest induction of facts,—that side, and that side alone, will stand.

[1] See Preface.

CHAPTER V.

THE ANTIQUITY OF THE TRADITIONAL TEXT [1].

I. WITNESS OF THE EARLY FATHERS.

§ 1. *Involuntary Evidence of Dr. Hort.*

OUR readers will have observed, that the chief obstacle in the way of an unprejudiced and candid examination of the sound and comprehensive system constructed by Dean Burgon is found in the theory of Dr. Hort. Of the internal coherence and the singular ingenuity displayed in Dr. Hort's treatise, no one can doubt : and I hasten to pay deserved and sincere respect to the memory of the highly accomplished author whose loss the students of Holy Scripture are even now deploring. It is to his arguments sifted logically, to the judgement exercised by him upon texts and readings, upon manuscripts and versions and Fathers, and to his collisions with the record of history, that a higher duty than appreciation of a Theologian however learned and pious compels us to demur.

But no searching examination into the separate links and details of the argument in Dr. Hort's Introduction to his Edition of the New Testament will be essayed now. Such a criticism has been already made by Dean Burgon in the 306th number of the Quarterly Review, and has

---

[1] This chapter and the next three have been supplied entirely by the Editor.

been republished in The Revision Revised [1].   The object here pursued is only to remove the difficulties which Dr. Hort interposes in the development of our own treatise. Dr. Hort has done a valuable service to the cause of Textual Criticism by supplying the rationale of the attitude of the School of Lachmann.   We know what it really means, and against what principles we have to contend. He has also displayed a contrast and a background to the true theory; and has shewn where the drawing and colouring are either ill-made or are defective.   More than all, he has virtually destroyed his own theory.

The parts of it to which I refer are in substance briefly the following:

'The text found in the mass of existing MSS. does not date further back than the middle of the fourth century. Before that text was made up, other forms of text were in vogue, which may be termed respectively Neutral, Western, and Alexandrian.   The text first mentioned arose in Syria and more particularly at Antioch.   Originally there had been in Syria an Old-Syriac, which after Cureton is to be identified with the Curetonian.   In the third century, about 250 A.D., "an authoritative revision, accepted by Syriac Christendom," was made, of which the locality would be either Edessa or Nisibis, or else Antioch itself.   "This revision was grounded probably upon an authoritative revision at Antioch" (p. 137) of the Greek texts which called for such a recension on account of their "growing diversity and confusion."   Besides these two, a second revision of the Greek texts, or a third counting the Syriac revision, similarly authoritative, was completed at Antioch "by 350 or thereabouts"; but what was now "the Vulgate Syriac" text, that is the Peshitto, did not again undergo any corresponding revision.   From the last Greek revision

---

[1] See also Miller's Textual Guide, chapter iv.   No answer has been made to the Dean's strictures.

issued a text which was afterwards carried to Constantinople—"Antioch being the true ecclesiastical parent of
Constantinople"—and thenceforward became the Text
dominant in Christendom till the present century. Nevertheless, it is not the true Text, for that is the "Neutral"
text, and it may be called "Syrian." Accordingly, in investigations into the character and form of the true Text,
"Syrian" readings are to be "rejected at once, as proved
to have a relatively late origin."'

A few words will make it evident to unprejudiced
judges that Dr. Hort has given himself away in this part
of his theory.

1. The criticism of the Canon and language of the
Books of the New Testament is but the discovery and
the application of the record of Testimony borne in history
to those books or to that language. For a proof of this
position as regards the Canon, it is sufficient to refer to
Bishop Westcott's admirable discussion upon the Canon
of the New Testament. And as with the Books generally,
so with the details of those Books—their paragraphs, their
sentences, their clauses, their phrases, and their words. To
put this dictum into other terms :—The Church, all down
the ages, since the issue of the original autographs, has
left in Copies or in Versions or in Fathers manifold
witness to the books composed and to the words written.
Dr. Hort has had the unwisdom from his point of view
to present us with some fifteen centuries, and—I must in
duty say it—the audacity to label those fifteen centuries of
Church Life with the title ' Syrian,' which as used by him
I will not characterize, for he has made it amongst his
followers a password to contemptuous neglect. Yet those
fifteen centuries involve everything. They commenced when
the Church was freeing herself from heresy and formulating
her Faith. They advanced amidst the most sedulous care
of Holy Scripture. They implied a consentient record from

the first, except where ignorance, or inaccuracy, or carelessness, or heresy, prevailed.   And was not Dr. Hort
aware, and do not his adherents at the present day know,
that Church Life means nothing arbitrary, but all that is
soundest and wisest and most complete in evidence, and
most large-minded in conclusions? Above all, did he fancy,
and do his followers imagine, that the HOLY GHOST who
inspired the New Testament could have let the true Text
of it drop into obscurity during fifteen centuries of its life,
and that a deep and wide and full investigation (which
by their premisses they will not admit) must issue in the
proof that under His care the WORD of GOD has been
preserved all through the ages in due integrity?—This
admission alone when stripped of its disguise, is plainly
fatal to Dr. Hort's theory.

2. Again, in order to prop up his contention, Dr. Hort
is obliged to conjure up the shadows of two or three
'phantom revisions,' of which no recorded evidence exists[1].
We must never forget that subjective theory or individual
speculation are valueless, when they do not agree with facts,
except as failures leading to some better system.   But
Dr. Hort, as soon as he found that he could not maintain
his ground with history as it was, instead of taking back
his theory and altering it to square with facts, tampered
with historical facts in order to make them agree with
his theory.   This is self-evident: no one has been able to
adduce, during the quarter of a century that has elapsed
since Dr. Hort published his book, passages to shew that
Dr. Hort was right, and that his supposed revisions
really took place.   The acute calculations of Adams and
Leverrier would have been very soon forgotten, if Neptune
had not appeared to vindicate their correctness.

But I shall not leave matters here, though it is evident

---

[1] See Dr. Scrivener's incisive criticism of Dr. Hort's theory, Introduction,
edit. 4, ii. 284–296.

that Dr. Hort is confuted out of his own mouth. The fifteen centuries of dominant evidence, which he admits to have been on our side, involve the other centuries that had passed previously, because the Catholic Church of Christ is ever consistent with itself, and are thus virtually decisive of the controversy; besides the collapse of his theory when superimposed upon the facts of history and found not to coincide with them. I proceed to prove from the surviving records of the first three or four centuries, during the long period that elapsed between the copying of the Vatican and Sinaitic MSS. and the days of the Evangelists, that the evidence of Versions and Fathers is on our side.

And first of the Fathers.

§ 2. *Testimony of the Ante-Chrysostom Writers.*

No one, I believe, has till now made a systematic examination of the quotations occurring in the writings of the Fathers who died before A. D. 400 and in public documents written prior to that date. The consequence is that many statements have been promulgated respecting them which are inconsistent with the facts of the case. Dr. Hort, as I shall shew, has offended more than once in this respect. The invaluable Indexes drawn up by Dean Burgon and those who assisted him, which are of the utmost avail in any exhaustive examination of Patristic evidence upon any given text, are in this respect of little use, the question here being, What is the testimony of all the Fathers in the first four centuries, and of every separate Father, as to the MSS. used by them or him, upon the controversy waged between the maintainers of the Traditional Text on the one side, and on the other the defenders of the Neologian Texts? The groundwork of such an examination evidently lies not in separate passages of the Gospels, but in the series of quotations from them found in the works of the collective or individual Fathers of the period under consideration.

I must here guard myself. In order to examine the text of any separate passage, the treatment must be exhaustive, and no evidence if possible should be left out. The present question is of a different kind. Dr. Hort states that the Traditional Text, or as he calls it 'the Syrian,' does not go back to the earliest times, that is as he says, not before the middle of the fourth century. In proving my position that it can be traced to the very first, it would be amply sufficient if I could shew that the evidence is half on our side and half on the other. It is really found to be much more favourable to us. We fully admit that corruption prevailed from the very first[1] : and so, we do not demand as much as our adversaries require for their justification. At all events the question is of a general character, and does not depend upon a little more evidence or a little less. And the argument is secondary in its nature : it relates to the principles of the evidence, not directly to the establishment of any particular reading. It need not fail therefore if it is not entirely exhaustive, provided that it gives a just and fair representation of the whole case. Nevertheless, I have endeavoured to make it exhaustive as far as my power would admit, having gone over the whole field a second time, and having employed all the care in either scrutiny that I could command.

The way in which my investigation has been accomplished is as follows :—A standard of reference being absolutely necessary, I have kept before me a copy of Dr. Scrivener's Cambridge Greek Testament, A. D. 1887, in which the disputed passages are printed in black type, although the

---

[1] The Revision Revised, pp. 323-324, 334.

Text there presented is the Textus Receptus from which the Traditional Text as revised by Dean Burgon and hereafter to be published differs in many passages. It follows therefore that upon some of these the record, though not unfavourable to us, has many times been included in our opponents' column. I have used copies of the Fathers in which the quotations were marked, chiefly those in Migne's Series, though I have also employed other editions where I could find any of superior excellence as well as Migne. Each passage with its special reading was entered down in my note-book upon one column or the other. Successive citations thus fell on either side when they witnessed upon the disputed points so presented. But all doubtful quotations (under which head were included all that were not absolutely clear) were discarded as untrustworthy witnesses in the comparison that was being made; and all instances too of mere spelling, because these latter might have been introduced into the text by copyists or editors through an adaptation to supposed orthography in the later ages when the text of the Father in question was copied or printed. The fact also that deflections from the text more easily catch the eye than undeviating rejection of deflections was greatly to the advantage of the opposite side. And lastly, where any doubt arose I generally decided questions against my own contention, and have omitted to record many smaller instances favourable to us which I should have entered in the other column. From various reasons the large majority of passages proved to be irrelevant to this inquiry, because no variation of reading occurred in them, or none which has been adopted by modern editors. Such were favourite passages quoted again and again as the two first verses of St. John's Gospel, ' I and My Father are one,' ' I am the way, the truth, and the life,' ' No man knoweth the Father but the Son,' and many others. In Latin books, more quotations had to be rejected than in Greek, because the verdict of a version cannot be so close as the witness of the original language.

An objection may perhaps be made, that the texts of the books of the Fathers are sure to have been altered in order to coincide more accurately with the Received Text. This is true of the Ethica, or Moralia, of Basil, and of the Regulae brevius Tractatae, which seem to have been read constantly at meals, or were otherwise in continual use in Religious Houses. The monks of a later age would not be content to hear every day familiar passages of Holy Scripture couched in other terms than those to which they were accustomed, and which they regarded as correct. This fact was perfectly evident upon examination, because these treatises were found to give evidence for the Textus Receptus in the proportion of about 6 : 1, whereas the other books of St. Basil yielded according to a ratio of about 8 : 3.

For the same reason I have not included Marcion's edition of St. Luke's Gospel, or Tatian's Diatessaron, in the list of books and authors, because such representations of the Gospels having been in public use were sure to have been revised from time to time, in order to accord with the judgement of those who read or heard them. Our readers will observe that these were self-denying ordinances, because by the inclusion of the works mentioned the list on the Traditional side would have been greatly increased. Yet our foundations have been strengthened, and really the position of the Traditional Text rests so firmly upon what is undoubted, that it can afford to dispense with services which may be open to some suspicion [1]. And the natural inference remains, that the difference between the witness of the Ethica and the Regulae brevius Tractatae on the one hand, and that of the other works of Basil on the

---

[1] Yet Marcion and Tatian may fairly be adduced as witnesses upon individual readings.

other, suggests that too much variation, and too much which
is evidently characteristic variation, of readings meets us in
the works of the several Fathers, for the existence of any
doubt that in most cases we have the words, though perhaps
not the spelling, as they issued originally from the author's
pen[1]. Variant readings of quotations occurring in different
editions of the Fathers are found, according to my experience, much less frequently than might have been
supposed. Where I saw a difference between MSS. noted
in the Benedictine or other editions or in copies from the
Benedictine or other prints, of course I regarded the
passage as doubtful and did not enter it. Acquaintance
with this kind of testimony cannot but render its general
trustworthiness the more evident. The habit of quotation
of authorities from the Fathers by Tischendorf and all
Textual Critics shews that they have always been taken
to be in the main trustworthy. It is in order that we may
be on sure ground that I have rejected many passages on
both sides, and a larger number of cases of pettier testimony on the Traditional side.

In the examination of the Greek Fathers, Latin Translations have generally been neglected (except in the case
of St. Irenaeus[2]), because the witness of a version is second-
hand, and Latin translators often employed a rendering
with which they were familiar in representing in Latin
passages cited from the Gospels in Greek. And in the
case even of Origen and especially of the later Fathers
before A.D. 400, it is not certain whether the translation,
such as that of Rufinus, comes within the limit of time
prescribed. The evidence of the Father as to whether he

---

[1] E. g. 'Many of the verses which he [Origen] quotes in different places shew
discrepancies of text that cannot be accounted for either by looseness of citation
or by corruption of the MSS. of his writings.' Hort, Introduction, p. 113.
See also the whole passage, pp. 113-4.

[2] See Hort, Introduction, p. 160. The most useful part of Irenaeus' works
in this respect is found in the Latin Translation, which is of the fourth century.

used a Text or Texts of one class or another is of course much better exhibited in his own Greek writing, than where some one else has translated his words into Latin. Accordingly, in the case of the Latin Fathers, only the clearest evidence has been admitted. Some passages adduced by Tischendorf have been rejected, and later experience has convinced me that such rejections made in the earlier part of my work were right. In a secondary process like this, if only the cup were borne even, no harm could result, and it is of the greatest possible importance that the foundation of the building should be sound.

The general results will appear in the annexed Table. The investigation was confined to the Gospels. For want of a better term, I have uniformly here applied the title 'Neologian' to the Text opposed to ours.

Fathers.	Traditional Text.	Neologian.
Patres Apostolici and Didachè	11	4
Epistle to Diognetus	1	0
Papias	1	0
Justin Martyr	17	20
Heracleon	1	7
Gospel of Peter	2	0
Seniores apud Irenaeum	2	0
Athenagoras	3	1
Irenaeus (Latin as well as Greek)	63	41
Hegesippus	2	0
Theophilus Antiochenus	2	4
Testament of Abraham	4	0
Epistola Viennensium et Lugdunensium	1	0
Clement of Alexandria	82	72
Tertullian	74	65
Clementines	18	7
Hippolytus	26	11
Callixtus (Pope)	1	0
Pontianus (Pope)	0	2
	311	234

Fathers.	Traditional Text.	Neologian.
Brought forward	311	. . . 234
Origen	460	. . . 491
Julius Africanus	1	. . . 1
Gregory Thaumaturgus	11	. . . 3
Novatian	6	. . . 4
Cornelius (Pope)	4	. . . 1
Synodical Letter	1	. . . 2
Cyprian	100	. . . 96
Concilia Carthaginiensia	8	. . . 4
Dionysius of Alexandria	12	. . . 5
Synodus Antiochena	3	. . . 1
Acta Pilati	5	. . . 1
Theognostus	0	. . . 1
Archelaus (Manes)	11	. . . 2
Pamphilus	5	. . . 1
Methodius	14	. . . 8
Peter of Alexandria	7	. . . 8
Alexander Alexandrinus	4	. . . 0
Lactantius	0	. . . 1
Juvencus	1	. . . 2
Arius	2	. . . 1
Acta Philippi	2	. . . 1
Apostolic Canons and Constitutions .	61	. . . 28
Eusebius (Caesarea)	315	. . . 214
Theodorus Heracleensis	2	. . . 0
Athanasius	179	. . . 119
Firmicus Maternus	3	. . . 1
Julius (Pope)	1	. . . 2
Serapion	5	. . . 1
Eustathius	7	. . . 2
Macarius Aegyptius or Magnus [1] . .	36	. . . 17
	1577	1252

[1] Or Magnus, or Major, which names were applied to him to distinguish him from his brother who was called Alexandrinus, and to whom some of his works have been sometimes attributed. Macarius Magnus or Aegyptius was a considerable writer, as may be understood from the fact that he occupies nearly 1000 pages in Migne's Series. His memory is still, I am informed, preserved in Egypt. But in some fields of scholarship at the present day he has met with strange neglect.

Fathers.	Traditional Text.	Neologian.
Brought forward	1577	1252
Hilary (Poictiers)	73	39
Candidus Arianus	0	1
Eunomius	1	0
Didymus	81	36
Victorinus of Pettau	4	3
Faustinus	4	0
Zeno	3	5
Basil	272	105
Victorinus Afer	14	14
Lucifer of Cagliari	17	20
Titus of Bostra	44	24
Cyril of Jerusalem	54	32
Pacianus	2	2
Optatus	10	3
Quaestiones ex Utroque Test.	13	6
Gregory of Nyssa	91	28
Philastrius	7	6
Gregory of Nazianzus	18	4
Amphilochius	27	10
Epiphanius	123	78
Ambrose	169	77
Macarius Magnes	11	5
Diodorus of Tarsus	1	0
Evagrius Ponticus	4	0
Esaias Abbas	1	0
Nemesius	0	1
Philo of Carpasus [1]	9	2
	2630	1753

The testimony therefore of the Early Fathers is emphatically, according to the issue of numbers, in favour of the Traditional Text, being about 3 : 2. But it is also necessary to inform the readers of this treatise, that here quality confirms quantity. A list will now be given of thirty important

[1] The names of many Fathers are omitted in this list, because I could not find any witness on one side or the other in their writings. Also Syriac writings are not here included.

passages in which evidence is borne on both sides, and it
will be seen that 530 testimonies are given in favour of the
Traditional readings as against 170 on the other side. In
other words, the Traditional Text beats its opponent in a
general proportion of 3 to 1. This result supplies a fair idea
of the two records. The Neologian record consists mainly
of unimportant, or at any rate of smaller alterations, such
as δέδωκα for ἔδωκα, ὁ οὐράνιος for ὁ ἐν οὐρανοῖς, φοβεῖσθε for
φοβηθῆτε, disarrangements of the order of words, omissions
of particles, besides of course greater omissions of more
or less importance. In fact, a great deal of the variations
suggest to us that they took their origin when the Church
had not become familiar with the true readings, the *verba
ipsissima*, of the Gospels, and when an atmosphere of much
inaccuracy was spread around. It will be readily understood how easily the text of the Holy Gospels might have
come to be corrupted in oral teaching whether from the
pulpit or otherwise, and how corruptions must have so
embedded themselves in the memories and in the copies of
many Christians of the day, that it needed centuries before
they could be cast out. That they were thus rooted
out to a large extent must have been due to the loving
zeal and accuracy of the majority. Such was a great
though by no means the sole cause of corruption. But
before going further, it will be best to exhibit the testimony referred to as it is borne by thirty of the most
important passages in dispute. They have been selected
with care : several which were first chosen had to be
replaced by others, because of their absence from the
quotations of the period under consideration. Of course,
the quotations are limited to that period. Quotations are
made in this list also from Syriac sources. Besides my own
researches, The Last Twelve Verses, and The Revision
Revised, of Dean Burgon have been most prolific of
apposite passages. A reference here and there has been

added from Resch's Ausser-Canonische Paralleltexte zu
den Evangelien, Leipzig, 1894–5.

1. St. Matt. i. 25. Πρωτότοκον.

On the Traditional side:—

Tatian (Diatessaron).

Athanasius (c. Apoll. i. 20; ii.
15).

Basil (Adv. Eunom. iv. (291); in
S. Xti. Gen. 5; i. 392; ii. 599,
600).

Didymus (Trin. iii. 4).

Cyril Jerus. (Cat. vii. 9).

Gregory Nyss. (ii. 229).

Ephraem Syrus (Commentary
on Diatessaron).

Epiphanius (Haer. II. li. 5; III.
lxxxviii. 17, &c.—5 times).

Ambrose (De Fid. I. xiv. 89)[1].

Against:—I can discover nothing.

2. St. Matt. v. 44 (some of the clauses).

Traditional:—Separate clauses are quoted by—

Didachè (§ 1).

Polycarp (x.).

Justin M. (Apol. i. 15).

Athenagoras (Leg. pro Christian.
11).

Tertullian (De Patient. vi.).

Theophilus Ant. (Ad Autoly-
cum).

Clemens Alex. (Paed. i. 8; Strom.
iv. 14; vii. 14).

Origen (De Orat. i.; Cels. viii.
35; 41).

Eusebius (Praep. Ev. xiii. 7;
Comment. in Isai. 66; Comment. in Ps. 3; 108).

Athanasius (De Incarnat. c.
Arian. 3; 13).

Apost. Const. (i. 1, all the
clauses; vii. 1).

Gregory Naz. (Orat. iv. 124).

Gregory Nyss. (In Bapt. Christ.;
In S. Stephanum).

Lucifer (Pro S. Athan. ii.).

Philo of Carpasus (I. 7).

Pacianus (Epist. ii.).

Hilary (Tract. in Ps. cxviii. 9. 9;
10. 16).

Ambrose (De Abrahamo ii. 30;
In Ps. xxxviii. 10; In Ps. cxviii.
12. 51).

Aphraates (Dem. ii.).

Apocryphal Acts of the Gospels
(p. 89).

Against:—

Cyprian (De Bono Patient. v.;
De Zelo xv.; Test. ad Jud.
iii. 49).

Irenaeus (Haer. III. xviii. 5).

Origen (Comment. on St. John
XX. xv.; xxvii.).

Eusebius (Dem. Evan. xiii. 7).

Gregory Nyss. (In Bapt. Christ.).

[1] See The Revision Revised, p. 123

3. St. Matt. vi. 13. Doxology.

Traditional :—

Didachè (viii, with variation).   with variation).
Apostol. Const. (iii. 18 ; vii. 25,   Ambrose (De Sacr. vi. 5. 24).

Against (?), i.e. generally silent about it :—

Tertullian (De Orat. 8).   Cyril Jerus. (Cat. xxiii., Myst. 5,
Cyprian (De Orat. Dom. 27).   18).
Origen (De Orat. 18).   Gregory Nyss. is doubtful (De
    Orat. Dom. end).

4. St. Matt. vii. 13, 14. Ἡ πύλη.

Traditional :—

Hippolytus (In Susannam v. 18).   Ambrose (Epist. I. xxviii. 6).
Testament of Abraham (5 times).   Esaias Abbas.
Origen (Select. in Ps. xvi. ;   Philo of Carpasus (iii. 73).
    Comment. in Matt. xii. 12).

Against :—

Hippolytus (Philosoph. v. 1.   Basil (Hom. in Ps. xxxiii. 4 ;
    1—bis).   xlv. 2).
Origen (Cels. vi. 17; Select. in Ps.   Cyril Jerus. (Cat. iii. 7).
    xlv. 2 ; cxvii.; c. Haeres. v. 8).   Gregory Nyss. (c. Fornicarios).
Cyprian (De Hab. Virg. xxi. ;   Ambrose (Exposit. in Luc. iv.
    Test. ad Jud. iii. 6).   37).
Eusebius (Eclog. Proph. iii. 4 ;   Philo of Carpasus (i. 7).
    Comment. in Ps. 3).   Macarius Aegypt. (Hom. xxviii.).
Clemens Alex. (Strom. IV. ii.; vi.;   Lucifer (De Athan. ii. ; Morien-
    v. 5 ; Cohort. ad Gent. p. 79).   dum esse).

5. St. Matt. ix. 13. εἰς μετάνοιαν. Mark ii. 17.

Traditional :—

Barnabas (5).   Hilary (Comment. in Matt. ad
Justin M. (Apol. i. 15).   loc.).
Irenaeus (III. v. 2).   Basil (De Poenitent. 3 ; Hom.
Origen (Comment. in Joh.   in Ps. xlviii. 1 ; Epist. Class. I.
    xxviii. 16).   xlvi. 6).
Eusebius (Comment. in Ps. cxlvi.).

Against :—

Clemens Rom. (ii. 2).

Hilary (in Mark ii. 17).

6. St. Matt. xi. 27.   βούληται ἀποκάλυψαι.

Traditional :—

Irenaeus (c. Haeres. IV. vi. 1).
Archelaus—Manes (xxxvii.).
Clementines (Recog. ii. 47;
Hom. xvii. 4; xviii. 4; 13).
Athanasius (Matt. xi. 27—com-
menting upon it ; De Incarn.
c. Arian. 7; 13; 47; 48; c.
Arianos iii. 26; 49; c. Sabell.
Greg. 4).
Didymus (De Trin. iii. 36).

Basil (Adv. Eunom. v. 314).
Victorinus Afer (Adv. Arium i.
15).
Ambrose (De Fide V. xvi. 201 ;
De Spir. S. II. xi. 123).
Gregory Nyss. (c. Eunom. i.).
Hilary (Comment. in Matt. ad
loc. ; De Trin. ii. 10; vi. 26 ;
ix. 50; Frag. xv.).
Quaestiones ex N. T. (124).

Against :—

Irenaeus (c. Haeres. I. xx. 3;
II. vi. 1 ; IV. vi. 3).
Clemens Alex. (Cohort. ad Gent.
i. end ; Paed. i. 5 ; Strom. i.
28; v. 13; vii. 10; 18; Quis
Div. Salv. viii.).
Justin M. (Apol. i. 63—bis ;
Dial. c. Tryph. 100).
Origen (Cels. vi. 17; Comm. in
Joh. i. 42).
Synodus Antiochena.

Athanasius (Hist. Arian. xii.; c.
Arian.i.12; 39; iv.23; Serm.
Maj. de Fide, 28).
Didymus (De Trin. ii. 16).
Eusebius (Eclog. Proph. i. 11 ;
De Eccles. Theol. I. xv; xvi.).
Basil (Adv. Eunom. v. 311).
Cyril Jerus. (Cat. vi. 6 ; x. 1).
Epiphanius (Adv. Haeres. i. 34.
18; ii. 54. 4; iii. 65. 4; 76.
4; 29; Ancor. 67).

7. St. Matt. xvii. 21.   The Verse.

Traditional :—

Clement Alex. Ἐκλογαὶ ἐκ τ.
προφ xv.
Origen (Comment. in Matt. xiii.
7; Hom. i.).
Athanasius (De Virg. vii.).
Basil (De Jejun. Hom. i. 9 ; Reg.
fus. tract. xviii. ; Hom. de

Jejun. iii.).
Juvencus (iii. vv. 381-2).
Ambrose (In Ps. xlv. 9 ; Epist.
Class. I. xlii. 11).
Hilary (Comment. in Matt. ad
loc.).

Against :—none, so far as I can find.

8. St. Matt. xviii. 11.   The Verse.

Traditional :—

Origen (ii. 147 ; Conc. v. 675).
Tertullian (Pudic. 9 ; Resurr. 9).

Ambrose (De Interpell. Dav. IV. ii. 4 ; Expos. in Luc. vii. 209 ; De Fid. Res. II. 6) [1].

Against :—none, so far as I can find.

9. St. Matt. xix. 16, 17.   ἀγαθέ, and περὶ τοῦ ἀγαθοῦ.

Traditional :—

Clemens Alex. (Strom. v. 10).
Origen—ἀγαθέ (Comment. in Matt. xv. 10).
Eusebius (Praep. Evan. xi. 21).
Athanasius (De Incarn. c. Arian. 7).
Cyril Jerus. (Cat. xviii. 30).

Gregory Naz. (i. 529).
Hilary (Comment. in Matt. ad loc.).
Epiphanius (Adv. Haeres. I. iii. 34. 18).
Macarius Magnes (i. 9) [2].

Against :—

Origen (Praep. Evan. xi. 19 ; Comment. in Matt. xv. 10.—bis).
Eusebius (Praep. Evan. xi. 21).

Novatian (De Trin. xxx.).
Hilary—omits ἀγαθέ (Comment. in loc.).

10. St. Matt. xxiii. 38.   ἔρημος.   St. Luke xiii. 35.

Traditional :—

Cyprian (Test. ad Jud. i. 6).
Irenaeus (c. Haeres. IV. xxxvi. 8 ; xxxvii. 5).
Clemens Alex. (Paed. i. 9).
Methodius (Serm. de Simeone et Anna).
Origen (Hom. in Jerem. vii.—

bis ; x. ; xiii. ; Select. in Jeremiam xv. ; in Threnos iv. 6).
Apostol. Const. (vi. 5).
Eusebius (Dem. Evan. II. iv. (38)—four times ; IV. xvi. (189) ; VI. (291) ; viii. (401) ; x. (481) ; Eclog. Proph. IV.

---

[1] The Revision Revised, p. 92.

[2] I have mentioned here only cases where the passage is quoted professedly from St. Matthew. The passage as given in St. Mark x. 17–18, and in St. Luke xviii. 18–19, is frequently quoted without reference to any one of the Gospels. Surely some of these quotations must be meant for St. Matthew.

i. ; Comment. in Ps. 73—bis ;
77 ; 79 ; in Isaiam 7–8 ; De
Theophan. vii.—tris).
Basil (Comment. in Isaiam i. 20).

Cyril Jerus. (Cat. xiii. 32).
Philo of Carpasus (iii. 83).
Ambrose (In Ps. xliii. 69 ; In
Cant. Cant. iv. 54).

Against :—

Didymus (Expos. in Ps. 67).
Epiphanius (Adv. Haeres. I.

iii. 40).
Zeno (xiv. 2).

11. St. Matt. xxvii. 34.   Ὄξος and οἶνον.

Traditional :—

Gospel of Peter (§ 5).
Acta Philippi (§ 26).
Barnabas (§ 7).
Irenaeus.
Tertullian.
Celsus.
Origen.

Eusebius of Emesa.
Theodore of Heraclea.
Didymus.
Gregory Naz.
Gregory Nyss.
Ephraem Syrus.
Titus of Bostra.

Against :—

Apocryphal Acts of the Apostles.
Macarius Magnes (ii. 12).

Gospel of Nicodemus [1].

12. St. Matt. xxviii. 2.   ἀπὸ τῆς θύρας.

Traditional :—

Gospel of Nicodemus.
Acta Philippi.
Apocryphal Acts of the Apostles.

Eusebius (ad Marinum, ii. 4).
Greg. Nyss. (De Christ. Resurr.
I. 390, 398) [2]?

Compare also Acta Pilati (ἀπὸ τοῦ στόματος τοῦ σπηλαίου,
and ἐκ τοῦ μνημείου), and Gospel of Peter (ἐπὶ τῆς θύρας—
ἐπὶ τῆς θύρας).

Against :—

Dionysius Alex. (Epist. Canon.
ad Basilidem).

Origen (c. Celsum, ii. 70).
Apostol. Can. (vii. 1).

[1] For the reff. see below, Appendix II.
[2] Compare The Revision Revised, pp. 162–3.

13. St. Matt. xxviii. 19. βαπτίζοντες.

Traditional :—

Irenaeus (c. Haeres. III. xvii. 1).
Hippolytus (c. Haeres. Noet. 14).
Apostolic Canons (pp. 29 ; 43 ; 49 (Lagarde) ; Const. ii. 26 ; iv. 1 ; vii. 22).
Concilia Carthaginiensia (vii.—tris).
Ps. Justin (Expos. Rect. Fid. v.).
Tertullian (De Baptismo xiii.).
Cyprian (Epist. ad Jubaianum v.; xxv. 2 tingentes; lxiii. 18 ; ad Novatianum Heret. iii.—3rd cent.; Testimon. II. xxvi. tingentes).
Eusebius (c. Marcell. I. i.).
Athanasius (Epist. Encycl. i.; Epist. ad Serap. i. 6 ; 28 ; ii. 6 ; iii. 6 ; iv. 5 ; de Syn. 23 ; De Titulis Ps. 148).
Basil (Adv. Eunom. v. 299 ; De Fide 4 ; De Bapt. I. 1 ; ii. 6 ;

Epist. Class. I. viii. 11 ; II. ccx. 3).
Didymus (De Trin. i. 30 ; 36 ; ii. 5 ; iii. 23).
Cyril Jerus. (Cat. xvi. 4).
Hilary (Comment. in Matt. ad loc.; c. Auxentium 14 ; De Syn. xxix.; De Trin. ii. 1).
Amphilochius (Epist. Synod.).
Gregory Nyss. (c. Eunom. xi.; In Bapt. Christ.; In Christ. Resurr.—bis; Epist. v.; xxiv.).
Victorinus of Pettau (In Apoc. i. 15).
Optatus (De Schism. Don. v. 5).
Firmicus Maternus (De Error. Profan. Relig. xxv.).
Ambrose (De Joseph. xii. 71).
Victorinus Afer (Adv. Arium iv. 18).
Epiphanius (Adv. Haeres. iii. 73. 3 ; 74. 5 ; ἀνακεφαλαίωσις, end).

Against :—none.

14. St. Mark i. 2. τοῖς προφήταις . . . Ἡσαΐᾳ.

Traditional :—

Titus of Bostra.
Origen.
Porphyry.

Irenaeus (III. xvi. 3).
Eusebius.
Ambrose [1].

Against :—

Irenaeus (III. xi. 8).
Origen (Cels. ii. 4 ; Comment. in John i. 14).

Titus of Bostra (Adv. Manich. iii. 4).
Epiphanius.

[1] For reff. see Vol. II. viii. For Mark i. 1, Υἱοῦ τοῦ Θεοῦ, see Appendix IV.

Basil (Adv. Eunom. ii. 15).
Epiphanius (Adv. Haeres. II. i.
51).

Serapion.
Victorinus of Pettau (In Apoc.
S. Joann.).

15. St. Mark xvi. 9–20.   Last Twelve Verses.

Traditional :—

Papias (Eus. H. E. iii. 39).
Justin Martyr (Tryph. 53 ; Apol.
i. 45).
Irenaeus (c. Haer. III. x. 6 ; iv.
56).
Tertullian (De Resurr. Carn.
xxxvii. ; Adv. Praxeam xxx.).
Clementines (Epit. 141).
Hippolytus (c. Haer. Noet.
ad fin.).
Vincentius (2nd Council of
Carthage—Routh, Rell. Sacr.
iii. p. 124).
Acta Pilati (xiv. 2).
Apost. Can. and Const. (can. 1 ;
v. 7 ; 19 ; vi. 15 ; 30 ; viii. 1).
Eusebius (Mai, Script. Vett.
Nov. Collect. i. p. 1).

Cyril Jerus. (Cat. xiv. 27).
Syriac Table of Canons.
Macarius Magnes (iii. 16 ; 24).
Aphraates (Dem. i.—bis).
Didymus (Trin. ii. 12).
Syriac Acts of the Apostles.
Epiphanius (Adv. Haer. I. xliv.
6).
Gregory Nyss.(In Christ. Resurr.
ii.).
Apocryphal Acts of the Gospel
—Wright (4 ; 17 ; 24).
Ambrose (Hexameron vi. 38 ;
De Interpell.ii.5 ; Apol.proph.
David II. iv. 26 ; Luc. vii.
81 ; De Poenit. I. viii. 35 ; De
Spir. S. II. xiii. 151).

Against :—

Eusebius (Mai, Script. Vett. Nov. Collect. i. p. 1)[1].

16. St. Luke i. 28.   εὐλογημένη, κ.τ.λ.

Traditional :—

Tertullian (De Virg. Vel. vi.).
Eusebius (Dem. Evan. vii. 329).

Aphraates (Dem. ix.).
Ambrose (Exposit. in loc.).

Against :—

Titus of Bostra (Exposit. in loc. ; Adv. Manich. iii.).

[1] The Revision Revised, pp. 423–440. Last Twelve Verses, pp. 42–51. The latitudinarian Eusebius on the same passage witnesses on both sides.

17. St. Luke ii. 14. Εὐδοκία.

Traditional :—

Irenaeus (III. x. 4).
Origen (c. Celsum i. 60 ; Selecta in Ps. xlv.; Comment. in Matt. xvii.; Comment. in Joh. i. 13).
Apostol. Const. (vii. 47 ; viii. 12).
Methodius (Serm. de Simeon. et Anna).
Eusebius (Dem. Ev. iv. (163); vii. (342)).
Gregory Thaumaturgus (De Fid. Cap. 12).
Aphraates (Dem. ix. ; xx.).
Titus of Bostra (Expos. in Luc. ad loc.).

Athanasius (De Tit. Pss. Ps. cxlviii.).
Didymus (De Trin. i. 27 ; Expos. in Ps. lxxxiv.).
Basil (In S. Christ. Gen. 5).
Gregory Naz. (Or. xlv. i.).
Philo of Carpasus (iii. 167).
Epiphanius (Haer. I. 30. 29 ; III. 78. 15).
Gregory Nyss. (In Ps. xiv.; In Cant. Cant. xv.; In Diem Nat. Christ. 1138 ; De Occurs. Dom. 1156).
Ephraem Syr.[1] (Gr. iii. 434).

Against:—

Irenaeus (III. x. 4).
Optatus (De Schism. Don. iv. 4).
Cyril Jerus. (Cat. xii. 72).

Ambrose (Exposit. in Luc. ad loc.).
Juvencus (II. v. 174).

18. St. Luke x. 41–2. Ὀλίγων χρεία ἐστίν, ἢ ἑνός.

Traditional :—

Basil (Const. Monast. i. 1).
Macarius Aegypt. (De Orat.).

Evagrius Ponticus.

Against :—

Titus of Bostra (Exposit. in Luc. ad loc. But μεριμνᾶς).

19. St. Luke xxii. 43–4. Ministering Angel and Agony.

Traditional :—

Justin M. (Tryph. 103).
Irenaeus (Haer. III. xxii. 2 ; IV. xxxv. 3).
Tatian (Ciasca, 556).
Hippolytus (c. Haer. Noet. 5 ; 18).
Marcion (ad loc.).

Dionysius Alex. (Hermen. in Luc. ad loc.).
Eusebius (Sect. 283).
Athanasius (Expos. in Ps. lxviii.).
Ephraem Syrus (ap. Theodor. Mops.).
Gregory Naz. (xxx. 16).

---

[1] The Revision Revised, pp. 420-1 ; Last Twelve Verses, pp. 42-3.

Didymus (Trin. iii. 21).

Titus of Bostra (In Luc. ad loc.).

Against:—none.

Epiphanius (Haer. II. (2) lxix. 19; 59; Ancor. 31; 37).

Arius (Epiph. Haer.lxix.19; 61)[1].

20. St. Luke xxiii. 34.   Our Lord's Prayer for His murderers.

Traditional :—

Hegesippus (Eus. H. E. ii. 23).

Ps. Justin (Quaest. et Respons. 108—bis).

Irenaeus (c. Haer. III. xviii. 5).

Archelaus (xliv.).

Marcion (in loc.).

Hippolytus (c. Noet. 18).

Clementines (Recogn. vi. 5; Hom. xi. 20).

Apost. Const. (ii. 16; v. 14).

Athanasius (De Tit. Pss., Ps. cv.).

Eusebius (canon x.).

Didymus (Trin. iii. 21).

Amphilochius (Orat. in d. Sabbati).

Hilary (De Trin. i. 32).

Ambrose (De Joseph. xii. 69;

De Interpell. III. ii. 6; In Ps. CXVIII. iii. 8; xiv. 28; Expos. Luc. v. 77; x. 62; Cant. Cant. i. 46).

Gregory Nyss. (De Perf. Christ. anim. forma—bis).

Titus of Bostra (Comment. Luc. ad loc.—bis).

Acta Pilati (x. 5).

Basil (Adv. Eunom. iv. 290).

Gregory Naz. (Orat. iv. 78).

Ephraem Syr. (ii. 321).

Acta Philippi (§ 26).

Quaestiones ex Utroque Test. (N. T. 67; Mixtae II. (1) 4).

Apocryphal Acts of the Gospels (Wright), 11; (16)[2].

Against:—none.

21. St. Luke xxiii. 38.   The Superscription.

Traditional :—

Marcion (ad loc.).

Eusebius (Eclog. Proph. II. xiv.).

Gospel of Peter (i. 11).

Acta Pilati (x. 1).

Gregory Nyss. (In Cant. Cant. vii.).

Titus of Bostra (In Luc. ad loc.).

Against:—none.

[1] The Revision Revised, pp. 79–82. The Dean alleges more than forty witnesses in all. What are quoted here, as in the other instances, are only the Fathers before St. Chrysostom.

[2] Ibid. pp. 82–5.

22. St. Luke xxiii. 45. ἐσκοτίσθη.

Traditional :—

Marcion (ad loc.).	i. 1006).
Gospel of Peter (§ 5).	Cyril Jerus. (Cat. xiii. 24).
Acta Pilati.	Macarius Magnes (iii. 17).
Anaphora Pilati (§ 7).	Julius Africanus (Chronicon, v.
Hippolytus (c. Haer. Noet. 18).	1).
Tertullian (Adv. Jud. xiii.).	Apocryphal Acts of the Gospels
Athanasius (De Incarn. Verb.	(Wright, p. 16).
49; ad Adelph. 3; ap. Epiph.	Ephraem Syrus (ii. 48).

Against :—

Origen (Cels. ii. 35).	Acta Pilati.

Eusebius mentions the reading ἐκλιπόντος, but appears afterwards to condemn it [1].

23. St. Luke xxiv. 40. The Verse.

Traditional :—

Marcion (ad loc.).	Eusebius (ap. Mai, ii. 294).
Tertullian (De Carne Christi 5).	Ambrose (ap. Theodoret, iv.
Athanasius (ad Epictet. 7 ;	141).
quoted by Epiph. i. 1003).	Epiphanius (Haer. III. lxxvii. 9) [2].

Against :—none.

24. St. Luke xxiv. 42. ἀπὸ μελισσίου κηρίου.

Traditional :—

Marcion (ad loc.).	Athanasius (c. Arian. iv. 35).
Justin Martyr (bis).	Cyril Jerus. (bis).
Clemens Alex.	Gregory Nyss.
Tertullian.	Epiphanius.

Against :—

Clemens Alex. Paed. i. 5 [3].

---

[1] The Revision Revised, pp. 61–65.
[2] Ibid. pp. 90–1.   [3] See below, Appendix I.

25. St. John i. 3–4.   Full stop at the end of the Verse?

Traditional :—

Athanasius (Serm. in Nativ.
  Christ. iii.).
Eusebius (Praep. Evan. xi. 19).
Didymus (De Trin. I. xv.).
Gregory Nyss. (c. Eunom. i. p.
  348—bis; ii. p. 450; p. 461;

Against :—

Irenaeus (I. viii. 5 (2); III. xi. 1).
Theodotus (ap. Clem. Alex. vi.).
Hippolytus (Philosoph. V. i. 8;
  17).
Clemens Alex. (Paed. ii. 9).
Valentinians (ap. Epiph. Haer.
  I. (xxxi.) 27).
Origen (c. Cels. vi. 5; Princip.
  II. ix. 4; IV. i. 30; In Joh.
  i. 22; 34; ii. 6; 10; 12; 13—
  bis; in Rom. iii. 10; 15; c.
  Haer. v. 151).

p. 468; iv. p. 584; v. p. 591).
Epiphanius (Haer. I. (xliii.) 1; II.
  (li.) 12; (lxv.) 3; (lxix.) 56;
  Ancoratus lxxv.).
Alexandrians and Egyptians
  (Ambrose In Ps. 36).

Eusebius (de Eccles. Theol. II.
  xiv.).
Basil (c. Eunom. V. 303).
Gregory Nyss. (De Cant. Cant.
  Hom. ii.).
Candidus Arianus (De Generat.
  Div.).
Victorinus Afer (Adv. Arium I.
  iv. 33; 41).
Hilary (De Trin. i. 10).
Ambrose (In Ps. xxxvi. 35 (4);
  De Fide III. vi. 41–2—tris)[1].

26. St. John i. 18.   Ὁ Μονογένης Υἱός.

Traditional :—

Irenaeus (c. Haeres. III. xi. 6;
  IV. xx. 6).
Tertullian (Adv. Praxean xv.).
Hippolytus (c. Haeres. Noeti 5).
Synodus Antiochena.
Archelaus (Manes) (xxxii.).
Origen (Comment. in Joh. vi.
  2; c. Celsum ii. 71).
Eusebius (De Eccles. Theol. I.
  ix.; II. xi.; xxiii.).
Alexander Alex. (Epist.).

Gregory Naz. (Orat. xxix. 17).
Cyril Jerus. (Cat. vii. 11).
Didymus (In Ps. cix.).
Athanasius (De Decr. Nic. Syn.
  xiii.; xxi.; c. Arianos ii. 62;
  iv. 26).
Titus of Bostra (Adv. Manichaeos iii. 6).
Basil (De Spir. S. xi.; Hom.
  in Ps. xxviii. 3; Epist.
  ccxxxiv.; Sermons xv. 3).

[1] Many of the Fathers quote only as far as οὐδὲ ἕν. But that was evidently
a convenient quotation of a stock character in controversy, just as πάντα δι' αὐτοῦ
ἐγένετο was even more commonly. St. Epiphanius often quotes thus, but remarks (Haer. II. (lxix.) 56, Ancor. lxxv.), that the passage goes on to ὃ γέγονεν.

I

Gregory Nyss. (c. Eunom. ii.
p. 522).
Hilary (De Trin. iv. 8; 42; vi.
39; 40).
Ambrose (De Interpell. I. x.
30; De Benedict. xi. 51;
Expos. in Luc. i. 25—bis; ii.
12; De Fide III. iii. 24; De

Against: —
Irenaeus (IV. xx. 11).
Theodotus (ap. Clem. vi.).
Clemens Alex. (Strom. v. 12).
Origen (Comment. in Joh. II.
29; XXXII. 13).
Eusebius (Υἱὸς or Θεός, De Eccles.
Theol. I. ix–x.).
Didymus(DeTrin.i.15; ii.5;16).

Spir. S. I. i. 26).
Eustathius (De Engastr. 18).
Faustinus (De Trin. ii. 5—tris).
Quaest. ex Utroque Test. (71;
91).
Victorinus Afer (De Generat.
Verb. xvi.; xx.; Adv. Arium
i. 2—bis; iv. 8; 32).

Arius (ap. Epiph. 73—Tisch.).
Basil (De Spiritu Sanct. vi.; c.
Eunom. i. p. 623).
Gregory Nyss. (c. Eunom. iii.
p. 577—bis; 581).
Epiphanius (Adv. Haeres. II.
(lxv.) 5; III. (lxx.) 7).

27. St. John iii. 13. Ὁ ὢν ἐν τῷ Οὐρανῷ.

Traditional :—
Hippolytus (c. Haer. Noet. 4).
Novatian (De Trin. 13).
Athanasius (i. 1275; Frag. p.
1222, apud Panopl. Euthym.
Zyg.).
Origen (In Gen. Hom. iv. 5; In
Rom. viii. 2—bis).
Basil (Adv. Eunom. iv. 2).
Amphilochius (Sentent. et
Excurs. xix.).
Didymus (De Trin. III. ix.).

Theodorus Heracleensis (In Is.
liii. 5).
Lucifer (Pro S. Athan. ii.).
Epiphanius (Haer. II. lvii. 7).
Eustathius (De Engastr. 18).
Zeno (xii. 1).
Hilary (Tract. in Ps. ii. 11;
cxxxviii. 22; De Trin. x. 16).
Ambrose (In Ps. xxxix. 17; xliii.
39; Expos. in Luc. vii. 74).
Aphraates (Dem. viii.).

Against:—some Fathers quote as far as these words
and then stop, so that it is impossible to know whether
they stopped because the words were not in their copies,
or because they did not wish to quote further. On some
occasions at least it is evident that it was not to their
purpose to quote further than they did, e.g. Greg. Naz.

Ep. ci. Eusebius (Eclog. Proph. ii.) is only less doubtful [1].
See Revision Revised, p. 134, note.

28. St. John x. 14. γινώσκομαι ὑπὸ τῶν ἐμῶν.

Traditional :—
Macarius Aegypt. (Hom. vi.).

Against :—
Eusebius (Comment. in Isaiam 8).

Gregory Naz. (orat. xv. end;
xxxiii. 15).

Basil (Hom. xxi.; xxiii.).
Epiphanius (Comm. in Ps. lxvi.) [2].

29. St. John xvii. 24. οὕς (or ὅ).

Traditional :—
Irenaeus (c. Haeres. IV. xiv. 1).
Cyprian (De Mortal. xxii.; Test.
ad Jud. iii. 58) [3].
Clemens Alex. (Paed. i. 8).
Athanasius (De Tit. Pss. Ps. iii.).
Eusebius (De Eccles. Theol. iii.
17—bis; c. Marcell. p. 292).

Hilary (Tract. in Ps. lxiv. 5;
De Trin. ix. 50).
Ambrose (De Bon. Mort. xii.
54; De Fide V. vi. 86; De
Spirit. S. II. viii. 76).
Quaestiones ex N. T. (75) [4].

Against :—
Clemens Alex. (140—Tisch.).

30. St. John xxi. 25. The Verse.

Traditional :—
Origen (Princ. II. vi.; vol. ii.
1=81; In Matt. XIV. 12;
In Luc. Hom. xxvii; xxix;
In Joh. I. 11; V. ap. Eus.
H. E. VI. 25; XIII. 5; XIX.
2; XX. 27; Cat. Corder.
p. 474).
Pamphilus (Apol. pro Orig. Pref.;

Against :—none.

iii. ap. Gall. iv. pp. 9, 15).
Eusebius (Mai, iv. 297; Eus.
H. E. vi. 25; Lat. iii. 964).
Gregory Nyss. (c. Eunom. xii.—
bis).
Gregory Naz. (Orat. xxviii. 20).
Ambrose (Expos. Luc. I. 11).
Philastrius (Gall. vii. 499) [5].

[1] See The Revision Revised, p. 133. [2] Ibid. pp. 220-1.
[3] Tischendorf quotes these on the wrong side.
[4] The Revision Revised, pp. 217-8.
[5] Ibid. pp. 23-4. See also an article in Hermathena, Vol. VIII., No. XIX.,
1893, written by the Rev. Dr. Gwynn with his characteristic acuteness and
ingenuity.

I 2

As far as the Fathers who died before 400 A. D. are
concerned, the question may now be put and answered.
Do they witness to the Traditional Text as existing from
the first, or do they not? The results of the evidence,
both as regards the quantity and the quality of the testimony, enable us to reply, not only that the Traditional
Text was in existence, but that it was predominant, during
the period under review. Let any one who disputes
this conclusion make out for the Western Text, or the
Alexandrian, or for the Text of B and ℵ, a case from the
evidence of the Fathers which can equal or surpass that
which has been now placed before the reader.

An objection may be raised by those who are not well
acquainted with the quotations in the writings of the
Fathers, that the materials of judgement here produced are
too scanty. But various characteristic features in their
mode of dealing with quotations should be particularly
noticed. As far as textual criticism is concerned, the
quotations of the Fathers are fitful and uncertain. They
quote of course, not to hand down to future ages a
record of readings, but for their own special purpose
in view. They may quote an important passage in dispute, or they may leave it wholly unnoticed. They often
quote just enough for their purpose, and no more. Some
passages thus acquire a proverbial brevity. Again, they
write down over and over again, with unwearied richness
of citation, especially from St. John's Gospel, words which
are everywhere accepted : in fact, all critics agree upon
the most familiar places. Then again, the witness of the
Latin Fathers cannot always be accepted as being free
from doubt, as has been already explained. And the
Greek Fathers themselves often work words of the New
Testament into the roll of their rhetorical sentences, so
that whilst evidence is given for the existence of a verse,
or a longer passage, or a book, no certain conclusions can

be drawn as to the words actually used or the order of them. This is particularly true of St. Gregory of Nazianzus to the disappointment of the Textual Critic, and also of his namesake of Nyssa, as well as of St. Basil. Others, like St. Epiphanius, quote carelessly. Early quotation was usually loose and inaccurate. It may be mentioned here, that the same Father, as has been known about Origen since the days of Griesbach, often used conflicting manuscripts. As will be seen more at length below, corruption crept in from the very first.

Some ideas have been entertained respecting separate Fathers which are not founded in truth. Clement of Alexandria and Origen are described as being remarkable for the absence of Traditional readings in their works [1]. Whereas besides his general testimony of 82 to 72 as we have seen, Clement witnesses in the list just given 8 times for them to 14 against them; whilst Origen is found 44 times on the Traditional side to 27 on the Neologian. Clement as we shall see used mainly Alexandrian texts which must have been growing up in his days, though he witnesses largely to Traditional readings, whilst Origen employed other texts too. Hilary of Poictiers is far from being against the Traditional Text, as has been frequently said: though in his commentaries he did not use so Traditional a text as in his De Trinitate and his other works. The texts of Hippolytus, Methodius, Irenaeus, and even of Justin, are not of that exclusively Western character which Dr. Hort ascribes to them [2]. Traditional readings occur almost equally with others in Justin's works, and predominate in the works of the other three.

But besides establishing the antiquity of the Traditional Text, the quotations in the early Fathers reveal the streams of corruption which prevailed in the first ages, till they were washed away by the vast current of the trans-

---

[1] Hort, Introduction, pp. 128, 127.   [2] Ibid. p. 113.

mission of the Text of the Gospels. Just as if we ascended in a captive balloon over the Mississippi where the volume of the Missouri has not yet become intermingled with the waters of the sister river, so we may mount up above those ages and trace by their colour the texts, or rather clusters of readings, which for some time struggled with one another for the superiority. But a caution is needed. We must be careful not to press our designation too far. We have to deal, not with distinct dialects, nor with editions which were separately composed, nor with any general forms of expression which grew up independently, nor in fact with anything that would satisfy literally the full meaning of the word ' texts,' when we apply it as it has been used. What is properly meant is that, of the variant readings of the words of the Gospels which from whatever cause grew up more or less all over the Christian Church, so far as we know, some have family likenesses of one kind or another, and may be traced to a kindred source. It is only in this sense that we can use the term Texts, and we must take care to be moderate in our conception and use of it.

The Early Fathers may be conveniently classed, according to the colour of their testimony, the locality where they flourished, and the age in which they severally lived, under five heads, viz., Early Traditional, Later Traditional, Syrio-Low Latin, Alexandrian, and what we may perhaps call Caesarean.

I. *Early Traditional.*

	Traditional.	Neologian.
Patres Apostolici and Didachè . .	11	4
Epistle to Diognetus	1	0
Papias	1	0
Epistola Viennensium et Lugdunensium	1	0
Hegesippus	2	0
Seniores apud Irenaeum	2	0
	18	4

	Traditional.	Neologian.
Brought forward	18	4
Justin [1]	17	20
Athenagoras	3	1
Gospel of Peter	2	0
Testament of Abraham	4	0
Irenaeus	63	41
Clementines	18	7
Hippolytus	26	11
	151	84

II. *Later Traditional.*

Gregory Thaumaturgus	11	3
Cornelius	4	1
Synodical Letter	1	2
Archelaus (Manes)	11	2
Apostolic Constitutions and Canons	61	28
Synodus Antiochena	3	1
Concilia Carthaginiensia	8	4
Methodius	14	8
Alexander Alexandrinus	4	0
Theodorus Heracleensis	2	0
Titus of Bostra	44	24
Athanasius (—except Contra Arianos)[2]	122	63
Serapion	5	1
Basil	272	105
Eunomius	1	0
Cyril of Jerusalem	54	32
Firmicus Maternus	3	1
Victorinus of Pettau	4	3
Gregory of Nazianzus	18	4
Hilary of Poictiers	73	39
	715	321

[1] It may perhaps be questioned whether Justin should be classed here : but the character of his witness, as on Matt. v. 44, ix. 13, and Luke xxii. 43-44, is more on the Traditional side, though the numbers are against that.

[2] Athanasius in his ' Orationes IV contra Arianos' used Alexandrian texts. See IV.

	Traditional.	Neologian.
Brought forward	715	321
Eustathius	7	2
Macarius Aegyptius or Magnus	36	17
Didymus	81	36
Victorinus Afer	14	14
Gregory of Nyssa	91	28
Faustinus	4	0
Optatus	10	3
Pacianus	2	2
Philastrius	7	6
Amphilochius (Iconium)	27	10
Ambrose	169	77
Diodorus of Tarsus	1	0
Epiphanius	123	78
Acta Pilati	5	1
Acta Philippi	2	1
Macarius Magnes	11	5
Quaestiones ex Utroque Testamento	13	6
Evagrius Ponticus	4	0
Esaias Abbas	1	0
Philo of Carpasus	9	2
	1332	609

III. *Western or Syrio-Low Latin.*

	Traditional	Neologian
Theophilus Antiochenus	2	4
Callixtus and Pontianus (Popes)	1	2
Tertullian	74	65
Novatian	6	4
Cyprian	100	96
Zeno, Bishop of Verona	3	5
Lucifer of Cagliari	17	20
Lactantius	0	1
Juvencus (Spain)	1	2
Julius (Pope)?	1	2
Candidus Arianus	0	1
Nemesius (Emesa)	0	1
	205	203

IV. *Alexandrian.*

	Traditional.	Neologian.
Heracleon	1	7
Clement of Alexandria	82	72
Dionysius of Alexandria	12	5
Theognostus	0	1
Peter of Alexandria	7	8
Arius	2	1
Athanasius (Orat. c. Arianos) . . .	57	56
	161	150

V. *Palestinian or Caesarean.*

Julius Africanus (Emmaus) . . .	1	1
Origen	460	491
Pamphilus of Caesarea	5	1
Eusebius of Caesarea	315	214
	781	707

The lessons suggested by the groups of Fathers just assembled are now sufficiently clear.

I. The original predominance of the Traditional Text is shewn in the list given of the earliest Fathers. Their record proves that in their writings, and so in the Church generally, corruption had made itself felt in the earliest times, but that the pure waters generally prevailed.

II. The tradition is also carried on through the majority of the Fathers who succeeded them. There is no break or interval: the witness is continuous. Again, not the slightest confirmation is given to Dr. Hort's notion that a revision or recension was definitely accomplished at Antioch in the middle of the fourth century. There was a gradual improvement, as the Traditional Text gradually established itself against the forward and persistent intrusion of corruption. But it is difficult, if not altogether impossible, to discover a ripple on the surface betokening any movement in the depths such as a revision or recension would necessitate.

III. A source of corruption is found in Low-Latin MSS. and especially in Africa. The evidence of the Fathers shews that it does not appear to have been so general as the name 'Western' would suggest. But this will be a subject of future investigation. There seems to have been a connexion between some parts of the West in this respect with Syria, or rather with part of Syria.

IV. Another source of corruption is fixed at Alexandria. This, as in the last case, is exactly what we should expect, and will demand more examination.

V. Syria and Egypt,—Europe, Asia, and Africa,—seem to meet in Palestine under Origen.

But this points to a later time in the period under investigation. We must now gather up the depositions of the earliest Versions.

CHAPTER VI.

THE ANTIQUITY OF THE TRADITIONAL TEXT.

II. WITNESS OF THE EARLY SYRIAC VERSIONS.

THE rise of Christianity and the spread of the Church in Syria was startling in its rapidity. Damascus and Antioch shot up suddenly into prominence as centres of Christian zeal, as if they had grown whilst men slept.

The arrangement of places and events which occurred during our Lord's Ministry must have paved the way to this success, at least as regards principally the nearer of the two cities just mentioned. Galilee, the scene of the first year of His Ministry—'the acceptable year of the Lord'—through its vicinity to Syria was admirably calculated for laying the foundation of such a development. The fame of His miracles and teaching extended far into the country. Much that He said and did happened on the Syrian side of the Sea of Galilee. Especially was this the case when, after the death of John the Baptist had shed consternation in the ranks of His followers, and the Galilean populace refused to accompany Him in His higher teaching, and the wiles of Herod were added as a source of apprehension to the bitter opposition of Scribes and Pharisees, He spent some months between the Passover and the Feast of Tabernacles in the north and north-east of Palestine. If Damascus was not one of the 'ten cities[1],' yet the report

---

[1] According to Pliny (N. II. v. 18), the towns of Decapolis were: 1. Scythopolis the chief, not far from Tiberias (Joseph. B. J. III. ix. 7); 2. Philadelphia;

of His twice feeding thousands, and of His stay at Caesarea Philippi and in the neighbourhood[1] of Hermon, must have reached that city. The seed must have been sown which afterwards sprang up men knew not how.

Besides the evidence in the Acts of the Apostles, according to which Antioch following upon Damascus became a basis of missionary effort hardly second to Jerusalem, the records and legends of the Church in Syria leave but little doubt that it soon spread over the region round about. The stories relating to Abgar king of Edessa, the fame of St. Addaeus or Thaddaeus as witnessed particularly by his Liturgy and 'Doctrine,' and various other Apocryphal Works[2], leave no doubt about the very early extension of the Church throughout Syria. As long as Aramaic was the chief vehicle of instruction, Syrian Christians most likely depended upon their neighbours in Palestine for oral and written teaching. But when—probably about the time of the investment of Jerusalem by Vespasian and Titus and the temporary removal of the Church's centre to Pella—through the care of St. Matthew and the other

---

3. Raphanae; 4. Gadara ; 5. Hippos ; 6. Dios; 7. Pella ; 8. Gerasa ; 9. Canatha (Otopos, Joseph.); 10. Damascus. This area does not coincide with that which is sometimes now marked in maps and is part of Galilee and Samaria. But the Gospel notion of Decapolis, is of a country east of Galilee, lying near to the Lake, starting from the south-east, and stretching on towards the mountains into the north. It was different from Galilee (Matt. iv. 25), was mainly on the east of the sea of Tiberias (Mark v. 20, Eusebius and Jerome OS². pp. 251, 89—'around Pella and Basanitis,'—Epiphanius Haer. i. 123), extended also to the west (Mark vii. 31), was reckoned in Syria (Josephus, passim, ' Decapolis of Syria '), and was generally after the time of Pompey under the jurisdiction of the Governor of Syria. The Encyclopaedia Britannica describes it well as ' situated, with the exception of a small portion, on the eastern side of the Upper Jordan and the sea of Tiberias.' Smith's Dictionary of the Bible, to which I am indebted for much of the evidence given above, is inconsistent. The population was in a measure Greek.

[1] Εἰς τὰς κώμας Καισαρείας τῆς Φιλίππου. What a condensed account of His sojourn in various ' towns ' !

[2] See Ancient Syriac Documents relative to the Earliest Establishment of Christianity in Edessa and the neighbouring countries, &c. edited by W. Cureton, D.D., with a Preface by the late Dr. Wright, 1864.

Evangelists the Gospel was written in Greek, some regular translation was needed and doubtless was made.

So far both Schools of Textual Criticism are agreed. The question between them is, was this Translation the Peshitto, or was it the Curetonian? An examination into the facts is required: neither School has any authority to issue decrees.

The arguments in favour of the Curetonian being the oldest form of the Syriac New Testament, and of the formation of the Peshitto in its present condition from it, cannot be pronounced to be strong by any one who is accustomed to weigh disputation. Doubtless this weakness or instability may with truth be traced to the nature of the case, which will not yield a better harvest even to the critical ingenuity of our opponents. May it not with truth be said to be a symptom of a feeble cause?

Those arguments are mainly concerned with the internal character of the two texts. It is asserted[1] (1) that the Curetonian was older than the Peshitto which was brought afterwards into closer proximity with the Greek. To this we may reply, that the truth of this plea depends upon the nature of the revision thus claimed[2]. Dr. Hort was perfectly logical when he suggested, or rather asserted dogmatically, that such a drastic revision as was necessary for turning the Curetonian into the Peshitto was made in the third century at Edessa or Nisibis. The difficulty lay in his manufacturing history to suit his purpose, instead of following it. The fact is, that the internal difference between the text of the Curetonian and the Peshitto is so great, that the former could only have arisen in very queer times such as the earliest, when inaccuracy and looseness,

---

[1] Cureton's Preface to ' An Antient Recension, &c.'

[2] Philip E. Pusey held that there was a revision of the Peshitto in the eighth century, but that it was confined to grammatical peculiarities. This would on general grounds be not impossible, because the art of copying was perfected by about that time.

infidelity and perverseness, might have been answerable for anything. In fact, the Curetonian must have been an adulteration of the Peshitto, or it must have been partly an independent translation helped from other sources: from the character of the text it could not have given rise to it [1].

Again, when (2) Cureton lays stress upon 'certain peculiarities in the original Hebrew which are found in this text, but not in the Greek,' he has not found others to follow him, and (3) the supposed agreement with the Apocryphal Gospel according to the Hebrews, as regards any results to be deduced from it, is of a similarly slippery nature. It will be best to give his last argument in his own words:—'It is the internal evidence afforded by the fact that upon comparing this text with the Greek of St. Matthew and the parallel passages of St. Mark and St. Luke, they are found to exhibit the same phenomena which we should, *a priori*, expect certainly to discover, had we the plainest and most incontrovertible testimony that they are all in reality translations from such an Aramaic original as this.' He seems here to be trying to establish his position that the Curetonian was at least based on the Hebrew original of St. Matthew, to which he did not succeed in bringing over any scholars.

The reader will see that we need not linger upon these arguments. When interpreted most favourably they carry us only a very short way towards the dethronement of the great Peshitto, and the instalment of the little Curetonian upon the seat of judgement. But there is more in what other scholars have advanced. There are resemblances between the Curetonian, some of the Old-Latin texts, the Codex Bezae, and perhaps Tatian's Diatessaron, which lead us to assign an early origin to many of the peculiar readings in this manuscript. Yet there is no reason, but all the reverse, for supposing that the Peshitto and the

[1] See Appendix VI.

Curetonian were related to one another in line-descent. The age of one need have nothing to do with the age of the other. The theory of the Peshitto being derived from the Curetonian through a process of revision like that of Jerome constituting a Vulgate rests upon a false parallel [1]. There are, or were, multitudes of Old-Latin Texts, which in their confusion called for some recension : we only know of two in Syriac which could possibly have come into consideration. Of these, the Curetonian is but a fragment : and the Codex Lewisianus, though it includes the greater part of the Four Gospels, yet reckons so many omissions in important parts, has been so determinedly mutilated, and above all is so utterly heretical [2], that it must be altogether rejected from the circle of purer texts of the Gospels. The disappointment caused to the adherents of the Curetonian, by the failure of the fresh MS. which had been looked for with ardent hopes to satisfy expectation, may be imagined. *Noscitur a sociis*: the Curetonian is admitted by all to be closely allied to it. and must share in the ignominy of its companion, at least to such an extent as to be excluded from the progenitors of a Text so near to the Traditional Text as the Peshitto must ever have been [3].

But what is the position which the Peshitto has occupied till the middle of the present century? What is the evidence of facts on which we must adjudicate its claim ?

Till the time of Cureton, it has been regarded as *the* Syriac Version, adopted at the time when the translation of the New Testament was made into that language, which

[1] This position is demonstrated in full in an article in the Church Quarterly Review for April, 1895, on 'The Text of the Syriac Gospels,' pp. 123–5.

[2] The Text of the Syriac Gospels, pp. 113-4 : also Church Times, Jan. 11, 1895. This position is established in both places.

[3] Yet some people appear to think, that the worse a text is the more reason there is to suppose that it was close to the Autograph Original. Verily this is evolution run wild.

must have been either the early part of the second century, or the end of the first,—adopted too in the Unchangeable East, and never deposed from its proud position. It can be traced by facts of history or by actual documents to the beginning of the golden period of Syriac Literature in the fifth century, when it is found to be firm in its sway, and it is far from being deserted by testimony sufficient to track it into the earlier ages of the Church.

The Peshitto in our own days is found in use amongst the Nestorians who have always kept to it[1], by the Monophysites on the plains of Syria, the Christians of St. Thomas in Malabar, and by 'the Maronites on the mountain-terraces of Lebanon[2].' Of these, the Maronites take us back to the beginning of the eighth century when they as Monothelites separated from the Eastern Church ; the Monophysites to the middle of the fifth century ; the Nestorians to an earlier date in the same century. Hostile as the two latter were to one another, they would not have agreed in reading the same Version of the New Testament if that had not been well established at the period of their separation. Nor would it have been thus firmly established, if it had not by that time been generally received in the country for a long series of years.

But the same conclusion is reached in the indubitable proof afforded by the MSS. of the Peshitto Version which exist, dating from the fifth century or thereabouts. Mr. Gwilliam in the third volume of Studia Biblica et Ecclesiastica[3] mentions two MSS. dating about 450 A.D., besides four of the fifth or sixth century, one of the latter, and three which bear actual dates also of the sixth. These, with the exception of one in the Vatican and one belonging

---

[1] Encyclopaedia Britannica, 9th ed., 'Syriac Literature,' by Dr. W. Wright, now published separately under the same title.

[2] Dr. Scrivener, Introduction (4th Edition), II. 7.

[3] See also Miller's Edition of Scrivener's Introduction (4th), II. 12.

to the Earl of Crawford, are from the British Museum
alone[1].   So that according to the manuscriptal evidence
the treasures of little more than one library in the world
exhibit a very *apparatus criticus* for the Peshitto, whilst
the Curetonian can boast only one manuscript and that in
fragments, though of the fifth century.   And it follows
too from this statement, that whereas only seven uncials
of any size can be produced from all parts of the world of
the Greek Text of the New Testament before the end
of the sixth century, no less than eleven or rather twelve
of the Peshitto can be produced already before the same
date.   Doubtless the Greek Text can boast certainly two,
perhaps three, of the fourth century : but the fact cannot but
be taken to be very remarkable, as proving, when compared
with the universal Greek original, how strongly the local
Peshitto Version was established in the century in which
' commences the native historical literature of Syria[2].'

The commanding position thus occupied leads back
virtually a long way.   Changes are difficult to introduce in
'the unchangeable East.'   Accordingly, the use of the

---

[1] Another very ancient MS. of the Peshitto Gospels is the Cod. Philipp. 1388,
in the Royal Library, Berlin (in Miller's Scrivener the name is spelt PHILLIPPS).
Dr. Sachau ascribes it to the fifth, or the beginning of the sixth century, thus
making it older than the Vatican Tetraevangelicum, No. 3, in Miller's Scrivener,
II. 12.   A full description will be found in Sachau's Catalogue of the Syr. MSS.
in the Berlin Library.

The second was collated by Drs. Guidi and Ugolini, the third, in St. John,
by Dr. Sachau.   The readings of the second and third are in the possession of
Mr. Gwilliam, who informs me that all three support the Peshitto text, and
are free from all traces of any pre-Peshitto text, such as according to Dr. Hort
and Mr. Burkitt the Curetonian and Lewis MSS. contain.   Thus every fresh
accession of evidence tends always to establish the text of the Peshitto Version
more securely in the position it has always held until quite recent years.

The interesting feature of all the above-named MSS. is the uniformity of
their testimony to the text of the Peshitto.   Take for example the evidence of
No. 10 in Miller's Scrivener, II. 13, No. 3, in Miller's Scrivener, II. 12, and
Cod. Philipp. 1388.   The first was collated by P. E. Pusey, and the results
are published in Studia Biblica, vol. i, ' A fifth century MS.'

[2] Dr. W. Wright's article in Encyclopaedia Britannica.   Dr. Hort could not
have been aware of this fact when he spoke of ' the almost total extinction of
Old Syriac MSS.' : or else he lamented a disappearance of what never appeared.

K

Peshitto is attested in the fourth century by Ephraem Syrus and Aphraates. Ephraem 'in the main used the Peshitto text'—is the conclusion drawn by Mr. F. H. Woods in the third volume of Studia Biblica [1]. And as far as I may judge from a comparison of readings [2], Aphraates witnesses for the Traditional Text, with which the Peshitto mainly agrees, twenty-four times as against four. The Peshitto thus reckons as its supporters the two earliest of the Syrian Fathers.

But the course of the examination of all the primitive Fathers as exhibited in the last section of this work suggests also another and an earlier confirmation of the position here taken. It is well known that the Peshitto is mainly in agreement with the Traditional Text. What therefore proves one, virtually proves the other. If the text in the latter case is dominant, it must also be in the former. If, as Dr. Hort admits, the Traditional Text prevailed at Antioch from the middle of the fourth century, is it not more probable that it should have been the continuance of the text from the earliest times, than that a change should have been made without a record in history, and that in a part of the world which has been always alien to change? But besides the general traces of the Traditional Text left in patristic writings in other districts of the Church, we are not without special proofs in the parts about Syria. Though the proofs are slight, they occur in a period which in other respects was for the present purpose almost 'a barren and dry land where no water is.' Methodius, bishop of Tyre in the early part of the fourth century, Archelaus, bishop in Mesopotamia in the latter half of the third, the Synodus Antiochena in A.D. 265, at a greater distance Gregory Thaumaturgus of Neocaesarea in Pontus who flourished about 243 and passed some time at Caesarea in Palestine, are found to have used mainly

[1] p. 107.　　[2] See Patrologia Syriaca, Graffin, P. I. vol. ii. Paris, 1895.

Traditional MSS. in Greek, and consequently witness to the use of the daughter text in Syriac. Amongst those who employed different texts in nearly equal proportions were Origen who passed his later years at Caesarea and Justin who issued from the site of Sychar. Nor is there reason, whatever has been said, to reject the reference made by Melito of Sardis about A.D. 170 in the words ὁ Σύρος. At the very least, the Peshitto falls more naturally into the larger testimony borne by the quotations in the Fathers, than would a text of such a character as that which we find in the Curetonian or the Lewis Codex.

But indeed, is it not surprising that the petty Curetonian with its single fragmentary manuscript, and at the best its short history, even with so discreditable an ally as the Lewis Codex, should try conclusions with what we may fairly term the colossal Peshitto? How is it possible that one or two such little rills should fill so great a channel?

But there is another solution of the difficulty which has been advocated by the adherents of the Curetonian in some quarters since the discovery made by Mrs. Lewis. It is urged that there is an original Syriac Text which lies at the back of the Curetonian and the Codex Lewisianus, and that this text possesses also the witness of the Diatessaron of Tatian :—that those MSS. themselves are later, but that the Text of which they give similar yet independent specimens is the Old Syriac,—the first Version made from the Gospels in the earliest ages of the Church.

The evidence advanced in favour of this position is of a speculative and vague nature, and moreover is not always advanced with accuracy. It is not 'the simple fact that no purely "Antiochene" [i.e. Traditional] reading occurs in the Sinai Palimpsest [1].' It is not true that 'in the Diatessaron

---

[1] See in St. Matt. alone (out of many instances) v. 22 (the translation of εἰκῇ), ix. 13 (of εἰς μετάνοιαν), xi. 23 ('which art exalted'), xx. 16 (of πολλοὶ γάρ εἰσι κλητοί, ὀλίγοι δὲ ἐκλεκτοί), xxvi. 42 (ποτήριον), 28 (καινῆς); besides

Joseph and Mary are never spoken of as husband and
wife,' because in St. Matt. i. 19 Joseph is expressly called
'her husband,' and in verse 24 it is said that Joseph
'took unto him Mary his wife.' It should be observed that
besides a resemblance between the three documents in
question, there is much divergence. The Cerinthian heresy,
which is spread much more widely over the Lewis Codex
than its adherents like to acknowledge, is absent from the
other two. The interpolations of the Curetonian are not
adopted by the remaining members of the trio. The Diatessaron, as far as we can judge,—for we possess no copy
either in Greek or in Syriac, but are obliged to depend
upon two Arabic Versions edited recently by Agostino
Ciasca, a Latin Translation of a commentary on it by
Ephraem Syrus, and quotations made by Aphraates or
Jacobus Nisibenus—, differs very largely from either.
That there is some resemblance between the three we
admit : and that the two Codexes are more or less made
up from very early readings, which we hold to be corrupt,
we do not deny. What we assert is, that it has never yet
been proved that a regular Text in Syriac can be constructed out of these documents which would pass muster
as the genuine Text of the Gospels ; and that, especially in
the light shed by the strangely heretical character of one
of the leading associates, such a text, if composed, cannot
with any probability have formed any stage in the transmission of the pure text of the original Version in Syriac
to the pages of the Peshitto. If corruption existed in the
earliest ages, so did purity. The Word of GOD could not
have been dragged only through the mire.

We are thus driven to depend upon the leading historical
facts of the case. What we do know without question is
this :—About the year 170 A D., Tatian who had sojourned

St. Luke ii. 14 (εὐδοκία), xxiii. 45 (ἐσκοτίσθη), John iii. 13 (though 'from
heaven'), xxi. 25 (the verse).

for some time at Rome drew up his Diatessaron, which is found in the earlier half of the third century to have been read in Divine service at Edessa [1]. This work was current in some parts of Syria in the time of Eusebius [2], to which assertion some evidence is added by Epiphanius [3]. Rabbūla, bishop of Edessa, A.D. 412–435 [4], ordered the presbyters and deacons of his diocese to provide copies of the distinct or *Mĕpharrĕshe* Gospels. Theodoret, Bishop of Cyrrhus near the Euphrates [5], writes in 453 A.D., that he had turned out about two hundred copies of Tatian's Diatessaron from his churches, and had put the Gospels of the four Evangelists in their place. These accounts are confirmed by the testimony of many subsequent writers, whose words together with those to which reference has just been made may be seen in Mr. Hamlyn Hill's book on the Diatessaron [6]. It must be added, that in the Curetonian we find 'The *Mĕpharrĕsha* Gospel of Matthew [7],' and the Lewis Version is termed 'The Gospel of the *Mĕpharrĕshe* four books'; and that they were written in the fifth century.

Such are the chief facts : what is the evident corollary ? Surely, that these two Codexes, which were written at the very time when the Diatessaron of Tatian was cast out of the Syrian Churches, were written purposely, and possibly amongst many other MSS. made at the same time, to supply the place of it—copies of the *Mĕpharrĕshe*, i.e. Distinct or Separate [8] Gospels, to replace the *Mĕhallĕte* or Gospel of the Mixed. When the sockets are found to have been prepared and marked, and the pillars lie fitted and labelled, what else can we do than slip the pillars into their own sockets? They were not very successful

---

[1] Doctrine of Addai, xxxv. 15-17. [2] H. E. iv. 29.
[3] Haer. xlvi. 1. [4] Canons. [5] Haer. i. 20.
[6] The Earliest Life of Christ, Appendix VIII.
[7] The MS. is mutilated at the beginning of the other three Gospels.
[8] It appears almost, if not quite, certain that this is the true meaning. Payne Smith's Thesaurus Syriacus, coll. 3303-4.

attempts, as might have been expected, since the **Peshitto**, or in some places amongst the Jacobites the **Philoxenian** or Harkleian, entirely supplanted them in future use, and they lay hidden for centuries till sedulous inquiry unearthed them, and the ingenuity of critics invested them with an importance not their own [1].

What was the origin of the mass of floating readings, of which some were transferred into the text of these two Codexes, will be considered in the next section. Students should be cautioned against inferring that the Diatessaron was read in service throughout Syria. There is no evidence to warrant such a conclusion. The mention of Edessa and Cyrrhus point to the country near the upper Euphrates; and the expression of Theodoret, relating to the Diatessaron being used ' in churches of our parts,' seems to hint at a circumscribed region. Plenty of room was left for a predominant use of the Peshitto, so far as we know : and no reason on that score can be adduced to counterbalance the force of the arguments given in this section in favour of the existence from the beginning of that great Version.

Yet some critics endeavour to represent that the Peshitto was brought first into prominence upon the supersession of the Diatessaron, though it is never found under the special title of *Mĕpharrĕsha.* What is this but to disregard the handposts of history in favour of a pet theory ?

---

[1] The Lewis Codex was in part destroyed, as not being worth keeping, while the leaves which escaped that fate were used for other writing. Perhaps others were treated in similar fashion, which would help to account for the fact mentioned in note 2, p. 129.

CHAPTER VII.

THE ANTIQUITY OF THE TRADITIONAL TEXT.

III. WITNESS OF THE WESTERN OR SYRIO-LOW-LATIN TEXT.

THERE are problems in what is usually termed the Western Text of the New Testament, which have not yet, as I believe, received satisfactory treatment. Critics, including even Dr. Scrivener[1], have too readily accepted Wiseman's conclusion[2], that the numerous Latin Texts all come from one stem, in fact that there was originally only one Old-Latin Version, not several.

That this is at first sight the conclusion pressed upon the mind of the inquirer, I readily admit. The words and phrases, the general cast and flow of the sentences, are so similar in these texts, that it seems at the outset extremely difficult to resist the inference that all of them began from the same translation, and that the differences between them arose from the continued effect of various and peculiar circumstances upon them and from a long course of copying. But examination will reveal on better acquaintance certain obstinate features which will not allow us to be guided by first appearances. And before investigating these, we may note that there are some considerations of a general character which take the edge off this phenomenon.

---

[1] Plain Introduction, II. 43–44.

[2] Essays on Various Subjects, i. Two Letters on some parts of the controversy concerning 1 John v. 7, pp. 23, &c. The arguments are more ingenious than powerful. Africa, e. g., had no monopoly of Low-Latin.

Supposing that Old-Latin Texts had a multiform origin, they must have gravitated towards more uniformity of expression: intercourse between Christians who used different translations of a single original must, in unimportant points at least, have led them to greater agreement. Besides this, the identity of the venerated original in all the cases, except where different readings had crept into the Greek, must have produced a constant likeness to one another, in all translations made into the same language and meant to be faithful. If on the other hand there were numerous Versions, it is clear that in those which have descended to us there must have been a survival of the fittest.

But it is now necessary to look closely into the evidence, for the answers to all problems must depend upon that, and upon nothing but that.

The first point that strikes us is that there is in this respect a generic difference between the other Versions and the Old-Latin. The former are in each case one, with no suspicion of various origination. Gothic, Bohairic, Sahidic, Armenian (though the joint work of Sahak and Mesrop and Eznik and others), Ethiopic, Slavonic :—each is one Version and came from one general source without doubt or question. Codexes may differ: that is merely within the range of transcriptional accuracy, and has nothing to do with the making of the Version. But there is no pre-eminent Version in the Old-Latin field. Various texts compete with difference enough to raise the question. Upon disputed readings they usually give discordant verdicts. And this discord is found, not as in Greek Codexes where the testifying MSS. generally divide into two hostile bodies, but in greater and more irregular discrepancy. Their varied character may be seen in the following Table including the Texts employed by Tischendorf, which has been constructed from that scholar's notes upon the basis of the chief passages in dispute, as revealed in the text of the Revised Version throughout the Gospels, the standard being the *Textus Receptus* :—

Brixianus, f	$\frac{286}{54}$*	= about $\frac{19}{3}$
Monacensis, q	$\frac{255}{97}$	= $\frac{5}{2}$+
Claromontanus, h (only in St. Matt.)	$\frac{46}{28}$	= $\frac{5}{3}$+
Colbertinus, c	$\frac{165}{152}$	= about $\frac{14}{13}$
Fragm. Sangall. n	$\frac{8}{8}$	= 1
Veronensis, b	$\frac{134}{184}$	= $\frac{2}{3}$+
Sangermanensis II, g²	$\frac{24}{36}$	= $\frac{2}{3}$
Corbeiensis II, ff²	$\frac{113}{180}$	= $\frac{2}{3}$—
Sangermanensis I, g²	$\frac{27}{46}$	= $\frac{3}{5}$—
Rehdigeranus, l	$\frac{104}{184}$	= $\frac{5}{8}$+
Vindobonensis, i	$\frac{37}{72}$	= $\frac{1}{2}$+
Vercellensis, a	$\frac{100}{214}$	= $\frac{1}{2}$—
Corbeiensis I, ff¹	$\frac{37}{73}$	= $\frac{1}{2}$—
Speculum, m	$\frac{8}{18}$	= $\frac{1}{2}$—
Palatinus, e	$\frac{48}{130}$	= $\frac{1}{3}$+
Frag. Ambrosiana, s	$\frac{2}{8}$	= $\frac{1}{4}$
Bobiensis, k	$\frac{25}{93}$	= $\frac{1}{4}$+

Looking dispassionately at this Table, the reader will surely observe that these MSS. shade off from one another by intervals of a somewhat similar character. They do not fall readily into classes : so that if the threefold division of Dr. Hort is adopted, it must be employed as not meaning very much. The appearances are against all being derived from the extreme left or from the extreme right. And some current modes of thought must be guarded against, as for instance when a scholar recently laid down as an axiom which all critics would admit, that *k* might be taken as the representative of the Old-Latin Texts, which would be about as true as if Mr. Labouchere at the present day were said to represent in opinion the Members of the House of Commons.

* The numerator in these fractions denotes the number of times throughout the Gospels when the text of the MS. in question agrees in the selected passages with the Textus Receptus : the denominator, when it witnesses to the Neologian Text.

The sporadic nature of these Texts may be further exhibited, if we take the thirty passages which helped us in the second section of this chapter. The attestation yielded by the Old-Latin MSS. will help still more in the exhibition of their character.

	Traditional.	*Neologian.*
St. Matt.		
i. 25	f. ff^1. g^2. q.	b. c. g^1. k.
v. 44	(1) c. f. h.	a. b. ff^1. g$^{1.2}$. k. l.
	(2) a. b. c. f. h.	
vi. 13	f. g^1. q.	a. b. c. ff^1. g^2. l.
vii. 13	f. ff^2. g$^{1.2}$. q.	a. b. c. h. k. m.
ix. 13	c. g$^{1.2}$.	a. b. f. ff^1. h. k. l. q.
xi. 27	All.	
xvii. 21	'Most' a. b. c. (?) g^1. . e. ff^1.	
xviii. 11	e. ff^1.	
xix. 17		
(1) ἀγαθέ	b. c. f. ff^2. g$^{1.2}$. h. q.	a. e. ff^1.
(2) τί με ἐρωτᾷς κ.τ.λ. }	f. q.	{ a. b. c. e. ff$^{1.2}$. g^1. h. l. (Vulg.)
(3) εἷς ἐστ. ὁ ἀγ.	f. g^1. m. q.	b. c. ff$^{1.2}$. l. (Vulg.)
xxiii. 38		
(Lk. xiii. 35)	All—except	ff^2.
xxvii. 34	c. f. h. q.	a. b. ff$^{1.2}$. g$^{1.2}$. l. (Vulg.)
xxviii. 2	f. h.	a. b. c. ff$^{1.2}$. g$^{1.2}$. l. n.
,, 19	All.	
St. Mark		
i. 2		All.
xvi. 9–20	All—except	k.
St. Luke		
i. 28	All.	
ii. 14		All.
x. 41–42	f. g$^{1.2}$. q. (Vulg.)	a. b. c. e. ff^2. i. l.
xxii. 43–44	a. b. c. e. ff^2. g$^{1.2}$. i. l. q.	f.
xxiii. 34	c. e. f. ff^2. l.	a. b. d.
,, 38	All—except	a.
,, 45	a. b. c. e. f. ff^2. l. q.	

	Traditional.	Neologian.

(St. Luke)

xxiv. 40 . . . c. f. q. . . . . . . a. b. d. e. ff². l.

  ,,   42 . . . a. b. f. ff². l. q. . . . . e.

St. John

i. 3–4 . . . . c. (Vulg.) . . . . . a. b. e. ff². q.

  ,,   18 . . . . a. b. c. e. f. ff².

            l. q.

iii. 13 . . . . All.

x. 14 . . . . All.

xvii. 24 . . . All (Vulg.) . . . . Vulg. MSS.

xxi. 25 . . . All.

It will be observed that in all of these thirty passages, Old-Latin MSS. witness on both sides and in a sporadic way, except in three on the Traditional side and six on the Neologian side, making nine in all against twenty-one. In this respect they stand in striking contrast with all the Versions in other languages as exhibiting a discordance in their witness which is at the very least far from suggesting a single source, if it be not wholly inconsistent with such a supposition.

Again, the variety of synonyms found in these texts is so great that they could not have arisen except from variety of origin. Copyists do not insert *ad libitum* different modes of expression. For example, Mr. White has remarked that ἐπιτιμᾶν is translated 'in no less than eleven different ways,' or adding *arguere*, in twelve, viz. by

admonere	emendare	minari	praecipere
comminari	imperare	obsecrare	prohibere
corripere[1]	increpare	objurgare	arguere (r).

It is true that some of these occur on the same MS., but the variety of expression in parallel passages hardly agrees with descent from a single prototype. Greek MSS. differ in readings, but not in the same way. Similarly

---

[1] Once in k by *comperire* probably a slip for *corripere*. Old Latin Texts, III. pp. xxiv–xxv.

δοξάζω, which occurs, as he tells us, thirty-seven times in the Gospels, is rendered by *clarifico, glorifico, honorem accipio, honorifico, honoro, magnifico*, some passages presenting four variations. So again, it is impossible to understand how συνοχή in the phrase συνοχὴ ἐθνῶν (St. Luke xxi. 25) could have been translated by *compressio* (Vercellensis, *a*), *occursus* (Brixianus, *f*), *pressura* (others), *conflictio* (Bezae, *d*), if they had a common descent. They represent evidently efforts made by independent translators to express the meaning of a difficult word. When we meet with *possidebo* and *haereditabo* for κληρονομήσω (St. Luke x. 25) *lumen* and *lux* for φῶς (St. John i. 9), *ante galli cantum* and *antequam gallus cantet* for πρὶν ἀλέκτορα φωνῆσαι (St. Matt. xxvi. 34), *locum* and *praedium* and *in agro* for χωρίον (xxvi. 35), *transfer a me calicem istum* and *transeat a me calix iste* for παρελθέτω ἀπ᾿ ἐμοῦ τὸ ποτήριον τοῦτο (xxvi. 39);—when we fall upon *vox venit de caelis, vox facta est de caelis, vox de caelo facta est, vox de caelis*, and the like ; or *qui mihi bene complacuisti, charissimus in te complacui, dilectus in quo bene placuit mihi, dilectus in te bene sensi* (St. Mark i. 11), or *adsumpsit (autem . . . duodecim), adsumens, convocatis* (St. Luke xviii. 31) it is clear that these and the instances of the same sort occurring everywhere in the Old-Latin Texts must be taken as fingerposts pointing in many directions. Various readings in Greek Codexes present, not a parallel, but a sharp contrast. No such profusion of synonyms can be produced from them.

The arguments which the Old-Latin Texts supply internally about themselves are confirmed exactly by the direct evidence borne by St. Augustine and St. Jerome. The well-known words of those two great men who must be held to be competent deponents as to what they found around them, even if they might fall into error upon the events of previous ages, prove (1) that a very large number of texts then existed, (2) that they differed greatly from one another, (3) that none had any special authority, and

(4) that translators worked on their own independent lines[1]. But there is the strongest reason for inferring that Augustine was right when he said, that 'in the earliest days of the faith whenever any Greek codex fell into the hands of any one who thought that he had slight familiarity (*aliquantulum facultatis*) with Greek and Latin, he was bold enough to attempt to make a translation[2].' For what else could have happened than what St. Augustine says actually did take place? The extraordinary value and influence of the sacred Books of the New Testament became apparent soon after their publication. They were most potent forces in converting unbelievers: they swayed the lives and informed the minds of Christians: they were read in the services of the Church. But copies in any number, if at all, could not be ordered at Antioch, or Ephesus, or Rome, or Alexandria. And at first no doubt translations into Latin were not to be had. Christianity grew almost of itself under the viewless action of the HOLY GHOST: there were no administrative means of making provision. But the Roman Empire was to a great extent bilingual. Many men of Latin origin were acquainted more or less with Greek. The army which furnished so many converts must have reckoned in its ranks, whether as officers or as ordinary soldiers, a large number who were accomplished Greek scholars. All evangelists and teachers would have to explain the new Books to those who did not understand Greek. The steps were but short from oral to written teaching, from answering questions and giving exposition to making regular translations in fragments or books and afterwards throughout the New Testament. The resistless energy of the Christian faith must have demanded such offices on behalf of the Latin-speaking members of the

[1] 'Tot sunt paene (exemplaria), quot codices,' Jerome, Epistola ad Damascum. 'Latinorum interpretum infinita varietas,' 'interpretum numerositas,' 'nullo modo numerari possunt,' De Doctrina Christiana, ii. 16, 21.
[2] De Doctr. Christ. ii. 16.

Church, and must have produced hundreds of versions, fragmentary and complete. Given the two languages side by side, under the stress of the necessity of learning and the eagerness to drink in the Words of Life, the information given by St. Augustine must have been amply verified. And the only wonder is, that scholars have not paid more attention to the witness of that eminent Father, and have missed seeing how natural and true it was.

It is instructive to trace how the error arose. It came chiefly, if I mistake not, from two ingenious letters of Cardinal Wiseman, then a young man, and from the familiarity which they displayed with early African Literature. So Lachmann, Tischendorf, Davidson, Tregelles, Scrivener, and Westcott and Hort, followed him. Yet an error lies at the root of Wiseman's argument which, if the thing had appeared now, scholars would not have let pass unchallenged and uncorrected.

Because the Bobbian text agreed in the main with the texts of Tertullian, Cyprian, Arnobius, and Primasius, Wiseman assumed that not only that text, but also the dialectic forms involved in it, were peculiar to Africa and took their rise there. But as Mr. White has pointed out [1], ' that is because during this period we are dependent almost exclusively on Africa for our Latin Literature.' Moreover, as every accomplished Latin scholar who is acquainted with the history of the language is aware, Low-Latin took rise in Italy, when the provincial dialects of that Peninsula sprang into prominence upon the commencement of the decay of the pure Latin race, occurring through civil and foreign wars and the sanguinary proscriptions, and from the consequent lapse in the predominance in literature of the pure Latin Language. True, that the pure Latin and the Low-Latin continued side by side for a long time, the former in the best literature, and the latter in ever

[1] Scrivener's Plain Introduction, IL 44, note 1.

increasing volume. What is most apposite to the question, the Roman colonists in France, Spain, Portugal, Provence, and Walachia, consisted mainly of Italian blood which was not pure Latin, as is shewn especially in the veteran soldiers who from time to time received grants of land from their emperors or generals. The six Romance Languages are mainly descended from the provincial dialects of the Italian Peninsula. It would be contrary to the action of forces in history that such and so strong a change of language should have been effected in an outlying province, where the inhabitants mainly spoke another tongue altogether. It is in the highest degree improbable that a new form of Latin should have grown up in Africa, and should have thence spread across the Mediterranean, and have carried its forms of speech into parts of the extensive Roman Empire with which the country of its birth had no natural communication. Low-Latin was the early product of the natural races in north and central Italy, and from thence followed by well-known channels into Africa and Gaul and elsewhere[1]. We shall find in these truths much light, unless I am deceived, to dispel our darkness upon the Western text.

The best part of Wiseman's letters occurs where he proves that St. Augustine used Italian MSS. belonging to what the great Bishop of Hippo terms the 'Itala,' and pronounces to be the best of the Latin Versions. Evidently the 'Itala' was the highest form of Latin Version—highest, that is, in the character and elegance of the Latin used in it, and consequently in the correctness of its rendering. So

---

[1] See Diez, Grammatik der Romanischen Sprachen, as well as Introduction to the Grammar of the Romance Languages, translated by C. B. Cayley. Also Abel Hovelacque, The Science of Language, English Translation, pp. 227-9. 'The Grammar of Frederick Diez, first published some forty years ago, has once for all disposed of those Iberian, Keltic, and other theories, which nevertheless crop up from time to time.' Ibid. p. 229. Brachet, Grammar of the French Language, pp. 3-5; Whitney, Language and the Study of Language, pp. 165, &c., &c.

here we now see our way. Critics have always had some difficulty about Dr. Hort's 'European' class, though there is doubtless a special character in *b* and its following. It appears now that there is no necessity for any embarrassment about the intermediate MSS., because by unlocalizing the text supposed to be African we have the Low-Latin Text prevailing over the less educated parts of Italy, over Africa, and over Gaul, and other places away from Rome and Milan and the other chief centres.

Beginning with the Itala, the other texts sink gradually downwards, till we reach the lowest of all. There is thus no bar in the way of connecting that most remarkable product of the Low-Latin Text, the Codex Bezae, with any others, because the Latin Version of it stands simply as one of the Low-Latin group.

Another difficulty is also removed. Amongst the most interesting and valuable contributions to Sacred Textual Criticism that have come from the fertile conception and lucid argument of Mr. Rendel Harris, has been the proof of a closer connexion between the Low-Latin Text, as I must venture to call it, and the form of Syrian Text exhibited in the Curetonian Version, which he has given in his treatment of the Ferrar Group of Greek MSS. Of course the general connexion between the two has been long known to scholars. The resemblance between the Curetonian and Tatian's Diatessaron, to which the Lewis Codex must now be added, on the one hand, and on the other the less perfect Old-Latin Texts is a commonplace in Textual Criticism. But Mr. Harris has also shewn that there was probably a Syriacization of the Codex Bezae, a view which has been strongly confirmed on general points by Dr. Chase: and has further discovered evidence that the text of the Ferrar Group of Cursives found its way into and out of Syriac and carried back, according to Mr. Harris' ingenious suggestion, traces of its sojourn there. Dr. Chase has very recently shed more light upon the subject in his book called 'The Syro-Latin Element of the Gospels [1].' So all these particulars exhibit in strong light the connexion between the Old-Latin and the Syriac. If we are dealing, not so much with the entire body of Western Texts, but as I contend with the Low-Latin part of them in its wide circulation, there is no difficulty in understanding how such a connexion arose. The Church in Rome shot up as noiselessly as the Churches of Damascus and Antioch. How and why? The key is given in the sixteenth chapter of St. Paul's Epistle to the Romans. How could he have known intimately so many of the leading Roman Christians, unless they had carried his teaching along the road of commerce from Antioch to Rome? Such travellers, and they would by no means be confined to the days of St. Paul, would understand Syriac as well as Latin. The stories and books, told or written in Aramaic, must have gone through all Syria, recounting the thrilling history of redemption before the authorized accounts were given in Greek. Accordingly, in the earliest times translations must have been made from Aramaic or Syriac into Latin, as afterwards from Greek. Thus a connexion between the Italian and Syrian Churches, and also between the teaching given in the two countries, must have lain embedded in the foundations of their common Christianity, and must have exercised an influence during very many years after.

This view of the interconnexion of the Syrian and Old-Latin readings leads us on to what must have been at first the chief origin of corruption. 'The rulers derided Him': 'the common people heard Him gladly.' It does not, I think, appear probable that the Gospels were written till after St. Paul left Jerusalem for Rome. Literature of a high kind arose slowly in the Church, and the great

---

[1] 'Syro-Latin' is doubtless an exact translation of 'Syro-Latinus': but as we do not say 'Syran' but 'Syrian,' it is not idiomatic English.

missionary Apostle was the pioneer.   It is surely impossible that the authors of the Synoptic Gospels should have seen one another's writings, because in that case they would not have differed so much from one another[1].   The effort of St. Luke (Pref.), made probably during St. Paul's imprisonment at Caesarea (Acts xxiv. 23), though he may not have completed his Gospel then, most likely stimulated St. Matthew.   Thus in time the authorized Gospels were issued, not only to supply complete and connected accounts, but to become accurate and standard editions of what had hitherto been spread abroad in shorter or longer narratives, and with more or less correctness or error.   Indeed, it is clear that before the Gospels were written many erroneous forms of the stories which made up the oral or written Gospel must have been in vogue, and that nowhere are these more likely to have prevailed than in Syria, where the Church took root so rapidly and easily.   But the readings thus propagated, of which many found their way, especially in the West, into the wording of the Gospels before St. Chrysostom, never could have entered into the pure succession.   Here and there they were interlopers and usurpers, and after the manner of such claimants, had to some extent the appearance of having sprung from the genuine stock.   But they were ejected during the period elapsing from the fourth to the eighth century, when the Text of the New Testament was gradually purified.

This view is submitted to Textual students for verification.

We have now traced back the Traditional Text to the earliest times.   The witness of the early Fathers has established the conclusion that there is not the slightest

---

[1] This is purely my own opinion.   Dean Burgon followed Townson in supposing that the Synoptic Evangelists in some cases saw one another's books.

uncertainty upon this point. To deny it is really a piece of pure assumption. It rests upon the record of facts. Nor is there any reason for hesitation in concluding that the career of the Peshitto dates back in like manner. The Latin Texts, like others, are of two kinds: both the Traditional Text and the forms of corruption find a place in them. So that the testimony of these great Versions, Syriac and Latin, is added to the testimony of the Fathers. There are no grounds for doubting that the causeway of the pure text of the Holy Gospels, and by consequence of the rest of the New Testament, has stood far above the marshes on either side ever since those sacred Books were written. What can be the attraction of those perilous quagmires, it is hard to understand. 'An highway shall be there, and a way'; 'the redeemed shall walk there'; 'the wayfaring men, though fools, shall not err therein [1].'

---

[1] Isaiah xxxv. 8, 9.

CHAPTER VIII.

ALEXANDRIA AND CAESAREA.

§ 1. *Alexandrian Readings, and the Alexandrian School.*

WHAT is the real truth about the existence of an Alexandrian Text? Are there, or are there not, sufficient elements of an Alexandrian character, and of Alexandrian or Egyptian origin, to constitute a Text of the Holy Gospels to be designated by that name?

So thought Griesbach, who conceived Origen to be the standard of the Alexandrian text. Hort, who appears to have attributed to his Neutral text much of the native products of Alexandria[1], speaks more of readings than of text. The question must be decided upon the evidence of the case, which shall now be in the main produced.

The Fathers or ancient writers who may be classed as Alexandrian in the period under consideration are the following :—

	Traditional.	Neologian.
Heracleon	1	7
Clement of Alexandria . .	82	72
Dionysius of Alexandria . .	12	5
Theognostus	0	1
Peter of Alexandria . . .	7	8
Arius	2	1
Athanasius (c. Arianos) . .	57	56
	161	150

[1] Introduction, pp. 127, &c.

Under the thirty places already examined, Clement, the most important of these writers, witnesses 8 times for the Traditional reading and 14 times for the Neologian. Origen, who in his earlier years was a leader of this school, testifies 44 and 27 times respectively in the order stated.

The Version which was most closely connected with Lower Egypt was the Bohairic, and under the same thirty passages gives the ensuing evidence :—

1. Matt. i. 25. Omits. One MS. says the Greek has 'her first-born son.'
2. ,, v. 44. Large majority, all but 5, omit. Some add in the margin.
3. ,, vi. 13. Only 5 MSS. have the doxology.
4. ,, vii. 13. All have it.
5. ,, ix. 13. 9 have it, and 3 in margin : 12 omit, besides the 3 just mentioned.
6. ,, xi. 27. All have βούληται.
7. ,, xvii. 21. Only 6 MSS. have it, besides 7 in margin or interlined : 11 omit wholly.
8. ,, xviii. 11. Only 4 have it.
9. ,, xix. 16. Only 7 have 'good,' besides a few corrections : 12 omit.
   ,, ,, 17. Only 1 has it.
10. ,, xxiii. 38. Only 6 have it.
11. ,, xxvii. 34. One corrected and one which copied the correction. All the rest have οἶνον[1].
12. ,, xxviii. 2. All have it.
13. ,, ,, 19. All have it.
14. Mark i. 2. All (i.e. 25) give, Ἡσαΐᾳ.
15. ,, xvi. 9-20. None wholly omit: 2 give the alternative ending.
16. Luke i. 28. Only 4 + 2 corrected have it : 12 omit.
17. ,, ii. 14. All have εὐδοκία.
18. ,, x. 41-2. Ὀλίγων δὲ (3 omit) ἐστὶ χρεία ἢ ἑνός : 1 omits ἢ ἑνός. 2 corrected add ' of them.'
19. ,, xxii. 43-4. Omitted by 18[1].
20. ,, xxiii. 34. All omit[1].

[1] Probably Alexandrian readings.

21. Luke xxiii. 38. All omit except 5 [1] (?).
22. „   „   45. All have ἐκλιπόντος [1].
23. „   xxiv. 40. All have it.
24. „   „   42. All omit [1].
25. John i.   3–4. All (except 1 which pauses at οὐδὲ ἓν) have it.
            The Sahidic is the other way.
26. „   „   18. All have Θεός [1].
27. „   iii. 13. Omitted by 9.
28. „   x.   14. All have 'mine know me.' The Bohairic has
            no passive : hence the error [1].
29. „   xvii. 24. The Bohairic could not express οὖς : hence
            the error [1].
30. „   xxi. 25. All have it.

The MSS. differ in number as to their witness in each place.

No manuscripts can be adduced as Alexandrian : and in fact we are considering the ante-manuscriptal period. All reference therefore to manuscripts would be consequent upon, not a factor in, the present investigation.

It will be seen upon a review of this evidence, that the most striking characteristic is found in the instability of it. The Bohairic wabbles from side to side. Clement witnesses on both sides upon the thirty places but mostly against the Traditional text, whilst his collected evidence in all cases yields a slight majority to the latter side of the contention. Origen on the contrary by a large majority rejects the Neologian readings on the thirty passages, but acknowledges them by a small one in his habitual quotations. It is very remarkable, and yet characteristic of Origen, who indeed changed his home from Alexandria to Caesarea, that his habit was to adopt one of the most notable of Syrio-Low-Latin readings in preference to the Traditional reading prevalent at Alexandria. St. Ambrose (in Ps. xxxvi. 35) in defending the reading of St. John i. 3–4, 'without Him was not anything made : that which was made was life in Him,' says that

[1] Probably Alexandrian readings.

Alexandrians and Egyptians follow the reading which is now adopted everywhere except by Lachmann, Tregelles, and W.-Hort. It has been said that Origen was in the habit of using MSS. of both kinds, and indeed no one can examine his quotations without coming to that conclusion.

Therefore we are led first of all to the school of Christian Philosophy which under the name of the Catechetical School has made Alexandria for ever celebrated in the early annals of the Christian Church. Indeed Origen was a Textual Critic. He spent much time and toil upon the text of the New Testament, besides his great labours on the Old, because he found it disfigured as he says by corruptions 'some arising from the carelessness of scribes, some from evil licence of emendation, some from arbitrary omissions and interpolations [1].' Such a sitting in judgement, or as perhaps it should be said with more justice to Origen such a pursuit of inquiry, involved weighing of evidence on either side, of which there are many indications in his works. The connexion of this school with the school set up at Caesarea, to which place Origen appears to have brought his manuscripts, and where he bequeathed his teaching and spirit to sympathetic successors, will be carried out and described more fully in the next section. Origen was the most prominent personage by far in the Alexandrian School. His fame and influence in this province extended with the reputation of his other writings long after his death. 'When a writer speaks of the "accurate copies," what he actually means is the text of Scripture which was employed or approved by Origen [2].' Indeed it was an elemental, inchoate school, dealing in an academical and eclectic spirit with evidence of various kinds, highly intellectual rather than original, as for ex-

[1] In Matt. xv. 14, quoted and translated by Dr. Bigg in his Bampton Lectures on The Christian Platonists of Alexandria, p. 123.
[2] Burgon, Last Twelve Verses, p. 236, and note z.

ample in the welcome given to the Syrio-Low-Latin variation of St. Matt. xix. 16, 17, and addicted in some degree to alteration of passages. It would appear that besides this critical temper and habit there was to some extent a growth of provincial readings at Alexandria or in the neighbourhood, and that modes of spelling which were rejected in later ages took their rise there. Specimens of the former of these peculiarities may be seen in the table of readings just given from the Bohairic Version. The chief effects of Alexandrian study occurred in the Caesarean school which now invites our consideration.

§ 2. *Caesarean School.*

In the year 231, as seems most probable, Origen finally left Alexandria. His head-quarters thenceforward may be said to have been Caesarea in Palestine, though he travelled into Greece and Arabia and stayed at Neo-Caesarea in Cappadocia with his friend and pupil Gregory Thaumaturgus. He had previously visited Rome : so that he must have been well qualified by his experience as well as probably by his knowledge and collection of MSS. to lay a broad foundation for the future settlement of the text. But unfortunately his whole career marks him out as a man of uncertain judgement. Like some others, he was a giant in learning, but ordinary in the use of his learning. He was also closely connected with the philosophical school of Alexandria, from which Arianism issued.

The leading figures in this remarkable School of Textual Criticism at Caesarea were Origen and Eusebius, besides Pamphilus who forms the link between the two. The ground-work of the School was the celebrated library in the city which was formed upon the foundation supplied by Origen, so far as the books in it escaped the general destruction of MSS. that occurred in the persecution of Diocletian. It is remarkable, that although there seems little doubt that the Vatican and Sinaitic MSS. were amongst the fruits of this school, as will be shewn in the next chapter, the witness of the writings of both Origen and Eusebius is so favourable as it is to the Traditional Text. In the case of Origen there is as already stated [1] not far from an equality between the totals on either side, besides a majority of 44 to 27 on the thirty important texts: and the numbers for Eusebius are respectively 315 to 214, and 41 to 11.

Palestine was well suited from its geographical position to be the site of the junction of all the streams. The very same circumstances which adapted it to be the arena of the great drama in the world's history drew to its shores the various elements in the representation in language of the most characteristic part of the Word of God. The Traditional Text would reach it by various routes : the Syrio-Low-Latin across the sea and from Syria : the Alexandrian readings from the near neighbourhood. Origen in his travels would help to assemble all. The various alien streams would thus coalesce, and the text of B and א would be the result. But the readings of MSS. recorded by Origen and especially by Eusebius prove that in this broad school the Traditional Text gained at least a decided preponderance according to the private choice of the latter scholar. Yet, as will be shewn, he was probably, not the writer of B and of the six conjugate leaves in א, yet as the executor of the order of Constantine the superintendent also in copying those celebrated MSS. Was he then influenced by the motives of a courtier in sending such texts as he thought would be most acceptable to the Emperor? Or is it not more in consonance with the facts of the case —especially as interpreted by the subsequent spread in

---

[1] Above, p. 100.

Constantinople of the Traditional Text[1]—, that we should infer that the fifty MSS. sent included a large proportion of Texts of another character? Eusebius, the Homoiousian or Semi-Arian, would thus be the collector of copies to suit different tastes and opinions, and his scholar and successor Acacius, the Homoean, would more probably be the writer of B and of the six conjugate leaves of א[2]. The trimming character of the latitudinarian, and the violent forwardness of the partisan, would appear to render such a supposition not unreasonable. Estimating the school according to principles of historical philosophy, and in consonance with both the existence of the Text denoted by B and א and also the subsequent results, it must appear to us to be transitional in character, including two distinct and incongruous solutions, of which one was afterwards proved to be the right by the general acceptation in the Church that even Dr. Hort acknowledges to have taken place.

An interesting inquiry is here suggested with respect to the two celebrated MSS. just mentioned. How is it that we possess no MSS. of the New Testament of any considerable size older than those, or at least no other such MSS. as old as they are? Besides the disastrous results of the persecution of Diocletian, there is much force in the reply of Dean Burgon, that being generally recognized as bad MSS. they were left standing on the shelf in their handsome covers, whilst others which were more correct were being thumbed to pieces in constant use. But the discoveries made since the Dean's death enables me to suggest another answer which will also help to enlarge our view on these matters.

The habit of writing on vellum belongs to Asia. The first mention of it that we meet with occurs in the 58th

[1] Hort, Introduction, p. 143.
[2] Eusebius suggested the Homoean theory, but his own position, so far as he had a position, is best indicated as above.

chapter of the 5th book of Herodotus, where the historian tells us that the Ionians wrote on the skins of sheep and goats because they could not get 'byblus,' or as we best know it, papyrus. Vellum remained in comparative obscurity till the time of Eumenes II, King of Pergamum. That intelligent potentate, wishing to enlarge his library and being thwarted by the Ptolemies who refused out of jealousy to supply him with papyrus, improved the skins of his country[1], and made the 'charta Pergamena,' from whence the term parchment has descended to us. It will be remembered that St. Paul sent to Ephesus for 'the books, especially the parchments[2].' There is evidence that vellum was used at Rome: but the chief materials employed there appear to have been waxen tablets and papyrus. Martial, writing towards the end of the first century, speaks of vellum MSS. of Homer, Virgil, Cicero, and Ovid[3]. But if such MSS. had prevailed generally, more would have come down to us. The emergence of vellum into general use is marked and heralded by the products of the library at Caesarea, which helped by the rising literary activity in Asia and by the building of Constantinople, was probably the means of the introduction of an improved employment of vellum. It has been already noticed[4], that Acacius and Euzoius, successively bishops of Caesarea after Eusebius, superintended the copying of papyrus manuscripts upon vellum. Greek uncials were not unlike in general form to the square Hebrew letters used at Jerusalem after the Captivity. The activity in Asiatic Caesarea synchronized with the rise in the use of vellum. It would seem that in moving there Origen deserted papyrus for the more durable material.

---

[1] Sir E. Maunde Thompson, Greek and Latin Palaeography. p. 35. Plin. at. Hist. xiii. 11.

[2] τὰ βιβλία, μάλιστα τὰς μεμβράνας, 2 Tim. iv. 13.

[3] Palaeography, p. 36.   [4] See above, p. 2.

A word to explain my argument. If vellum had been in constant use over the Roman Empire during the first three centuries and a third which elapsed before B and ℵ were written, there ought to have been in existence some remains of a material so capable of resisting the tear and wear of use and time. As there are no vellum MSS. at all except the merest fragments dating from before 330 A. D., we are perforce driven to infer that a material for writing of a perishable nature was generally employed before that period. Now not only had papyrus been for 'long the recognized material for literary use,' but we can trace its employment much later than is usually supposed. It is true that the cultivation of the plant in Egypt began to wane after the capture of Alexandria by the Mahommedans in 638 A. D., and the destruction of the famous libraries : but it continued in existence during some centuries afterwards. It was grown also in Sicily and Italy. 'In France papyrus was in common use in the sixth century.' Sir E. Maunde Thompson enumerates books now found in European Libraries of Paris, Genoa, Milan, Vienna, Munich, and elsewhere, as far down as the tenth century. The manufacture of it did not cease in Egypt till the tenth century. The use of papyrus did not lapse finally till paper was introduced into Europe by the Moors and Arabs [1], upon which occurrence all writing was executed upon tougher substances, and the cursive hand drove out uncial writing even from parchment.

---

[1] Palaeography, pp. 27–34. Paper was first made in China by a man named 蔡倫 Ts'ai Lun, who lived about A. D. 90. He is said to have used the bark of a tree ; probably Broussonetia papyrifera, Vent. from which a coarse kind of paper is still made in northern China. The better kinds of modern Chinese paper are made from the bamboo, which is soaked and pounded to a pulp. See Die Erfindung des Papiers in China, von Friedrich Hirth. Published in Vol. I. of the T'oung Pao (April, 1890). S. J. Brille: Leide. (Kindly communicated by Mr. H. A. Giles, H. B. M. Consul at Ningpo, author of 'A Chinese-English Dictionary,' &c., through my friend Dr. Alexander Prior of Park Terrace, N. W., and Halse House, near Taunton.)

The knowledge of the prevalence of papyrus, as to which any one may satisfy himself by consulting Sir E. Maunde Thompson's admirable book, and of the employment of the cursive hand before Christ, must modify many of the notions that have been widely entertained respecting the old Uncials.

1. In the first place, it will be clear that all the Cursive MSS. are not by any means the descendants of the Uncials. If the employment of papyrus in the earliest ages of the Christian Church was prevalent over by far the greater part of the Roman Empire, and that description is I believe less than the facts would warrant —then more than half of the stems of genealogy must have originally consisted of papyrus manuscripts. And further, if the use of papyrus continued long after the date of B and ℵ, then it would not only have occupied the earliest steps in the lines of descent, but much later exemplars must have carried on the succession. But in consequence of the perishable character of papyrus those exemplars have disappeared and live only in their cursive posterity. This aspect alone of the case under consideration invests the Cursives with much more interest and value than many people would nowadays attribute to them.

2. But beyond this conclusion, light is shed upon the subject by the fact now established beyond question, that cursive handwriting existed in the world some centuries before Christ [1]. For square letters (of course in writing interspersed with circular lines) we go to Palestine and Syria, and that may not impossibly be the reason why uncial Greek letters came out first, as far as the evidence of extant remains can guide us, in those countries. The change

---

[1] . . . 'the science of palaeography, which now stands on quite a different footing from what it had twenty, or even ten, years ago. Instead of beginning practically in the fourth century of our era, with the earliest of the great vellum codices of the Bible, it now begins in the third century before Christ. . . .' Church Quarterly Review for October, 1894, p. 104.

from uncial to cursive letters about the tenth century is most remarkable. Must it not to a great extent have arisen from the contemporary failure of papyrus which has been explained, and from the cursive writers on papyrus now trying their hand on vellum and introducing their more easy and rapid style of writing into that class of manuscripts[1]? If so, the phenomenon shews itself, that by the very manner in which they are written, Cursives mutely declare that they are not solely the children of the Uncials. Speaking generally, they are the progeny of a marriage between the two, and the papyrus MSS. would appear to have been the better half.

Such results as have been reached in this chapter and the last have issued from the advance made in discovery and research during the last ten years. But these were not known to Tischendorf or Tregelles, and much less to Lachmann. They could not have been embraced by Hort in his view of the entire subject when he constructed his clever but unsound theory some forty years ago[2]. Surely our conclusion must be that the world is leaving that school gradually behind.

[1] ... 'it is abundantly clear that the textual tradition at about the beginning of the Christian era is substantially identical with that of the tenth or eleventh century manuscripts, on which our present texts of the classics are based. Setting minor differences aside, the papyri, with a very few exceptions, represent the same texts as the vellum manuscripts of a thousand years later.' Church Quarterly, pp. 98, 99. What is here represented as unquestionably the case as regards Classical manuscripts is indeed more than what I claim for manuscripts of the New Testament. The Cursives were in great measure successors of papyri.

[2] Introduction, p. 16. He began it in the year 1853, and as it appears chiefly upon Lachmann's foundation.

CHAPTER IX.

THE OLD UNCIALS. THE INFLUENCE OF ORIGEN.

§ 1 [1].

CODEX B was early enthroned on something like speculation, and has been maintained upon the throne by what has strangely amounted to a positive superstition. The text of this MS. was not accurately known till the edition of Tischendorf appeared in 1867[2] : and yet long before that time it was regarded by many critics as the Queen of the Uncials. The collations of Bartolocci, of Mico, of Rulotta, and of Birch, were not trustworthy, though they far surpassed Mai's two first editions. Yet the prejudice in favour of the mysterious authority that was expected to issue decrees from the Vatican[3] did not wait till the clear light of criticism was shed upon its eccentricities and its defalcations. The same spirit, biassed by sentiment not ruled by reason, has remained since more has been disclosed of the real nature of this Codex[4].

A similar course has been pursued with respect to Codex א. It was perhaps to be expected that human infirmity should have influenced Tischendorf in his treatment of the treasure-trove by him : though his character

---

[1] By the Editor.

[2] Tischendorf's fourteen brief days' work is a marvel of accuracy, but must not be expected to be free from all errors. Thus he wrongly gives Ευρακυλων instead of Ευρακυδων, as Vercellone pointed out in his Preface to the octavo ed. of Mai in 1859, and as may be seen in the photographic copy of B.

[3] Cf. Scrivener's Introduction, (4th ed.) II. 283.

[4] See Kuenen and Cobet's Edition of the Vatican B, Introduction.

for judgement could not but be seriously injured by the
fact that in his eighth edition he altered the mature conclusions of his seventh in no less than 3.572[1] instances,
chiefly on account of the readings in his beloved Sinaitic
guide.

Yet whatever may be advanced against B may be alleged
even more strongly against ℵ. It adds to the number of
the blunders of its associate: it is conspicuous for habitual
carelessness or licence: it often by itself deviates into
glaring errors[2]. The elevation of the Sinaitic into the
first place, which was effected by Tischendorf as far as his
own practice was concerned, has been applauded by only
very few scholars: and it is hardly conceivable that they
could maintain their opinion, if they would critically and
impartially examine this erratic copy throughout the New
Testament for themselves.

The fact is that B and ℵ were the products of the school
of philosophy and teaching which found its vent in
Semi-Arian or Homoean opinions. The proof of this
position is somewhat difficult to give, but when the nature
of the question and the producible amount of evidence are
taken into consideration, is nevertheless quite satisfactory.

In the first place, according to the verdict of all critics
the date of these two MSS. coincides with the period when
Semi-Arianism or some other form of Arianism were in the
ascendant in the East, and to all outward appearance
swayed the Universal Church. In the last years of his
rule, Constantine was under the domination of the
Arianizing faction; and the reign of Constantius II over
all the provinces in the Roman Empire that spoke Greek,
during which encouragement was given to the great
heretical schools of the time, completed the two central

[1] Gregory's Prolegomena to Tischendorf's 8th Ed. of New Testament, (I)
p. 286.
[2] See Appendix V.

decades of the fourth century[1]. It is a circumstance that cannot fail to give rise to suspicion that the Vatican and Sinaitic MSS. had their origin under a predominant influence of such evil fame. At the very least, careful investigation is necessary to see whether those copies were in fact free from that influence which has met with universal condemnation.

Now as we proceed further we are struck with another most remarkable coincidence, which also as has been before noticed is admitted on all hands, viz. that the period of the emergence of the Orthodox School from oppression and the settlement in their favour of the great Nicene controversy was also the time when the text of B and ℵ sank into condemnation. The Orthodox side under St. Chrysostom and others became permanently supreme : so did also the Traditional Text. Are we then to assume with our opponents that in the Church condemnation and acceptance were inseparable companions? That at first heresy and the pure Text, and afterwards orthodoxy and textual corruption, went hand in hand? That such ill-matched couples graced the history of the Church? That upon so fundamental a matter as the accuracy of the written standard of reference, there was precision of text when heretics or those who dallied with heresy were in power, but that the sacred Text was contaminated when the Orthodox had things their own way? Is it indeed come to this, that for the pure and undefiled Word of GOD we must search, not amongst those great men who under the guidance of the Holy Spirit ascertained and settled for ever the main Articles of the Faith, and the Canon of Holy Scripture, but amidst the relics of those who were unable to agree with one another, and whose fine-drawn subtleties in creed and policy have been the despair of the historians,

---

[1] Constantine died in 337, and Constantius II reigned till 360.

M

and a puzzle to students of Theological Science? It is not too much to assert, that Theology and History know no such unscientific conclusions.

It is therefore a circumstance full of significance that Codexes B and ℵ were produced in such untoward times [1], and fell into neglect on the revival of orthodoxy, when the Traditional Text was permanently received. But the case in hand rests also upon evidence more direct than this.

The influence which the writings of Origen exercised on the ancient Church is indeed extraordinary. The fame of his learning added to the splendour of his genius, his vast Biblical achievements and his real insight into the depth of Scripture, conciliated for him the admiration and regard of early Christendom. Let him be freely allowed the highest praise for the profundity of many of his utterances, the ingenuity of almost all. It must at the same time be admitted that he is bold in his speculations to the verge, and beyond the verge, of rashness; unwarrantedly confident in his assertions; deficient in sobriety; in his critical remarks even foolish. A prodigious reader as well as a prodigious writer, his words would have been of incalculable value, but that he seems to have been so saturated with the strange speculations of the early heretics, that he sometimes adopts their wild method; and in fact has not been reckoned among the orthodox Fathers of the Church.

But (and this is the direction in which the foregoing remarks have tended) Origen's ruling passion is found to have been textual criticism [2]. This was at once his forte

---

[1] In his Last Twelve Verses of St. Mark, pp. 291–4, Dean Burgon argued that a lapse of about half a century divided the date of ℵ from that of B. But it seems that afterwards he surrendered the opinion which he embraced on the first appearance of ℵ in favour of the conclusion adopted by Tischendorf and Scrivener and other experts, in consequence of their identifying the writing of the six conjugate leaves of ℵ with that of the scribe of B. See above, pp. 46, 52.

[2] The Revision Revised, p. 292.

and his foible. In the library of his friend Pamphilus at Caesarea were found many Codexes that had belonged to him, and the autograph of his Hexapla, which was seen and used by St. Jerome[1]. In fact, the collection of books made by Pamphilus, in the gathering of which at the very least he was deeply indebted to Origen, became a centre from whence, after the destruction of copies in the persecution of Diocletian, authority as to the sacred Text radiated in various directions. Copying from papyrus on vellum was assiduously prosecuted there[2]. Constantine applied to Eusebius for fifty handsome copies[3], amongst which it is not improbable that the manuscripts ($\sigma\omega\mu\alpha\tau\acute{\iota}\alpha$) B and $\aleph$ were to be actually found[4]. But even if that is not so, the Emperor would not have selected Eusebius for the order, if that bishop had not been in the habit of providing copies : and Eusebius in fact carried on the work which he had commenced under his friend Pamphilus, and in which the latter must have followed the path pursued by Origen. Again, Jerome is known to have resorted to this quarter[5], and various entries in MSS. prove that others did the same[6]. It is clear that the celebrated library of Pamphilus exercised great influence in the province of

---

[1] The above passage, including the last paragraph, is from the pen of the Dean.

[2] See above, Introduction, p. 2.

[3] It is remarkable that Constantine in his Semi-Arian days applied to Eusebius, whilst the orthodox Constans sent a similar order afterwards to Athanasius. Apol. ad Const. § 4 (Montfaucon, Vita Athan. p. xxxvii), *ap.* Wordsworth's Church History, Vol. II. p. 45.

[4] See Canon Cook's ingenious argument. Those MSS. are handsome enough for an imperial order. The objection of my friend, the late Archdeacon Palmer (Scrivener's Introduction, I. 119, note), which I too hastily adopted on other grounds also in my Textual Guide, p. 82, note 1, will not stand, because $\sigma\omega\mu\alpha\tau\acute{\iota}\alpha$ cannot mean ' collections [of writings],' but simply, according to the frequent usage of the word in the early ages of the Church, ' vellum manuscripts.' The difficulty in translating $\tau\rho\iota\sigma\sigma\grave{\alpha}$ $\kappa\alpha\grave{\iota}$ $\tau\epsilon\tau\rho\alpha\sigma\sigma\acute{\alpha}$ ' of three or four columns in a page ' is not insuperable.

[5] Scrivener, Vol. II. 269 (4th ed.).

[6] Scrivener, Vol. I. 55 (4th ed.).

Textual Criticism ; and the spirit of Origen was powerful throughout the operations connected with it, at least till the Origenists got gradually into disfavour and at length were finally condemned at the Fifth General Council in A.D. 553.

But in connecting B and ℵ with the Library at Caesarea we are not left only to conjecture or inference. In a well-known colophon affixed to the end of the book of Esther in ℵ by the third corrector, it is stated that from the beginning of the book of Kings to the end of Esther the MS. was compared with a copy 'corrected by the hand of the holy martyr Pamphilus,' which itself was written and corrected after the Hexapla of Origen[1]. And a similar colophon may be found attached to the book of Ezra. It is added that the Codex Sinaiticus (τόδε τὸ τεῦχος) and the Codex Pamphili (τὸ αὐτὸ παλαιώτατον βιβλίον) manifested great agreement with one another. The probability that ℵ was thus at least in part copied from a manuscript executed by Pamphilus is established by the facts that a certain 'Codex Marchalianus' is often mentioned which was due to Pamphilus and Eusebius; and that Origen's recension of the Old Testament, although he published no edition of the Text of the New, possessed a great reputation. On the books of Chronicles, St. Jerome mentions manuscripts executed by Origen with great care, which were published by Pamphilus and Eusebius. And in Codex H of St. Paul it is stated that that MS. was compared with a MS. in the library of Caesarea 'which was written by the hand of the holy Pamphilus[2].' These notices added to the frequent

---

[1] The colophon is given in full by Wilhelm Bousset in a number of the well-known 'Texte und Untersuchungen,' edited by Oscar von Gebhardt and Adolf Harnack, entitled 'Textkritische Studien zum Neuen Testament,' p. 45. II. Der Kodex Pamphili, 1894, to which my notice was kindly drawn by Dr. Sanday.

[2] Miller's Scrivener, I. 183-4. By Euthalius, the Deacon, afterwards Bp. of Sulci.

reference by St. Jerome and others to the critical (ἀκριβῆ) MSS., by which we are to understand those which were distinguished by the approval of Origen or were in consonance with the spirit of Origen, shew evidently the position in criticism which the Library at Caesarea and its illustrious founder had won in those days. And it is quite in keeping with that position that אַ should have been sent forth from that 'school of criticism.'

But if אַ was, then B must have been;—at least, if the supposition certified by Tischendorf and Scrivener be true, that the six conjugate leaves of אַ were written by the scribe of B. So there is a chain of reference, fortified by the implied probability which has been furnished for us from the actual facts of the case.

Yet Dr. Hort is 'inclined to surmise that B and אַ were both written in the West, probably at Rome; that the ancestors of B were wholly Western (in the geographical, not the textual sense) up to a very early time indeed; and that the ancestors of אַ were in great part Alexandrian, again in the geographical, not the textual sense[1].' For this opinion, in which Dr. Hort stands alone amongst authorities, there is nothing but 'surmise' founded upon very dark hints. In contrast with the evidence just brought forward there is an absence of direct testimony: besides that the connexion between the Western and Syrian Texts or Readings, which has been recently confirmed in a very material degree, must weaken the force of some of his arguments.

§ 2[2].

The points to which I am anxious rather to direct attention are (1) the extent to which the works of Origen were studied by the ancients: and (2) the curious

---

[1] Introduction, p. 267. Dr. Hort controverts the notion that B and אַ were written at Alexandria (not Caesarea), which no one now maintains.

[2] By the Dean.

discovery that Codexes אB, and to some extent D, either belong to the same class as those with which Origen was chiefly familiar ; or else have been anciently manipulated into conformity with Origen's teaching. The former seems to me the more natural supposition ; but either inference equally satisfies my contention: viz. that Origen, and mainly BאD, are not to be regarded as wholly independent authorities, but constitute a class.

The proof of this position is to be found in various passages where the influence of Origen may be traced, such as in the omission of Ὑιοῦ τοῦ Θεοῦ—'The Son of God'—in Mark i. 1[1] ; and of ἐν Ἐφέσῳ—'at Ephesus'— in Eph. i. 1[2] ; in the substitution of Bethabara (St. John i. 28) for Bethany[3] ; in the omission of the second part of the last petition the Lord's Prayer in St. Luke[4], of ἔμπροσθέν μου γέγονεν in John i. 27[5].

He is also the cause why the important qualification εἰκῆ ('without a cause') is omitted by Bא from St. Matt. v. 22 ; and hence, in opposition to the whole host of Copies, Versions[6], Fathers, has been banished from the sacred Text by Lachmann, Tischendorf, W. Hort and the Revisers[7]. To the same influence, I am persuaded, is to be attributed the omission from a little handful of copies (viz. A, B–א, D*, F–G, and 17*) of the clause τῇ ἀληθείᾳ μὴ πείθεσθαι

---

[1] See Appendix IV, and Revision Revised, p. 132. Origen, c. Celsum, Praef. ii. 4 ; Comment. in John ix. Followed here only by א*.

[2] See Last Twelve Verses, pp. 93-99. Also pp. 66, note, 85, 107, 235.

[3] Migne, viii. 96 d. Ταῦτα ἐγένετο ἐν Βηθανίᾳ. ὅσα δὲ τῶν ἀντιγράφων ἀκριβέστερον ἔχει, ἐν Βηθαβαρᾷ, φησιν. ἡ γὰρ Βηθανία οὐχὶ πέραν τοῦ Ἰορδάνου, οὐδὲ ἐπὶ τῆς ἐρήμου ἦν· ἀλλ' ἐγγύς που τῶν Ἱεροσολύμων. This speedily assumed the form of a *scholium*, as follows :—Χρὴ δὲ γινώσκειν, ὅτι τὰ ἀκριβῆ τῶν ἀντιγράφων ἐν Βηθαβαρᾷ περιέχει· ἡ γὰρ Βηθανία οὐχὶ πέραν τοῦ Ἰορδάνου, ἀλλ' ἐγγύς που τῶν Ἱεροσολύμων :—which is quoted by the learned Benedictine editor of Origen in M. iv. 401 (at top of the left hand column),—evidently from Coisl. 23, our Evan. 39,—since the words are found in Cramer, Cat. ii. 191 (line 1-3).

[4] Origen, i. 265 ; coll. I. 227, 256.

[5] Origen, Comment. in John vi.

[6] The word is actually transliterated into Syriac letters in the Peshitto.

[7] See The Revision Revised, pp. 358-61.

('that you should not obey the truth') Gal. iii. 1. Jerome duly acknowledges those words while commenting on St. Matthew's Gospel[1]; but when he comes to the place in Galatians[2], he is observed, first to admit that the clause 'is found in some copies,' and straightway to add that 'inasmuch as it is not found in the copies of Adamantius[3], he omits it.' The clue to his omission is supplied by his own statement that in writing on the Galatians he had made Origen his guide[4]. And yet the words stand in the Vulgate.

For :—

C Dᶜ E K L P, 46 Cursives.	Theodoret ii. 40.
Vulg. Goth. Harkl. Arm. Ethiop.	J. Damascene ii. 163.
Orig. ii. 373.	Theodorus Studita,—433, 1136.
Cyril Al. ii. 737.	Hieron. vii. 418. c. Legitur in
Ephr. Syr. iii. 203.	quibusdam codicibus, 'Quis
Macarius Magnes (or rather the	vos fascinavit non credere
heathen philosopher with	veritati?' Sed hoc, quia in
whom he disputed), — 128.	exemplaribus Adamantii non
ps.-Athanas. ii. 454.	habetur, omisimus.

Against :—

ℵ A B D* F G 17*.	Exemplaria Adamantii.
d e f g—fu.	Cyril 429.
Peshitto, Bohairic.	Theodoret i. 658 (= Mai vii[2] 150).
Chrys.	Theodorus Mops.
Euthal. ᶜᵒᵈ.	Hier. vii. 418. c.

In a certain place Origen indulges in a mystical exposition of our LORD'S two miracles of feeding[5]; drawing marvellous inferences, as his manner is, from the details of

---

[1] vii. 52.   [2] vii. 418.
[3] A name by which Origen was known.
[4] Imbecillitatem virium mearum sentiens, Origenis Commentarios sum sequutus.   Scripsit ille vir in epistolam Pauli ad Galatas quinque proprie volumina, et decimum Stromatum suorum librum commatico super explanatione ejus sermone complevit.—Praefatio, vii. 370.
[5] iii. 509-10.

either miracle. We find that Hilary[1], that Jerome[2], that Chrysostom [3], had Origen's remarks before them when they in turn commented on the miraculous feeding of the 4000. At the feeding of the 5000, Origen points out that our LORD 'commands the multitude to sit down' (St. Matt. xiv. 19): but at the feeding of the 4000, He does not 'command' but only 'directs' them to sit down. (St. Matt. xv. 35[4])... From which it is plain that Origen did not read as we do in St. Matt. xv. 35, καὶ ἐκέλευσε τοῖς ὄχλοις—but παρήγγειλε τῷ ὄχλῳ ἀναπεσεῖν; which is the reading of the parallel place in St. Mark (viii. 6). We should of course have assumed a slip of memory on Origen's part; but that אBD are found to exhibit the text of St. Matt. xv. 35 in conformity with Origen[5]. He is reasoning therefore from a MS. which he has before him; and remarking, as his unfortunate manner is, on what proves to be really nothing else but a palpable depravation of the text.

Speaking of St. John xiii. 26, Origen remarks,—'It is not written "He it is to whom I shall give the sop"; but with the addition of "I shall dip": for it says, "I shall dip the sop and give it."' This is the reading of BCL and is adopted accordingly by some Editors. But surely it is a depravation of the text which may be ascribed with confidence to the officiousness of Origen himself. *Who*, at all events, on such precarious evidence would surrender the established reading of the place, witnessed to as it is by

---

[1] 686–7. [2] vii. 117–20. [3] vii. 537 seq.

[4] I endeavour in the text to make the matter in hand intelligible to the English reader. But such things can scarcely be explained in English without more words than the point is worth. Origen says :—κἀκεῖ μὲν κελεύει τοὺς ὄχλους ἀνακλιθῆναι (Matt. xiv. 19), ἢ ἀναπεσεῖν ἐπὶ τοῦ χόρτου. (καὶ γὰρ ὁ Λουκᾶς (ix. 14) κατακλίνατε αὐτούς, ἀνέγραψε· καὶ ὁ Μάρκος (vi. 39), ἐπέταξε, φησίν, αὐτοῖς πάντας ἀνακλῖναι·) ἐνθάδε δὲ οὐ κελεύει, ἀλλὰ παραγγέλλει τῷ ὄχλῳ ἀνακλιθῆναι. iii. 509 f, 510 a.

[5] The only other witnesses are from Evan. 1, 33, and the lost archetype of 13, 124, 346. The Versions do not distinguish certainly between κελεύω and παραγγέλλω. Chrysostom, the only Father who quotes this place, exhibits ἐκέλευσε . . . καὶ λαβών (vii. 539 c).

every other known MS. and by several of the Fathers? The grounds on which Tischendorf reads βάψω τὸ ψωμίον καὶ δώσω αὐτῷ, are characteristic, and in their way a curiosity [1].

Take another instance of the same phenomenon. It is plain, from the consent of (so to speak) all the copies, that our Saviour rejected the Temptation which stands second in St. Luke's Gospel with the words,—'Get thee behind Me, Satan [2].' But Origen officiously points out that this (quoting the words) is precisely what our LORD did not say. He adds a reason,—'He said to Peter, "Get thee behind Me, Satan"; but to the Devil, "Get thee hence," without the addition "behind Me"; for to be behind Jesus is a good thing [3].'

---

[1] Lectio ab omni parte commendatur, et a correctore alienissima: βαψω και δωσω ab usu est Johannis, sed elegantius videbatur βαψας επιδωσω vel δωσω.

[2] Luke iv. 8.

[3] Πρὸς μὲν τὸν Πέτρον εἶπεν· ὕπαγε ὀπίσω μου, Σατανᾶ· πρὸς δὲ τὸν διάβολον. ὕπαγε, Σατανᾶ, χώρις τῆς ὀπίσω μου προσθήκης· τὸ γὰρ ὀπίσω τοῦ Ἰησοῦ εἶναι ἀγαθόν ἐστι. iii. 540. I believe that Origen is the sole cause of the perplexity. Commenting on Matt. xvi. 23 υπαγε οπισω μου Σατανα (the words addressed to Simon Peter), he explains that they are a rebuke to the Apostle for having for a time at Satan's instigation *desisted from following Him.* Comp. (he says) these words spoken to Peter (υπ. οπ. μου Σ.) with those addressed to Satan at the temptation *without the* οπισω μου 'for to be *behind Christ* is a good thing.'... I suppose he had before him a MS. of St. Matt. *without* the οπισω μου. This gloss is referred to by Victor of Antioch (173 Cat. Poss., i. 348 Cramer). It is even repeated by Jerome on Matt. vii. 21 d e: Non ut plerique putant eâdem Satanas et Apostolus Petrus sententiâ condemnantur. Petro enim dicitur, ' *Vade retro me,* Satana ;' id est ' Sequere me, qui contrarius es voluntati meae.' Hic vero audit, ' *Vade Satana :* ' et non ei dicitur ' *retro me,*' ut subaudiatur, ' vade in ignem aeternum.' *Vade Satana* (Irenaeus, 775, also Hilary, 620 a). Peter Alex. has υπαγε Σατανα, γεγραπται γαρ, ap. Routh, Reliqq. iv. 24 (on p. 55). Audierat diabolus a Domino, *Recede Sathanas, scandalum mihi es.* Scriptum est, *Dominum Deum tuum adorabis et illi soli servies,* Tertullian, Scorp. c. 15. Οὐκ εἶπεν "Υπαγε ὀπίσω μου· οὐ γὰρ ὑποστρέψαι οἷός τε· ἀλλά· "Υπαγε Σατανᾶ, ἐν οἷς ἐπελέξω.— Epist. ad Philipp. c. xii. Ignat. interpol. According to some Critics (Tisch., Treg., W.-Hort) there is *no* υπαγε οπισω μου Σ. in Lu. iv. 8, and *only* υπαγε Σ. in Matt. iv. 10, so that υπαγε οπισω μου Σατανα occurs in *neither* accounts of the temptation. But I believe υπαγε οπισω μου Σ. is the correct reading in *both* places. Justin M. Tryph. ii. 352. Origen interp. ii. 132 b (Vade retro), so Ambrose, i. 671; so Jerome, vi. 809 e; redi retro S., Aug. iv. 47 e; redi post me S., Aug. iii. 842 g. Theodoret, ii. 1608. So Maximus Taur., Vigil. Taps.

Our Saviour on a certain occasion (St. John viii. 38) thus addressed his wicked countrymen:—'I speak that which I have seen with My Father; and ye likewise do that which you have seen with your father.' He contrasts His own gracious doctrines with their murderous deeds; and refers them to their respective 'Fathers,'—to 'My Father,' that is, GOD; and to 'your father,' that is, the Devil[1]. That this is the true sense of the place appears plainly enough from the context. 'Seen with' and 'heard from[2]' are the expressions employed on such occasions, because sight and hearing are the faculties which best acquaint a man with the nature of that whereof he discourses.

Origen, misapprehending the matter, maintains that GOD is the 'Father' spoken of on either side. He I suspect it was who, in order to support this view, erased 'My' and 'your'; and in the second member of the sentence, for 'seen with,' substituted 'heard from';—as if a contrast had been intended between the manner of the Divine and of the human knowledge,—which would be clearly out of place. In this way, what is in reality a revelation, becomes converted into a somewhat irrelevant precept: 'I speak the things which I have seen with the Father.' 'Do ye the things which ye have heard from the Father,'—which is how Lachmann, Tischendorf, Tregelles, Alford exhibit the place. Cyril Alex. employed a text thus impaired. Origen also puts ver. 39 into the form of a precept (ἐστέ...

Vade retro S. *ap.* Sabattier. '*Vade post me Satana.* Et sine dubio ire post Deum servi est.' Et iterum quod ait ad illum, '*Dominum Deum tuum adorabis, et ipsi soli servies.*' Archelaus et Man. disput. (Routh, Reliqq. v. 120), A.D. 277. St. Antony the monk, *apud* Athanas. '*Vita Ant.*' i. 824 c d (= Galland. iv. 647 a). A.D. 300. *Retro vade Satana,* ps.-Tatian (Lu.), 49. Athanasius, i. 272 d, 537 c, 589 f. Nestorius ap. Marium Merc. (Galland. viii. 647 c) *Vade retro S.* but only *Vade S.* viii. 631 c. Idatius (A.D. 385) *apud* Athanas. ii. 605 b. Chrys. vii. 172 *bis* (Matt.) J. Damascene, ii. 450. ps.-Chrys. x. 734, 737. Opus Imperf. ap. Chrys. vi. 48 *bis.* Apocryphal Acts, Tisch. p. 250.

[1] See ver. 44.
[2] St. John viii. 40; xv. 15.

ποιεῖτε); but he has all the Fathers[1] (including himself),
—all the Versions,—all the copies against him, being
supported only by B.

But the evidence against 'the restored reading' to which
Alford invites attention, (viz. omitting μου and substituting
ἠκούσατε παρὰ τοῦ Πατρός for ἑωράκατε παρὰ τῷ Πατρὶ ὑμῶν.)
is overwhelming. Only five copies (BCLTX) omit μου:
only four (BLT, 13) omit ὑμῶν: a very little handful are for
substituting ἠκούσατε with the genitive for ἑωράκατε. Chrys.,
Apolinaris, Cyril Jerus., Ammonius, as well as every ancient
version of good repute, protest against such an exhibition
of the text. In ver. 39, only five read ἐστέ (אBDLT):
while ποιεῖτε is found only in Cod. B. Accordingly, some
critics prefer the imperfect ἐποιεῖτε, which however is only
found in אDLT. 'The reading is remarkable' says Alford.
Yes, and clearly fabricated. The ordinary text is right.

§ 3.

Besides these passages, in which there is actual evidence
of a connexion subsisting between the readings which they
contain and Origen, the sceptical character of the Vatican
and Sinaitic manuscripts affords a strong proof of the
alliance between them and the Origenistic School. It
must be borne in mind that Origen was not answerable
for all the tenets of the School which bore his name,
even perhaps less than Calvin was responsible for all that
Calvinists after him have held and taught. Origenistic
doctrines came from the blending of philosophy with
Christianity in the schools of Alexandria where Origen
was the most eminent of the teachers engaged[2].

---

[1] Orig., Euseb., Epiph., both Cyrils, Didymus, Basil, Chrysostom.
[2] For the sceptical passages in B and א see Appendix V.

CHAPTER X.

§ 1[1].

IT is specially remarkable that the Canon of Holy
Scripture, which like the Text had met with opposition,
was being settled in the later part of the century in which
these two manuscripts were produced, or at the beginning
of the next. The two questions appear to have met
together in Eusebius. His latitudinarian proclivities seem
to have led him in his celebrated words[2] to lay undue
stress upon the objections felt by some persons to a few of
the Books of the New Testament; and cause us therefore
not to wonder that he should also have countenanced those
who wished without reason to leave out portions of the
Text. Now the first occasion, as is well known, when we
find all the Books of the New Testament recognized with
authority occurred at the Council of Laodicea in 363 A. D.,
if the passage is genuine[3], which is very doubtful; and the

---

[1] By the Editor.

[2] Eusebius (Hist. Eccles. iii. 25) divides the writings of the Church into
three classes :—

    1. The Received Books (ὁμολογούμενα), i. e. the Four Gospels, Acts, the
        Fourteen Epistles of St. Paul, 1 Peter, 1 John, and the Revelation (?).
    2. Doubtful (ἀντιλεγόμενα), i. e. James, 2 Peter, 2 and 3 John, Jude (cf.
        ii. 23 fin.).
    3. Spurious (νόθα), Acts of St. Paul, Shepherd of Hermas, Revelation of
        St. Peter, Epistle of Barnabas, the so-called Διδαχαί, Revelation of
        St. John (?).

This division appears to need confirmation, if it is to be taken as representing
the general opinion of the Church of the time.

[3] See Westcott, Canon, &c. pp. 431-9.

settlement of the Canon which was thus initiated, and was accomplished by about the end of the century, was followed, as was natural, by the settlement of the Text. But inasmuch as the latter involved a large multitude of intricate questions, and corruption had crept in and had acquired a very firm hold, it was long before universal acquiescence finally ensued upon the general acceptance effected in the time of St. Chrysostom. In fact, the Nature of the Divine Word, and the character of the Written Word, were confirmed about the same time : — mainly, in the period when the Nicene Creed was re-asserted at the Council of Constantinople in 381 A.D. ; for the Canon of Holy Scripture was fixed and the Orthodox Text gained a supremacy over the Origenistic Text about the same time:—and finally, after the Third Council of Constantinople in 680 A.D., at which the acknowledgement of the Natures of the Son of Man was placed in a position superior to all heresy; for it was then that the Traditional Text began in nearly perfect form to be handed down with scarce any opposition to future ages of the Church.

Besides the multiplicity of points involved, three special causes delayed the complete settlement of the Text, so far as the attainment was concerned all over the Church of general accuracy throughout the Gospels, not to speak of all the New Testament.

1. Origenism, going beyond Origen, continued in force till it was condemned by the Fifth General Council in 553 A.D., and could hardly have wholly ended in that year. Besides this, controversies upon fundamental truths agitated the Church, and implied a sceptical and wayward spirit which would be ready to sustain alien variations in the written Word, till the censure passed upon Monothelitism at the Sixth General Council in 680 A.D.

2. The Church was terribly tried by the overthrow of the Roman Empire, and the irruption of hordes of Barbarians:

and consequently Churchmen were obliged to retire into extreme borders, as they did into Ireland in the fifth century [1], and, to spend their energies in issuing forth from thence to reconquer countries for the Kingdom of Christ. The resultant paralysis of Christian effort must have been deplorable. Libraries and their treasures, as at Caesarea and Alexandria under the hands of Mahommedans in the seventh century, were utterly destroyed. Rest and calmness, patient and frequent study and debate, books and other helps to research, must have been in those days hard to get, and were far from being in such readiness as to favour general improvement in a subject of which extreme accuracy is the very breath and life.

3. The Art of Writing on Vellum had hardly passed its youth at the time when the Text advocated by B and ℵ fell finally into disuse. Punctuation did but exist in the occasional use of the full stop : breathings or accents were perhaps hardly found : spelling, both as regards consonants and vowels, was uncertain and rudimental. So that the Art of transcribing on vellum even so far as capital letters were concerned, did not arrive at anything like maturity till about the eighth century.

But it must not be imagined that manuscripts of substantial accuracy did not exist during this period, though they have not descended to us. The large number of Uncials and Cursives of later ages must have had a goodly assemblage of accurate predecessors from which they were copied. It is probable that the more handsome and less correct copies have come into our hands, since such would have been not so much used, and might have been in the possession of the men of higher station whose heathen

---

[1] See particularly Haddan's Remains, pp. 258–294, Scots on the Continent. The sacrifice of that capable scholar and excellent churchman at a comparatively early age to the toil which was unavoidable under want of encouragement of ability and genius has entailed a loss upon sacred learning which can hardly be over-estimated.

ancestry had bequeathed to them less orthodox tenden-
cies, and the material of many others must have been
too perishable to last. Arianism prevailed during much of
the sixth century in Italy, Africa, Burgundy, and Spain.
Ruder and coarser volumes, though more accurate, would
be readily surrendered to destruction, especially if they
survived in more cultured descendants. That a majority of
such MSS. existed, whether of a rougher or more polished
sort, both in vellum and papyrus, is proved by citations of
Scripture found in the Authors of the period. But those
MSS. which have been preserved are not so perfect as the
others which have come from the eighth and following
centuries.

Thus Codex A, though it exhibits a text more like the
Traditional than either B or ℵ, is far from being a sure
guide. Codex C, which was written later in the fifth
century, is only a fragmentary palimpsest, i. e. it was
thought to be of so little value that the books of
Ephraem the Syrian were written over the Greek: it
contains not more than two-thirds of the New Testament,
and stands as to the character of its text between A and
B. Codex Q, a fragment of 235 verses, and Codex I of
135, in the same century, are not large enough to be taken
into consideration here. Codexes Φ and Σ, recently discovered, being products of the end of the fifth or beginning
of the sixth, and containing St Matthew and St. Mark
nearly complete, are of a general character similar to A,
and evince more advancement in the Art. It is unfortunate indeed that only a fragment of either of them, though
that fragment in either case is pretty complete as far as it
goes, has come into our hands. After them succeeds
Codex D, or Codex Bezae, now in the Cambridge Library,
having been bequeathed to the University by Theodore
Beza, whose name it bears. It ends at Acts xxii. 29.

§ 2. CODEX D [1].

No one can pretend fully to understand the character of this Codex who has not been at the pains to collate every word of it with attention. Such an one will discover that it omits in the Gospels alone no less than 3,704 words; adds to the genuine text 2,213; substitutes 2,121; transposes 3,471, and modifies 1,772. By the time he has made this discovery his esteem for Cod. D will, it is presumed, have experienced serious modification. The total of 13,281 deflections from the Received Text is a formidable objection to explain away. Even Dr. Hort speaks of 'the prodigious amount of error which D contains [2].'

But the intimate acquaintance with the Codex which he has thus acquired has conducted him to certain other results, which it is of the utmost importance that we should particularize and explain.

I. And first, this proves to be a text which in one Gospel is often assimilated to the others. And in fact the assimilation is carried sometimes so far, that a passage from one Gospel is interpolated into the parallel passage in another. Indeed the extent to which in Cod. D interpolations from St. Mark's Gospel are inserted into the Gospel according to St. Luke is even astounding. Between verses 14 and 15 of St. Luke v. thirty-two words are interpolated from the parallel passage in St. Mark i. 45–ii. 1: and in the 10th verse of the vith chapter twelve words are introduced from St. Mark ii. 27, 28. In St. Luke iv. 37, ἡ ἀκοή, 'the report,' from St. Mark i. 28, is substituted for ἦχος, 'the sound,' which is read in the other manuscripts. Besides the introduction into St. Luke i. 64

---

[1] The reader is now in the Dean's hands. See Mr. Rendel Harris' ingenious and suggestive 'Study of Codex Bezae' in the Cambridge Texts and Studies, and Dr. Chase's 'The Old Syriac Element in the Text of Codex Bezae.' But we must demur to the expression 'Old Syriac.'

[2] Introduction, p. 149.

of ἐλύθη from St. Mark vii. 35, which will be described below, in St. Luke v. 27 seven words are brought from the parallel passage in St. Mark ii. 14, and the entire passage is corrupted[1]. In giving the Lord's Prayer in St. Luke xi. 2, the scribe in fault must needs illustrate the Lord's saying by interpolating an inaccurate transcription of the warning against 'vain repetitions' given by Him before in the Sermon on the Mount. Again, as to interpolation from other sources, grossly enough, St. Matt. ii. 23 is thrust in at the end of St. Luke ii. 39 ; that is to say, the scribe of D, or of some manuscript from which D was copied, either directly or indirectly, thought fit to explain the carrying of the Holy Child to Nazareth by the explanation given by St. Matthew, but quoting from memory wrote 'by the prophet' in the singular, instead of 'by the prophets' in the plural[2]. Similarly, in St. Luke iv. 31 upon the mention of the name of Capernaum, D must needs insert from St. Matt. iv. 13, 'which is upon the sea-coast within the borders of Zabulon and Nephthalim' (τὴν παραθαλασσιον (sic) εν οριοις Ζαβουλων και Νεφθαλειμ). Indeed, no adequate idea can be formed of the clumsiness, the coarseness of these operations, unless some instances are given : but a few more must suffice.

1. In St. Mark iii. 26, our LORD delivers the single statement, 'And if Satan is risen against himself (ἀνέστε ἐφ' ἑαυτόν) and is divided (καὶ μεμέρισται) he cannot stand, but hath an end (ἀλλὰ τέλος ἔχει).' Instead of this, D exhibits, 'And if Satan cast out Satan, he is divided against himself : his kingdom cannot stand, but hath the end (ἀλλὰ

---

[1] The same wholesale corruption of the deposit prevails in what follows, viz. the healing of the paralytic borne of four (v. 17–26), and the call of St. Matthew (27–34) : as well as in respect of the walk through the cornfields on the Sabbath day (vi. 1–5), and the healing of the man with the withered hand (6–11). Indeed it is continued to the end of the call of the Twelve (12–19). The particulars are too many to insert here.

[2] καθως ερεθη δια του προφητου, instead of ὅπως πληρωθῇ διὰ τῶν προφητῶν.

N

τὸ τέλος ἔχει).' Now this is clearly an imitation, not
a copy, of the parallel place in St. Matt. xii. 26, where
also a twofold statement is made, as every one may see.
But the reply is also a clumsy one to the question asked
in St. Mark, but not in St. Matthew, 'How can Satan cast
out Satan?' Learned readers however will further note
that it is St. Matthew's ἐμερίσθη, where St. Mark wrote
μεμέρισται, which makes the statement possible for him
which is impossible according to the representation given
by D of St. Mark.

2. At the end of the parable of the pounds, the scribe
of D, or one of those whom he followed, thinking that the
idle servant was let off too easily, and confusing with this
parable the other parable of the talents,—blind of course
to the difference between the punishments inflicted by
a 'lord' and those of a new-made king,—inserts the 30th
verse of St. Matt. xxv. at the end of St. Luke xix. 27.

3. Again, after St. Matt. xx. 28, when the LORD had
rebuked the spirit of ambition in the two sons of Zebedee,
and had directed His disciples not to seek precedence,
enforcing the lesson from His own example as shewn in
giving His Life a ransom for many, D inserts the following
tasteless passage: 'But ye seek to increase from a little,
and from the greater to be something less[1].' Nor is this
enough :—an addition is also made from St. Luke xiv.
8-10, being the well-known passage about taking the
lowest room at feasts. But this additional interpolation
is in style and language unlike the words of any Gospels,
and ends with the vapid piece of information, 'and this
shall be useful to thee.' It is remarkable that, whereas D
was alone in former errors, here it becomes a follower in
one part or other of the passage of twelve Old Latin
manuscripts[2]: and indeed the Greek in the passage in D is

[1] Ὑμεις δε ζητειτε εκ μικρου αυξησαι, και εκ μειζονος ελαττον ειναι.
[2] I.e. a b c d e ff¹·² g¹·² h m n.

evidently a version of the Syrio-Low-Latin. The following words, or forms of words or phrases, are not found in the rest of the N. T.: παρακληθέντες (aor. part. *rogati* or *vocati*), ἀνακλίνεσθε (*recumbite*), ἐξέχοντας (*eminentioribus*), δειπνοκλήτωρ (*invitator caenae*), ἔτι κάτω χώρει (*adhuc infra accede*), ἥττονα τόπον (*loco inferiori*), ἥττων (*inferior*), σύναγε ἔτι ἄνω (*collige adhuc superius*). These Latin expressions are taken from one or other of the twelve Old Latin MSS. Outside of the Latin, the Curetonian is the sole ally, the Lewis being mutilated, of the flighty Old Uncial under consideration.

These passages are surely enough to represent to the reader the interpolations of Codex D, whether arising from assimilation or otherwise. The description given by the very learned editor of this MS. is in the following words:—
'No known manuscript contains so many bold and extensive interpolations (six hundred, it is said, in the Acts alone), countenanced, where they are not absolutely unsupported, chiefly by the Old Latin and the Curetonian version[1].'

II. There are also traces of extreme licentiousness in this copy of the Gospels which call for distinct notice. Sometimes words or expressions are substituted: sometimes the sense is changed, and utter confusion introduced: delicate terms or forms are ignored: and a general corruption ensues.

I mean for example such expressions as the following, which are all found in the course of a single verse (St. Mark iv. 1).

St. Mark relates that once when our SAVIOUR was teaching 'by the sea-side' (παρά) there assembled so vast a concourse of persons that 'He went into the ship, and

---

[1] Scrivener's Introduction, I. 130 (4th ed.). The reader will recollect the suggestion given above in Chapter VII that some of these corruptions may have come from the earliest times before the four Gospels were written. The interpolation just noticed may very well have been such a survival.

sat in the sea,' all the multitude being 'on the land,
towards the sea': i. e. with their faces turned in the
direction of the ship in which He was sitting. Was
a plain story ever better told?

But according to D the facts of the case were quite
different. First, it was our SAVIOUR who was teaching
'towards the sea' (πρός). Next, in consequence of the
crowd, He crossed over, and 'sat on the other side of the
sea' (πέραν). Lastly, the multitude—followed Him, I suppose; for they also—'were on the other side of the sea'
(πέραν). . . Now I forgive the scribe for his two transposi-
tions and his ungrammatical substitution of ὁ λαός for ὄχλος.
But I insist that a MS. which circulates incidents after
this fashion cannot be regarded as trustworthy. Verse 2
begins in the same licentious way. Instead of,—'And He
taught them many things (πολλά) in parables,' we are informed that 'He taught them in many parables' (πολλαῖς).
Who will say that we are ever safe with such a guide?

§ 3.

All are aware that the two Evangelical accounts of our
LORD'S human descent exhibit certain distinctive features.
St. Matthew distributes the 42 names in 'the book of the
generations of JESUS CHRIST, the son of David, the son
of Abraham,' into three fourteens; and requires us to
recognize in the Ἰεχονίας of ver. 11 a different person (viz.
Jehoiakim) from the Ἰεχονίας of ver. 12 (viz. Jehoiachin).
Moreover, in order to produce this symmetry of arrangement, he leaves out the names of 3 kings,—Ahaziah, Joash,
Amaziah: and omits at least 9 generations of Zorobabel's
descendants[1]. The mystical correspondence between the
42 steps in our SAVIOUR'S human descent from Abraham,
and the 42 stations of the Israelites on their way to Canaan[2],

---

[1] The number of the generations in St. Luke's Gospel is 18.
[2] Num. xxxiii. coll. xxi. 18, 19 and Deut. x. 6, 7.

has been often remarked upon. It extends to the fact that the stations also were, historically, far more than 42. And so much for what is contained in St. Matthew's Gospel.

St. Luke, who enumerates the 77 steps of his genealogy in backward order, derives the descent of 'JESUS, the son of Joseph' from 'Adam, the son of GOD.' He traces our LORD'S descent from David and again from Zorobabel through a different line of ancestry from that adopted by St. Matthew. He introduces a second 'Cainan' between Arphaxad and Sala (ver. 35, 36). The only names which the two tables of descent have in common are these five,— David, Salathiel, Zorobabel, Joseph, JESUS.

But Cod. D— (from which the first chapter of St. Matthew's Gospel has long since disappeared)—in St. Luke iii. exhibits a purely fabricated table of descent. To put one name for another,—as when A writes 'Shem' instead of Seth: to misspell a name until it ceases to be recognizable,—as when ℵ writes 'Balls' for Boaz: to turn one name into two by cutting it in half,—as where ℵ writes 'Admin' *and* 'Adam' instead of Aminadab: or again, in defiance of authority, to leave a name out,—as when A omits Mainan and Pharez; or to put a name in,—as when Verona Lat. (b) inserts 'Joaram' after Aram:—with all such instances of licence the 'old Uncials' have made us abundantly familiar. But we are not prepared to find that in place of the first 18 names which follow those of 'JESUS' and 'Joseph' in St. Luke's genealogy (viz. Heli to Rhesa inclusive), D in- troduces the 9 immediate ancestors of Joseph (viz. Abiud to Jacob) as enumerated by St. Matthew,—thus abbreviating St. Luke's genealogy by 9 names. Next,—'Zorobabel' and 'Salathiel' being common to both genealogies,—in place of the 20 names found in St. Luke between Salathiel and David (viz. Neri to Nathan inclusive), Cod. D presents us with the 15 royal descendants of David enumerated by

St. Matthew (viz. Solomon to Jehoiachin [1] inclusive);—
infelicitously inventing an imaginary generation, by styling
Jehoiakim 'the son of Eliakim,'—being not aware that
'Jehoiakim' and 'Eliakim' are one and the same person:
and, in defiance of the first Evangelist, supplying the names
of the 3 kings omitted by St. Matthew (i. 8), viz. Ahaziah,
Joash, and Amaziah. Only 34 names follow in Cod. D;
the second 'Cainan' being omitted. In this way, the
number of St. Luke's names is reduced from 77 to 66.
A more flagrant instance of that licentious handling of
the deposit which was a common phenomenon in Western
Christendom is seldom to be met with [2]. This particular
fabrication is happily the peculiar property of Cod. D; and
we are tempted to ask, whether it assists in recommend-
ing that singular monument of injudicious and arbitrary
textual revision to the favour of one of the modern schools
of Critics.

§ 4.

We repeat that the ill treatment which the deposit has
experienced at the hands of those who fabricated the text
of Cod. D is only to be understood by those who will be

---

[1] Note, that whereas the 'Ιεχονίας of St. Matt. i. 11 is *Jehoiakim*, and the
'Ιεχονίας of ver. 12, *Jehoiachin*,—Cod. D writes them respectively Ιωακειμ and
Ιεχονιας.

[2] Cureton's Syriac is the only known copy of the Gospels in which the three
omitted kings are found in St. Matthew's Gospel: which, I suppose, explains
why the learned editor of that document flattered himself that he had therein
discovered the lost original of St. Matthew's Gospel. Cureton (Pref., p. viii)
shews that in other quarters also (e. g. by Mar Yakub the Persian, usually
known as Aphraates) 63 generations were reckoned from Adam to JESUS
exclusive: *that* number being obtained by adding 24 of St. Matthew's
names and 33 of St. Luke's to the 3 names common to both Evangelists
(viz. David, Salathiel, and Zorobabel); and to these, adding the 3 omitted
kings.

The testimony of MSS. is not altogether uniform in regard to the number of
names in the Genealogy. In the Textus Receptus (including our SAVIOUR'S
name and the name of the Divine AUTHOR of Adam's being) the number of
the names is 77. So Basil made it; so Greg. Naz. and his namesake of Nyssa;
so Jerome and Augustine.

at the pains to study its readings throughout. Constantly to substitute the wrong word for the right one ; or at all events to introduce a less significant expression : on countless occasions to mar the details of some precious incident ; and to obscure the purpose of the Evangelist by tastelessly and senselessly disturbing the inspired text,—*this* will be found to be the rule with Cod. D throughout. As another example added to those already cited :—In St. Luke xxii, D omits verse 20, containing the Institution of the Cup, evidently from a wish to correct the sacred account by removing the second mention of the Cup from the record of the third Evangelist.

St. Mark (xv. 43) informs us that, on the afternoon of the first Good Friday, Joseph of Arimathaea 'taking courage *went in* (εἰσῆλθε) to Pilate and requested to 'have the *body* (σῶμα) of Jesus': that 'Pilate wondered (ἐθαύμασεν) [at hearing] that He *was dead* (τέθνηκε) already: and sending for the centurion [who had presided at the Crucifixion] inquired of him if [JESUS] had been dead long?' (εἰ πάλαι ἀπέθανε)

But the author of Cod. D, besides substituting '*went*' (ἦλθεν) for ' went *in*,'—'*corpse*' (πτῶμα) for 'body' (which by the way he repeats in ver. 45),—and a sentiment of 'continuous wonder' (ἐθαύμαζεν) for the fact of astonishment which Joseph's request inspired,—having also substituted the prosaic τεθνήκει for the graphic τέθνηκε of the Evangelist, —represents Pilate as inquiring of the centurion ' if [indeed JESUS] was dead already?' (εἰ ἤδη τεθνήκει ; *si jam mortuus esset?*), whereby not only is all the refinement of the original lost, but the facts of the case also are seriously misrepresented. For Pilate did not doubt Joseph's tidings. He only wondered at them. And his inquiry was made not with a view to testing the veracity of his informant, but for the satisfaction of his own curiosity as to the time when his Victim had expired.

Now it must not be supposed that I have fastened unfairly on an exceptional verse and a half (St. Mark xv. half of v. 43 and all v. 44) of the second Gospel. The reader is requested to refer to the note [1], where he will find set down a collation of *eight consecutive verses* in the selfsame context: viz. St. Mark xv. 47 to xvi. 7 inclusive; after an attentive survey of which he will not be disposed to deny that only by courtesy can such an exhibition of the original verity as Cod. D be called 'a copy' at all. Had the genuine text been *copied* over and over again till the crack of doom, the result could never have been this. There are in fact but 117 words to be transcribed: and of these no less than 67—much more than half—have been either omitted (21), or else added (11); substituted (10), or else transposed (11); depraved (12, as by writing ανατελλοντος for ἀνατείλαντος), or actually blundered (2, as by writing ερχονται ημιον for ἔρχονται ἡμῖν). Three times the construction has been altered,—once indeed very seriously, for the Angel at the sepulchre is made to personate Christ. Lastly, five of the corrupt readings are the result of Assimilation. Whereas the evangelist wrote καὶ ἀναβλέψασαι θεωροῦσιν ὅτι ἀποκεκύλισται ὁ λίθος, what else but a licentious

---

[1] ἡ δὲ Μαρία (D—η) Μαγδαληνὴ καὶ Μαρία Ἰωσῆ (D Ἰακωβου) ἐθεώρουν (D εθεασαντο) ποῦ (D οπου) τίθεται (D τεθειται). Καὶ διαγενομένου τοῦ σαββάτου, Μαρία ἡ Μαγδαληνὴ καὶ Μαρία ἡ τοῦ Ἰακώβου καὶ Σαλώμη (D omits the foregoing thirteen words) (D + πορευθεισαι) ἠγόρασαν ἀρώματα, ἵνα ἐλθοῦσαι (D—ελθουσαι) ἀλείψωσιν αὐτόν (D αυτ. αλειψ.) καὶ (D + ερχορται) λίαν (D—λιαν) πρωΐ τῆς (D—της) μιᾶς σαββάτων (D σαββατου) ἔρχονται (D see above) ἐπὶ τὸ μνημεῖον, ἀνατείλαντος (D ανατελλοντος) τοῦ ἡλίου. καὶ ἔλεγον πρὸς ἑαυτὰς (D εαυτους), Τίς ἀποκυλίσει ἡμῖν (D ημιον αποκ.) τὸν λίθον ἐκ (D απο) τῆς θύρας τοῦ μνημείου; (D + ην γαρ μεγας σφοδρα). Καὶ ἀναβλέψασαι θεωροῦσιν (D ερχονται και ευρισκουσιν) ὅτι ἀποκεκύλισται ὁ λίθος (D αποκεκυλισμενον τον λιθον)· ἦν γὰρ μέγας σφόδρα. (D see above.) καὶ .... εἶδον νεανίσκον (D νεαν. ειδ.) καθήμενον .... καὶ ἐξεθαμβήθησαν (D εθανβησαν). ὁ δὲ λέγει αὐταῖς (D και λεγει αυτοις) (D + ο αγγελος). Μὴ ἐκθαμβεῖσθε (D φοβεισθαι) (D + τον) Ἰησοῦν ζητεῖτε τὸν Ναζαρηνὸν (D—τον Ναζ.) .... ἴδε (D ειδετε) ὁ τύπος (D εκει τοπον αυτου) ὅπου ἔθηκαν αὐτόν. ἀλλ' (D αλλα) ὑπάγετε (D + και) εἴπατε .... ὅτι (D + ιδου) προάγει (D προαγω) ὑμᾶς εἰς τὴν Γαλιλαίαν· ἐκεῖ αὐτὸν (D με) ὄψεσθε, καθὼς εἶπεν (D ειρηκα) ὑμῖν. St. Mark xv. 47—xvi. 7.

paraphrase is the following,—ερχονται και ευρισκουσιν αποκεκυλισμενον τον λιθον? This is in fact a fabricated, not an honestly transcribed text: and it cannot be too clearly understood that such a text (more or less fabricated, I mean) is exhibited by Codexes BℵD throughout.

§ 5.

It is remarkable that whenever the construction is somewhat harsh or obscure, D and the Latin copies are observed freely to transpose,—to supply,—and even slightly to paraphrase,—in order to bring out the presumed meaning of the original. An example is furnished by St. Luke i. 65, where the Evangelist, having related that Zacharias wrote—'His name is John,' adds,—'and all wondered. And his mouth was opened immediately, and his tongue, and he spake praising GOD.' The meaning of course is that his tongue 'was loosed.' Accordingly D actually supplies ἐλύθη,—the Latin copies, 'resoluta est.' But D does more. Presuming that what occasioned the 'wonder' was not so much what Zacharias wrote on the tablet as the restored gift of speech, it puts that clause first,—ingeniously transposing the first two words (παραχρημα και); the result of which is the following sentence:—'And immediately his tongue was loosed; and all wondered. And his mouth was opened, and he spake praising GOD'..... In the next verse it is related that 'fear came upon all who dwelt round about them.' But the order of the words in the original being unusual (καὶ ἐγένετο ἐπὶ πάντας φόβος τοὺς περιοικοῦντας αὐτούς), D and the Latin copies transpose them: (indeed the three Syriac do the same): but D b c gratuitously introduce an epithet,—και εγενετο φοβος μεγας επι παντας τους περιοικουντας αυτον..... In ver. 70, the expression τῶν ἀπ' αἰῶνος προφητῶν αὐτοῦ appearing harsh was (by transposing the words) altered into this, which is the easy

and more obvious order: προφητων αυτον των απ' αιωνος.....
So again in ver. 71 : the phrase σωτηρίαν ἐξ ἐχθρῶν seeming
obscure, the words ἐκ χειρός (which follow) were by D
substituted for ἐξ. The result (σωτηρίαν ἐκ χειρὸς ἐχθρῶν
ἡμῶν [compare ver. 74], καὶ πάντων τῶν μισούντων ἡμᾶς) is
certainly easier reading : but—like every other change
found in the same context—it labours under the fatal
condemnation of being an unauthorized human gloss.

The phenomenon however which perplexes me most in
Cod. D is that it abounds in fabricated readings which
have nothing whatever to recommend them. Not con-
tented with St. Luke's expression 'to thrust out *a little*
(ὀλίγον) from the land' (v. 3), the scribe writes οσον οσον.
In ver. 5, instead of 'I will let down the net' (χαλάσω τὸ
δίκτυον) he makes St. Peter reply, 'I will not neglect
to obey' (ου μη παρακουσομαι). So, for 'and when they had
this done,' he writes 'and when they had straightway let
down the nets': and immediately after, instead of διερρή-
γνυτο δὲ τὸ δίκτυον αὐτῶν we are presented with ωστε τα
δικτυα ρησσεσθαι. It is very difficult to account for this,
except on an hypothesis which I confess recommends itself
to me more and more : viz. that there were in circulation in
some places during the earliest ages of the Church Evangelical paraphrases, or at least free exhibitions of the chief
Gospel incidents,—to which the critics resorted ; and from
which the less judicious did not hesitate to borrow
expressions and even occasionally to extract short passages.
Such loose representations of passages must have prevailed
both in Syria, and in the West where Greek was not so
well understood, and where translators into the vernacular
Latin expressed themselves with less precision, whilst they
attempted also to explain the passages translated.

This notion, viz. that it is within the province of a Copyist
to interpret the original before him, clearly lies at the root
of many a so-called 'various reading.'

Thus for the difficult ἐπιβαλὼν ἔκλαιε (in St. **Mark xiv.** 72), 'when he thought thereon' (i. e. 'when in **self-abandonment** he flung himself upon the thought '), ' he **wept**,' D exhibits καὶ ἤρξατο κλαίειν, 'and he began to weep,' a much easier and a very natural expression, only that it is not the right one, and does not express all that the true words convey. Hence also the transposition by D and some Old Latin MSS. of the clause ἦν γὰρ μέγας σφόδρα 'for it was very great' from xvi. 4, where it seems to be out of place, to ver. 3 where it seems to be necessary. Eusebius is observed to have employed a MS. similarly corrupt.

Hence again the frequent unauthorized insertion of a nominative case to determine the sense: e.g. ὁ ἄγγελος 'the angel,' xvi. 6, ὁ δὲ Ἰωσήφ ' Joseph,' xv. 46, or the substitution of the name intended for the pronoun,—as της Ελισαβεδ (sic) for αὐτῆς in St. Luke i. 41.

Hence in xvi. 7, instead of, ' He goeth before you into Galilee, there shall ye see Him as He said unto you,'— D exhibits,—'Behold, I go before you into Galilee, there shall ye see Me, as I told you.' As if it had been thought allowable to recall in this place the fact that our SAVIOUR had once (St. Matt. xxvi. 32, St. Mark xiv. 28) spoken these words in His own person.

And in no other way can I explain D's vapid substitution, made as if from habit, of 'a Galilean city' for 'a city of Galilee, named Nazareth' in St. Luke i. 26.

Hence the frequent insertion of a wholly manufactured clause in order to impart a little more clearness to the story—as of the words τὸ ὄνομα αὐτοῦ 'his name' (after κληθήσεται 'shall be called')—into St. Luke i. 60.

These passages afford expressions of a feature in this Manuscript to which we must again invite particular attention. It reveals to close observation frequent indications of an attempt, not to supply a faithful representation of the very words of Holy Scripture and nothing more than those words, but to interpret, to illustrate,—in a word,—to be a Targum. Of course, such a design or tendency is absolutely fatal to the accuracy of a transcriber. Yet the habit is too strongly marked upon the pages of Codex D to admit of any doubt whether it existed or not[1].

In speaking of the character of a MS. one is often constrained to distinguish between the readings and the scribe. The readings may be clearly fabricated : but there may be evidence that the copyist was an accurate and painstaking person. On the other hand, obviously the scribe may have been a considerable blunderer, and yet it may be clear that he was furnished with an admirable archetype. In the case of D we are presented with the alarming concurrence of a fabricated archetype and either a blundering scribe, or a course of blundering scribes.

But then further,—One is often obliged (if one would be accurate) to distinguish between the penman who actually produced the MS., and the critical reader for whom he toiled. It would really seem however as if the actual transcriber of D, or the transcribers of the ancestors of D, had invented some of those monstrous readings as they went on. The Latin version which is found in this MS. exactly reflects, as a rule, the Greek on the opposite page : but sometimes it bears witness to the admitted truth of Scripture, while the Greek goes off *in alia omnia*[2].

§ 6.

It will of course be asked,—But why may not D be in every respect an exact copy,—line for line, word for word, letter for letter,—of some earlier archetype? To establish

---

[1] So for example at the end of the same passage in St. Luke, the difficult αὕτη ἡ ἀπογραφὴ πρώτη ἐγένετο (ii. 2) becomes αυτη εγενετο απογραφη πρωτη ; ἐπλήσθησαν is changed into the simpler ετελεσθησαν ; φόβος μέγας (ii. 9) after ἐφοβήθησαν into σφοδρα ; και (ii. 10) is inserted before παντὶ τῷ λαῷ.

[2] Yet not unfrequently the Greek is unique in its extravagance, e. g. Acts v. 8 ; xiii. 14 ; xxi. 28, 29.

the reverse of *this*, so as to put the result beyond the reach of controversy, is impossible. The question depends upon reasons purely critical, and is not of primary importance. For all practical purposes, it is still Codex D of which we speak. When I name 'Codex D' I mean of course nothing else but Codex D according to Scrivener's reprint of the text. And if it be a true hypothesis that the actual Codex D is nothing else but the transcript of another Codex strictly identical with itself, then it is clearly a matter of small importance of which of the two I speak. When 'Codex D' is cited, it is the contents of Codex D which are meant, and no other thing.

And upon this point it may be observed, that D is chiefly remarkable as being the only Greek Codex[1] which exhibits the highly corrupt text found in some of the Old Latin manuscripts, and may be taken as a survival from the second century.

The genius of this family of copies is found to have been—

1. To substitute one expression for another, and generally to paraphrase.

2. To remove difficulties, and where a difficult expression presented itself, to introduce a conjectural emendation of the text. For example, the passage already noticed about the Publican going down to his house 'justified rather than the other' is altered into 'justified more than that Pharisee' (μαλλον παρ' εκεινον τον Φαρισαιον. St. Luke xviii. 14)[2].

3. To omit what might seem to be superfluous. Thus the verse, 'Lord, he hath ten pounds' (St. Luke xix. 25) is simply left out[3].

Enough has been surely said to prove amply that the text of Codex D is utterly untrustworthy. Indeed, the

---

[1] Cureton's Syriac is closely allied to D, and the Lewis Codex less so.
[2] See b c e f ff² i l q Vulg.   [3] So b e g² Curetonian, Lewis.

habit of interpolation found in it, the constant tendency to explain rather than to report, the licentiousness exhibited throughout, and the isolation in which this MS. is found, except in cases where some of the Low-Latin Versions and Cureton's Syriac, and perhaps the Lewis, bear it company, render the text found in it the foulest in existence. What then is to be thought of those critics who upon the exclusive authority of this unstable offender and of a few of the Italic copies occasionally allied with it, endeavour to introduce changes in face of the opposition of all other authorities? And since their ability is unquestioned, must we not seek for the causes of their singular action in the theory to which they are devoted?

§ 7.

Before we take leave of the Old Uncials, it will be well to invite attention to a characteristic feature in them, which is just what the reader would expect who has attended to all that has been said, and which adds confirmation to the doctrine here propounded.

The clumsy and tasteless character of some at least of the Old Uncials has come already under observation. This was in great measure produced by constantly rubbing off delicate expressions which add both to the meaning and the symmetry of the Sacred Record. We proceed to give a few examples, not to prove our position, since it must surely be evident enough to the eyes of any accomplished scholar, but as specimens, and only specimens, of the loss which the Inspired Word would sustain if the Old Uncials were to be followed. Space will not admit of a full discussion of this matter.

An interesting refinement of expression, which has been hopelessly obscured through the proclivity of אBD to fall into error, is found in St. Matt. xxvi. 71. The Evangelist describing the second of St. Peter's denials notes that the damsel who saw him said to the bystanders, 'This man *too* (καί) was with Jesus of Nazareth.' The three MSS. just mentioned omit the καί. No other MS., Uncial or Cursive, follows them. They have only the support of the unstable Sahidic [1]. The loss inflicted is patent : comment is needless.

Another instance, where poverty of meaning would be the obvious result if the acceptance by some critics of the lead of the same trio of Uncials were endorsed, may be found in the description of what the shepherds did when they had seen the Holy Child in the manger. Instead of 'they made known abroad' (διεγνώρισαν), we should simply have 'they made known' (ἐγνώρισαν). We are inclined to say, 'Why this clipping and pruning to the manifest disadvantage of the sacred deposit.' Only the satellite L and Ξ and six Cursives with a single passage from Eusebius are on the same side. The rest in overwhelming majority condemn such rudeness [2].

§ 8.

The undoubtedly genuine expression καὶ τίς ἐστι, Κύριε (which is the traditional reading of St. John ix. 36), loses its characteristic KAI in Cod. ℵ*AL,—though it retains it in the rest of the uncials and in all the cursives. The καί is found in the Complutensian,—because the editors followed their copies : it is not found in the Textus Receptus only because Erasmus did not as in cases before mentioned follow his. The same refinement of expression recurs in the Traditional Text of ch. xiv. 22 (Κύριε, KAÌ τί γέγονεν),

---

[1] St. Chrysostom (vii. 84. d), Origen (iii. 902. d *int.*), Victor of Antioch (335) insert the καί.

[2] So too ἀνακειμένους (BCLΔ. 42) for συνανακειμένους (St. Mark vi. 26) : omit δὲ (ℵBC*LΔ. six curs.) in καὶ ἄλλα δὲ πλοῖα (iv. 36): ἐγείρουσιν (ℵB*C*ΔΠ. few curs.) for διεγείρουσιν (iv. 38): ἔθηκεν (ℵBC²DL. few curs.) for κατέθηκεν (xv. 46): μέγαλα (ℵ* et cᵈ BD*L) for μεγαλεῖα (St. Luke i. 49): ἀναπεσών (ℵᶜBC*KLXΠ* few curs.) for ἐπιπεσών (St. John xiii. 25): &c., &c.

and experienced precisely the same fate at the hands of the
two earliest editors of the printed Greek Text. It is also
again faithfully upheld in its integrity by the whole body
of the cursives,—always excepting ' 33.' But (as before)
in uncials of bad character, as BDL (even by AEX) the
καὶ is omitted,—for which insufficient reason it has been
omitted by the Revisers likewise,—notwithstanding the
fact that it is maintained in all the other uncials. As is
manifest in most of these instances, the Versions, being
made into languages with other idioms than Greek, can
bear no witness ; and also that these delicate embellish-
ments would be often brushed off in quotations, as well as
by scribes and so-called correctors.

We have not far to look for other instances of this.
St. Matthew (i. 18) begins his narrative,—μνηστευθείσης ΓΑ῾Ρ
τῆς μητρὸς αὐτοῦ Μαρίας τῷ Ἰωσήφ. Now, as readers of
Greek are aware, the little untranslated (because untrans-
lateable) word exhibited in capitals[1] stands with peculiar
idiomatic force and propriety immediately after the first
word of such a sentence as the foregoing, being employed
in compliance with strictly classical usage[2] : and though it
might easily come to be omitted through the carelessness
or the licentiousness of copyists, yet it could not by any
possibility have universally established itself in copies of
the Gospel—as it has done—had it been an unauthorized
accretion to the text. We find it recognized in St. Matt. i.
18 by Eusebius[3], by Basil[4], by Epiphanius[5], by Chrysostom[6], by Nestorius[7], by Cyril[8], by Andreas Cret.[9] : which
is even extraordinary ; for the γάρ is not at all required for
purposes of quotation. But the essential circumstance as

---

[1] Owing to differences of idiom in other languages, it is not represented here
in so much as a single ancient Version.

[2] ' *Est enim* τοῦ ΓΑΡ *officium inchoare narrationem.*' Hoogeveen, De Partic.
Cf. Prom. Vinct. v. 666. See also St. Luke ix. 44.

[3] Dem. Ev. 320 b.   [4] ii. 597 : 278.   [5] i. 1040 b.

[6] viii. 314 a : (Eclog.) xii. 694 d.   [7] *Ap.* Cyril, v². 28 a.

[8] v¹. 676 e.   [9] 30 b (= Gall. xiii. 109 d).

usual is, that γάρ is found besides in the whole body of the manuscripts. The only uncials in fact which omit the idiomatic particle are four of older date, viz. BℵC*Z.

This same particle (γάρ) has led to an extraordinary amount of confusion in another place, where its idiomatic propriety has evidently been neither felt nor understood,— viz. in St. Luke xviii. 14. 'This man' (says our LORD) 'went down to his house justified rather than' (ἢ γάρ) 'the other.' Scholars recognize here an exquisitely idiomatic expression, which in fact obtains so universally in the Traditional Text that its genuineness is altogether above suspicion. It is vouched for by 16 uncials headed by A, and by the cursives in the proportion of 500 to 1. The Complutensian has it, of course : and so would the Textus Receptus have it, if Erasmus had followed his MS. : but '*praefero*' (he says) '*quod est usitatius apud probos autores.*' Uncongenial as the expression is to the other languages of antiquity, ἢ γάρ is faithfully retained in the Gothic and in the Harkleian Version [1]. Partly however, because it is of very rare occurrence and was therefore not understood [2], and partly because when written in uncials it easily got perverted into something else, the expression has met with a strange fate. ΗΓΑΡ is found to have suggested, or else to have been mistaken for, both ΗΠΕΡ [3] and ΥΠΕΡ [4]. The prevailing expedient however was, to get rid of the Η,—to turn ΓΑΡ into ΠΑΡ,—and, for ἐκεῖνος to write ἐκεῖνον [5]. The

<hr />

[1] So, in Garnier's MSS. of Basil ii. 278 a, note. Also in Cyril *apud* Mai ii. 378.

[2] So Mill, *Prolegg.* 1346 and 1363.—Beza says roundly, '*Quod plerique Graeci codices scriptum habent* ἢ γὰρ ἐκεῖνος, *sane non intelligo ; nisi dicam* γάρ *redundare.*'

[3] ἤ,περ ἐκεῖνος is exhibited by the printed text of Basil ii. 278 a.

[4] ὑπὲρ αὐτόν is found in Basil ii. 160 b:—ὑπὲρ ἐκεῖνον, in Dorotheus (A.D. 596) *ap.* Galland. xii. 403 d:—ὑπὲρ τὸν Φαρισαῖον, in Chrysostom iv. 536 a; vi. 142 d— (where one of the Manuscripts exhibits παρὰ τὸν Φαρισαῖον).—Nilus the Monk has the same reading (ὑπὲρ τὸν Φαρισαῖον),—i. 280.

[5] Accordingly, παρ' ἐκεῖνον is found in Origen i. 490 b. So also reads the author

uncials which exhibit this strange corruption of the text
are exclusively that quaternion which have already come
so often before us,—viz. BℵDL. But D improves upon
the blunder of its predecessors by writing, like a Targum,
μᾶλλον ΠΑΡ' αἰκεῖνον (sic), and by adding (with the Old
Latin and the Peshitto) τὸν Φαρισαῖον,—an exhibition of the
text which (it is needless to say) is perfectly unique[1].

And how has the place fared at the hands of some
Textual critics? Lachmann and Tregelles (forsaken by
Tischendorf) of course follow Codd. BℵDL. The Revisers
(with Dr. Hort)—not liking to follow BℵDL, and unable
to adopt the Traditional Text, suffer the reading of the
Textus Receptus (ἢ ἐκεῖνος) to stand,—though a solitary
cursive (Evan. 1) is all the manuscript authority that can
be adduced in its favour. In effect, ἢ ἐκεῖνος may be said to
be without manuscript authority[2].

The point to be noticed in all this is, that the true reading of St. Luke xviii. 14 has been faithfully retained by the
MSS. in all countries and all down the ages, not only by
the whole body of the cursives, but by every uncial in
existence except four. And those four are BℵDL.

But really the occasions are without number when
minute words have dropped out of ℵB and their allies,—
and yet have been faithfully retained, all through the
centuries, by the later Uncials and despised Cursive copies.
In St. John xvii. 2, for instance, we read—δόξασόν σου τὸν

of the scholium in Cramer's Cat. ii. 133,—which is the same which Matthaei
(*in loc.*) quotes out of Evan. 256. And so Cyril (*ap.* Mai, ii. 180),—παρ' ἐκεῖνον
τὸν Φαρισαῖον.—Euthymius (A. D. 1116), commenting on the traditional text
of Luke xviii. 14 (see Matthaei's *Praefat.* i. 177), says ΠΑΡ ὃ ἐκεῖνος ἤγουν οὐκ
ἐκεῖνος.

[1] The μᾶλλον is obviously added by way of interpretation, or to help out the
meaning. Thus, in Origen (iv. 124 d) we meet with μᾶλλον αὐτοῦ:—in
Chrysostom (i. 151 c), μᾶλλον ὑπὲρ τὸν Φαρισαῖον : and in Basil Sel. (p. 184 c),
μᾶλλον ἢ ὁ Φαρισαῖος.

[2] It is found however in ps.-Chrysostom (viii. 119 c) :—in Antiochus Mon.
(p. 1102 = ed. Migne, vol. 89, p. 1579 c) : and in Theophylact (i. 433 c). At
p. 435 b, the last-named writes ἢ ἐκεῖνος, ἀντὶ τοῦ ΠΑΡ' ὃ ἐκεῖνος.

υἱόν, ἵνα ΚΑΙ ὁ υἱός ϹΟΥ δοξάσῃ σέ: where καί is omitted by אABCD : and σου (after ὁ υἱός) by אBC. Some critics will of course insist that, on the contrary, both words are spurious accretions to the text of the cursives; and they must say so, if they will. But does it not sensibly impair their confidence in א to find that it, and it only, exhibits λελάληκεν (for ἐλάλησεν) in ver. 1,—δώσω αὐτῷ (for δώσῃ αὐτοῖς) in ver. 2, while אB are peculiar in writing 'Ιησοῦς without the article in ver. 1 ?

Enough has surely been said to exhibit and illustrate this rude characteristic of the few Old Copies which out of the vast number of their contemporaries are all that we now possess. The existence of this characteristic is indubitable and undoubted : it is in a measure acknowledged by Dr. Hort in words on which we shall remark in the ensuing chapter[1]. Our readers should observe that the 'rubbing off' process has by no means been confined to particles like καί and γάρ, but has extended to tenses, other forms of words, and in fact to all kinds of delicacies of expression. The results have been found all through the Gospels : sacred and refined meaning, such as accomplished scholars will appreciate in a moment, has been pared off and cast away. If people would only examine B, א and D in their bare unpresentableness, they would see the loss which those MSS. have sustained, as compared with the Text supported by the overwhelming mass of authorities: and they would refuse to put their trust any longer in such imperfect, rudimentary, and ill-trained guides.

[1] Introduction, p. 135.

CHAPTER XI.

THE LATER UNCIALS AND THE CURSIVES.

§ 1[1].

THE nature of Tradition is very imperfectly understood in many quarters; and mistakes respecting it lie close to the root, if they are not themselves the root, of the chief errors in Textual Criticism. We must therefore devote some space to a brief explanation of this important element in our present inquiry.

Tradition is commonly likened to a stream which, as is taken for granted, contracts pollution in its course the further it goes. Purity is supposed to be attainable only within the neighbourhood of the source: and it is assumed that distance from thence ensures proportionally either greater purity or more corruption.

Without doubt there is much truth in this comparison: only, as in the case of nearly all comparisons there are limits to the resemblance, and other features and aspects are not therein connoted, which are essentially bound up with the subject believed to be illustrated on all points in this similitude.

In the first place, the traditional presentment of the New Testament is not like a single stream, but resembles rather a great number of streams of which many have

---

[1] For all this section except the early part of ' 4 ' the Editor is responsible.

remained pure, but some have been corrupted. One cluster of bad streams was found in the West, and, as is most probable, the source of very many of them was in Syria : another occurred in the East with Alexandria and afterwards Caesarea as the centre, where it was joined by the currents from the West. A multitude in different parts of the Church were kept wholly or mainly clear of these contaminants, and preserved the pure and precise utterance as it issued from the springs of the Written Word.

But there is another pitfall hidden under that imperfect simile which is continually employed on this subject either by word of mouth or in writing. The Tradition of the Church does not take shape after the model of a stream or streams rolling in mechanical movement and unvaried flow from the fountain down the valley and over the plain. Like most mundane things, it has a career. It has passed through a stage when one manuscript was copied as if mechanically from another that happened to be at hand. Thus accuracy except under human infirmity produced accuracy ; and error was surely procreative of error. Afterwards came a period when both bad and good exemplars offered themselves in rivalry, and the power of refusing the evil and choosing the good was in exercise, often with much want of success. As soon as this stage was accomplished, which may be said roughly to have reached from Origen till the middle of the fourth century, another period commenced, when a definite course was adopted, which was followed with increasing advantage till the whole career was fixed irrevocably in the right direction. The period of the two Gregories, Basil, Chrysostom, and others, was the time when the Catholic Church took stock of truth and corruption, and had in hand the duty of thoroughly casting out error and cleansing her faith. The second part of the Creed was thus permanently defined ; the third part which, besides the Divinity of the Holy Ghost, relates to His action in the Church, to the Written Word, inclusive both of the several books generally and the text of those books, to the nature of the Sacraments, to the Ministry, to the character of the unity and government of the Church, was on many points delayed as to special definition by the ruin soon dealt upon the Roman Empire, and by the ignorance of the nations which entered upon that vast domain : and indeed much of this part of the Faith remains still upon the battlefield of controversy.

But action was taken upon what may be perhaps termed the Canon of St. Augustine[1]: 'What the Church of the time found prevailing throughout her length and breadth, not introduced by regulations of Councils, but handed down in unbroken tradition, that she rightly concluded to have been derived from no other fount than Apostolic authority.' To use other words, in the accomplishment of her general work, the Church quietly and without any public recension examined as to the written Word the various streams that had come down from the Apostles, and followed the multitude that were purest, and by gradual filtration extruded out of these nearly all the corruption that even the better lines of descent had contracted.

We have now arrived at the period, when from the general consentience of the records, it is discovered that the form of the Text of the New Testament was mainly settled. The settlement was effected noiselessly, not by public debate or in decrees of general or provincial councils, yet none the less completely and permanently. It was the Church's own operation, instinctive, deliberate, and in the main universal. Only a few witnesses here and there lifted up their voices against the prevalent decisions, themselves to be condemned by the dominant sense of Christendom. Like the repudiation of Arianism, it was

---

[1] See above, p. 61, note.

a repentance from a partial and temporary encouragement of corruption, which was never to be repented of till it was called in question during the general disturbance of faith and doctrine in the nineteenth century. Doubtless, the agreement thus introduced has not attained more than a general character. For the exceeding number of questions involved forbids all expectation of an universal coincidence of testimony extending to every single case.

But in the outset, as we enter upon the consideration of the later manuscripts, our way must be cleared by the removal of some fallacies which are widely prevalent amongst students of Sacred Textual Criticism.

It is sometimes imagined (1) that Uncials and Cursives differ in kind; (2) that all Cursives are alike; (3) that all Cursives are copies of Codex A, and are the results of a general Recension; and (4) that we owe our knowledge of the New Testament entirely to the existing Uncials. To these four fallacies must be added an opinion which stands upon a higher footing than the preceding, but which is no less a fallacy, and which we have to combat in this chapter, viz. that the Text of the later Uncials and especially the Text of the Cursives is a debased Text.

1. The real difference between Uncials and Cursives is patent to all people who have any knowledge of the subject. Uncials form a ruder kind of manuscripts, written in capital letters with no space between them till the later specimens are reached, and generally with an insufficient and ill-marked array of stops. Cursives show a great advance in workmanship, being indited, as the name suggests, in running and more easily flowing letters, with 'a system of punctuation much the same as in printed books.' As contrasted with one another, Uncials as a class enjoy a great superiority, if antiquity is considered; and Cursives are just as much higher than the sister class, if workmanship is to be the guiding principle

of judgement. Their differences are on the surface, and are such that whoso runs may read.

But Textual Science, like all Science, is concerned, not with the superficial, but with the real;—not with the dress in which the text is presented, but with the text itself;—not again with the bare fact of antiquity, since age alone is no sure test of excellence, but with the character of the testimony which from the nature of the subject-matter is within reach. Judging then the later Uncials, and comparing them with the Cursives, we make the discovery that the texts of both are mainly the same. Indeed, they are divided by no strict boundary of time: they over-lap one another. The first Cursive is dated May 7, 835[1]: the last Uncials, which are Lectionaries, are referred to the eleventh, and possibly to the twelfth, century[2]. One, Codex Λ, is written partly in uncials, and partly in cursive letters, as it appears, by the same hand. So that in the ninth, tenth, and eleventh centuries both uncials and cursives must have issued mainly and virtually from the same body of transcribers. It follows that the difference lay in the outward investiture, whilst, as is found by a comparison of one with another, there was a much more important similarity of character within.

2. But when a leap is made from this position to another sweeping assertion that all cursives are alike, it is necessary to put a stop to so illicit a process. In the first place, there is the small handful of cursive copies which is associated with B and ℵ. The notorious 1,—handsome outwardly like its two leaders but corrupt in text,—33, 118, 131, 157, 205, 209[3], and others;—the Ferrar Group, containing 13, 69, 124, 346, 556, 561, besides 348, 624, 788;—

---

[1] 481 of the Gospels: from St. Saba, now at St. Petersburg.

[2] The Evangelistaria 118, 192. Scrivener, Introduction, I. pp. 335, 340.

[3] Scrivener, I. App. F, p. 398*. Of these, 205 and 209 are probably from the same original. Burgon, Letters in *Guardian* to Dr. Scrivener.

these are frequently dissentients from the rest of the Cursives. But indeed, when these and a few others have been subtracted from the rest and set apart in a class by themselves, any careful examination of the evidence adduced on important passages will reveal the fact that whilst almost always there is a clear majority of Cursives on one side, there are amply enough cases of dissentience more or less to prove that the Cursive MSS. are derived from a multiplicity of archetypes, and are endued almost severally with what may without extravagance be termed distinct and independent personality. Indeed, such is the necessity of the case. They are found in various countries all over the Church. Collusion was not possible in earlier times when intercommunication between countries was extremely limited, and publicity was all but confined to small areas. The genealogies of Cursive MSS., if we knew them, would fill a volume. Their stems must have been extremely numerous; and like Uncials, and often independently of Uncials, they must have gone back to the vast body of early papyrus manuscripts.

3. And as to the Cursives having been copies of Codex A, a moderate knowledge of the real character of that manuscript, and a just estimate of the true value of it, would effectually remove such a hallucination. It is only the love of reducing all knowledge of intricate questions to the compass of the proverbial nutshell, and the glamour that hangs over a very old relic, which has led people, when they had dropped their grasp of B, to clutch at the ancient treasure in the British Museum. It is right to concede all honour to such a survival of so early a period : but to lift the pyramid from its ample base, and to rest it upon a point like A, is a proceeding which hardly requires argument for its condemnation. And next, when the notion of a Recension is brought forward, the answer is, What and when and how and where? In the absence

of any sign or hint of such an event in records of the past, it is impossible to accept such an explanation of what is no difficulty at all. History rests upon research into documents which have descended to us, not upon imagination or fiction. And the sooner people get such an idea out of their heads as that of piling up structures upon mere assumption, and betake themselves instead to what is duly attested, the better it will be for a Science which must be reared upon well authenticated bases, and not upon phantom theories.

4. The case of the Cursives is in other respects strangely misunderstood, or at least is strangely misrepresented. The popular notion seems to be, that we are indebted for our knowledge of the true text of Scripture to the existing Uncials entirely; and that the essence of the secret dwells exclusively with the four or five oldest of those Uncials. By consequence, it is popularly supposed that since we are possessed of such Uncial Copies, we could afford to dispense with the testimony of the Cursives altogether. A more complete misconception of the facts of the case can hardly be imagined. For the plain truth is that all the phenomena exhibited by the Uncial MSS. are reproduced by the Cursive Copies. A small minority of the Cursives, just as a small minority of the Uncials, are probably the depositaries of peculiar recensions.

It is at least as reasonable to assert that we can afford entirely to disregard the testimony of the Uncials, as to pretend that we can afford entirely to disregard the testimony of the Cursives. In fact of the two, the former assertion would be a vast deal nearer to the truth. Our inductions would in many cases be so fatally narrowed, if we might not look beyond one little handful of Uncial Copies.

But the point to which the reader's attention is specially invited is this:—that so far from our being entirely dependent on Codexes B℧CD, or on some of them, for certain of the most approved corrections of the Received Text, we should have been just as fully aware of every one of those readings if neither B nor ℧, C nor D, had been in existence. Those readings are every one to be found in one or more of the few Cursive Codexes which rank by themselves, viz. the two groups just mentioned and perhaps some others. If they are not, they may be safely disregarded; they are readings which have received no subsequent recognition [1].

Indeed, the case of the Cursives presents an exact parallel with the case of the Uncials. Whenever we observe a formal consensus of the Cursives for any reading, there, almost invariably, is a grand consensus observable for the same reading of the Uncials.

The era of greater perfection both in the outer presentment and in the internal accuracy of the text of copies of the New Testament may be said, as far as the relics which have descended to us are concerned, to have commenced with the Codex Basiliensis or E of the Gospels. This beautiful and generally accurate Codex must have been written in the seventh century [2]. The rest of the later

---

[1] I am not of course asserting that any known cursive MS. is an exact counterpart of one of the oldest extant Uncials. Nor even that every reading however extraordinary, contained in Codd. B℧D, is also to be met with in one of the few Cursives already specified. But what then? Neither do any of the oldest Uncials contain all the textual avouchings discoverable in the same Cursives.

The thing asserted is only this : that, as a rule, every principal reading discoverable in any of the five or seven oldest Uncials, is also exhibited in one or more of the Cursives already cited or in others of them ; and that generally when there is consent among the oldest of the Uncials, there is also consent among about as many of the same Cursives. So that it is no exaggeration to say that we find ourselves always concerned with the joint testimony of the same little handful of Uncial and Cursive documents : and therefore, as was stated at the outset, if the oldest of the Uncials had never existed, the readings which they advocate would have been advocated by MSS. of the eleventh, twelfth, thirteenth, and fourteenth centuries.

[2] *Manuscript Evangelia in foreign Libraries*, Letters in the *Guardian* from Dean Burgon to Dr. Scrivener, *Guardian*, Jan. 29, 1873. 'You will not be dating it too early if you assign it to the seventh century.'

Uncials are ordinarily found together in a large or considerable majority: whilst there is enough dissent to prove that they are independent witnesses, and that error was condemned, not ignored. Thus the Codex Regius (L, eighth century), preserved at Paris, generally follows B and ℵ : so does the Codex Sangallensis (Δ, ninth century), the Irish relic of the monastery of St. Gall, in St. Mark alone: and the Codex Zacynthius (Ξ, an eighth century palimpsest) now in the Library of the Bible Society, in St. Luke[1]. The isolation of these few from the rest of their own age is usually conspicuous. The verdict of the later uncials is nearly always sustained by a large majority.

In fact, as a rule, every principal reading discoverable in any of the oldest Uncials is also exhibited in one, two, or three of the later Uncials, or in one or more of the small handful of dissentient Cursives already enumerated. Except indeed in very remarkable instances, as in the case of the last twelve verses of St. Mark, such readings are generally represented : yet in the later MSS. as compared with the oldest there is this additional feature in the representation, that if evidence is evidence, and weight, number, and variety are taken into account, those readings are altogether condemned.

§ 2[2].

But we are here confronted with the contention that the text of the Cursives is of a debased character. Our opponents maintain that it is such that it must have been compounded from other forms of text by a process of con-

---

[1] The other uncials which have a tendency to consort with B and ℵ are of earlier date. Thus T (Codex Borgianus I) of St. Luke and St. John is of the fourth or fifth century, R of St. Luke (Codex Nitriensis in the British Museum) is of the end of the sixth, Z of St. Matthew (Codex Dublinensis), a palimpsest, is of the sixth : Q and P, fragments like the rest, are respectively of the fifth and sixth.

[2] By the Editor.

flation so called, and that in itself it is a text of a character greatly inferior to the text mainly represented by B and ℵ.

Now in combating this opinion, we are bound first to remark that the burden of proof rests with the opposite side. According to the laws which regulate scientific conclusions, all the elements of proof must be taken into consideration. Nothing deserves the name of science in which the calculation does not include all the phenomena. The base of the building must be conterminous with the facts. This is so elementary a principle that it seems needless to insist more upon it.

But then, this is exactly what we endeavour to accomplish, and our adversaries disregard. Of course they have their reasons for dismissing nineteen-twentieths of the evidence at hand : but—this is the point—it rests with them to prove that such dismissal is lawful and right. What then are their arguments? Mainly three, viz. the supposed greater antiquity of their favourite text, the superiority which they claim for its character, and the evidence that the Traditional Text was as they maintain formed by conflation from texts previously in existence.

Of these three arguments, that from antiquity has been already disposed of, and illustration of what has been already advanced will also be at hand throughout the sequel of this work. As to conflation, a proof against its possible applicability to the Traditional Text was supplied as to particles and other words in the last chapter, and will receive illustration from instances of words of a greater size in this. Conflation might be possible, supposing for a moment that other conditions favoured it, and that the elements to be conflated were already in existence in other texts. But inasmuch as in the majority of instances such elements are found nowhere else than in the Traditional Text, conflation as accounting for the changes which upon this theory must have been made is simply impossible. On the other hand, the Traditional Text might have been very easily chipped and broken and corrupted, as will be shewn in the second part of this Treatise, into the form exhibited by B and ℵ[1].

Upon the third argument in the general contention, we undertake to say that it is totally without foundation. On the contrary, the text of the Cursives is greatly the superior of the two. The instances which we proceed to give as specimens, and as specimens only, will exhibit the propriety of language, and the taste of expression, in which it is pre-eminent[2]. Let our readers judge fairly and candidly, as we doubt not that they will, and we do not fear the result.

But before entering upon the character of the later text, a few words are required to remind our readers of the effect of the general argument as hitherto stated upon this question. The text of the later Uncials is the text to which witness is borne, not only by the majority of the Uncials, but also by the Cursives and the Versions and the Fathers, each in greater numbers. Again, the text of the Cursives enjoys unquestionably the support of by very far the largest number among themselves, and also of the Uncials and Versions and Fathers. Accordingly, the text of which we are now treating, which is that of the later Uncials and the Cursives combined, is incomparably superior under all the external Notes of Truth. It possesses in nearly all cases older attestation[3]: there is no sort of question as to the greater number of witnesses that bear evidence to its claims : nor to their variety : and hardly ever to the explicit proof of their continuousness ; which indeed is also generally—nay, universally—implied owing to the nature of the case : their weight is certified upon strong grounds : and as a matter of fact, the context in nearly all instances testifies on their side. The course of doctrine pursued in the history of the Universal Church is

---

[1] Above, pp. 80-81.   [2] Hort, Introduction, p. 135.
[3] Chapters V, VI, VII.

immeasurably in their favour. We have now therefore only to consider whether their text, as compared with that of BℵD and their allies, commends itself on the score of intrinsic excellence. And as to this consideration, if as has been manifested the text of B-ℵ, and that of D, are bad, and have been shewn to be the inferior, this must be the better. We may now proceed to some specimen instances exhibiting the superiority of the Later Uncial and Cursive text.

§ 3.

Our SAVIOUR'S lament over Jerusalem ('If thou hadst known, even thou, at least in this thy day, the things which belong unto thy peace!') is just one of those delicately articulated passages which are safe to suffer by the process of transmission. Survey St. Luke's words (xix. 42), Εἰ ἔγνως καὶ σύ, καί γε ἐν τῇ ἡμέρᾳ σου ταύτῃ, τὰ πρὸς εἰρήνην σου,—and you will perceive at a glance that the vulnerable point in the sentence, so to speak, is καὶ σύ, καί γε. In the meanwhile, attested as those words are by the Old Latin[1] and by Eusebius[2], as well as witnessed to by the whole body of the copies beginning with Cod. A and including the lost original of 13–69–124–346 &c.,—the very *order* of those words is a thing quite above suspicion. Even Tischendorf admits this. He retains the traditional reading in every respect. Eusebius however twice writes καί γε σύ[3]; once, καὶ σύ γε[4]; and once he drops καί γε entirely[5]. Origen drops it 3 times[6]. Still, there is at least a general *consensus* among Copies, Versions and Fathers for beginning the sentence with the characteristic words, εἰ ἔγνως καὶ σύ; the phrase being

---

[1] Vercell.:—*Si scires tu, quamquam in hac tuâ die, quae ad pacem tuam.* So Amiat. and Aur.:—*Si cognovisses et tu, et quidem in hâc die tuâ, quae ad pacem tibi.*

[2] Mai, iv. 129.

[3] Ibid., and H. E. iii. 7.

[4] Montf. ii. 470.

[5] Montf. i. 700.

[6] iii. 321; *interp.* 977; iv. 180.

witnessed to by the Latin, the Bohairic, the Gothic, and the Harkleian Versions ; by Irenaeus [1],—by Origen [2],— by ps.-Tatian [3],—by Eusebius [4],—by Basil the Great [5],—by Basil of Seleucia [6],—by Cyril [7].

What then is found in the three remaining Uncials, for C is defective here? D exhibits ει εγνως και συ, εν τη ημερα ταυτη, τα προς ειρηνην σοι : being supported only by the Latin of Origen in one place [8]. Lachmann adopts this reading all the same. Nothing worse, it must be confessed, has happened to it than the omission of καί γε, and of the former σου. But when we turn to Bℵ, we find that they and L, with Origen once [9], and the Syriac heading prefixed to Cyril's homilies on St. Luke's Gospel [10], exclusively exhibit,—ει εγνως εν τη ημερα ταυτη και συ τα προς ειρηνην : thus, not only omitting καί γε, together with the first and second σου, but by transposing the words καὶ σύ — ἐν τῇ ἡμέρᾳ ταύτῃ, obliterating from the passage more than half its force and beauty. This maimed and mutilated exhibition of our LORD's words, only because it is found in Bℵ, is adopted by W.-Hort, who are in turn followed by the Revisers [11]. The Peshitto by the way omits καὶ σύ, and transposes the two clauses which remain [12]. The Curetonian Syriac runs wild, as usual, and the Lewis too [13].

Amid all this conflict and confusion, the reader's attention is invited to the instructive fact that the whole body of cursive copies (and all the uncials but four) have retained

---

[1] i. 220: also the *Vet. interp.*, 'Si cognovisses et tu.' And so *ap. Epiph.* i. 254 b.

[2] iii. 321, 977.

[3] *Evan. Conc.* 184, 207.

[4] In all 5 places.

[5] *Mor.* ii. 272 b.

[6] 205.

[7] *In Luc.* (Syr.) 686.

[8] *Int.* iii. 977.

[9] iv. 180.

[10] *In Luc.* (Syr.) 607.

[11] In their usual high-handed way, these editors *assume, without note or comment,* that Bℵ are to be followed here. The 'Revisers' of 1881 *do the same.* Is this to deal honestly with the evidence and with **the English** reader?

[12] Viz.—ει ἔγνως τὰ πρὸς εἰρήνην σου, καί γε ἐν τῇ ἡμέρᾳ σου **ταύτῃ.**

[13] Viz.—ει καὶ ἐν τῇ ἡμέρᾳ ταύτῃ ἔγνως τὴν εἰρήνην σου.

in this passage all down the ages uninjured every exquisite lineament of the inspired archetype. The truth, I say, is to be found in the cursive copies, not in the licentious BℵDL, which as usual stand apart from one another and from A. Only in respect of the first σου is there a slight prevarication on the part of a very few witnesses[1]. Note however that it is overborne by the consent of the Syriac, the Old Latin and the Gothic, and further that the testimony of ps.-Tatian is express on this head[2]. There is therefore nothing to be altered in the traditional text of St. Luke xix. 42, which furnishes an excellent instance of fidelity of transmission, and of an emphatic condemnation of B–ℵ.

§ 4.

It is the misfortune of inquiries like the present that they sometimes constrain us to give prominence to minute details which it is difficult to make entertaining. Let me however seek to interest my reader in the true reading of St. Matt. xx. 22, 23 : from which verses recent critical Editors reject the words, 'and to be baptized with the baptism that I am baptized with,' καὶ τὸ βάπτισμα ὃ ἐγὼ βαπτίζομαι βαπτισθῆναι.

About the right of the same words to a place in the corresponding part of St. Mark's Gospel (x. 38), there is no difference of opinion : except that it is insisted that in St. Mark the clause should begin with ἤ instead of καί.

Next, the reader is requested to attend to the following circumstance : that, except of course the four (ℵBDL) and Z which omit the place altogether and one other (S), all the Uncials together with the bulk of the Cursives, and the

---

[1] It is omitted by Eus. iv. 129, Basil ii. 272, Cod. A, Evann. 71, 511, Evst. 222, 259. For the second σου still fewer authorities exhibit σοι : while some few (as Irenaeus) omit it altogether.

[2] '*Hanc diem tuam.* Si ergo dies ejus erat, quanto magis et tempus ejus!' p. 184, and so 207.

Peshitto and Harkleian and several Latin Versions, concur in reading ἢ τὸ βάπτισμα in St. Matthew : all the Uncials but eight (אBCDLWΔΣ), together with the bulk of the Cursives and the Peshitto, agree in reading καὶ τὸ βάπτισμα in St. Mark. This delicate distinction between the first and the second Gospel, obliterated in the Received Text, is faithfully maintained in nineteen out of twenty of the Cursive Copies.

In the meantime we are assured on the authority of אBDLZ —with most of the Latin Copies, including of course Hilary and Jerome, the Cureton, the Lewis, and the Bohairic, besides Epiphanius,—that the clause in question has no right to its place in St. Matthew's Gospel. So confidently is this opinion held, that the Revisers, following Griesbach, Lachmann, Tischendorf, Tregelles, Alford, have ejected the words from the Text. But are they right? Certainly not, I answer. And I reason thus.

If this clause has been interpolated into St. Matthew's Gospel. how will you possibly account for its presence in every MS. in the world except 7, viz. 5 uncials and 2 cursives? It is pretended that it crept in by assimilation from the parallel place in St. Mark. But I reply,—

1. Is this credible? Do you not see the glaring improbability of such an hypothesis? Why should the Gospel most in vogue have been assimilated in all the Copies but seven to the Gospel least familiarly known and read in the Churches?

2. And pray when is it pretended that this wholesale falsification of the MSS. took place? The Peshitto Syriac as usual sides with the bulk of the Cursives : but it has been shewn to be of the second century. Some of the Latin Copies also have the clause. Codex C, Chrysostom and Basil of Seleucia also exhibit it. Surely the preponderance of the evidence is overwhelmingly one way. But then

3. As a matter of fact the clause cannot have come

in from St. Mark's Gospel,—for the very conclusive reason that the two places are delicately discriminated,—as on the testimony of the Cursives and the Peshitto has been shewn already. And

4. I take upon myself to declare without fear of contradiction on the part of any but the advocates of the popular theory that, on the contrary, it is St. Matthew's Gospel which has been corrupted from St. Mark's. A conclusive note of the assimilating process is discernible in St. Mark's Gospel where ἡ has intruded,—not in St. Matthew's.

5. Why St. Matthew's Gospel was maimed in this place, I am not able to explain. Demonstrable it is that the Text of the Gospels at that early period underwent a process of Revision at the hands of men who apparently were as little aware of the foolishness as of the sinfulness of all they did : and that Mutilation was their favourite method. And, what is very remarkable, the same kind of infatuation which is observed to attend the commission of crime, and often leads to its detection, is largely recognizable here. But the Eye which never sleeps has watched over the Deposit, and provided Himself with witnesses.

§ 5.

Singular to relate, the circumstances under which Simon and Andrew, James and John were on the last occasion called to Apostleship (St. Matt. iv. 17–22 : St. Mark i. 14–20: St. Luke v. 1–11) have never yet been explained[1]. The facts were as follows.

It was morning on the Sea of Galilee. Two boats were

---

[1] 'Having been wholly unsuccessful [in their fishing], two of them, seated on the shore, were occupying their time in washing,—and two, seated in their boat . . . were mending —their nets.' (Farrar's Life of Christ, i. 241-2.) The foot note appended to this 'attempt to combine *as far as it is possible* in one continuous narrative' the 'accounts of the Synoptists,' is quite a curiosity.

moored to the shore. The fishermen having 'toiled all the night and taken nothing[1],'—'were gone out of them and had washed out ($\dot{a}\pi\acute{\epsilon}\pi\lambda\upsilon\nu\alpha\nu$) their nets ($\tau\grave{a}$ $\delta\acute{\iota}\kappa\tau\upsilon\alpha$)[2].' But though fishing in deep water had proved a failure, they knew that by wading into the shallows, they might even now employ a casting-net with advantage. Accordingly it was thus that our SAVIOUR, coming by at this very juncture, beheld Simon and Andrew employed ($\beta\acute{a}\lambda\lambda o\nu\tau\alpha s$ $\dot{a}\mu\phi\acute{\iota}\beta\lambda\eta\eta\tau\rho o\nu$)[3]. Thereupon, entering Simon's boat, 'He prayed him that he would thrust out a little from the land[4].' The rest requires no explanation.

Now, it is plain that the key which unlocks this interesting story is the graphic precision of the compound verb employed, and the well-known usage of the language which gives to the aorist tense on such occasions as the present a pluperfect signification[5]. The Translators of 1611, not understanding the incident, were content, as Tyndale, following the Vulgate[6], had been before them, to render $\dot{a}\pi\acute{\epsilon}\pi\lambda\upsilon\nu\alpha\nu$ $\tau\grave{a}$ $\delta\acute{\iota}\kappa\tau\upsilon\alpha$,—'were washing their nets.' Of this rendering, so long as the Greek was let alone, no serious harm could come. The Revisers of 1881, however, by not only retaining the incorrect translation ' were washing their nets,' but, by making the Greek tally with the English— by substituting in short $\acute{\epsilon}\pi\lambda\upsilon\nu o\nu$ for $\dot{a}\pi\acute{\epsilon}\pi\lambda\upsilon\nu\alpha\nu$,—have so effectually darkened the Truth as to make it simply irrecoverable by ordinary students. The only point in the meantime to which the reader's attention is just now invited is this:—that the compound verb in the aorist tense ($\dot{a}\pi\acute{\epsilon}\pi\lambda\upsilon\nu\alpha\nu$) has been retained by the whole body of the Cursives, as transmitted all down the ages : while the

[1] St. Luke v. 5.   [2] Ibid., verses 1, 2.
[3] St. Matt. iv. 18 = St. Mark i. 16.   [4] St. Luke v. 3.
[5] As in St. Matt. xxvii. 2, 60 ; St. Luke v. 4; xiii. 16; St. John xviii. 24; xxi. 15 ; Acts xii. 17 ; Heb. iv. 8, &c., &c.
[6] *lavabant retia*, it. vulg. The one known exception is (1) the Cod. Rehdigeranus [VII] (Tischendorf).

barbarous ἐπλυνον is only found at this day in the two corrupt uncials BD[1] and a single cursive (Evan. 91)[2].

§ 6.

' How hardly shall they that *have riches* enter into the Kingdom of Heaven,' exclaimed our LORD on a memorable occasion. The disciples were amazed. Replying to their thoughts,—' Children,' He added, ' how hard is it for them that *trust in riches* to enter into the Kingdom of GOD.' (St. Mark x. 23, 24). Those familiar words, vouched for by 16 uncials and all the cursives, are quite above suspicion. But in fact all the Versions support them likewise. There is really no pretext for disturbing what is so well attested, not to say so precious. Yet Tischendorf and Westcott and Hort eject τοὺς πεποιθότας ἐπὶ τοῖς χρήμασιν from the text, on the sole ground that the clause in question is omitted by אBΔ, one copy of the Italic (k), and one copy of the Bohairic. Aware that such a proceeding requires an apology,—' I think it unsafe,' says Tischendorf, ' to forsake in this place the very ancient authorities which I am accustomed to follow ': i. e. Codexes א and B. But of what nature is this argument? Does the critic mean that he must stick to antiquity? If this be his meaning, then let him be reminded that Clemens[3], a more ancient authority than אB by 150 years,—not to say the Latin and the Syriac Versions, which are more ancient still,—recognizes the words in question[4]. Does however the learned critic mean no more than this,—That it is with him a fundamental principle of Textual Criticism to uphold at all

---

[1] The same pair of authorities are *unique* in substituting βαπτίσαντες (for βαπτίζοντες) in St. Matt. xxviii. 19 ; i. e. the Apostles were to baptize people first, and make them disciples afterwards.

[2] אC exhibit ἐπλυναν : A (by far the purest of the five ' old uncials ') retains the traditional text.

[3] p. 938.

[4] So does Aphraates, a contemporary of B and א, p. 392.

hazards the authority of B and ℵ ? He cannot mean that ; **as I** proceed to explain.

For the strangest circumstance is behind. Immediately after he has thus (in ver. 24) proclaimed the supremacy of ℵB, Tischendorf is constrained to reject the combined evidence of ℵBCΔ. In ver. 26 those 4 copies advocate the absurd reading λέγοντες πρὸς AYTON Καὶ τίς δύναται σωθῆναι; whereas it was evidently to themselves (πρὸς ἑαυτούς) that the disciples said it. Aware that this time the 'antiquissimae quas sequi solet auctoritates ' stand self-condemned, instead of ingenuously avowing the fact, Tischendorf grounds his rejection of προς αυτον on the consideration that 'Mark never uses the expression λεγειν προς αυτον.' Just as if the text of one place in the Gospel is to be determined by the practice of the same Evangelist in another place,—and not by its own proper evidence ; which in the present instance is (the reader may be sure) simply overwhelming !

Westcott and Hort erroneously suppose that all the copies but four,—all the versions but one (the Bohairic),— may be in error : but that B-ℵ, C, and Cod. Δ which is curious in St. Mark, must needs be in the right.

§ 7.

There are many occasions—as I remarked before,— where the very logic of the case becomes a powerful argument. Worthless in and by themselves,—in the face, I mean, of general testimony,—considerations derived from the very reason of the thing sometimes vindicate their right to assist the judgement wherever the evidence is somewhat evenly balanced. But their cogency is felt to be altogether overwhelming when, after a careful survey of the evidence alone, we entertain no doubt whatever as to what must be the right reading of a place. They seem then to sweep the field. Such an occasion is presented by St. Luke

xvi. 9,—where our LORD, having shewn what provision the
dishonest steward made against the day when he would
find himself houseless,—the Divine Speaker infers that
something analogous should be done by ourselves with our
own money,—'in order' (saith He) 'that *when ye fail*, ye
may be received into the everlasting tabernacles.' The
logical consistency of all this is as exact, as the choice of
terms in the Original is exquisite : the word employed to
designate Man's departure out of this life (ἐκλίπητε), con-
veying the image of one fainting or failing at the end of
his race. It is in fact the word used in the LXX to denote
the peaceful end of Abraham, and of Ishmael, and of Isaac,
and of Jacob[1].

But instead of this, אBDLRΠ with AX present us with
εκλιπη or εκλειπη,—shewing that the author of this reading
imagined without discrimination, that what our LORD meant
to say was that when at last our money 'fails' us, we may
not want a home. The rest of the Uncials to the number
of twelve, together with two correctors of א, the bulk of
the Cursives, and the Old Latin copies, the Vulgate,
Gothic, Harkleian, and Ethiopic Versions, with Irenaeus[2],
Clemens Alex.[3], Origen[4], Methodius[5], Basil[6], Ephraem
Syrus[7], Gregory Naz.[8], Didymus[9], Chrysostom[10], Severianus[11], Jerome[12], Augustine[13], Eulogius[14], and Theodoret[15], also Aphraates (A. D. 325)[16], support the reading
ἐκλίπητε. Cyril appears to have known both readings[17].

---

[1] Gen. xxv. 8, 17; xxxv. 29; xlix. 33. Also Jer. xlii. 17, 22 ; Lament. i. 20;
Job xiii. 19 ; Ps. ciii. 30.
[2] 268, 661. [3] 942, 953 (Lat. Tr.). [4] 162, 338 (Lat. Tr.), 666.
[5] *ap.* Phot. 791. [6] i. 353. [7] iii. 120.
[8] i. 861. [9] 280. [10] i. 920; iii. 344; iv. 27; vi. 606.
[11] vi. 520. [12] i. 859 b. [13] 3ʲ. 772.
[14] Mai, 2. [15] i. 517. [16] 388.
[17] In one place of the Syriac version of his Homilies on St. Luke (Luc. 110),
the reading is plainly ἵνα ὅταν ἐκλίπητε : but when the Greek of the same
passage is exhibited by Mai (ii. 196, line 28–38) it is observed to be destitute of
the disputed clause. On the other hand, at p 512 of the Syriac, the reading is
ἐκλίπῃ. But then the entire quotation is absent from the Greek original (Mai,

His testimony, such as it is, can only be divined from his fragmentary remains; and 'divination' is a faculty to which I make no pretence.

In p. 349, after ὀεῖ δὲ πάντως αὐτοὺς ἀποπεσεῖν τῆς οἰκονομίας ἐπιπηδῶντος θανάτου, καὶ τῶν καθ' ἡμᾶς πραγμάτων ἐξελκότος. ἀδιάφυκτον γὰρ ἀνθρώπῳ παντὶ τοῦ θανάτου τὸν λίνον,—Cyril is represented as saying (6 lines lower down) ὅταν αὐτοὺς ὁ ἐπίγειος ἐκλείπῃ ΠΛΟΥΤΟΣ, with which corresponds the Syriac of Luc. 509. But when we encounter the same passage in Cramer's Catena (p. 122), besides the reference to death, ἀποπεσοῦνται πάντως τῆς οἰκονομίας, ἐπιπηδῶντος αὐτοῖς τοῦ θανάτου (lines 21–3), we are presented with ὅταν αὐτοὺς ἡ ἐπίγειος ἐκλείποι Ζωή, which clearly reverses the testimony. If Cyril wrote *that*, he read (like every other Father) ἐκλίπητε. It is only right to add that ἐκλίπῃ is found besides in pp. 525, 526 (= Mai ii. 358) and 572 of Cyril's Syriac Homilies on St. Luke. This however (like the quotation in p. 5c6) may well be due to the Peshitto. I must avow that amid so much conflicting evidence, my judgement concerning Cyril's text is at fault.

§ 8.

There is hardly to be found a more precious declaration concerning the guiding and illuminating office of the Holy Ghost, than our Lord's promise that 'when He, the Spirit of Truth shall come, He shall guide you into all the Truth': ὁδηγήσει ὑμᾶς εἰς πᾶσαν τὴν ἀλήθειαν (St. John xvi. 13). Now, the six words just quoted are found to have experienced an extraordinary amount of perturbation; far more than can be due to the fact that they happen to be the concluding words of a lection. To be brief,—every

ii. 349, line 11 from bottom). In Mai, ii. 380, Cyril's reading is certainly ἐκλίπητε.

known variety in reading this passage may be brought under one of three heads:—

1. With the first,—which is in fact a gloss, not a reading (διηγήσεται ὑμῖν τὴν ἀλήθειαν πᾶσαν),—we need not delay ourselves. Eusebius in two places [1], Cyril Jer. [2], copies of the Old Latin [3], and Jerome [4] in a certain place, so read the place. Unhappily the same reading is also found in the Vulgate [5]. It meets with no favour however, and may be dismissed.

2. The next, which even more fatally darkens our Lord's meaning, might have been as unceremoniously dealt with, the reading namely of Cod. L (ὁδηγήσει ὑμᾶς ἐν τῇ ἀληθείᾳ πάσῃ), but that unhappily it has found favour with Tischendorf,—I suppose, because with the exception of πάσῃ it is the reading of his own Cod. א [6]. It is thus that Cyril Alex. [7] thrice reads the place : and indeed the same thing practically is found in D [8]; while so many copies of the Old Latin exhibit *in omni veritate,* or *in veritate omni* [9], that one is constrained to inquire, How is ἐν ἀληθείᾳ πάσῃ to be accounted for?

We have not far to look. Ὁδηγεῖν followed by ἐν occurs in the LXX, chiefly in the Psalms, more than 16 times. Especially must the familiar expression in Ps. xxiv. 5 (ὁδήγησόν με ἐν τῇ ἀληθείᾳ σου, *Dirige me in veritate tua*), by inopportunely suggesting itself to the mind of some early copyist, have influenced the text of St. John xvi. 13 in this fatal way. One is only astonished that so acute a critic as Tischendorf should have overlooked so plain

---

[1] Eus. ᵐᵃʳᵉ 330, ·ᵖˢ 251 (—πᾶσαν).   [2] Cyr ʰʳ 270.

[3] e, *inducet vobis veritatem omnem* : m, *disseret vobis omnem veritatem.*

[4] *docebit vos omnem veritatem* (ii. 301).

[5] Cod. *am.* (which exhibits *docebit vos in omnem,* &c.) clearly confuses two distinct types.

[6] א om. πάσῃ.   [7] Cyr. Alex. iv. 347 ; v. 369, 593.

[8] D, ἐκεῖνος ὑμᾶς ὁδηγήσει ἐν τῇ ἀληθείᾳ πάσῃ.

[9] So Cod. b, *deducet vos in veritate omni.* Cod. c, *docebit vos in veritate omni.*

a circumstance. The constant use of the Psalm in Divine Service, and the entire familiarity with the Psalter resulting therefrom, explains sufficiently how it came to pass, that in this as in other places its phraseology must have influenced the memory.

3. The one true reading of the place (ὁδηγήσει ὑμᾶς εἰς πᾶσαν τὴν ἀλήθειαν) is attested by 12 of the uncials (EGHI[b]KMSUΓΔΛΠ), the whole body of the cursives, and by the following Fathers,—Didymus [1], Epiphanius [2], Basil [3], Chrysostom [4], Theodotus, bp. of Antioch [5], Cyril Alex.[6], Theodoret [7]; besides Tertullian in five places, Hilary and Jerome in two [8].

But because the words πᾶσαν τὴν ἀλήθειαν are found transposed in ABY alone of manuscripts, and because Peter Alex.[9], and Didymus[10] once, Origen [11] and Cyril Alex. [12] in two places, are observed to sanction the same infelicitous arrangement (viz. τὴν ἀλήθειαν πᾶσαν),—Lachmann, Tregelles, Alford, Westcott and Hort, adopt without hesitationt his order of the words [13]. It cannot of course be maintained. The candid reader in the meantime will not fail to note that as usual the truth has been preserved neither by A nor B nor D: least of all by ℵ: but comes down to us unimpaired in the great mass of MS. authorities, uncial and cursive, as well as in the oldest Versions and Fathers.

---

[1] Did. 278, 446, 388 (πρos), 443 (− την).   [2] Epiph. i. 898 ; ii. 78.
[3] Bas. iii. 42 (πρos: and so Evan. 249. Codd. of Cyril Alex. (ἐπι).
[4] Chrys. viii. 527: also 460, 461 (− την).   [5] Theod. ant 541, ap. Wegn.
[6] Cyr. Alex. txt iv. 923 : v. 628.   [7] Thdt. iii. 15 (ἐκεῖ. os ὑμ. ὁδ.).
[8] Tert. i. 762, 765, 884; ii. 11, 21. Hil. 805, 959. Jer. ii. 140. 141. There are many lesser variants :—' (diriget vos Tert. i. 884, deducet vos Tert. ii. 21, Vercell. vos deducet ; i. 762 vos ducet : Hil. 805, vos diriget) in omnem veritatem.' Some few (as D, Tert. i. 762 ; ii. 21. Cod. a, Did. 388. Thdrt. iii. 15) prefix ἐκεῖνος.
[9] Pet. Alex. ap. Routh, p. 9.   [10] Did. 55.
[11] Orig. i. 387, 388.   [12] Cyr. Alex. iv. 925, 986.
[13] εἰς τὴν ἀλ.ήθ. πᾶσαν L., Tr., W.-H.: ἐν τῇ ἀληθ. πάσῃ T.

§ 9.

It may have been anticipated by the readers of these pages that the Divine Author of Scripture has planted here and there up and down the sacred page—often in most improbable places and certainly in forms which we should have least of all imagined—tests of accuracy, by attending to which we may form an unerring judgement concerning the faithfulness of a copy of the sacred Text. This is a discovery which at first astonished me: but on mature reflection, I saw that it was to have been confidently anticipated. Is it indeed credible that Almighty Wisdom—which is observed to have made such abundant provision for the safety of the humblest forms of animal life, for the preservation of common seeds, often seeds of noxious plants,—should yet have omitted to make provision for the life-giving seed of His own Everlasting Word?

For example, strange to relate, it is a plain fact (of which every one may convince himself by opening a copy of the Gospels furnished with a sufficient critical apparatus), that although in relating the healing of the centurion's servant (St. Matt. viii. 5–13) the Evangelist writes ἑκατον-ταρχ̣ΟΣ in verses 5 and 8, he writes ἑκατονταρχῌ instead of -ΧΩ̣ in ver. 13. This minute variety has been faithfully retained by uncials and cursives alike. *Only* one uncial (viz. א) has ventured to assimilate the two places, writing ἑκατουταρχης throughout. With the blindness proverbially ascribed to parental love, Tischendorf follows א, though the carelessness that reigns over that MS. is visible to all who examine it.

The matter is a trifle confessedly. But so was the scrap of a ballad which identified the murderer, another scrap of it being found with the bullet in the body of the murdered man.

When we find καί disappearing before κρίσιν (in the

solemn statement ἐξουσίαν ἔδωκεν αὐτῷ [sc. ὁ Πατὴρ] ΚΑΙ κρίσιν ποιεῖν)[1], it nothing moves us to discover that 4 Greek Codexes (ABL 33), as many ancient versions[2], and as many ancient Fathers[3] are without that little but significant word. The fact that *all other Greek copies have it*, is conclusive for retaining it. And why? Because while nothing is more easily accounted for than the absence of καί in this place from a little handful of documents, quite inexplicable is its presence in all the rest[4] except on the hypothesis that it was found in the autograph of St. John.

§ 10.

Again, that pathetic anticipation of the lord of the vineyard (St. Luke xx. 13) that when the servants had once 'seen' his 'beloved son' (ἰδόντες), they would reverence him,—disappears under the baneful influence of אBCDLQ, and their little handful of adherents. (Consider in connexion with this the latter part of Is. liii. 2.) Does not the very repetition of ἰδόντες δέ, in the next verse, seem to demand the presence of the word which the Cursives almost to a manuscript have so jealously retained, but which Lachmann, Tischendorf, Tregelles, Alford, Westcott and Hort have expunged? .... Then further, the inward thoughts of the heart, those πονηροὶ διαλογισμοί of which our Saviour elsewhere speaks[5], and which were never more conspicuous than in the men who compassed His shameful death, become wellnigh obliterated from the parable. It was '*within* themselves' (St. Matt. xxi. 38)—'*to*

---

[1] St. John v. 27. [2] Bohairic, Cureton, Armenian, Ethiopic.

[3] Origen, ii. 548, 558; iv. 41, 359, 360; Didymus, Trin. iii. 17, *ap*. Chrys. viii. 230 a; Paul of Samos, Ath. Gen. v. 168 c; Thdrt. v. 1108.

[4] In the Old Lat., Peshitto and Harkleian, Chrys. viii. 229 d e; Cyril, iv. 235; v.[1] 562; v.[2] 177, 179 (= Conc. iii. 310, 311); Gennadius, Cord. Cat. in Ps i. 69.

[5] St. Matt. xv. 19.

themselves' (St. Mark xii. 7), He says, that those sinful men declared their murderous purpose. Their hearts it was, not their lips, which spoke. Hence St. Luke says plainly, 'they thought to themselves' (xx. 14). But we are now invited on yet slenderer evidence than before, instead of διελ. πρὸς ἑαυτούς, to read πρὸς ἀλλήλους, which is certainly wrong. .... Lastly, that murderous resolve of the servants, 'This is the heir: come, let us kill him' (Δεῦτε ἀποκτείνωμεν),—which (as every student knows) is nothing else but a quotation from the Septuagint version of Genesis (xxxvii. 19), is robbed of its characteristic word in deference to ARMQΠ and the Latin copies: Tischendorf, sheltering himself complacently behind the purblind as well as tasteless dictum of Schulz, —'Lucas nunquam usus est hoc verbo ': as if that were any reason why he might not quote the Septuagint! In this way, the providential care which caused that the same striking expression should find place in all the three Evangelists, is frustrated ; and it might even be overlooked by a reader of the third Gospel that Joseph is a divinely intended type of our Saviour Christ.

§ 11.

The instances which have been given in this chapter of the superiority of the text exhibited in the later Uncials and the Cursives might have been increased in number to almost any extent out of the papers left by Dean Burgon. The reader will find many more illustrations in the rest of these two volumes. Even Dr. Hort admits that the Traditional Text which is represented by them is 'entirely blameless on either literary or religious grounds as regards vulgarized or unworthy diction [1],' while 'repeated and

---

[1] Introduction, p. 135. The rest of his judgement is unfounded in fact. Constant and careful study combined with subtle appreciation will not reveal ' feebleness' or ' impoverishment' either in ' sense ' or ' force.'

diligent study ' can only lead, if conducted with deep and wide research, to the discovery of beauties and meanings which have lain unrevealed to the student before.

Let it be always borne in mind, that (*a*) the later Uncials and Cursives are the heirs in succession of numerous and varied lines of descent spread throughout the Church ; that (*b*) their verdict is nearly always decisive and clear ; and that nevertheless (*c*) such unanimity or majority of witnesses is not the testimony of mechanical or suborned testifiers, but is the coincidence, as facts unquestionably prove, except in certain instances of independent deponents to the same story.

Let me be allowed to declare [1] in conclusion that no person is competent to pronounce concerning the merits or demerits of cursive copies of the Gospels, who has not himself, in the first instance, collated with great exactness at least a few of them. He will be materially assisted, if it has ever fallen in his way to familiarize himself however partially with the text of vast numbers. But nothing can supply the place of exact collation of at least a few copies: of which labour, if a man has had no experience at all, he must submit to be assured that he really has no right to express himself confidently in this subject-matter. He argues, not from facts, but from his own imagination of what the facts of the case will probably be. Those only who have minutely collated several copies, and examined with considerable attention a large proportion of all the Sacred Codexes extant, are entitled to speak with authority here. Further, I venture to assert that no conviction will force itself so irresistibly on the mind of him who submits to the labour of exactly collating a few Cursive copies of the Gospels, as that the documents in question have been executed with even extraordinary diligence, fidelity, and skill. That history confirms this conviction, we have only

---

[1] These are the Dean's words to the end of the paragraph.

to survey the elaborate arrangements made in monasteries for carrying on the duty, and perfecting the art, of copying the Holy Scriptures.

If therefore this body of Manuscripts be thus declared by the excellence of its text, by the evident pains bestowed upon its production, as well as by the consentience with it of other evidence, to possess high characteristics; if it represents the matured settlement of many delicate and difficult questions by the Church which after centuries of vacillation more or less, and indeed less rather than more, was to last for a much larger number of centuries ; must it not require great deference indeed from all students of the New Testament? Let it always be remembered, that no single Cursive is here selected from the rest or advanced to any position whatsoever which would invest its verdicts with any special authority. It is the main body of the Cursives, agreeing as they generally do with the exception of a few eccentric groups or individuals, which is entitled to such respect according to the measure of their agreement. And in point of fact, the Cursives which have been collated are so generally consentient, as to leave no doubt that the multitude which needs collation will agree similarly. Doubtless, the later Uncials and the Cursives are only a class of the general evidence which is now before us : but it is desirable that those Textual Students who have been disposed to undervalue this class should weigh with candour and fairness the arguments existing in favour of it, which we have attempted to exhibit in this chapter.

CHAPTER XII.

CONCLUSION.

THE Traditional Text has now been traced, from the earliest years of Christianity of which any record of the New Testament remains, to the period when it was enshrined in a large number of carefully-written manuscripts in main accord with one another. Proof has been given from the writings of the early Fathers, that the idea that the Traditional Text arose in the middle of the fourth century is a mere hallucination, prompted by only a partial acquaintance with those writings. And witness to the existence and predominance of that form of Text has been found in the Peshitto Version and in the best of the Latin Versions, which themselves also have been followed back to the beginning of the second century or the end of the first. We have also discovered the truth, that the settlement of the Text, though mainly made in the fourth century, was not finally accomplished till the eighth century at the earliest; and that the later Uncials, not the oldest, together with the cursives express, not singly, not in small batches or companies, but in their main agreement, the decisions which had grown up in the Church. In so doing, attention has been paid to all the existing evidence : none has been omitted. *Quod semper, quod ubique, quod ab omnibus*, has been the underlying principle. The foundations of the building have been laid as deeply and as broadly as our power would allow. No other course would be in consonance with scientific procedure. The seven notes of truth have been made as comprehensive as possible. Antiquity, number, variety, weight, continuity, context, and internal evidence, include all points of view and all methods of examination which are really sound. The characters of the Vatican, Sinaitic, and Bezan manuscripts have been shewn to be bad, and the streams which led to their production from Syrio-Old-Latin and Alexandrian sources to the temporary school of Caesarea have been traced and explained. It has been also shewn to be probable that corruption began and took root even before the Gospels were written. The general conclusion which has grown upon our minds has been that the affections of Christians have not been misdirected; that the strongest exercise of reason has proved their instincts to have been sound and true; that the Text which we have used and loved rests upon a vast and varied support; that the multiform record of Manuscripts, Versions, and Fathers, is found to defend by large majorities in almost all instances those precious words of Holy Writ, which have been called in question during the latter half of this century.

We submit that it cannot be denied that we have presented a strong case, and naturally we look to see what has been said against it, since except in some features it has been before the World and the Church for some years. We submit that it has not received due attention from opposing critics. If indeed the opinions of the other School had been preceded by, or grounded upon, a searching examination, such as we have made in the case of B and ℵ, of the vast mass of evidence upon which we rest,—if this great body of testimony had been proved to be bad from overbalancing testimony or otherwise,—we should have found reason for doubt, or even for a reversal of our decisions. But Lachmann, Tregelles, and Tischendorf laid down principles chiefly, if not exclusively, on the score of their intrinsic probability. Westcott and Hort built up their own theory upon reasoning internal to it, without clearing the ground first by any careful and detailed scrutiny. Besides which, all of them constructed their buildings before travellers by railways and steamships had placed within their reach the larger part of the materials which are now ready for use. We hear constantly the proclamation made in dogmatic tones that they are right: no proof adequate to the strength of our contention has been worked out to shew that we are wrong.

Nevertheless, it may be best to listen for a moment to such objections as have been advanced against conclusions like these, and which it may be presumed will be urged again.

1. 'After all it cannot be denied that B and ℵ are the oldest manuscripts of the New Testament in existence, and that they must therefore be entitled to the deference due to their age.' Now the earlier part of this allegation is conceded by us entirely: *prima facie* it constitutes a very strong argument. But it is really found on examination to be superficial. Fathers and Versions are virtually older, and, as has been demonstrated, are dead against the claim set up on behalf of those ancient manuscripts, that they are the possessors of the true text of the Gospels. Besides which antiquity is not the sole note of truth any more than number is. So much has been already said on this part of the subject, that it is needless to enter into longer discussion here.

2. 'The testimony of witnesses ought to be weighed before it is reckoned.' Doubtless: this also is a truism, and allowance has been made for it in the various 'notes of truth.' But this argument, apparently so simple, is really intended to carry a huge assumption involved in an elaborate maintenance of the (supposed) excellent character of B and ℵ and their associates. After so much

that has been brought to the charge of those two MSS. in this treatise, it is unnecessary now to urge more than that they appeared in strange times, when the Church was convulsed to her centre ; that, as has been demonstrated, their peculiar readings were in a very decided minority in the period before them ; and, as all admit, were rejected in the ages that passed after the time of their date.

3. It is stated that the Traditional is a conflate text, i.e. that passages have been put together from more than one other text, so that they are composite in construction instead of being simple. We have already treated this allegation, but we reply now that it has not been established : the opinion of Canon Cooke who analysed all the examples quoted by Hort[1], of Scrivener who said they proved nothing[2], and of many other critics and scholars has been against it. The converse position is maintained, that the text of B and ℵ is clipped and mutilated. Take the following passage, which is fairly typical of the large class in question : 'For we are members of His Body' (writes St. Paul[3]) 'of His flesh and of His bones' ($\dot{\epsilon}\kappa$ $\tau\hat{\eta}s$ $\sigma\alpha\rho\kappa\dot{o}s$ $\alpha\dot{v}\tau o\hat{v}$ $\kappa\alpha\dot{\iota}$ $\dot{\epsilon}\kappa$ $\tau\hat{\omega}\nu$ $\dot{o}\sigma\tau\dot{\epsilon}\omega\nu$ $\alpha\dot{v}\tau o\hat{v}$). But those last 9 words are disallowed by recent editors, because they are absent from B-ℵ, A, 8, and 17, and the margin of 67, besides the Bohairic version. Yet are the words genuine. They are found in DFGKLP and the whole body of the cursives : in the Old Latin and Vulgate and the two Syriac versions : in Irenaeus[4],—in Theodorus of Mopsuestia[5],—in Nilus[6],— in Chrysostom[7] more than four times,— in Severianus[8],— in Theodoret[9],— in Anastasius Sinaita[10],— and in John Damascene[11]. They were probably read by

---

[1] Revised Version, &c., pp. 205-218.
[2] Introduction, i. 292-93.
[3] Ephes. v. 30.
[4] 718 (Mass. 294), Gr. and Lat.
[5] *In loc.* ed. Swete, Gr. and Lat.
[6] i. 95, 267.
[7] iii. 215 b, 216 a ; viii. 272 c ; xi. 147 a b c d.
[8] *Ap.* Cramer, vi. 205, 2c8.
[9] iii. 434.
[10] (A.D. 560), 1004 a, 1007 a.
[11] ii. 190 e.

Origen[1] and by Methodius[2]. Many Latin Fathers, viz. Ambrose[3], — Pacian[4], — Esaias abb.[5], — Victorinus[6], — Jerome[7], — Augustine[8] — and Leo P.[9] recognise them.

Such ample and such varied attestation is not to be set aside by the vapid and unsound dictum 'Western and Syrian,'—or by the weak suggestion that the words in dispute are an unauthorized gloss, fabricated from the LXX version of Gen. ii. 23. That St. Paul's allusion is to the oracular utterance of our first father Adam, is true enough : but, as Alford after Bengel well points out, it is incredible that any forger can have been at work here.

Such questions however, as we must again and again insist, are not to be determined by internal considerations : no, — nor by dictation, nor by prejudice, nor by divination, nor by any subjective theory of conflation on which experts and critics may be hopelessly at issue : but by the weight of the definite evidence actually producible and

---

[1] Rufinus (iii. 61 c) translates,—'quia membra sumus corporis ejus, *et reliqua.*' What else can this refer to but the very words in dispute?

[2] *Ap.* Galland. iii. 688 c:—ὅθεν ὁ Ἀπόστολος εὐθυβόλως εἰς Χριστὸν ἀνηκόντισε τὰ κατὰ τὸν Ἀδάμ· οὕτως γὰρ ἂν μάλιστα ἐκ τῶν ὀστῶν αὐτοῦ καὶ τῆς σαρκὸς τὴν ἐκκλησίαν συμφωνήσει γεγονέναι.   And lower down (e, and 689 a) :—ὅπως αὐξηθῶσιν οἱ ἐν αὐτῷ οἰκοδομηθέντες ἅπαντες, οἱ γεγεννημένοι διὰ τοῦ λουτροῦ, ἐκ τῶν ὀστῶν καὶ ἐκ τῆς σαρκός, τουτέστιν ἐκ τῆς ἁγιωσύνης αὐτοῦ, καὶ ἐκ τῆς δόξης προσειληφότες· ὀστᾶ γὰρ καὶ σάρκα Σοφίας ὁ λέγων εἶναι σύνεσιν καὶ ἀρετήν, ὀρθότατα λέγει.   From this it is plain that Methodius read Ephes. v. 30 as we do ; although he had before quoted it (iii. 614 b) *without* the clause in dispute. Those who give their minds to these studies are soon made aware that it is never safe to infer from the silence of a Father that he disallowed the words he omits,—especially if those words are in their nature parenthetical, or supplementary, or not absolutely required for the sense. Let a short clause be beside his immediate purpose, and a Father is as likely as not to omit it. This subject has been discussed elsewhere : but it is apt to the matter now in hand that I should point out that Augustine *twice* (iv. 297 c, 1438 c) closes his quotation of the present place abruptly : 'Apostolo dicente, *Quoniam membra sumus corporis ejus.*' And yet, elsewhere (iii. 794), he gives the words in full. It is idle therefore to urge on the opposite side, as if there were anything in it, the anonymous commentator on St. Luke in Cramer's Cat. p. 88.

[3] i. 1310 b. Also Ambrosiaster, ii. 248 d.

[4] *Ap.* Galland. vii. 262 e (A.D. 372).

[5] Ibid. 314 c.

[6] Mai, iii. 140.

[7] vii. 659 b.

[8] See above, end of note 2.

[9] Concil. iv. 50 b.

produced on either side. And when, as in the present
instance, Antiquity, Variety of testimony, Respectability
of witnesses, and Number are overwhelmingly in favour
of the Traditional Text, what else is it but an outrage
on the laws of evidence to claim that the same little
band of documents which have already come before us
so often, and always been found in error, even though
aided by speculative suppositions, shall be permitted to
outweigh all other testimony?

To build therefore upon a conflate or composite character
in a set of readings would be contrary to the evidence:—or
at any rate, it would at the best be to lay foundations upon
ground which is approved by one school of critics and
disputed by the other in every case. The determination
of the text of Holy Scripture has not been handed over
to a mere conflict of opposite opinions, or to the uncertain
sands of conjecture.

Besides, as has been already stated, no amount of
conflation would supply passages which the destructive
school would wholly leave out. It is impossible to 'conflate'
in places where B$\aleph$ and their associates furnish no materials for the supposed conflation. Bricks cannot be made
without clay. The materials actually existing are those
of the Traditional Text itself. But in fact these questions
are not to be settled by the scholarly taste or opinions of
either school, even of that which we advocate. They must
rest upon the verdict found by the facts in evidence: and
those facts have been already placed in array.

4. Again, stress is laid upon Genealogy. Indeed, as Dean
Burgon himself goes on to say, so much has lately been
written about 'the principle' and 'the method' 'of genealogy,' that it becomes in a high degree desirable that we
should ascertain precisely what those expressions lawfully
mean. No fair controversialist would willingly fail to
assign its legitimate place and value to any principle for

which he observes an opponent eagerly contending. But here is a 'principle' and here is a 'method' which are declared to be of even paramount importance. 'Documents ... are all fragments, usually casual and scattered fragments, of a genealogical tree of transmission, sometimes of vast extent and intricacy. The more exactly we are able to trace the chief ramifications of the tree, and to determine the places of the several documents among the branches, the more secure will be the foundations laid for a criticism capable of distinguishing the original text from its successive corruptions [1].'

The expression is metaphorical; belonging of right to families of men, but transferred to Textual Science as indicative that similar phenomena attend families of manuscripts. Unfortunately the phenomena attending transmission,—of Natures on the one hand, of Texts on the other,—are essentially dissimilar. A diminutive couple may give birth to a race of giants. A genius has been known to beget a dunce. A brood of children exhibiting extraordinary diversities of character, aspect, ability, sometimes spring from the same pair. Nothing like this is possible in the case of honestly-made copies of MSS. The analogy breaks down therefore in respect of its most essential feature. And yet, there can be no objection to the use of the term 'Genealogy' in connexion with manuscripts, provided always that nothing more is meant thereby than derivation by the process of copying: nothing else claimed but that 'Identity of reading implies identity of origin [2].'

Only in this limited way are we able to avail ourselves of the principle referred to. Of course if it were a well-ascertained fact concerning three copies (XYZ), that Z was copied from Y, and Y from X, XYZ might reasonably be spoken of as representing three descents in a pedigree; although the interval between Z and Y were only six

---

[1] Hort, Introduction, p. 40.   [2] Ibid. p. 46.

months,—the interval between Y and X, six hundred years. Moreover, these would be not three independent authorities, but only one. Such a case, however,—(the fact cannot be too clearly apprehended),—is simply non-existent. What is known commonly lies on the surface:—viz. that occasionally between two or more copies there exists such an amount of peculiar textual affinity as to constrain us to adopt the supposition that they have been derived from a common original. These peculiarities of text, we tell ourselves, cannot be fortuitous. Taking our stand on the true principle that 'identity of reading implies identity of origin,' we insist on reasoning from the known to the unknown: and (at our humble distance) we are fully as confident of our scientific fact as Adams and Le Verrier would have been of the existence of Neptune had they never actually obtained sight of that planet.

So far are we therefore from denying the value and importance of the principle under discussion that we are able to demonstrate its efficacy in the resolution of some textual problems which have been given in this work. Thus E, the uncial copy of St. Paul, is 'nothing better,' says Scrivener, 'than a transcript of the Cod. Claromontanus' D. 'The Greek is manifestly worthless, and should long since have been removed from the list of authorities[1].' Tischendorf nevertheless, not Tregelles, quotes it on every page. He has no business to do so, Codexes D and E, to all intents and purposes, being *strictly one Codex*. This case, like the two next, happily does not admit of diversity of opinion. Next, F and G of St. Paul's Epistles, inasmuch as they are confessedly derived from one and the same archetype, are not to be reckoned as two authorities, but as one.

Again, the correspondence between the nine MSS. of the Ferrar group—Evann. 13 at Paris, 69 at Leicester, 124 at

[1] Miller's Scrivener, Introduction, I. p. 177.

Vienna, 346 at Milan, 556 in the British Museum, 561 at Bank House, Wisbech,—and in a lesser degree, 348 at Milan, 624 at Crypta Ferrata, 788 at Athens, — is so extraordinary as to render it certain that these copies are in the main derived from one common archetype[1]. Hence, though one of them (788) is of the tenth century, three (348, 561, 624) are of the eleventh, four (13, 124, 346, 556) of the twelfth, and one (69) of the fourteenth, their joint evidence is held to be tantamount to the recovery of a lost uncial or papyrus of very early date, — which uncial or papyrus, by the way, it would be convenient to indicate by a new symbol, as F^r. standing for Ferrar, since Φ which was once attributed to them is now appropriated to the Codex Beratinus.   If indicated numerically, the figures should at all events be connected by a hyphen (13-69-124-346-&c.); not as if they were independent witnesses, as Tischendorf quotes them.   And lastly, B and ℵ are undeniably, more than any other two Codexes which can be named, the depositaries of one and the same peculiar, all but unique, text.

I propose to apply the foregoing remarks to the solution of one of the most important of Textual problems.   That a controversy has raged around the last twelve verses of St. Mark's Gospel is known to all.   Known also it is that a laborious treatise was published on the subject in 1871, which, in the opinion of competent judges, has had the effect of removing the 'Last Twelve Verses of St. Mark' beyond the reach of suspicion.   Notwithstanding this, at the end of ten years an attempt was made to revive the old plea.   The passage, say Drs. Westcott and Hort, 'manifestly cannot claim any Apostolic authority; but is doubtless founded on some tradition of the Apostolic age,' of which the 'precise date must remain **unknown**.'   It is 'a **very** early interpolation' (pp. 51, 46).   **In a word**, 'the

---

[1] Introduction, I. Appendix F, p. 398*.

last twelve verses' of St. Mark's Gospel, according to Drs. Westcott and Hort, are spurious. But what is their ground of confidence? for we claim to be as competent to judge of testimony as they. It proves to be 'the unique criterion supplied by the concord of the independent attestations of ℵ and B' (p. 46).

'Independent attestations'! But when two copies of the Gospel are confessedly derived from one and the same original, how can their 'attestations' be called 'independent'? This is however greatly to understate the case. The non-independence of B and ℵ in respect of St. Mark xvi. 9–20 is absolutely unique : for, strange to relate, it so happens that the very leaf on which the end of St. Mark's Gospel and the beginning of St. Luke's is written (St. Mark xvi. 2–Luke i. 56), is one of the six leaves of Cod. ℵ which are held to have been written by the scribe of Cod. B. 'The inference,' remarks Scrivener, 'is simple and direct, that at least in these leaves Codd. Bℵ make but one witness, not two[1].'

The principle of Genealogy admits of a more extended and a more important application to this case, because B and ℵ do not stand quite alone, but are exclusively associated with three or four other manuscripts which may be regarded as being descended from them. As far as we can judge, they may be regarded as the founders, or at least as prominent members of a family, whose descendants were few, because they were generally condemned by the generations which came after them. Not they, but other families upon other genealogical stems, were the more like to the patriarch whose progeny was to equal the stars of heaven in multitude.

Least of all shall I be so simple as to pretend to fix the

---

[1] Introduction, II. 337, note 1. And for Dean Burgon's latest opinion on the date of ℵ see above, pp. 46, 52, 162. The present MS., which I have been obliged to abridge in order to avoid repetition of much that has been already said, was one of the Dean's latest productions. See Appendix VII.

precise date and assign a definite locality to the fontal source, or sources, of our present perplexity and distress. But I suspect that in the little handful of authorities which have acquired such a notoriety in the annals of recent Textual Criticism, at the head of which stand Codexes B and ℵ, are to be recognized the characteristic features of a lost family of (once well known) second or third-century documents, which owed their existence to the misguided zeal of some well-intentioned but utterly incompetent persons who devoted themselves to the task of correcting the Text of Scripture; but were entirely unfit for the undertaking [1].

Yet I venture also to think that it was in a great measure at Alexandria that the text in question was fabricated. My chief reasons for thinking so are the following: (1) There is a marked resemblance between the peculiar readings of Bℵ and the two Egyptian Versions,— the Bohairic or Version of Lower Egypt especially. (2) No one can fail to have been struck by the evident sympathy between Origen,—who at all events had passed more than half his life at Alexandria, — and the text in question. (3) I notice that Nonnus also, who lived in the Thebaid, exhibits considerable sympathy with the text which I deem so corrupt. (4) I cannot overlook the fact that Cod. ℵ was discovered in a monastery under the sway of the patriarch of Alexandria, though how it got there no evidence remains to point out. (5) The licentious handling so characteristic of the Septuagint Version of the O. T.,—the work of Alexandrian Jews,—points in the same direction, and leads me to suspect that Alexandria was the final source of the text of B-ℵ. (6) I further observe that the sacred Text (κείμενον) in Cyril's Homilies

[1] Since Dean Burgon's death, there has been reason to identify this set of readings with the Syrio-Low-Latin Text, the first origin of which I have traced to the earliest times before the Gospels were written — by St. Matthew, St. Mark, and St. Luke, and of course St. John.

on St. John is often similar to B-א; and this, I take for granted, was the effect of the school of Alexandria,—not of the patriarch himself. (7) Dionysius of Alexandria complains bitterly of the corrupt Codexes of his day: and certainly (8) Clemens habitually employed copies of a similar kind. He too was of Alexandria[1].

Such are the chief considerations which incline me to suspect that Alexandria contributed largely to our Textual troubles.

The readings of B-א are the consequence of a junction of two or more streams and then of derivation from a single archetype. This inference is confirmed by the fact that the same general text which B exhibits is exhibited also by the eighth-century Codex L, the work probably of an Egyptian scribe[2]: and by the tenth-century Codex 33 : and by the eleventh-century Codex 1 : and to some extent by the twelfth-century Codex 69.

We have already been able to advance to another and a very important step. There is nothing in the history of the earliest times of the Church to prove that vellum manuscripts of the New Testament existed in any number before the fourth century. No such documents have come down to us. But we do know, as has been shewn above[3], that writings on papyrus were transcribed on vellum in the library of Caesarea. What must we then conclude? That, as has been already suggested, papyrus MSS. are mainly the progenitors of the Uncials, and probably of the oldest Uncials. Besides this inference, we have seen that it is also most probable that many of the Cursives were transcribed directly from papyrus books or rolls. So that the Genealogy of manuscripts of the New Testament includes a vast number of descendants, and many lines of descent, which ramified from one stem on the original start from

---

[1] So with St. Athanasius in his earlier days. See above, p. 119, note 2.
[2] Miller's Scrivener, Introduction, I. 138.   [3] pp. 2, 155.

the autograph of each book. The Vatican and the Sinaitic do not stand pre-eminent because of any great line of parentage passing through them to a multitudinous posterity inheriting the earth, but they are members of a condemned family of which the issue has been small. The rejected of the fourth century has been spurned by succeeding centuries. And surely now also the fourth century, rich in a roll of men conspicuous ever since for capacity and learning, may be permitted to proclaim its real sentiments and to be judged from its own decisions, without being disfranchised by critics of the nineteenth.

The history of the Traditional Text, on the contrary, is continuous and complete under the view of Genealogy. The pedigree of it may be commended to the examination of the Heralds' College. It goes step by step in unbroken succession regularly back to the earliest time. The present printed editions may be compared for extreme accuracy with the text passed by the Elzevirs or Beza as the text received by all of their time. Erasmus followed his few MSS. because he knew them to be good representatives of the mind of the Church which had been informed under the ceaseless and loving care of mediaeval transcribers: and the text of Erasmus printed at Basle agreed in but little variation with the text of the Complutensian editors published in Spain, for which Cardinal Ximenes procured MSS. at whatever cost he could. No one doubts the coincidence in all essential points of the printed text with the text of the Cursives. Dr. Hort certifies the Cursive Text as far back as the middle of the fourth century. It depends upon various lines of descent, and rests on the testimony supplied by numerous contemporary Fathers before the year 1000 A. D., when co-existing MSS. failed to bear witness in multitudes. The acceptance of it by the Church of the fifth century, which saw the settlement of the great doctrinal controversies either made or confirmed, proves that the seal was set upon the validity of the earliest pedigrees by the illustrious intellects and the sound faith of those days. And in the fifth chapter of this work, contemporary witness is carried back to the first days. There is thus a cluster of pedigrees, not in one line but in many parallel courses of descent, not in one country but in several, ranging over the whole Catholic Church where Greek was understood, attested by Versions, and illustrated copiously by Fathers, along which without break in the continuity the Traditional Text in its main features has been transmitted. Doubtless something still remains for the Church to do under the present extraordinary wealth of authorities in the verification of some particulars issuing in a small number of alterations, not in challenging or changing like the other school anything approaching to one-eighth of the New Testament[1]: for that we now possess in the main the very Words of the Holy Gospels as they issued from their inspired authors, we are taught under the principle of Genealogy that there is no valid reason to doubt.

To conclude, the system which we advocate will be seen to contrast strikingly with that which is upheld by the opposing school, in three general ways :

I. We have with us width and depth against the narrowness on their side. They are conspicuously contracted in the fewness of the witnesses which they deem worthy of credence. They are restricted as to the period of history which alone they consider to deserve attention. They are confined with regard to the countries from which their testimony comes. They would supply Christians with a shortened text, and educate them under a cast-iron system. We on the contrary champion the many against the few : we welcome all witnesses, and weigh all testimony : we uphold all the ages against one or two, and

---

[1] Hort, Introduction, p. 2.

all the countries against a narrow space. We maintain the genuine and all-round Catholicism of real Christendom against a discarded sectarianism exhumed from the fourth century. If we condemn, it is because the evidence condemns. We cling to all the precious Words that have come down to us, because they have been so preserved to our days under verdicts depending upon overwhelming proof.

II. We oppose facts to their speculation. They exalt B and ℵ and D because in their own opinion those copies are the best. They weave ingenious webs, and invent subtle theories, because their paradox of a few against the many requires ingenuity and subtlety for its support. Dr. Hort revelled in finespun theories and technical terms, such as 'Intrinsic Probability,' 'Transcriptional Probability,' 'Internal evidence of Readings,' 'Internal evidence of Documents,' which of course connote a certain amount of evidence, but are weak pillars of a heavy structure. Even conjectural emendation [1] and inconsistent decrees [2] are not rejected. They are infected with the theorizing which spoils some of the best German work, and with the idealism which is the bane of many academic minds, especially at Oxford and Cambridge. In contrast with this sojourn in cloudland, we are essentially of the earth though not earthy. We are nothing, if we are not grounded in facts : our appeal is to facts, our test lies in facts, so far as we can we build testimonies upon testimonies and pile facts on facts. We imitate the procedure of the courts of justice in decisions resulting from the converging product of all the evidence, when it has been cross-examined and sifted. As men of business, not less than students, we endeavour to pursue the studies of the library according to the best methods of the world.

III. Our opponents are gradually getting out of date : the world is drifting away from them. Thousands of

[1] Hort, Introduction, p. 7.   [2] Quarterly Review, No. 363, July, 1895.

manuscripts have been added to the known stores since Tischendorf formed his system, and Hort began to theorize, and their handful of favourite documents has become by comparison less and less. Since the deaths of both of those eminent critics, the treasures dug up in Egypt and elsewhere have put back the date of the science of palaeography from the fourth century after the Christian era to at least the third century before, and papyrus has sprung up into unexpected prominence in the ancient and mediaeval history of writing. It is discovered that there was no uncial period through which the genealogy of cursives has necessarily passed. Old theories on those points must generally be reconstructed if they are to tally with known facts. But this accession of knowledge which puts our opponents in the wrong, has no effect on us except to confirm our position with new proof. Indeed, we welcome the unlocking of the all but boundless treasury of ancient wealth, since our theory, being as open as possible, and resting upon the visible and real, remains not only uninjured but strengthened. If it were to require any re-arrangement, that would be only a re-ordering of particulars, not of our principles which are capacious enough to admit of any addition of materials of judgement. We trust to the Church of all the ages as the keeper and witness of Holy Writ, we bow to the teaching of the HOLY GHOST, as conveyed in all wisdom by facts and evidence: and we are certain, that, following no preconceived notions of our own, but led under such guidance, moved by principles so reasonable and comprehensive, and observing rules and instructions appealing to us with such authority, we are in all main respects

STANDING UPON THE ROCK.

APPENDIX I.

HONEYCOMB—ἀπὸ μελισσίου κηρίου.

[The Dean left positive instructions for the publication of this Dissertation, as being finished for Press.]

I PROPOSE next to call attention to the omission from St. Luke xxiv. 42 of a precious incident in the history of our Lord's Resurrection. It was in order effectually to convince the Disciples that it was Himself, in His human body, who stood before them in the upper chamber on the evening of the first Easter Day, that He inquired, [ver. 41] 'Have ye here any meat? [ver. 42] and they gave Him a piece of a broiled fish, AND OF AN HONEYCOMB.' But those four last words (καὶ ἀπὸ μελισσίου κηρίου) because they are not found in six copies of the Gospel, are by Westcott and Hort ejected from the text. Calamitous to relate, the Revisers of 1881 were by those critics persuaded to exclude them also. How do men suppose that such a clause as that established itself universally in the sacred text, if it be spurious? 'How do you suppose,' I shall be asked in reply, 'if it be genuine, that such a clause became omitted from any manuscript at all?'

I answer,—The omission is due to the prevalence in the earliest age of fabricated exhibitions of the Gospel narrative; in which, singular to relate, the incident recorded in St. Luke xxiv. 41–43 was identified with that other mysterious repast which St. John describes in his last chapter[1].

[1] St. John xxi. 9–13.

It seems incredible, at first sight, that an attempt would
ever be made to establish an enforced harmony between
incidents exhibiting so many points of marked contrast :
for St. Luke speaks of (1) 'broiled fish [ἰχθύος ὀπτοῦ] and
honeycomb,' (2) which '*they* gave *Him*,' (3) 'and *He* did
eat' (4) on the first Easter Day, (5) at evening, (6) in
a chamber, (7) at Jerusalem :—whereas St. John specifies
(1) '*bread*, and fish [ὀψάριον] likewise,' (2) which *He* gave
them, (3) and of which it is not related that Himself partook. (4) The occasion was subsequent : (5) the time,
early morning : (6) the scene, the sea-shore : (7) the country, Galilee.

Let it be candidly admitted on the other hand, in the
way of excuse for those ancient men, that 'broiled fish'
was common to both repasts ; that they both belong to the
period subsequent to the Resurrection : that the same
parties, our LORD namely and His Apostles, were concerned in either transaction ; and that both are prefaced
by similar words of inquiry. Waiving this, it is a plain
fact that Eusebius in his 9th Canon, makes the two incidents parallel ; numbering St. Luke (xxix. 41-3), § 341 ;
and St. John (xxi. 9, 10, 12, first half, and 13), severally
§§ 221, 223, 225. The Syriac sections which have hitherto
escaped the attention of critical scholars[1] are yet more
precise. Let the intention of their venerable compiler—
whoever he may have been—be exhibited in full. It has
never been done before :—

'(ST. LUKE xxiv.)

'§ 397. [Jesus] said unto
them, Have ye here any meat?
(ver. 41.)
'*Id.* . . . .

'(ST. JOHN xxi.)

'§ 255. Jesus saith unto them,
Children, have ye any meat?
They answered Him, No. (ver. 5.)
'§ 259. . . . As soon then as
they were come to land, they saw

[1] In Studia Biblica et Eccles. II. vi. (G. H. Gwilliam), published two years
after the Dean's death, will be found a full description of this form of sections.

(St. Luke xxiv.)	(St. John xxi.)
	a fire of coals there, and fish laid thereon, and bread. (ver. 9.)
'§ 398. And they gave Him a piece of a broiled fish and of an honeycomb. (ver. 42.)	'§ 264. Jesus then cometh and taketh bread, and giveth them, and fish likewise. (ver. 13.)
'§ 399. And He took it and did eat before them. (ver. 43.)'	'§ 262. Jesus saith unto them, Come and dine. (ver. 12.)'

The intention of all this is unmistakable. The places are deliberately identified. But the mischief is of much older date than the Eusebian Canons, and must have been derived in the first instance from a distinct source. Eusebius, as he himself informs us, did but follow in the wake of others. Should the Diatessaron of Ammonius or that of Tatian ever be recovered, a flood of light will for the first time be poured over a department of evidence where at present we must be content to grope our way[1].

But another element of confusion I suspect is derived from that lost Commentary on the Song of Solomon in which Origen is said to have surpassed himself[2]. Certain of the ancients insist on discovering in St. Luke xxiv. 42 the literal fulfilment of the Greek version of Cant. v. 1, ' I ate my *bread* with *honey*.' Cyril of Jerusalem remarks that those words of the spouse 'were fulfilled' when 'they gave Him a piece of a broiled fish and of an honeycomb[3]': while Gregory Nyss. points out (alluding to the same place) that 'the true Bread,' when He appeared to His Disciples, ' was by honeycomb made sweet[4].' Little did those

[1] As far as we know at present about Tatian's Diatessaron, he kept these occurrences distinct.—ED.
[2] 'Origenes, quum in caeteris libris omnes vicerit, in Cantico Canticorum ipse se vicit.'—Hieron. Opp. iii. 499 ; i. 525.
[3] After quoting Luke xxiv. 41, 42 *in extenso*, he proceeds,—βλέπεις πῶς πεπλήρωται τό· Ἔφαγον ἄρτον μου μετὰ μέλιτός μου (p. 210 b): and καὶ μετὰ τὴν ἀναστασιν ἔλεγεν, Ἔφαγον τὸν ἄρτον μετὰ μέλιτός μου. ἔδωκαν γὰρ αὐτῷ ἀπὸ μελισσίου κηρίου (p. 341 a).
[4] Ἄρτος γίνεται, οὐκέτι ἐπὶ πικρίδων ἐσθιόμενος ... ἀλλ' ὄψον ἑαυτῷ τὸ μέλι

Fathers imagine the perplexity which at the end of 15 centuries their fervid and sometimes fanciful references to Scripture would occasion!

I proceed to shew how inveterately the ancients have confused these two narratives, or rather these two distinct occasions. 'Who knows not,' asks Epiphanius, 'that our SAVIOUR ate, after His Resurrection from the dead? As the holy Gospels of Truth have it, "There was given unto Him" [which is a reference to St. Luke], " bread and part of a broiled fish." [but it is St. John who mentions the bread];—"and He took and ate" [but only according to St. Luke], "and gave to His disciples," [but only according to St. John. And yet the reference must be to St. Luke's narrative, for Epiphanius straightway adds,] " as He *also* did at the sea of Tiberias ; both eating," [although *no* eating on His part is recorded concerning *that* meal,] "and distributing¹."' Ephraem Syrus makes the same misstatement. 'If He was not flesh,' he asks, ' who was it, at the sea of Tiberias, who ate²?' 'While Peter is fishing,' says Hesychius³, (with plain reference to the narrative in St. John), 'behold in the LORD'S hands bread and honeycomb⁴': where the ' honeycomb' has clearly lost its way, and has thrust out the ' fish.' Epiphanius elsewhere even more fatally confuses the two incidents. 'JESUS' (he says) 'on a second occasion after His Resurrection ate both a piece of a broiled fish and some honeycomb⁵.' One would have set this down to sheer inadvertence, but that

ποιούμενος. And, ὁ μετὰ τὴν ἀνάστασιν προφανεὶς τοῖς μαθηταῖς ἄρτος ἐστί, τῷ κηρίῳ τοῦ μέλιτος ἡδυνόμενος,—i. 624 a b. See more concerning this quotation below, p. 249 note.

¹ Epiph. i. 143.   ² Ephr. Syr. ii. 48 e.

³ Or whoever else was the author of the first Homily of the Resurrection, wrongly ascribed to Gregory Nyss. (iii. 382-99). Hesychius was probably the author of the second Homily. (Last Twelve Verses, &c., pp. 57-9.) Both are *compilations* however, into which precious passages of much older Fathers have been unscrupulously interwoven,—to the infinite perplexity of every attentive reader.

⁴ *Apud* Greg. Nyss. iii. 399 d.   ⁵ Epiph. i. 652 d.

Jerome circumstantially makes the self-same assertion :—
' In John we read that while the Apostles were fishing, He
stood upon the shore, and ate part of a broiled **fish and
honeycomb**. At Jerusalem He is not related to have done
anything of the kind[1].' From whom can Jerome have
derived that wild statement[2]? It is certainly not his own.
It occurs in his letter to Hedibia where he is clearly
a translator only[3]. In another place, Jerome says, ' He
sought fish broiled upon the coals, in order to confirm
the faith of His doubting Apostles, who were afraid to
approach Him, because they thought they saw a spirit,
—not a solid body[4]': which is a mixing up of St. John's
narrative with that of St. Luke. Clemens Alex., in a passage which has hitherto escaped notice, deliberately affirms
that ' the LORD blessed the loaves and the broiled fishes
with which He feasted His Disciples[5].' Where did he find
that piece of information ?

One thing more in connexion with the ' broiled fish *and
honeycomb*.' Athanasius—and Cyril Alex.[6] after him—
rehearse the incident with entire accuracy ; but Athanasius
adds the apocryphal statement that ' He took what remained
over, and gave it unto them[7]': which tasteless appendix is
found besides in Cureton's Syriac [not in the Lewis],—in
the Bohairic, Harkleian, Armenian, and Ethiopic Versions ;
and must once have prevailed to a formidable extent, for

---

[1] In Joanne legimus quod piscantibus Apostolis, in littore steterit, et partem
assi piscis, favumque comederit, quae verae resurrectionis indicia sunt. In
Jerusalem autem nihil horum fecisse narratur.—Hieron. i. 825 a.

[2] Not from Eusebius' Qu. ad Marinum apparently. Compare however
Jerome, i. 824 d with Eusebius (*ap.* Mai), iv. 295 (cap. x).

[3] See Last Twelve Verses, &c., pp. 51–6.   [4] i. 444 b.

[5] p. 172.   [6] iv. 1108 c.

[7] Athanas. i. 644 : καὶ φαγὼν ἐνώπιον αὐτῶν, ΛΑΒΩΝ ΤΑ ΕΠΙΛΟΙΠΑ,
ἀπέδωκεν αὐτοῖς. This passage reappears in the fragmentary Commentary
published by Mai (ii. 582), divested only of the words καὶ ἀπὸ μελ. κηρ.—The
characteristic words (in capitals) do not appear in Epiphanius (i. 143 c), who
merely says καὶ ἔδωκε τοῖς μαθηταῖς,—confusing the place in St. Luke with the
place in St. John.

it has even established itself in the Vulgate[1]. It is witnessed to, besides, by two ninth-century uncials (ΚΠ) and ten cursive copies[2]. The thoughtful reader will say to himself,—'Had only Cod. B joined itself to this formidable conspiracy of primitive witnesses, we should have had this also thrust upon us by the new school as indubitable Gospel: and remonstrances would have been in vain!'

Now, as all must see, it is simply incredible that these many Fathers, had they employed honestly-made copies of St. Luke's and of St. John's Gospel, could have fallen into such frequent and such strange misrepresentations of what those Evangelists actually say. From some fabricated Gospel—from some 'Diatessaron' or ' Life of Christ,' once famous in the Church, long since utterly forgotten,— from some unauthentic narrative of our Saviour's Death and Resurrection, I say, these several depravations of the sacred story must needs have been imported into St. Luke's Gospel. And lo, out of all that farrago, the only manuscript traces which survive at this distant day, are found in the notorious B-ℵ, with A, D, L, and Π,—one copy each of the Old Latin (e) and the Bohairic [and the Lewis],—which exclusively enjoy the unenviable distinction of omitting the incident of the 'honeycomb': while the confessedly spurious appendix, ' He gave them what remained over,' enjoys a far more ancient, more varied, and more respectable attestation.—and yet has found favour with no single Editor of the Sacred Text: no, nor have our Revisers seen fit by a marginal note to apprize the ordinary English reader that ' many uncial authorities ' are disfigured in this particular way. With this latter accretion to the inspired verity, therefore, we need not delay ourselves : but that, so

---

[1] Aug. iii. P. 2, 143 (A. D. 400); viii. 472 (A. D. 404).

[2] To the 9 specified by Tisch.—(Evann. 13, 42, 88 (τα περισσευματα), 130 (το επαναλειφθεν), 161, 300, 346, 400, 507,—add Evan. 33, in which the words καὶ τὰ ἐπίλοιπα ἔδωκεν αὐτοῖς have been overlooked by Tregelles.

many disturbing influences having resulted, at the end of seventeen centuries, in the elimination of the clause καὶ ἀπὸ μελισσίου κηρίου from six corrupt copies of St. Luke's Gospel,—a fixed determination or a blundering tendency should now be exhibited to mutilate the Evangelical narrative in respect of the incident which those four words embody,—this may well create anxiety. It makes critical inquiry an imperative duty: not indeed for our own satisfaction, but for that of others.

Upon ourselves, the only effect produced by the sight of half a dozen Evangelia,—whether written in the uncial or in the cursive character we deem a matter of small account, —opposing themselves to the whole body of the copies, uncial and cursive alike, is simply to make us suspicious of those six Evangelia. Shew us that they have been repeatedly tried already and as often have been condemned, and our suspicion becomes intense. Add such evidence of the operation of a disturbing force as has been already set before the reader ; and further inquiry in our own minds we deem superfluous. But we must answer those distinguished Critics who have ruled that Codexes B-ℵ, D, L, can hardly if ever err.

The silence of the Fathers is really not of much account. Some critics quote Clemens Alexandrinus. But let that Father be allowed to speak for himself. He is inveighing against gluttony. 'Is not variety consistent with simplicity of diet?' (he asks); and he enumerates olives, vegetables, milk, cheese, &c. If it must be flesh, he proceeds, let the flesh be merely broiled. '"Have ye here any meat?" said our Lord to His disciples after His Resurrection. Whereupon, having been by Him taught frugality in respect of diet, "they gave Him a piece of a broiled fish."...Yet may the fact not be overlooked that those who sup as The Word approves may partake besides of "honeycomb." The fittest food, in a word, we consider to be that which requires no cooking: next, as I began by explaining, cheap and ordinary articles of diet[1].' Shall I be thought unreasonable if I insist that so far from allowing that Clemens is 'silent' concerning the 'honeycomb,' I even regard his testimony to the traditionary reading of St. Luke xxiv. 42 as express? At the end of 1700 years, I am as sure that 'honeycomb' was found in his copy, as if I had seen it with my eyes.

Origen, who is next adduced, in one place remarks concerning our SAVIOUR—'It is plain that after His Resurrection, He ate of a fish[2].' The same Father elsewhere interprets mystically the circumstance that the Disciples 'gave Him a piece of a broiled fish[3].' Eusebius in like manner thrice mentions the fact that our LORD partook of 'broiled fish[4]' after His Resurrection. And because these writers do not also mention 'honeycomb,' it is assumed by Tischendorf and his school that the words καὶ ἀπὸ μελισσίου κηρίου cannot have existed in their copies of St. Luke[5]. The proposed inference is plainly inadmissible. Cyril, after quoting accurately St. Luke xxiv. 36 to 43 ('honeycomb' and all)[6], proceeds to remark exclusively on the incident of the 'fish'[7]. Ambrose and Augustine certainly recognized the incident of 'the honeycomb': yet the latter merely remarks that 'to eat fish with the LORD is better than to eat lentiles with Esau[8];' while the former draws a mystical inference from 'the record in the Gospel that JESUS ate *broiled fishes*[9].' Is it

---

[1] Πρὸς τούτοις οὐδὲ τραγημάτων κηρίων ἀμείρους περιορατέον τοὺς δειπνοῦντας κατὰ Λόγον.—p. 174.

[2] i. 384.　　[3] iii. 477.　　[4] *Apud* Mai, iv. 294, 295 *bis*.

[5] 'Ibi τὸ κηρίον praeterire non poterat [*sc.* Origenes] si in exemplis suis additamentum reperisset.' (From Tischendorf's note on Luke xxiv. 42.)

[6] iv. 1108 b c.

[7] Κατεδήδοκε γὰρ τὸ προκομισθὲν ἰχθύδιον, ἤτοι τὸ ἐξ αὐτοῦ μέρος.—Ibid. d. Similarly in the fragments of Cyril's Commentary on St. Luke, he is observed to refer to the incident of the piece of broiled fish exclusively. (Mai, ii. 442, 443, which reappears in P. Smith, p. 730.)

[8] iii. P. i. p. 51. For the honeycomb, see iii. P. ii. p. 143 a : viii. 472 d.

[9] i. 215.

not obvious that the more conspicuous incident,—that of
the ‘broiled fish,’—being common to both repasts, stands
for all that was partaken of on either occasion? in other
words, represents the entire meal? It excludes neither
the ‘honeycomb’ of the upper chamber, nor the ‘bread’
which was eaten beside the Galilean lake. Tertullian[1],
intending no slight either to the ‘broiled fish’ or to the
‘bread,’ makes mention only of our Lord’s having ‘eaten
honeycomb’ after His Resurrection. And so Jerome,
addressing John, bishop of Jerusalem, exclaims —‘Why
did the Lord eat honeycomb? Not in order to give thee
licence to eat honey, but in order to demonstrate the truth
of His Resurrection[2].’ To draw inferences from the rhetorical
silence of the Fathers as if we were dealing with a mathematical problem or an Act of Parliament, can only result
in misconceptions of the meaning of those ancient men.

As for Origen, there is nothing in either of the two
places commonly cited from his writings[3], where he only
mentions the partaking of ‘fish,’ to preclude the belief that
Origen knew of the ‘honeycomb’ also in St. Luke xxiv. 42.
We have but fragments of his Commentary on St. Luke[4],
and an abridged translation of his famous Commentary
on Canticles. Should these works of his be hereafter
recovered in their entirety, I strongly suspect that a certain
scholium in Cordier’s Catena on St. Luke[5], which contains
a very elaborate recognition of the ‘honeycomb,’ will be
found to be nothing else but an excerpt from one or other
of them. At foot the learned reader will be gratified by
the sight of the original Greek of the scholium referred to[6],

---

[1] ‘*Favos* post fella gustavit.’—De Coronâ, c. 14 (i. p. 455).
[2] ii. 444 a.   [3] i. 384; iii. 477.
[4] Opp. iii. 932-85: with which comp. Galland. xiv. Append. 83-90 and
91-109.
[5] Cat. (1628), p. 622. Cordier translates from ‘Venet. 494’ (our ‘Evan. 466’).
[6] What follows is obtained (June 28, 1884) by favour of Sig. Veludo, the
learned librarian of St. Mark’s, from the Catena on St. Luke’s Gospel at
Venice (cod. 494 = our Evan. 466), which Cordier (in 1628) translated into

which Cordier so infelicitously exhibits in Latin. He will
at least be made aware that if it be not Origen who there
speaks to us, it is some other very ancient father, whose
testimony to the genuineness of the clause now under consideration is positive evidence in its favour which greatly
outweighs the negative evidence of the archetype of B-ℵ.
But in fact as a specimen of mystical interpretation, the
passage in question is quite in Origen's way[1]—has all his
fervid wildness,—in all probability is actually *his*.

Latin. The Latin of this particular passage is to be seen at p. 622 of his
badly imagined and well-nigh useless work. The first part of it (συνέφαγε ...
ἐναπογράψονται) is occasionally found as a scholium, e.g. in Cod. Marc. Venet.
27 (our Evan. 210), and is already known to scholars from Matthaei's N. T.
(note on Luc. xxiv. 42). The rest of the passage (which now appears for the
first time) I exhibit for the reader's convenience parallel with a passage of
Gregory of Nyssa's Christian Homily on Canticles. If the author of what is
found in the second column is not quoting what is found in the first, it is at
least certain that both have resorted to, and are here quoting from the same
lost original:—

Συνέφαγεν δὲ καὶ τῷ ὀπτῷ ἰχθύῳ (*sic*) τὸ κηρίον τοῦ μέλιτος· δηλῶν ὡς οἱ
πυρωθέντες διὰ τῆς θείας ἐνανθρωπήσεως καὶ μετασχόντες αὐτοῦ τῆς θεότητος, ὡς
μέλι μετ' ἐπιθυμίας τὰς ἐντολὰς αὐτοῦ παραδέξονται· κηρῷ ὥσπερ τοὺς νόμους
ἐναπογράψαντες· ὅτι ὁ μὲν τοῦ πάσχα

ἄρτος ἐπὶ πικρίδων ἠσθίετο καὶ ὁ νόμος διεκελεύετο·	.... ἄρτος .... οὐκέτι ἐπὶ πικρίδων ἐσθιόμενος, ὡς ὁ νόμος διακελεύεται·
πρὸς γὰρ τὸ παρὸν ἡ πικρία·	πρὸς γὰρ τὸ παρόν ἐστιν ἡ πικρίς·
ὁ δὲ μετὰ τὴν ἀνάστασιν ἄρτος τῷ κηρίῳ τοῦ μέλιτος ἡδύνετο·	(.... ὁ μετὰ τὴν ἀνάστασιν τοῦ κυρίου προσφανεὶς τοῖς μαθηταῖς ἄρτος ἐστί, τῷ κηρίῳ τοῦ μέλιτος ἡδυνόμινος.)
ὄψον γὰρ ἑαυτοῖς τὸ μέλι ποιησόμεθα, ὅταν ἐν τῷ ἰδίῳ κηρῷ ὁ καρπὸς τῆς ἀρετῆς καταγλυκαίνει τὰ τῆς ψυχῆς αἰσθητήρια.	ἀλλ' ὕψον ἑαυτῷ τὸ μέλι ποιούμενος, ὅταν ἐν τῷ ἰδίῳ καιρῷ ὁ καρπὸς τῆς ἀρετῆς καταγλυκαίνῃ τὰ τῆς ψυχῆς αἰσθητήρια.
ANON. *apud Corderium* (fol. 58): see above.	GREG. NYSS. in Cant. (Opp. i. a); the sentence in brackets being trans- posed.

Quite evident is it that, besides Gregory of Nyssa, HESYCHIUS (or whoever
else was the author of the first Homily on the Resurrection) had the same
original before him when he wrote as follows:—ἀλλ' ἐπειδὴ ὁ πρὸ τοῦ πάσχα
σῖτος ὁ ἄζυμος, ὄψον τὴν πικρίδα ἔχει, ἴδωμεν τίνι ἡδύσματι ὁ μετὰ τὴν ἀνάστασιν
ἄρτος ἡδύνεται. ὁρᾷς τοῦ Πέτρου ἁλιεύοντος ἐν ταῖς χερσὶ τοῦ κυρίου ἄρτον καὶ
κηρίον μέλιτος νόησον τί σοι ἡ πικρία τοῦ βίου κατασκευάζεται. οὐκοῦν ἀνα-
στάντες καὶ ἡμεῖς ἐκ τῆς τῶν λόγων ἁλείας, ἤδη τῷ ἄρτῳ προσδράμωμεν, ὃν
καταγλυκαίνει τὸ κηρίον τῆς ἀγαθῆς ἐλπίδος. (*ap.* Greg. Nyss. Opp. iii. 399 c d.)

[1] So Matthaei: 'Haec interpretatio sapit ingenium Origenis.' (N.T. iii. 498.)

The question however to be decided is clearly not
whether certain ancient copies of St. Luke were without
the incident of the honeycomb; but only whether it is
reasonable to infer from the premisses that the Evangelist
made no mention of it. And I venture to anticipate that
readers will decide this question with me in the negative.
That, from a period of the remotest antiquity, certain disturbing forces have exercised a baneful influence over this
portion of Scripture is a plain fact: and that their combined
agency should have resulted in the elimination of the
incident of the ' honeycomb ' from a few copies of St. Luke
xxiv. 42, need create no surprise. On the other hand, this
Evangelical incident is attested by the following witnesses:—

In the second century, by Justin M.[1],— by Clemens
Alexandrinus[2],—by Tertullian[3],—by the Old-Latin,—and
by the Peshitto Version:

In the third century, by Cureton's Syriac,—and by the
Bohairic:

In the fourth century, by Athanasius[4],— by Gregory of
Nyssa[5],—by Epiphanius[6],—by Cyril of Jerusalem[7],—by
Jerome[8],—by Augustine[9],—and by the Vulgate:

In the fifth century, by Cyril of Alexandria[10],— by
Proclus[11],—by Vigilius Tapsensis[12],—by the Armenian,—
and Ethiopic Versions:

In the sixth century, by Hesychius and Cod. N[13]:

In the seventh century, by the Harkleian Version.

Surely an Evangelical incident attested by so many,
such respectable, and such venerable witnesses as these, is
clearly above suspicion. Besides its recognition in the

[1] Καὶ ἔφαγε κηρίον καὶ ἰχθύν,—ii. 240. From the fragment De Resurrectione
preserved by John Damascene,—ii. 762 a.
[2] See above, note 1, p. 247.	[3] See above, note 1, p. 248.
[4] i. 644 (see above, p. 244, n. 7).	[5] i. 624 (see above, p. 242, n. 3).
[6] pp. 210, 431 (see above, p. 243).	[7] i. 652 d (see above, p. 247).
[8] i. 825 a ; ii. 444 a.	[9] See above, note 1, p. 245.
[10] iv. 1108.	[11] Apud Galland. ix. 633.
[12] Varim. i. 56.	[13] Apud Greg. Nyss. iii. 399.

ancient scholium to which attention has been largely
invited already[1], we find the incident of the 'honeycomb'
recognized by 13 ancient Fathers,—by 8 ancient Versions,
—by the unfaltering Tradition of the universal Church,—
above all, by every copy of St. Luke's Gospel in existence
(as far as is known), uncial as well as cursive—except *six*.
That it carries on its front the impress of its own genuineness, is what no one will deny[2]. Yet was Dr. Hort for
dismissing it without ceremony. 'A singular interpolation
evidently from an extraneous source, written or oral,' he
says. A singular hallucination, we venture to reply, based
on ideal grounds and 'a system [of Textual Criticism]
hopelessly self-condemned[2];' seeing that that ingenious
and learned critic has nothing to urge except that the
words in dispute are omitted by B-א,—by A seldom found
in the Gospels in such association,—by D of the sixth
century,—by L of the eighth,—by Π of the ninth.

I have been so diffuse on this place because I desire
to exhibit an instance shewing that certain perturbations
of the sacred Text demand laborious investigation,—have
a singular history of their own,—may on no account be
disposed of in a high-handed way, by applying to them
any cut and dried treatment,—nay I must say, any arbitrary
shibboleth. The clause in dispute enjoys in perfection
every note of a genuine reading: viz. number, antiquity,
variety, respectability of witnesses, besides continuity of
attestation: every one of which notes are away from that
exhibition of the text which is contended for by my
opponents[4]. Tischendorf conjectures that the 'honeycomb'

---

[1] See above, p. 248, note 6.
[2] 'The words could hardly have been an interpolation.' (Alford, *in loc*)
[3] Scrivener's Introd. II. p. 358.
[4] It is well known that Dean Burgon considered B, א, and D to be bad
manuscripts. When I wrote my Textual Guide, he was angry with me for not
following him in this. Before his death, the logic of facts convinced me that he
was right and I was wrong. We came together upon independent investigation.

may have been first brought in from the 'Gospel of the
Hebrews.' What if, on the contrary, by the Valentinian
'Gospel of Truth,'—a composition of the second century,—
the 'honeycomb' should have been first thrust out[1]? The
plain statement of Epiphanius (quoted above[2]) seems to
establish the fact that his maimed citation was derived
from that suspicious source.

Let the foregoing be accepted as a specimen of the injury
occasionally sustained by the Evangelical text in a very
remote age from the evil influence of the fabricated narratives, or *Diatessarons*, which anciently abounded. The
genuineness of the clause καὶ ἀπὸ μελισσίου κηρίου, it is
hoped, will never more be seriously called in question.
Surely it has been demonstrated to be quite above
suspicion[3].

I find that those MSS. in disputed passages are almost always wrong—mainly,
if not entirely, the authors of our confusion. What worse could be said of
them? And nothing less will agree with the facts from our point of view.
Compromise on this point which might be amiable shrinks upon inquiry before
a vast array of facts.—E. M.

[1] Compare Epiphanius (i. 143 c) *ut supra* (Haer. xxx. c. 19) with Irenaeus
(iii. c. 11, § 9): 'Hi vero qui sunt a Valentino . . . in tantum processerunt
audaciae, uti quod ab his non olim conscriptum est *Veritatis Evangelium*
titulent.'

[2] See above, p. 243.

[3] There is reason for thinking that the omission was an Alexandrian reading.
Egyptian asceticism would be alien to so sweet a food as honeycomb. See
above, p. 150. The Lewis Cod. omits the words. But it may be remembered
that it restricts St. John Baptist's food to locusts 'and the honey of the
mountain.'—E. M.

APPENDIX II.

Ὄξος — VINEGAR.

[The Dean thought this to be one of his most perfect papers.]

WHEN He had reached the place called Golgotha, there were some who *offered* to the Son of Man (ἐδίδουν 'were for giving' Him) a draught of wine drugged with myrrh[1]. He would not so much as taste it. Presently, the soldiers gave Him while hanging on the Cross vinegar mingled with gall[2]. This He tasted, but declined to drink. At the end of six hours, He cried, 'I thirst': whereupon one of the soldiers ran, filled a sponge with vinegar, and gave Him to drink by offering the sponge up to His mouth secured to the summit of the reed of aspersion: whereby (as St. John significantly remarks) it covered the bunch of ceremonial hyssop which was used for sprinkling the people[3]. This time He drank; and exclaimed, 'It is finished.'

Now, the ancients, and indeed the moderns too, have hopelessly confused this pathetic story by identifying the 'vinegar and gall' of St. Matt. xxvii. 34 with the 'myrrhed wine' of St. Mark xv. 23; shewing therein a want of critical perception which may reasonably excite astonishment; for

---

[1] Ἐσμυρμισμένον οἶνον, Mark xv. 23.
[2] Ὄξος μετὰ χολῆς μεμιγμένον, Matt. xxvii. 34 (= Luke xxiii. 37).
[3] Πλήσαντες σπόγγον ὄξους, καὶ ἰσσώπῳ περιθέντες, John xix. 29.

'wine' is not 'vinegar,' neither is 'myrrh' 'gall.' And surely, the instinct of humanity which sought to alleviate the torture of crucifixion by administering to our Saviour a preliminary soporific draught, was entirely distinct from the fiendish malice which afterwards with a nauseous potion strove to aggravate the agony of dissolution. Least of all is it reasonable to identify the leisurely act of the insolent soldiery at the third hour [1], with what 'one of them' (evidently appalled by the darkness) 'ran' to do at the ninth [2]. Eusebius nevertheless, in his clumsy sectional system, brackets [3] together these three places (St. Matt. xxvii. 34, St. Mark xv. 23, St. John xix. 29): while moderns (as the excellent Isaac Williams) and ancients (as Cyril of Jerusalem) [4] alike strenuously contend that the two first must needs be identical. The consequence might have been foreseen. Besides the substitution of 'wine' for 'vinegar' (οἶνον for ὄξος) which survives to this day in nineteen copies of St. Matt. xxvii. 34, the words 'and gall' are found improperly thrust into four or five copies of St. John xix. 29. As for Eusebius and Macarius Magnes, they read St. John xix. 29 after such a monstrous fashion of their own, that I propose to invite separate attention to it in another place. Since however the attempt to assimilate the fourth Gospel to the first (by exhibiting ὄξος μετὰ χολῆς in St. John xix. 29) is universally admitted to be indefensible, it need not occupy us further.

I return to the proposed substitution of οἶνον for ὄξος in St. Matt. xxvii. 34, and have only to point out that it is as

---

[1] Matt. xxvii. 34 (= Luke xxiii. 37).

[2] Καὶ εὐθέως ἥραμὰν εἰς ἐξ αὐτῶν, Matt. xxvii. 48 (= Mark xv. 36).

[3] Not so the author of the Syriac Canons. Like Eusebius, he identifies (1) Matt. xxvii. 34 with Mark xv. 23; and (2) Matt. xxvii. 48 with Mark xv. 36 and Luke xxiii. 36; but unlike Eusebius, he makes John xix. 29 parallel with these last three.

[4] The former,—pp. 286-7: the latter,—p. 197. The Cod. Fuld. ingeniously— 'Et dederunt ei vinum murratum bibere cum felle mixtum' (Ranke, p. 154).

plain an instance of enforced harmony as can be produced. That it exists in many copies of the Old-Latin, and lingers on in the Vulgate: is the reading of the Egyptian, Ethiopic, and Armenian Versions and the Lewis Cod.; and survives in BℵDKLΠ, besides thirteen of the cursives [1];—all this will seem strange to those only who have hitherto failed to recognize the undeniable fact that Codd. B-ℵ DL are among the foulest in existence. It does but prove how inveterately, as well as from how remote a period, the error under discussion has prevailed. And yet, the great and old Peshitto Version,—Barnabas [2],—Irenaeus [3],—Tertullian [4],—Celsus [5],—Origen [6],—the Sibylline verses in two places [7] (quoted by Lactantius),—and ps.-Tatian [8],—are more ancient

---

[1] Evann. 1, 22, 33, 63, 69, 73, 114, 122, 209, 222, 253, 507, 513.

[2] § 7.

[3] Pp. 526, 681 (Mass. 212, 277).

[4] De Spect. written A.D. 198 (see Clinton, App. p. 413), c. xxx.—i. p. 62.

[5] '" Et dederunt ei bibere *acetum* et fel." Pro eo quod dulci suo vino eos laetificarat, *acetum* ei porrexerunt; pro felle autem magna ejus miseratio amaritudinem gentium dulcem fecit.' Evan. Conc. p. 245.

[6] Celsus τὸ ὄξος καὶ τὴν χολὴν ὀνειδίζει τῷ Ἰησοῦ,—writes Origen (i. 416 c d e), quoting the blasphemous language of his opponent and refuting it, but accepting the reference to the Gospel record. This he does twice, remarking on the second occasion (i. 703 b c) that such as Celsus are for ever offering to JESUS 'gall and *vinegar*.' (These passages are unknown to many critics because they were overlooked by Griesbach.)—Elsewhere Origen twice (iii. 920 d e, 921 b) recognizes the same incident, on the second occasion contrasting the record in Matt. xxvii. 34 with that in Mark xv. 23 in a way which shews that he accounted the places parallel:—' Et hoc considera, quod secundum Matthaeum quidem Jesus accipiens *acetum cum felle permixtum* gustavit, et noluit bibere: secundum Marcum autem, cum daretur et *myrrhatum vinum*, non accepit.'—iii. 921 b.

[7] Lib. i. 374 and viii. 303 (assigned by Alexander to the age of Antoninus Pius), *ap.* Galland. i. 346 a, 395 c. The line (εἰς δὲ τὸ βρῶμα χολήν, καὶ εἰς δίψαν ὄξος ἔδωκαν,) is also found in Montfaucon's Appendix (Palaeogr. 246). Sibyll. lib. i. 374, Gall. i. 346 a εἰς δὲ τὸ βρῶμα χολην, καὶ εἰς πότον ὄξος ἄκρατον; ibid. viii. 303, 395 c . . . πιεῖν ὄξος ἔδωκαν; quoted by Lactantius, lib. iv. c. 18, A.D. 320, Gall. iv. 300 a . . . εἰς δίψαν ὄξος ἔδωκαν, which is the way the line is quoted from the Sibyl in Montfaucon's Appendix (Pal. Graec. 246). Lactantius a little earlier (Gall. iv. 299 b) had said,—' Dederunt ei cibum fellis, et miscuerunt ei aceti potionem.'

[8] Referring to the miracle at Cana, where (viz. in p. 55) the statement is repeated. Evan. Conc. p. 245. See above, note 5.

authorities than any of the preceding, and they all yield adverse testimony.

Coming down to the fourth century, (to which B-ℵ belong,) those two Codexes find themselves contradicted by Athanasius[1] in two places,—by another of the same name[2] who has been mistaken for the patriarch of Alexandria,— by Eusebius of Emesa[3],—by Theodore of Heraclea[4],—by Didymus[5],—by Gregory of Nyssa[6],—and by his namesake of Nazianzus[7],—by Ephraem Syrus[8],—by Lactantius[9],— by Jerome[10],— by Rufinus[11],— by Chrysostom[12],— by Severianus of Gabala[13],—by Theodore of Mopsuestia[14],—by Cyril of Alexandria[15],—and by Titus of Bostra[16]. Now these are more respectable contemporary witnesses to the text of Scripture by far than Codexes B-ℵ and D (who also have to reckon with A, Φ, and Σ—C being mute at the place), as well as outnumber them in the proportion of 24 to 2. To these (8 + 16 =) 24 are to be added the

---

[1] *Apud* Montf. ii. 63 ; Corderii, Cat in Luc. p. 599.

[2] The Tractatus [ii. 305 b] at the end of the Quaestt. ad Antiochum (Ath. ii. 301-6), which is certainly of the date of Athanasius, and which the editor pronounces to be not unworthy of him (Praefat. II. viii-ix).

[3] Opusc. ed. Augusti, p. 16.

[4] Cord. Cat. in Ps. ii. 393.

[5] Cord. Cat. in. Ps. ii. 409.

[6] Οὐ σπογγιὰ χολῇ τε καὶ ὄξει διάβροχος, οἵαν οἱ Ἰουδαῖοι τῷ εὐεργέτῃ τὴν φιλοτησίαν ἐνδεικνύμενοι διὰ τοῦ καλάμου προτείνουσι.—i. 624 b (where it should be noted that the contents of verses 34 and 48 (in Matt. xxvii) are confused).

[7] i. 481 a, 538 d, 675 b. More plainly in p. 612 e,— μιᾶς τῆς χολῆς, ἑνὸς ὄξους, δι᾽ ὧν τὴν πικρὰν γεῦσιν ἐθεραπεύθημεν (=Cat. Nic. p. 788).

[8] ii. 48 c, 284 a.

[9] Lib. iv. c. 18. See above, last page, note 7.

[10] vii. 236 c d, quoted next page.

[11] ' Refertur etiam quod aceto potatus sit, vel vino myrrhato, quod est amarius felle.' Rufinus, in Symb. § 26.

[12] vii. 819 a b (= Cat. Nic. p. 792). See also a remarkable passage ascribed to Chrys. in the Catena of Nicetas, pp. 371-2.

[13] 'Jesus *de felle una cum aceto* amaritudinis libavit.' (Hom. translated by Aucher from the Armenian.—Venice. 1827, p. 435).

[14] *Apud* Mai, N. Bibl. PP. iii. 455.

[15] *Apud* Mai, ii. 66; iii. 42. Is this the same place which is quoted in Cord. Cat. in Ps. ii. 410?

[16] *Apud* Galland. v. 332.

Apocryphal 'Gospel of Nicodemus[1],' which Tischendorf
assigns to the third century; the 'Acts of Philip[2],' and the
Apocryphal 'Acts of the Apostles[3],' which Dr. Wright
claims for the fourth; besides Hesychius[4], Amphilochius[5],
ps.-Chrysostom[6], Maximus[7], Severus of Antioch[8], and
John Damascene[9],—nine names which far outweigh in antiquity and importance the eighth and ninth-century Codexes
KLΠ. Those critics in fact who would substitute 'wine'
for 'vinegar' in St. Matt. xxvii. 34 have clearly no case.
That, however, which is absolutely decisive of the question
against them is the fact that *every uncial and every cursive
copy in existence*, except the very few specimens already
quoted, attest that the oldest known reading of this place
is the true reading. In fact, the Church has affirmed in
the plainest manner, from the first, that ὄξος (not οἶνον) is
to be read here. We are therefore astonished to find her
deliberate decree disregarded by Lachmann, Tischendorf,
Tregelles, Westcott and Hort, in an attempt on their part
to revive what is a manifest fabrication, which but for
the Vulgate would long since have passed out of the
memory of Christendom. Were they not aware that
Jerome himself knew better? 'Usque hodie' (he says)
'Judaei et omnes increduli Dominicae resurrectionis, *aceto
et felle* potant Jesum; et dant ei *vinum myrrhatum* ut eum
consopiant, et mala eorum non videat[10]:'—whereby he both
shews that he read St. Matt. xxvii. 34 according to the
traditional text (see also p. 233 c), and that he bracketed
together two incidents which he yet perceived were essentially distinct, and in marked contrast with one another.
But what most offends me is the deliberate attempt of the
Revisers in this place. Shall I be thought unreasonable

[1] Or Acta Pilati, pp. 262, 286. [2] p. 85. [3] p. 16.
[4] Cord. Cat. in Ps. ii. 410. [5] p. 87. [6] x. 829.
[7] ii. 84. 178. [8] Cramer, Cat. i. 235.
[9] i. 228, 549. [10] vii. 236 c d.

S

if I avow that it exceeds my comprehension how such
a body of men can have persuaded themselves that it is
fair to eject the reading of an important place of Scripture
like the present, and to substitute for it a reading resting
upon so slight a testimony *without furnishing ordinary
Christian readers with at least a hint of what they had
done?* They have considered the evidence in favour of
'*wine*' (in St. Matt. xxvii. 34) not only 'decidedly preponderating,' but the evidence in favour of '*vinegar*' so slight
as to render the word undeserving even of a place in the
margin. Will they find a sane jury in Great Britain to be
of the same opinion? Is this the candid and equitable
action befitting those who were set to represent the Church
in this momentous business?

APPENDIX III.

THE RICH YOUNG MAN.

THE eternal Godhead of CHRIST was the mark at which, in the earliest age of all, Satan persistently aimed his most envenomed shafts. St. John, in many a well-known place, notices this; begins and ends his Gospel by proclaiming our Saviour's Eternal Godhead[1]; denounces as 'deceivers,' 'liars,' and 'antichrists,' the heretical teachers of his own day who denied this[2];—which shews that their malice was in full activity before the end of the first century of our era; ere yet, in fact, the echoes of the Divine Voice had entirely died out of the memory of very ancient men. These Gnostics found something singularly apt for their purpose in a famous place of the Gospel, where the blessed Speaker seems to disclaim for Himself the attribute of 'goodness,'—in fact seems to distinguish between Himself and GOD. Allusion is made to an incident recorded with remarkable sameness of expression by St. Matthew (xix. 16, 17), St. Mark (x. 17, 18) and St. Luke (xviii. 18, 19), concerning a certain rich young Ruler. This man is declared by all three to have approached our LORD with one and the same question,—to have prefaced it with one and the same glozing address, '*Good* Master!'—and to

---

[1] St. John i. 1–3, 14; xx. 31.
[2] 1 St. John ii. 18, 22, 23; iv. 1, 2, 3, 15; v. 10, 11, 12, 20; 2 St. John ver. 7, 9, 10. So St. Jude ver. 4.

S 2

have been checked by the object of his adulation with one and the same reproof;—'Why dost thou [who takest me for an ordinary mortal like thyself[1]] call me *good*? No one is good [essentially good[2]] save one,' that is 'GOD.'

. . . See, said some old teachers, fastening blindly on the letter,—He disclaims being good : ascribes goodness exclusively to the Father : separates Himself from very and eternal God[3]. . . . The place was accordingly eagerly fastened on by the enemies of the Gospel[4] : while, to vindicate the Divine utterance against the purpose to which it was freely perverted, and to establish its true meaning, is found to have been the endeavour of each of the most illustrious of the Fathers in turn. Their pious eloquence would fill a volume[5]. Gregory of Nyssa devotes to this subject the eleventh book of his treatise against Eunomius[6].

In order to emphasize this impious as well as shallow gloss the heretic Valentinus (A. D. 120),—with his

---

[1] So Athanasius excellently :—ὁ θεὸς συναριθμήσας ἑαυτὸν μετὰ τῶν ἀνθρώπων, κατὰ τὴν σάρκα αὐτοῦ τοῦτο εἶπε, καὶ πρὸς τὸν νοῦν τοῦ προσελθόντος αὐτῷ· ἐκεῖνος γὰρ ἄνθρωπον αὐτὸν ἐνόμιζε μόνον καὶ οὐ θεόν, καὶ τοῦτον ἔχει τὸν νοῦν ἡ ἀπόκρισις. Εἰ μὲν γὰρ ἄνθρωπον, φησί, νομίζεις με καὶ οὐ θεόν, μή με λέγε ἀγαθόν· οὐδεὶς γὰρ ἀγαθός· οὐ γὰρ διαφέρει [is not an attribute or adornment of] ἀνθρωπίνῃ φύσει τὸ ἀγαθόν, ἀλλὰ θεῷ.—i. 875 a. So Macarius Magnes, p. 13.— See also below, note 2, p. 262.

[2] So, excellently Cyril Alex. V. 310 d, Suicer's Thesaurus ; see Pearson on the Creed, on St. Matt. xix. 17.

[3] So Marcion (*ap.* Epiph.),—εἶπέ τις πρὸς αὐτόν· διδάσκαλε ἀγαθέ, τί ποιήσας ζωὴν αἰώνιον κληρονομήσω; ὁ δέ, μή με λέγετε ἀγαθόν, εἷς ἐστιν ἀγαθός, ὁ Θεὸς ὁ Πατήρ [i. 339 a]. Note, that it was thus Marcion exhibited St. Luke xviii. 18, 19. See Hippol. Phil. 254,—Τί με λέγετε ἀγαθόν ; εἷς ἐστιν ἀγαθός.

[4] So Arius (*ap.* Epiphanium),—εἶτα πάλιν φησὶ ὁ μανιώδης Ἀρείος, πῶς εἶπεν ὁ Κύριος, Τί με λέγεις ἀγαθόν ; εἷς ἐστιν ἀγαθὸς ὁ Θεός. ὡς αὐτοῦ ἀρνουμένου τὴν ἀγαθότητα [i. 742 b].—From this, Arius inferred a separate essence :—καὶ ἀφώρισεν ἑαυτὸν ἐντεῦθεν ἀπὸ τῆς τοῦ Πατρὸς οὐσίας τε καὶ ὑποστάσεως. τὸ δὲ πᾶν ἐστι γελοιῶδες [i. 780 c].—Note, that this shews how St. Luke's Gospel was quoted by the Arians.

[5] E. g. ps.-Tatian, Evan. Conc. 173, 174.—Ambrose, ii. 473 e-476 d.— Gregory Naz. i. 549.—Didymus, Trin. 50-3.—Basil, i. 291 c.—Epiphanius, i. 780-1.—Macarius Magnes, 12-14.—Theodoret, v. 930-2.—Augustine is very eloquent on the subject.

[6] ii. 689. See the summary of contents at p. 281.

disciples, Heracleon and Ptolemaeus, the Marcosians, the Naassenes, Marcion (A.D. 150), and the rest of the Gnostic crew,—not only substituted 'One is good' for 'No one is good but one,'—but evidently made it a great point besides to introduce the name of the FATHER, either in place of, or else in addition to, the name of 'GOD[1].' So plausible a depravation of the text was unsuspiciously adopted by not a few of the orthodox. It is found in Justin Martyr[2],— in pseudo-Tatian[3],—in the Clementine homilies[4]. And many who, like Clemens Alex.,—Origen,— the Dialogus,—and pseudo-Tatian (in five places), are careful to retain the Evangelical phrase 'No one is good but one [that is] GOD,'—even they are observed to conclude the sentence with the heretical addition 'THE FATHER[5].' I am not of course denying that the expression is theologically correct : but only am requesting the reader to note that,

---

[1] Thus, Valentinus (ap. Clem. Alex.),—εἶς δέ ἐστιν ἀγαθός, οὗ παρουσία ἡ διὰ τοῦ υἱοῦ φανέρωσις . . . . ὁ μόνος ἀγαθὸς Πατήρ [Strom. ii. 409].—Heracleon (ap. Orig.),—ὁ γὰρ πέμψας αὐτὸν Πατήρ, ... οὗτος καὶ μόνος ἀγαθός, καὶ μείζων τοῦ πεμφθέντος [iv. 139 b].—Ptolemaeus to Flora (ap. Epiphanium),—καὶ εἰ ὁ τέλειος Θεὸς ἀγαθός ἐστι κατὰ τὴν ἑαυτοῦ φύσιν, ὥσπερ καὶ ἔστιν· ἕνα γὰρ μόνον εἶναι ἀγαθὸν Θεόν, τὸν ἑαυτοῦ Πατέρα, ὁ Σωτὴρ ἡμῶν ἀπεφήνατο, ὃν αὐτὸς ἐφανέρωσεν [i. 221 c].—The Marcosian gloss was,—εἶς ἐστὶν ἀγαθός, ὁ Πατὴρ ἐν τοῖς οὐρανοῖς [ap. Irenaeum, p. 92].—The Naassenes substituted,—εἶς ἐστὶν ἀγαθός, ὁ Πατήρ μου ὁ ἐν τοῖς οὐρανοῖς, ὃς ἀνατελεῖ τὸν ἥλιον αὐτοῦ κ.τ.λ. [ap. Hippolyt. Philosoph. 102].—Marcion introduced the same gloss even into St. Luke's Gospel,—εἶς ἐστιν ἀγαθός, ὁ Θεὸς ὁ Πατήρ [ap. Epiphan. i. 339 d, and comp. 315 c].

[2] Εἶς ἐστιν ἀγαθός, ὁ Πατήρ μου ὁ ἐν τοῖς οὐρανοῖς. — Tryph. c. 101 [vol. ii. 344].

[3] 'Unus tantum' (ait) 'est bonus, Pater qui in coelis est.'—Evan. Conc. p. 173 and on p. 169,—'Unus tantum' (ait) 'est bonus': ast post haec non tacuit, sed adjecit 'Pater.'

[4] Μή με λέγε ἀγαθόν· ὁ γὰρ ἀγαθὸς εἶς ἐστιν (ap. Galland. ii. 752 d). And so at p. 759 a and d, adding—ὁ Πατὴρ ὁ ἐν τοῖς οὐρανοῖς. This reference will be found vindicated below : in note 8, p. 269.

[5] For the places in Clemens Alex. see below, note 3, p. 263.—The places in Origen are at least six :—Τί με λέγεις ἀγαθόν ; οὐδεὶς ἀγαθὸς εἰ μὴ εἶς, ὁ Θεὸς ὁ Πατήρ [i. 223 c, 279 a, 586 a ; iv. 41 d : and the last nine words, iv. 65 d, 147 a].—For the places in ps.-Tatian, see below, note 2, p. 263.—The place in the *Dialogus* is found ap. Orig. i. 804 b :—λέγοντος τοῦ Χριστοῦ· οὐδεὶς ἀγαθὸς εἰ μὴ εἶς ὁ Πατήρ—words assigned to Megethius the heretic.

on the present occasion, it is clearly inadmissible ; seeing
that it was no part of our Saviour's purpose, as Didymus,
Ambrose, Chrysostom, Theodoret point out, to reveal
Himself to such an one as the rich young ruler in His
own essential relation to the Eternal Father[1],—to proclaim in short, in this chance way, the great mystery of
the Godhead : but only (as the ancients are fond of pointing out) to reprove the man for his fulsomeness in addressing one of his fellows (as he supposed) as 'good[2].' In the
meantime, the extent to which the appendix under discussion prevails in the Patristic writings is a singular illustration of the success with which, within 60 or 70 years of
its coming into being, the text of Scripture was assailed ;
and the calamitous depravation to which it was liable.
Surprising as well as grievous to relate, in every recent
critical recension of the Greek text of St. Matthew's
Gospel, the first four words of the heretical gloss ($\epsilon\hat{\iota}s\ \dot{\epsilon}\sigma\tau\iota\nu$
$\dot{o}\ \dot{a}\gamma\alpha\theta\dot{o}s$) have been already substituted for the seven words
before found there ($o\dot{v}\delta\epsilon\hat{\iota}s\ \dot{a}\gamma\alpha\theta\dot{o}s\ \epsilon\hat{\iota}\ \mu\dot{\eta}\ \epsilon\hat{\iota}s,\ \dot{o}\ \Theta\epsilon\dot{o}s$); and
(more grievous still) now, at the end of 1700 years, an
effort is being made to establish this unauthorized formula
in our English Bibles also. This is done, be it observed, in
opposition to the following torrent of ancient testimony:—
viz., in the second century, the Peshitto Version,—Justin

---

[1] Didymus,—$o\dot{v}\kappa\ \epsilon\hat{\iota}\pi\epsilon\nu\ \mu\dot{\epsilon}\nu\ o\dot{v}\delta\epsilon\hat{\iota}s\ \dot{a}\gamma\alpha\theta\dot{o}s\ \epsilon\hat{\iota}\ \mu\dot{\eta}\ \epsilon\hat{\iota}s\ \dot{o}\ \Pi\alpha\tau\dot{\eta}\rho\cdot\ \dot{a}\lambda\lambda'\ o\dot{v}\delta\epsilon\hat{\iota}s\ \dot{a}\gamma\alpha\theta\dot{o}s$
$\epsilon\hat{\iota}\ \mu\dot{\eta}\ \epsilon\hat{\iota}s\ \dot{o}\ \Theta\epsilon\dot{o}s$ [p. 51].—And Ambrose,—' Circumspectione coelesti non dixit,
Nemo bonus nisi unus Pater, sed *Nemo bonus nisi unus Deus*' [ii. 474 b].—
And Chrysostom,—$\dot{\epsilon}\pi\dot{\eta}\gamma\alpha\gamma\epsilon\nu,\ \epsilon\hat{\iota}\ \mu\dot{\eta}\ \epsilon\hat{\iota}s\ \dot{o}\ \Theta\epsilon\dot{o}s.\ \kappa\alpha\dot{\iota}\ o\dot{v}\kappa\ \epsilon\hat{\iota}\pi\epsilon\nu,\ \epsilon\hat{\iota}\ \mu\dot{\eta}\ \dot{o}\ \Pi\alpha\tau\dot{\eta}\rho\ \mu o\nu,$
$\check{\iota}\nu\alpha\ \mu\dot{a}\theta\eta s\ \check{o}\tau\iota\ o\dot{v}\kappa\ \dot{\epsilon}\xi\epsilon\kappa\dot{a}\lambda\nu\psi\epsilon\nu\ \dot{\epsilon}\alpha\nu\tau\dot{o}\nu\ \tau\hat{\omega}\ \nu\epsilon\alpha\nu\dot{\iota}\sigma\kappa\omega$ [vii. 628 b : quoted by Victor,
Ant. in Cat. p. 220].—And Theodoret (wrongly ascribed to Maximus, ii. 392,
396),—$O\dot{v}\kappa\ \epsilon\check{\iota}\rho\eta\tau\alpha\iota,\ O\dot{v}\delta\epsilon\hat{\iota}s\ \dot{a}\gamma\alpha\theta\dot{o}s,\ \epsilon\hat{\iota}\ \mu\dot{\eta}\ \epsilon\hat{\iota}s,\ \dot{o}\ \Pi\alpha\tau\dot{\eta}\rho.\ \dot{a}\lambda\lambda',\ O\dot{v}\delta\epsilon\hat{\iota}s\ \dot{a}\gamma\alpha\theta\dot{o}s,\ \epsilon\hat{\iota}\ \mu\dot{\eta}$
$\epsilon\hat{\iota}s,\ \dot{o}\ \Theta\epsilon\dot{o}s$ [v. p. 931]. Epiphanius [see the references above, in note 1, p. 261]
expressly mentions that this unauthorized addition (to Luke xviii. 18) was the
work of the heretic Marcion.

[2] 'Dicendo autem " *Quid me vocas bonum*," opinionem eius qui interrogaverat
suo responso refutavit, *quia iste putabat Christum de hâc terrâ et sicut unum
ex magistris Israelitarum esse*,'—ps.-Tatian, Evan. Conc. p. 174.—' Dives per
adulationem honoravit Filium . . . *sicut homines sociis suis grata nomina dare
volunt*.' Ibid. p. 168.

Martyr[1],—ps.-Tatian (5 times)[2],—Clemens Alex. (twice)[3]:
—in the third century, the Sahidic Version,—ps.-Dionysius
Areopag.[4]:—in the fourth century, Eusebius (3 times)[5],
Macarius Magnes (4 times)[6],— Basil[7], —Chrysostom[8] :—
Athanasius[9],—Gregory Nyss. (3 times)[10],—and Didymus
apparently (twice)[11] :—in the fifth century, Cod. C,—
Augustine in many places[12],—Cyril Alex.[13],—and Theodoret
(8 times)[14]:—in the sixth century, Antiochus mon.[15],—the
Opus imperf.[16]—with the Harkleian and the Ethiopic Version.

. . . When to these 21 authorities have been added *all the
known copies*, except six of dissentients,—an amount of
ancient evidence has been adduced which must be held to
be altogether decisive of a question like the present[17].

For what, after all, is the proper proof of the genuineness of any reading, but the prevailing consent of Copies,

---

[1] Apol. i. c. 16 [i. 42], —quoted below in note 2, p. 265.

[2] 'Cui respondit, "*Non est aliquis bonus*," ut tu putasti, "*nisi tantum unus
Deus Pater*" . . . . "*Nemo*" (sit) "*bonus, nisi tantum unus, Pater qui est in
coelis*" [Evan. Conc. p. 169]. "*Non est bonus, nisi tantum unus*" [Ibid.].
"*Non est bonus, nisi tantum unus qui est in coelis*" [p. 170]. "*Non est bonus
nisi tantum unus*"' [p. 173].

[3] Οὐ μὴν ἀλλὰ καὶ ὁπηνίκα διαρρήδην λέγει· Οὐδεὶς ἀγαθός, εἰ μὴ ὁ Πατήρ μου,
ὁ ἐν τοῖς οὐρανοῖς [p. 141]. And overleaf,—ἀλλὰ καὶ οὐδεὶς ἀγαθός, εἰ μὴ ὁ
Πατὴρ αὐτοῦ [p. 142]. Tischendorf admits the reference.

[4] i. 315 b. The quotation is given below, in note 7, p. 269.

[5] Praep. Evan. 542 b ; Ps. 426 d ; *ap.* Mai, iv. 101.

[6] Οὐδεὶς ἀγαθὸς εἰ μὴ εἷς, ὁ Θεός (p. 12).

[7] ii. 242 e and 279 e. (See also i. 291 e and iii. 361 a.)

[8] vii. 628 b,—οὐ γὰρ εἶπε, τί με λέγεις ἀγαθόν ; οὐκ εἰμὶ ἀγαθός· ἀλλ', οὐδεὶς
ἀγαθός . . . . εἰ μὴ εἷς ὁ Θεός. See also vii. 329.

[9] i. 875 a. The quotation is proved to be from St. Matt. xix. (17-21) by all
that follows.

[10] ii. 691 d ; 694 b c. See below, note 10, p. 267.   [11] Trin. 50, 51.

[12] '*Nemo bonus nisi unus Deus*':—iv. 383 c ; v. 488 b ; viii. 770 d, 772 b.

[13] v. P. i. 310 d, and 346 a (= 672 b).

[14] v. 931-3. Note that Ambrose, Didymus, Chrysostom, Theodoret, all four
hang together in this place, which is plain from the remark that is common to
all four, quoted above in note 1, last page. There is nothing to shew from
which Gospel Nilus (ii. 362) quotes the words οὐδεὶς ἀγαθός, εἰ μὴ εἷς ὁ Θεός.

[15] p. 1028, unequivocally.   [16] *Ap.* Chrys. vi. 137 d, 138 b.

[17] Besides these positive testimonies, the passage is quoted frequently as it is
given in St. Mark and St. Luke, *but with no special reference.* Surely some of
these must refer to St. Matthew ?

Fathers, Versions? This fundamental truth, strangely
overlooked in these last days, remains unshaken. For
if the universal consent of Copies, when sustained by a free
appeal to antiquity, is not to be held definitive,—what in
the world is? Were the subject less solemn there would
be something diverting in the *naïveté* of the marginal note
of the revisers of 1881,—'Some ancient authorities read . . .
"None is good save one [even] God."' How many
'ancient authorities' did the Revisers suppose exhibit
anything else?

But all this, however interesting and instructive, would
have attracted little attention were it not for the far more
serious corruption of the Sacred Text, which has next to
be considered. The point to be attended to is, that at the
very remote period of which we are speaking, it appears
that certain of the Orthodox,—with the best intentions
doubtless, but with misguided zeal,—in order to counteract
the pernicious teaching which the enemies of Christianity
elicited from this place of Scripture, deliberately falsified
the inspired record[1]. Availing themselves of a slight
peculiarity in St. Matthew's way of exhibiting the words
of the young Ruler,—(namely, 'What *good thing* shall
I do,')—they turned our LORD'S reply, 'Why callest thou
me good?' in the first Gospel, into this,—'*Why askest thou
me concerning the good?*' The ensuing formula which the
heretics had devised,—'*One there is that is good,*' with
some words of appendix concerning God the Father, as
already explained,—gave them no offence, because it occasioned them no difficulty. It even suited their purpose
better than the words which they displaced. On the other
hand, they did not fail to perceive that the epithet 'good,'
'Good Master,' if suffered to remain in the text, would
witness inconveniently against them, by suggesting our

---

[1] For other instances of this indiscreet zeal, see Vol. II.

LORD'S actual reply,—viz. 'Why callest thou me good?'
Accordingly, in an evil hour, they proceeded further to
erase the word ἀγαθέ from their copies. It is a significant
circumstance that the four uncial Codexes (BℵDL) which
exclusively exhibit τί με ἐρωτᾷς περὶ τοῦ ἀγαθοῦ; are exclusively the four which omit the epithet ἀγαθέ.

The subsequent history of this growth of error might
have been foreseen. Scarcely had the passage been pieced
together than it began to shew symptoms of disintegration;
and in the course of a few centuries, it had so effectually
disappeared, that tokens of it here and there are only to
be found in a few of the earliest documents. First, the
epithet (ἀγαθέ) was too firmly rooted to admit of a sentence
of perpetual banishment from the text. Besides retaining
its place in every known copy of the Gospels except eight[1],
it survives to this hour in a vast majority of the most
ancient documents. Thus, ἀγαθέ is found in Justin Martyr[2]
and in ps.-Tatian[3] :—in the remains of the Marcosian[4],—
and of the Naassene[5] Gnostics;—as well as in the Peshitto,
—and in the Old Latin versions :—in the Sahidic,—and the
Bohairic version,—besides in the Clementine Homilies[6], in
Cureton and Lewis,—and in the Vulgate:—in Origen[7],—in

[1] BℵDL, 1, 22, 479, Evst. 5.
[2] Καὶ προσελθόντος αὐτῷ τινος καὶ εἰπόντος· Διδάσκαλε ἀγαθέ, ἀπεκρίνατο
λέγων· Οὐδεὶς ἀγαθὸς εἰ μὴ μόνος ὁ Θεὸς ὁ ποιήσας τὰ πάντα.—Apol. I. c. 16
[vol. i. p. 42]. And so in Tryph. c. 101 [vol. ii. p. 344],—λέγοντος αὐτῷ
τινος· Διδάσκαλε ἀγαθέ· κ.τ.λ.
[3] 'Ad iudicem dives venit, donis dulcis linguae eum capturus.' (The
reference, therefore, is to St. Matthew's Gospel: which is further proved by
the quotation lower down of the latter part of ver. 17: also by the inquiry,—
'Quid adhuc mihi deest?') 'Ille dives bonum eum vocavit.' 'Dives
Dominum "Magistrum bonum" vocaverat sicut unum ex bonis magistris.'—
Evan. Conc. 168, 169.
[4] Ap. Irenaeum,—p. 92. See below, note 2, p. 267.
[5] Ap. Hippolytum, Philosoph. 102. See below, note 3, p. 267.
[6] Μή με λέγε ἀγαθόν (ap. Galland. ii. 759 d: comp. 752 b). For the
reference, and its indication, see below, note 8, p. 269.
[7] Comment. in Matt. xv. (in loc.).

Athanasius[1],—and in Basil[2],—and in Cyril of Jerusalem[3]:
—in Ephraem Syrus[4], and in Gregory of Nyssa[5]: in
Macarius Magnes[6],—and in Chrysostom[7] :—in Juvencus[8],
—Hilary[9],—Gaudentius[10],—Jerome[11],—and Augustine[12];—
lastly in Vigilius Tapsensis[13]:—in Cyril Alex.[14],—in Theodoret[15],—in Cod. C,—in the Harkleian Version,—and in the
Opus imperfectum[16]. So that, at the end of 1700 years,
6 witnesses of the second century,—3 of the third,—14 of
the fourth,—4 of the fifth,—2 of the sixth, come back
from all parts of Christendom to denounce the liberty
taken by the ancients, and to witness to the genuineness
of the traditional text.

So much then,—(1) For the unauthorized omission of
ἀγαθέ, and—(2) For the heretical substitution of εἷς ἐστιν
ὁ ἀγαθός in the room of οὐδεὶς ἀγαθὸς εἰ μὴ εἷς ὁ Θεός. We
have still to inquire after the fate of the most conspicuous
fabrication of the three: viz.—(3) The substitution of
Τί με ἐρωτᾷς περὶ τοῦ ἀγαθοῦ; for τί με λέγεις ἀγαθόν ; What

---

[1] i. 875 a,—clearly a quotation from memory of St. Matt. xix. 17, 18, 19, 20, 21.

[2] Adv. Eunom. i. 291 e,—ἀγαθὲ διδάσκαλε, ἀκούσας.   Again in ii. 242 c, and 279 e, expressly. See also iii. 361 a.

[3] Καθὼς ἀπεκρίνατο τῷ προσελθόντι καὶ εἰπόντι, Διδάσκαλε ἀγαθέ, τί ποιήσω ἵνα ζωὴν αἰώνιον ἔχω ;—Catech. 299.

[4] iii. 296 d (certainly from St. Matthew).

[5] Προσῄει θωπεύων τῇ τοῦ ἀγαθοῦ προσηγορίᾳ τὸ Κύριον . . . . Διδάσκαλον ἀγαθὸν ὀνομάζων.—Contr. Eunom. ii. 692 b. Also πρὸς τὸν νεάνισκον ἀγαθὸν αὐτὸν προσαγορεύσαντα· Τί με λέγεις ἀγαθόν ; (*ap.* Mai, iv. 12).

[6] Ὁ νεανίσκος ἐκεῖνος . . . . προσελθὼν διελέγετο φάσκων· Διδάσκαλε ἀγαθέ,— p. 12.

[7] vii. 628 b.   [8] lib. iii. 503.

[9] 994 c.   [10] *Ap.* Sabatier.

[11] vii. 147-8.

[12] iii.¹ 761 d ; iii.² 82 d [ibi enim et *bonum* nominavit] ; iv. 1279 g ; v. 196 g.

[13] *Ap.* Sabatier.

[14] v. P. i. 346 a (= 672 b),—προσέρχεταί τις ἐν τοῖς εὐαγγελίοις, καὶ φησί . . . . Διδάσκαλε ἀγαθέ.

[15] Τί με λέγεις ἀγαθόν ;—v. 931. See note 1, p. 262.

[16] *Magister bone, quid boni faciam ut vitam aeternam possideam?*—(*ap.* Chrysost. vi. 137 d, 138 b).

support do the earliest witnesses lend to the inquiry,—
' *Why askest thou me concerning the good?*' ... That
patent perversion of the obvious purport of our Saviour's
address, I answer, is disallowed by Justin Martyr[1]
(A.D. 140),—by the Marcosians[2],—and the Naassenes[3]
(A.D. 150),—by the Clementine homilies[4],— and ps.-
Tatian[5] (third century);—by the Peshitto and the Thebaic
version;— by Macarius Magnes[6],— Athanasius[7], — and
Basil[8];—by Hilary[9],—Gregory of Nyssa[10];—by Chrysostom[11],—by Cyril Alex.[12],—by Theodoret[13],—by the *Opus
imperfectum*[14],—by the Harkleian,—and the Armenian
versions. I have produced 18 witnesses,—4 belonging to the
second century : 3 to the third : 6 to the fourth : 5 to the
fifth. Moreover they come from every part of ancient
Christendom. Such an amount of evidence, it must be
again declared, is absolutely decisive of a question of this

---

[1] Λέγοντος αὐτῷ τινός, Διδάσκαλε ἀγαθέ, ἀπεκρίνατο· Τί με λέγεις ἀγαθόν; εἰς
ἐστιν ἀγαθός, ὁ Πατήρ μου ὁ ἐν τοῖς οὐρανοῖς [Tryph. c. 101, vol. ii. 344]. And
see the place (Apol. i. 16) quoted above, note 2, p. 265.

[2] Marcosians (*ap*. Irenaeum),—Καὶ τῷ εἰπόντι αὐτῷ, Διδάσκαλε ἀγαθέ, τὸν
ἀληθῶς ἀγαθὸν Θεὸν ὡμολογηκέναι εἰπόντα, Τί με λέγεις ἀγαθόν; εἷς ἐστιν
ἀγαθός, ὁ Πατὴρ ἐν τοῖς οὐρανοῖς [p. 92]. No one who studies the question will
affect to doubt that this quotation and the next are from St. Matthew's
Gospel.

[3] The Naassenes (*ap*. Hippolytum),—Τὸ ὑπὸ τοῦ Σωτῆρος λεγόμενον· Τί με
λέγεις ἀγαθόν ; εἷς ἐστιν ἀγαθός, ὁ Πατήρ μου ὁ ἐν τοῖς οὐρανοῖς, ὃς ἀνατελεῖ τὸν
ἥλιον αὐτοῦ ἐπὶ δικαίους καὶ ἀδίκους, καὶ βρέχει ἐπὶ ὁσίους καὶ ἁμαρτωλούς
[Philosoph. 102]. See the remark in the former note 5, p. 265.

[4] See below, note 8, p. 269.

[5] ' *Cur vocas me bonum*, quum in eo quod a me discere vis, iustus sim?'—
Evan. Conc. p. 168. And so in pp. 173, 174. See above, note 3, p. 265.

[6] This is in fact a double testimony, for the difficulty had been raised by the
heathen philosopher whom Macarius is refuting. Τί με λέγεις ἀγαθόν ;—pp.
12 and 13 (ed. 1876). See above, note 6, p. 263.

[7] i. 875 a. See last page, note 9.   [8] ii. 279 e.

[9] *Quid me vocas bonum ?*—703.

[10] ii. 692 d. Also *ap*. Mai, iv. 7, 12 (πρὸς τὸν νεάνισκον).

[11] vii 628 b. The place is quoted in note 1, p. 262.

[12] v.¹ 346 a (προσέρχεταί τις ἐν τοῖς εὐαγγελίοις κ.τ.λ.) = p. 672 b.

[13] v. 931,—which clearly is a reproduction of the place of Chrysostom
(vii. 628 b) referred to in the last note but one. Read the whole page.

[14] *Ap*. Chrysost. vi. 137 d, 138 b.

nature. Whether men care more for Antiquity or for
Variety of testimony ; whether Respectability of witnesses
or vastly preponderating Numbers, more impresses the
imagination,—they must needs admit that the door is here
closed against further debate. The traditional text of
St. Matt. xix. 16, 17 is certainly genuine, and must be
allowed to stand unmolested.

For it is high time to inquire,—What, after all, is the
evidence producible on the other side ? The exhibition of
the text, I answer, which recommends itself so strongly to
my opponents that they have thrust it bodily into the
Gospel, is found in its entirety only with that little band
of witnesses which have already so often come before us ;
and always with false testimony. I am saying that Origen[1]
in the third century,—Codd. B-ℵ in the fourth,—Cod. D
in the fifth,—Cod. L in the eighth,—besides a couple of
cursive Codexes (Evann. 1 and 22),—are literally the whole
of the producible evidence for the Revisers' text in its
entirety. Not that even these seven so-called consentient
witnesses are in complete accord among themselves. On
the contrary. The discrepancy between them is perpetual.
A collation of them with the traditional text follows :—

Και ιδου εις προσελθων ειπεν (D [*not* Orig. BℵL] λεγει)
αυτω (Bℵ [*not* Orig. DL] αυτω ειπε), Διδασκαλε αγαθε (Orig.
BℵDL—αγαθε), τι αγαθον ποιησω (ℵL [*not* Orig. BD] ποιη-
σας) ι,α εχω (Orig. BD [*not* ℵL] σχω) ζωην αιωνιον (Orig.
⁶⁶⁴ᵇ ℵL [*not* Orig. ⁶⁶⁴ᵃ BD] ζωην αιωνιον κληρονομησω) ;
ο δε ειπεν αυτω, Τι με λεγεις αγαθον (Orig. ⁶⁶¹⁻⁵ BℵDL
τι με ερωτας [Orig. ⁶⁶⁶ᵇ επερωτας] περι του (Orig. ⁶⁶⁴ᶜ D
[*not* Orig. ⁶⁶⁵ᶜ ⁶⁶⁶ᵇ BℵL]—του) αγαθου); ουδεις αγαθος ει μη
εις ο Θεος (BℵDL εις εστιν ο (D [*not* Orig. BℵL]—ο) αγαθυς).

---

[1] Καὶ ἰδού, εἷς προσελθὼν εἶπεν αὐτῷ· Διδάσκαλε, τί ἀγαθὸν ποιήσω, ἵνα σχῶ
ζωὴν αἰώνιον ; (but at the end of eight lines, Origen exhibits (like the five
authorities specified in note 8, next page) ἵνα ζωὴν αἰώνιον κληρονομήσω ;) ... Τί
με ἐρωτᾷς περὶ τοῦ (but τοῦ six lines lower down) ἀγαθοῦ ; εἷς ἐστιν ὁ ἀγαθός.
—in Matt. iii. 664 a b. And so p. 665 c. Cf. 666 b.

Can it be possibly reasonable to avow that such an amount of discrepancy between witnesses which claim to be consentient, inspires confidence rather than distrust in every one of them?

The reader is next to be told that there survive, as might have been expected, traces in sundry quarters of this threefold ancient fraud (as it seems to be rather than blunder);—as in Justin[1], and the Marcosian[2], and Naassene heretics[3]; the Latin Versions[4]; the Bohairic[5]; the Cureton and Lewis[6]; pseudo-Dionysius[7], the Clementine homilies[8] and Eusebius[9]; Cyril Alex.[10] and Antiochus the monk[11] (A.D. 614); Hilary[12], Jerome[13], and Augustine[14];

[1] See above, note 2, p. 261.   [2] See above, note 2, p. 261.
[3] See above, note 2, p. 261.
[4] a e ff¹ omit *bone*; b c f ff² g^{1-2} h–q Vulg. insert it; a b c e ff^{1.2} g¹ h l Vulg. write *de bono*, f q *bonum*; a b c ff^{1.2} l Vulg. write *unus*; f g¹ h m q *nemo*.
[5] See above, p. 149.
[6] This wild performance is unique in its testimony (see below, p. 277). Cureton renders the text thus:—'Why askest thou me concerning good? for One is good, GOD.' And Mrs. Lewis thus:—'Why askest thou me concerning the good? for One is the good one.'
[7] Τί με ἐρωτᾷς περὶ τοῦ ἀγαθοῦ; οὐδεὶς ἀγαθός, εἰ μὴ μόνος ὁ Θεός.—i. 315 b.
[8] Αὐτὸς ὁ διδάσκαλος ἡμῶν τῷ εἰπόντι Φαρισαίῳ, Τί ποιήσας ζωὴν αἰώνιον κληρονομήσω; πρῶτον ἔφη, Μή με λέγε ἀγαθόν. ὁ γὰρ ἀγαθὸς εἷς ἐστιν, ὁ Πατὴρ ὁ ἐν τοῖς οὐρανοῖς (*ap.* Galland. ii. 759 d e). — Note, the reference is certainly to St. Matthew's Gospel, as all that follows proves: the inquiry in ver. 16 (by assimilation from Luke xviii. 18) being similarly exhibited in ℵ, L,—Irenaeus, Int. p. 241; Orig. iii. 664 b; Cyril, Alex. v.¹ 310 d; Basil, ii. 279 e; and Chrysostom, iii. 182; vii. 627-8; viii. 234.
[9] Eusebius—Τί με ἐρωτᾷς περὶ τοῦ ἀγαθοῦ; Οὐδεὶς ἀγαθός, εἰ μὴ εἷς ὁ Θεός,—Praep. Evan. 542 b.—The last seven words are also found in Ps. (ed. Montf.) 426 d; and *ap.* Mai, iv. 101.
[10] Διδάσκαλε, τί ἀγαθὸν ποιήσας, ζωὴν αἰώνιον κληρονομήσω; ὁ δὲ εἶπεν αὐτῷ, Τί με ἐρωτᾷς περὶ τοῦ ἀγαθοῦ; οὐδεὶς ἀγαθὸς εἰ μὴ εἷς ὁ Θεός. (Note, that all but the last seven words exactly = ℵ, L, and Basil, ii. 279 e.)—V.¹ 310 d.—But elsewhere (also quoting St. Matthew) Cyril exhibits—διδάσκαλε ἀγαθέ . . . τί με λέγεις ἀγαθόν; οὐδεὶς ἀγαθὸς εἰ μὴ εἷς ὁ Θεός.—Ibid. p. 346 a (= p. 672 b).
[11] Τί με ἐρωτᾷς περὶ τοῦ ἀγαθοῦ; οὐδεὶς ἀγαθός, εἰ μὴ εἷς ὁ Θεός.—p. 1028.
[12] *Magister, quid boni faciam, ut habeam vitam aeternam.* Cui Dominus, *Quid me vocas bonum* (703):—*Unus enim bonus est*, ait Dominus (489). But elsewhere, *Magister bone, quid boni faciam* (994 c).
[13] *Magister bone, quid boni faciam ut habeam vitam aeternam? Qui dicit ei, Quid me interrogas de bono? Unus est bonus Deus.*—vii. 147-8.
[14] For '*bone*,' see above, note 12, p. 266: for '*nemo*,' &c., see note 12, p. 263.

besides in Evann. 479 and 604, and Evst. 5. But the
point to be attended to is, that not one of the foregoing
authorities sanctions the text which Lachmann, Tischendorf, Tregelles, W.-Hort, and the Revisers of 1881 unani-
mously adopt. This first. And next, that no sooner are
these sixteen witnesses fairly confronted, than they set
about hopelessly contradicting one another : so that it
fares with them as it fared with the Philistines in the days
of Saul :—' Behold, every man's sword was against his
fellow, and there was a very great discomfiture[1].' This
will become best understood by the reader if he will allow
' (I),' to represent the *omission* of the epithet ἀγαθέ :—'(II),'
the *substitution* of τί με ἐρωτᾷς περὶ τοῦ ἀγαθοῦ :—and '(III),'
the *substitution* of εἷς ἐστιν ὁ ἀγαθός with or without
appendix.   For it will appear that,—

(*a*) Evan. 479 and Evst. 5, though they witness *in favour
of* (I), yet witness *against* (II) and (III):—and that,

(*b*) The Latin and the Bohairic Versions, with Jerome
and Evan. 604, though they witness *in favour of* (II) and
(III), yet witness *against* (I).

Note, that Cureton and Lewis do the same : but then the
Cureton stultifies itself by omitting from the introductory
inquiry the underlined and clearly indispensable word,—
' What *good* [thing] must I do ? '   The same peculiarity is
exhibited by the Thebaic Version and by Cyril of Jer.[2]
Now this is simply fatal to the testimony of Cureton's
Syr. concerning '(II),'—seeing that, without it, the proposed reply cannot have been spoken.—It appears further
that,

(*c*) Augustine, though he witnesses in favour of (II), yet
witnesses against both (I) and (III) :—and that,

(*d*) Hilary, though he witnesses in favour of (III), and
yields uncertain testimony concerning (I), yet witnesses
against (II) :—and that,

---

[1] 1 Sam. xiv. 20.   [2] p. 299.

(e) Justin M. (in one place) and the Marcosian and Naassene heretics, together with the Clementine homilies, though they witness in favour of (III), yet witness against (I) and (II) :—and that,

(f) ps.-Dionysius, Eusebius, and Antiochus mon. (A.D. 614), though they witness in favour of (II), yet witness against (III).

(g) Cyril also, though he delivers uncertain testimony concerning (I) and (II), yet witnesses against (III).

The plain fact is that the place before us exhibits every chief characteristic of a clumsy fabrication. No sooner had it with perverse ingenuity been pieced together, than the process of disintegration set in. The spurious phrases τί με ἐρωτᾷς περὶ τοῦ ἀγαθοῦ, and εἷς ἐστιν ἀγαθός, having no lawful dwelling-place of their own, strayed out of the first Gospel into the third as soon as they were invented. Cureton in St. Luke xviii. 19 has both phrases, Lewis neither,— Marcion, in his heretical recension of St. Luke's Gospel (A.D. 150), besides the followers of Arius, adopt the latter[1]. 'The key of the whole position,' as Scrivener points out, 'is the epithet "good" before "Master" in ver. 16: for if this be genuine, the only pertinent answer is contained in the Received Text[2].' Precisely so: and it has been proved to be genuine by an amount of continuous attestation which is absolutely overwhelming. We just now analyzed the inconsistent testimony of sixteen ancient authorities ; and found that only the two cursive copies favour the omission of ἀγαθέ, while nine of the oldest witnesses are for retaining it. Concerning the expression τί με ἐρωτᾷς περὶ τοῦ ἀγαθοῦ, these inconsistent witnesses are evenly divided, —seven being for it, seven against it. All, in fact, is error,

---

[1] Epiphanius [i. 339 d], and Hippolytus [Phil. 254], shew that Marcion so read Luke xviii. 19.—Epiphanius [i. 742 b] quotes Arius. See the words above, in notes 3, 4, p. 260.

[2] Six Lectures on the Text (1875),—p. 130.

confusion, discord, the instant we get outside the traditional text.

The reason of all this contrariety has been assigned already. Before Christianity was a hundred years old, two opposite evil influences were at work here: one, heretical —which resulted in (III): the other, orthodox,—which resulted in (II) and (I). These influences, proceeding from opposite camps, were the cause that copies got independently propagated of two archetypes. But the Church, in her corporate capacity, has declined to know anything of either. She has been careful all down the ages that the genuine reading shall be rehearsed in every assembly of the faithful on the 12th Sunday after Pentecost; and behold, at this hour it is attested by every copy in the world—except that little handful of fabricated documents, which it has been the craze of the last fifty years to cry up as the only authentic witnesses to the truth of Scripture, viz. Codd. BℵDL and Origen. Now, as to the first two of these, Dr. Scrivener has pronounced [1] that (Bℵ), 'subsequent investigations have brought to light so close a relation as to render it impossible to regard them as independent witnesses;' while every page of the Gospel bears emphatic witness to the fact that Codd. BℵDL are, as has been said, the depositaries of a hopelessly depraved text.

But how about Origen? He, in A.D. 250, commenting on the present place of St. Matthew's Gospel, has a great deal to say concerning the grievously corrupt condition of the copies hereabouts. Now, the copies he speaks of must have been older, by at least 100 years, than either Cod. B or Cod. ℵ. He makes this admission casually in the course of some remarks which afford a fair sample of his critical method and therefore deserve attention:—He infers from Rom. xiii. 9 that if the rich young ruler really did 'love his

[1] Plain Introduction (ed. 4), II. p. 329.

neighbour as himself,' which, according to the three Evangelists, he virtually said he did [1], he was perfect [2]! Yet our Saviour's rejoinder to him is,—'*If* thou wilt be perfect,' go and do such and such things. Having thus invented a difficulty where none exists, Origen proposes, as a way out of it, to regard the precept (in St. Matt. xix. 20,—'Thou shalt love thy neighbour as thyself') as an unauthorized accretion to the Text,— the work of some tasteless scribe [3]. The reasonableness of suspecting its genuineness (he says) is heightened by the fact that neither in St. Mark's nor yet in St. Luke's parallel narrative, are the words found about 'loving one's neighbour as oneself.' As if that were not rather a reason for presuming it to be genuine! To be sure (proceeds Origen) it would be monstrous to regard these words, 'Thou shalt love thy neighbour as thyself,' as an interpolation, were it not for the existence of so many other discrepancies hereabouts. The copies of St. Matthew are in fact all at strife among themselves. And so are the copies of the other Gospels. Vast indeed, and with this he concludes, is the discrepancy in St. Matthew [4]: whether it has proceeded from the carelessness of the scribes ;—or from criminal audacity on the part of correctors of Scripture ;—or whether, lastly, it has been the result of licentiousness on the part of those who, pretending to 'correct' the text, have added or omitted according to their own individual caprice [5].

---

[1] Matt. xix. 20 = Mark x. 20 = Luke xviii. 21.

[2] iii. 669 c d.

[3] Πρόσχες οὖν εἰ δυνάμεθα πρὸς τὴν προκειμένην ζήτησιν ... οὕτως ἀπαντῆσαι, ὅτι μήποτε τό· ἀγαπήσεις τὸν πλουσίον σου ὡς ἑαυτόν. ὑπονοεῖσθαι δύναται, ὡς οὐχ ὑπὸ τοῦ Σωτῆρος ἐνταῦθα παρειλῆφθαι, ἀλλ' ὑπό τινος τὴν ἀκρίβειαν μὴ νοήσαντος τῶν λεγομένων, προστεθεῖσθαι.—iii. 670 a b.

[4] Καὶ εἰ μὲν μὴ καὶ περὶ ἄλλων πολλῶν διαφωνία ἦν πρὸς ἄλληλα τῶν ἀντιγράφων ὥστε πάντα τὰ κατὰ Ματθαῖον μὴ συνᾴδειν ἀλλήλοις, ὁμοίως δὲ καὶ τὰ λοιπὰ εὐαγγέλια, κ.τ.λ.—iii. 671 b.

[5] Νυνὶ δὲ δηλονότι πολλὴ γέγονεν ἡ τῶν ἀντιγράφων διαφορά, εἴτε ἀπὸ ῥᾳθυμίας τινῶν γραφέων, εἴτε ἀπὸ τόλμης τινῶν μοχθηρᾶς τῆς διορθώσεως τῶν γραφομένων,

T

Now all this is very instructive. Here is the most famous Critic of antiquity estimating the genuineness of a clause in the Gospel, not by the amount of external attestation which it enjoys, but by his own self-evolved fancies concerning it. As a matter of fact, no extant copy, Father, or Version is without the clause under discussion. By proposing therefore that it shall be regarded as spurious, Origen does but convict himself of rashness and incompetency. But when this same Critic,—who, by his own shewing, has had the evil hap to alight on a collection of singularly corrupt documents,— proceeds to handle a text of Scripture which has demonstrably had a calamitous history from the first days of the Gospel until now ;—two inconvenient questions force themselves on our attention :— The first,—What confidence can be reposed in his judgement? The second —What is there to conciliate our esteem for the particular Codex from which he happens to quote? On the other hand, the reader has been already shewn by a more open appeal to antiquity than has ever before been attempted, that the reading of St. Matt. xix. 16,17 which is exclusively found in BℵDL and the copy from which Origen quotes, is deficient in external attestation.

Now, when it is considered that Bℵ confessedly represent one and the same archetype, which may very well have been of the date of Origen himself,—how is it possible to resist the conviction that these three are not independent voices, but echoes of one and the same voice? And, What if certain Codexes preserved in the library of Caesarea in Palestine[1] ;—Codexes which were handled in turn by Origen, by Eusebius, by Jerome, and which also furnished the archetype from which B and ℵ were derived ;—what, I say, if it shall some day come to be generally admitted, that

εἴτε καὶ ἀπὸ τῶν τὰ ἑαυτοῖς δοκοῦντα ἐν τῇ διορθώσει προστιθέντων ἢ ἀφαιρούντων.—iii. 671 c.

[1] See above, pp. 152-4.

those Caesarean Codexes are most probably the true *fons et origo* of much of our past perplexity and of our present trouble? Since 'coincidence of reading infallibly implies identity of ancestry[1],' are we not even led by the hand to see that there must have existed in the famous library of Caesarea a little nest of copies credited, and justly so, with containing every 'last new thing' in the way of Textual Criticism, to which Critics of the type of Origen and Jerome, and perhaps Eusebius, must have been only too fond of resorting? A few such critically corrected copies would furnish a complete explanation of every peculiarity of reading exhibited exclusively by Codexes B and ℵ, and [fondled, perhaps with some critical cynicism, by] those three Fathers.

Yet it is to be remembered, (with reference to the place before us,) that 'Origen, Eusebius, and Jerome' are not in accord here, except in reading τί με ἐρωτᾷς περὶ τοῦ ἀγαθοῦ;—for Eusebius differs from Origen and Jerome in proceeding with the traditional text οὐδεὶς ἀγαθὸς εἰ μὴ εἷς: while Jerome and even Origen concur with the traditional text in recognizing the epithet ἀγαθέ,—a circumstance which, as already explained, may be regarded as fatal to the formula τί με ἐρωτᾷς κ.τ.λ. which follows.

This however by the way. That so ill-supported a fraud should have imposed upon Griesbach, Lachmann, Tischendorf, Tregelles, Alford, Westcott and Hort, and the Revisers of 1881, including Scrivener,—is to me unintelligible. The substituted reading is an impossible one to begin with, being inconsistent with its context. And although I hold the introduction of intrinsic probability into these inquiries to be unlawful, until the truth has been established on grounds of external evidence; yet, when that has been accomplished, not only do internal considerations claim

---

[1] W.-Hort, p. 287.

a hearing, but their effect is often, as in the present case, entirely to sweep the field. It is impossible, so at least it seems to me, to survey the narrative by the light of internal probability, without being overcome by the incoherence and essential foolishness of the reading before us. This is a point which deserves attention.

1. That our LORD actually *did* remonstrate with the young ruler for calling Him 'good,' is at least certain. Both St. Mark (x. 17, 18) and St. Luke (xviii. 18, 19) record that fact, and the text of neither is disputed. How grossly improbable then is the statement that He also reproved the young man for inviting Him to a philosophical discussion concerning τὸ ἀγαθόν,—which yet the young man clearly had not done. According to two out of the three Evangelists, if not to the third also, his question had not been about the abstract quality; but concerning the concrete thing, as a means to an end :—'What *good work must I do* in order that I may inherit eternal life?'— a purely practical question. Moreover, the pretended inquiry is not touched by the proposed rejoinder,—'One there is who is good,'—or 'There is none good but one, that is GOD.' Does not the very wording of that rejoinder shew that it must needs have been preceded by the inquiry, 'Why callest thou Me good?' The young man is told besides that if he desires to 'inherit eternal life' he must keep God's commandments. The question and the answer in the genuine text are strictly correlative. In the fabricated text, they are at cross purposes and inconsistent with one another in a high degree.

2. Let it however be supposed for an instant that our LORD'S reply actually was,—'Why askest thou Me concerning abstract goodness?' Note what results. Since it cannot be thought that such an interrogation is substantially equivalent to 'Why callest thou Me good?' the saying,—if uttered at all,—must have been spoken in

addition. Was it then spoken to the same man?—'Yes,'
replies the author of Cureton's Syriac: 'the rejoinder ran
thus,—"Why callest thou Me good?" and, "Why askest
thou Me respecting the good[1]?"'—'Not exactly,' remarks
the author of Evan. 251, 'The second of those two inquiries
was interposed after the word "Which?" in ver. 18.'—'Not
so,' cries the author of the Gospel to the Hebrews. 'The
men who came to our Lord were two in number[2].' There
is reason for suspecting that certain of the early heretics
were of the same opinion[3]. Will not every candid reader
admit that the more closely we look into the perplexed
tangle before us, the more intolerable it becomes,—the
more convinced we feel of its essential foolishness? And—
Is it too much to hope that after this deliberate exposure
of the insufficiency of the evidence on which it rests, no
further efforts will be made to bolster up a reading so
clearly indefensible?

Nothing more, I suppose, need be added. I have been
so diffuse concerning the present place of Scripture because
I ardently desire to see certain of the *vexatae quaestiones*
in Textual Criticism fairly threshed out and settled. And
this is a place which has been famous from the earliest
times,—a θρυλλούμενον κεφάλαιον as Macarius Magnes (p. 12)
calls it, in his reply to the heathen philosopher who had
proposed it as a subject for discussion. It is (in the opinion
of modern critics) 'quite a test passage[4].' Tischendorf
made this the subject of a separate dissertation in 1840[5].
Tregelles, who discusses it at great length[6], informs us

[1] So Cureton renders St. Luke xviii. 19.
[2] 'Scriptum est in evangelio quodam quod dicitur secundum Hebraeos, ...
Dixit ei alter divitum: Magister quid boni faciens vivam?'—(Orig. Vet.
Interp. iii. 670.) I suppose the mention of εἰς προσελθών, in ver. 16, suggested
this.
[3] The Marcionite Gospel exhibited Μή με λέγετε ἀγαθόν (Hippol. Phil. 254;
Epiph. i. 315 c).—Comp. the Clement. Hom. (*ap.* Galland. ii. 752 b, 759 a d).
[4] Hammond, quoted approvingly by Scrivener,—I. 328 (ed. 4).
[5] C. R. Gregory's Prolegomena, p. 7.   [6] Printed Text, pp. 133-8.

that he even 'relies on this one passage as supplying an argument on the whole question' which underlies his critical Recension of the Greek Text. It has caused all the Critics—Griesbach, Lachmann, Tischendorf, Tregelles, Alford, W.-Hort, the Revisers, even Scrivener[1], to go astray. Critics will spend their strength in vain if they seek any further to establish on a rational basis alterations made on the strength of testimony which is both restricted and is at variance with itself.

Let it be noted that our persistent appeal concerning St. Matt. xix. 17, 18 has been made to Antiquity. We reject the proposed innovation as undoubtedly spurious, because of the importance and overwhelming number of the witnesses of the second, third, and fourth centuries which come forward to condemn it ; as well as because of the plain insufficiency and want of variety in the evidence which is adduced in its support. Whenever a proposed correction of the Sacred Text is insufficiently attested, and especially when that attestation is destitute of Variety,— we claim that the traditional reading shall stand.

[1] Introduction (1883),—pp. 573-6. [Also Vol. II. (1894), pp. 327-9. I did not as Editor think myself entitled to alter Dr. Scrivener's expressed opinion. E. M.]

APPENDIX IV.

ST. MARK'S Gospel opens as follows:—'The beginning of the Gospel of Jesus Christ, THE SON OF GOD.' The significancy of the announcement is apparent when the opening of St. Matthew's Gospel is considered,—'The book of the generation of Jesus Christ, the Son of David.' Surely if there be a clause in the Gospel which carries on its front the evidence of its genuineness, it is this[1]. But in fact the words are found in every known copy but three (ℵ, 28, 255); in all the Versions; in many Fathers. The evidence in its favour is therefore overwhelming. Yet it has of late become the fashion to call in question the clause—Ὑιοῦ τοῦ Θεοῦ. Westcott and Hort shut up the words in brackets. Tischendorf ejects them from the text. The Revisers brand them with suspicion. High time is it to ascertain how much of doubt really attaches to the clause which has been thus assailed.

Tischendorf relies on the testimony of ten ancient Fathers, whom he quotes in the following order,—Irenaeus, Epiphanius, Origen, Basil, Titus, Serapion, Cyril of Jerusalem, Severianus, Victorinus, Jerome. But the learned

---

[1] It is right to state that Tischendorf thought differently. 'Videtur illud huic quidem loco parum apte illatum.' He can only bring himself to admit that the text had been 'jam Irenaei tempore nobili additamento auctum.' He insists that it is absurd, as well as at variance with the entire history of the sacred text, to suppose that the title 'SON OF GOD' has here been removed by unscrupulous Unbelief, rather than thrust in by officious Piety.

critic has to be reminded (1) that *pro hac vice*, Origen,
Serapion, Titus, Basil, Victorinus and Cyril of Jerusalem are
not six fathers, but only one.   Next (2), that Epiphanius
delivers no testimony whatever on the point in dispute.
Next (3), that Jerome[1] is rather to be reckoned with the
upholders, than the impugners, of the disputed clause :
while (4) Irenaeus and Severianus bear emphatic witness
in its favour.   All this quite changes the aspect of the
Patristic testimony.   The scanty residuum of hostile
evidence proves to be Origen and three Codexes,—of which
two are cursives.   I proceed to shew that the facts are
as I have stated them.

As we might expect, the true author of all the mischief was Origen.   At the outset of his commentary on
St. John, he writes with reference to St. Mark i. 1,—' Either
the entire Old Testament (represented by John Baptist) is
here spoken of as "the beginning" of the New ; or else,
only the end of it (which John quotes) is so spoken of, on
account of this linking on of the New Testament to the
Old.   For Mark says,—" The beginning of the Gospel of
Jesus Christ, as it is written in Isaiah the prophet, Behold,
I send my messenger, &c.   The voice of one, &c."   I can
but wonder therefore at those heretics,'— he means the
followers of Basilides, Valentinus, Cerdon, Marcion, and
the rest of the Gnostic crew, — 'who attribute the two
Testaments to two different Gods ; seeing that this very
place sufficiently refutes them.   For how can John be " the
beginning of the Gospel," if, as they pretend, he belongs
to another God, and does not recognize the divinity of the
New Testament ?'   Presently,—' In illustration of the
former way of taking the passage, viz. that John stands
for the entire Old Testament, I will quote what is found
in the Acts [viii. 35] " Beginning at the same Scripture of

[1] v. 10; vii. 17; and in the Vulgate.   Twice however (viz. i. 311 and
vi. 969) Jerome *omits* the clause.

Isaiah, He was brought as a lamb, &c., Philip preached to the eunuch the Lord Jesus." How could Philip, beginning at the prophet, preach unto him Jesus, unless Isaiah be some part of " the beginning of the Gospel¹?"' From the day that Origen wrote those memorable words [A. D. 230], an appeal to St. Mark i. 1–3 became one of the common-places of Theological controversy. St. Mark's assertion that the voices of the ancient Prophets, were 'the beginning of the Gospel'— of whom John Baptist was assumed to be the symbol,—was habitually cast in the teeth of the Manichaeans.

On such occasions, not only Origen's reasoning, but often Origen's mutilated text was reproduced. The heretics in question, though they rejected the Law, professed to hold fast the Gospel. 'But' (says Serapion) 'they do not understand the Gospel; for they do not receive the beginning of it:—" The beginning of the Gospel of Jesus Christ, as it is written in Isaiah the prophet²."' What the author of this curt statement meant, is explained by Titus of Bostra, who exhibits the quotation word for word as Serapion, following Origen, had exhibited it before him; and adding that St. Mark in this way 'connects the Gospel with the Law; recognizing the Law as the beginning of the Gospel³.' How does this prove that either Serapion or Titus disallowed the words υἱοῦ τοῦ Θεοῦ? The simple fact is that they are both reproducing Origen: and besides availing themselves of his argument, are content to adopt the method of quotation with which he enforces it.

Next, for the testimony of Basil. His words are,—' Mark makes the preaching of John the beginning of the Gospel,

---

¹ In Joan. iv. 15, 16.—See also contra Cels. i. 389 d e f, where Origen says the same thing more briefly. The other places are iv. 125 and 464.

² Οὔτε ἐπιστήμην τοῦ εὐαγγελίου ἔχουσι, τὴν τῶν εὐαγγελίων ἀρχὴν μὴ παρα-λαβόντες· ἀρχὴ τοῦ εὐαγγελίου Ἰησοῦ Χριστοῦ. καθὼς γέγραπται ἐν Ἡσαΐα τῷ προφήτῃ. adv. Manichaeos (ap. Galland. v. 61).

³ ap. Galland. v. 329.

saying, "The beginning of the Gospel of Jesus Christ . . .
as it is written in Isaiah the prophet . . . The voice of one
crying in the wilderness [1].'" This certainly shews that
Basil was treading in Origen's footsteps ; but it no more
proves that he disallowed the three words in dispute in
ver. 1, than that he disallowed the sixteen words not in
dispute in ver. 2.—from which it is undeniable that he
omits them intentionally, knowing them to be there. As
for Victorinus (A.D. 290), his manner of quoting the
beginning of St. Mark's Gospel is identical with Basil's[2],
and suggests the same observation.

If proof be needed that what precedes is the true account
of the phenomenon before us, it is supplied by Cyril of
Jerusalem, with reference to this very passage. He points
out that ' John was the end of the prophets, for "All the
prophets and the Law were until John ;" but the beginning
of the Gospel dispensation, for it says, "The beginning of
the Gospel of Jesus Christ," and so forth. John was bap-
tizing in the wilderness[3].' Cyril has therefore passed
straight from the middle of the first verse of St. Mark i.
to the beginning of ver. 4 : not, of course, because he
disallowed the eight and thirty words which come in
between ; but only because it was no part of his purpose
to quote them. Like Serapion and Titus, Basil and Cyril
of Jerusalem are in fact reproducing Origen : but unlike
the former two, the two last-named quote the Gospel ellip-
tically. The liberty indeed which the ancient Fathers
freely exercised, when quoting Scripture for a purpose,—
of leaving out whatever was irrelevant; of retaining just
so much of the text as made for their argument,— may
never be let slip out of sight. Little did those ancient
men imagine that at the end of some 1500 years a school
of Critics would arise who would insist on regarding every

[1] i. 250.   [2] *ap.* Galland. iv. 55.   [3] p. 42.

irregularity in such casual appeals to Scripture, as a deliberate assertion concerning the state of the text 1500 years before. Sometimes, happily, they make it plain by what they themselves let fall, that their citations of Scripture may not be so dealt with. Thus, Severianus. bishop of Gabala, after appealing to the fact that St. Mark begins his Gospel by styling our Saviour Υἱὸς Θεοῦ, straightway quotes ver. 1 without that record of Divine Sonship,— a proceeding which will only seem strange to those who omit to read his context. Severianus is calling attention to the considerate reserve of the Evangelists in declaring the eternal Generation of Jesus Christ. ' Mark does indeed say "Son of God"; but straightway, in order to soothe his hearers, he checks himself and cuts short that train of thought; bringing in at once about John the Baptist: saying,—" The beginning of the Gospel of Jesus Christ . . . as it is written in Isaiah the prophet, Behold," &c. No sooner has the Evangelist displayed the torch of Truth, than he conceals it [1].' How could Severianus have made his testimony more emphatic?

And now the reader is in a position to understand what Epiphanius has delivered. He is shewing that whereas St. Matthew begins his Gospel with the history of the Nativity, 'the holy Mark makes what happened at Jordan the introduction of the Gospel: saying,—The beginning of the Gospel . . . as it is written in Isaiah the prophet . . . The voice of one crying in the wilderness [2].' This does not of course prove that Epiphanius read ver. 1 differently from

---

[1] A. D. 400. De Sigill. ap. Chrys. xii. 412:—ὁ μακάριος Μάρκος, καθεὶς ἑαυτὸν εἰς τὸ εὐαγγέλιον, καὶ θαρσήσας τοῖς προγεγυμνασμένοις, λέγει μὲν " υἱὸν Θεοῦ," ἀλλ' εὐθέως συνέστειλε τὸν λόγον, καὶ ἐκολόβωσε τὴν ἔννοιαν, ἵνα μαλάξῃ τὸν ἀκροατήν. ἐπάγει οὖν εὐθέως τὰ κατὰ τὸν Βαπτιστήν, λέγων, " ἀρχὴ τοῦ εὐαγγελίου Ἰησοῦ Χριστοῦ, καθὼς γέγραπται ἐν Ἡσαίᾳ τῷ προφήτῃ ἰδοὺ " κ.τ.λ. ἔδειξε τὴν λαμπάδα τῆς ἀληθείας, καὶ εὐθέας ἀπέκρυψε.

[2] i. 427 :—ἀρχὴ τοῦ εὐαγγελίου . . . . ὡς γέγραπται ἐν Ἡσαίᾳ τῷ προφήτῃ . . . . φωνὴ βοῶντος ἐν τῇ ἐρήμῳ.

ourselves. He is but leaving out the one and twenty words
(5 in ver. 1 : 16 in ver. 2) which are immaterial to his
purpose. Our Lord's glorious designation (' Jesus Christ,
the Son of God,') and the quotation from Malachi which
precedes the quotation from Isaiah, stand in this writer's
way : his one object being to reach ' the voice of one crying
in the wilderness.' Epiphanius in fact is silent on the
point in dispute.

But the most illustrious name is behind. Irenaeus
(A.D. 170) unquestionably read Υἱοῦ τοῦ Θεοῦ in this place.
He devotes a chapter of his great work to the proof that
Jesus is the Christ,—very God as well as very Man ; and
establishes the doctrine against the Gnostics, by citing the
Evangelists in turn. St. Mark's testimony he introduces
by an apt appeal to Rom. i. 1–4, ix. 5, and Gal. iv. 4, 5 :
adding,—' The Son of God was made the Son of Man, in
order that by Him we might obtain the adoption : Man
carrying, and receiving, and enfolding the Son of God.
Hence, Mark says,—" The beginning of the Gospel of
Jesus Christ, the Son of God, as it is written in the
prophets[1]." ' Irenaeus had already, in an earlier chapter,
proved by an appeal to the second and third Gospels that
Jesus Christ is God. ' Quapropter et Marcus,' (he says)
' interpres et sectator Petri, initium Evangelicae conscrip-
tionis fecit sic: " Initium Evangelii Jesu Christi Filii Dei,
quemadmodum scriptum est in Prophetis," &c.[2] ' This at
all events is decisive. The Latin of either place alone
survives : yet not a shadow of doubt can be pretended as
to how the man who wrote these two passages read the
first verse of St. Mark's Gospel [3].

---

[1] i. 506 (lib. iii. cap. xvi).　　　　　[2] i. 461 (lib. iii. cap. x).

[3] Midway between the two places cited above, Irenaeus shews how the four
Gospels may be severally identified with the four living creatures described in
the Apocalypse. He sees the lion in St. John, who says: ' *In the beginning*

Even more interesting is the testimony of Victor of
Antioch ; for though he reproduces Origen's criticism, he
makes it plain that he will have nothing to say to Origen's
text [1]. He paraphrases, speaking in the person of the
Evangelist, the two opening verses of St. Mark's Gospel,
as follows!—' I shall make "the beginning of the Gospel"
from John : of the Gospel, I say "of the Son of God :"
for so "it is written in the prophets," viz. that He is the
Son of God. . . . Or, you may connect " as it is written in
the prophets" with "Behold, I send my messenger": in
which case, I shall make "the beginning of the Gospel of
the Son of God" that which was spoken by the prophets
concerning John.' And again,—' Mark says that John,
the last of the prophets, is "the beginning of the Gospel":
adding, " as it is written in the prophets, Behold," &c., &c.[2]'
It is therefore clear how Victor at least read the place.

*was the Word: and . . . . all things were made by him : and without him was
not anything made:*' the flying eagle in St. Mark, because he begins his
gospel with an appeal to 'the prophetic spirit which comes down upon men
from on high ; saying, " *The beginning of the Gospel . . . . as it is written in
the prophets.*" Hence the Evangelists' concise and elliptical manner, which is a
characteristic of prophecy' (lib. iii. cap. xi. § 8, p. 470). Such quotations as
these (18 words being omitted in one case, 5 in the other) do not help us. I
derive the above notice from the scholium in Evan. 238 (Matthaei's e,—N. T.
ii. 21); Curzon's ' 73. 8.'

The lost Greek of the passage in Irenaeus was first supplied by Grabe from
a MS. of the Quaestiones of Anastasius Sinaita) in the Bodleian (Barocc.
206, fol. πβ). It is the solution of the 144th Quaestio. But it is to be found in
many other places besides. In Evan. 238, by the way, twelve more of the lost
words of Irenaeus are found : viz. Οὔτε πλείονα τὸν ἀριθμόν, οὔτε ἐλάττονα
ἐνδέχεται εἶναι τὰ εὐαγγέλια· ἐπεὶ γάρ . . . . Germanus also (A.D. 715, ap.
Gall. xiii. 215) quoting the place, confirms the reading ἐν τοῖς προφήταις,—
which must obviously have stood in the original.

[1] Note, that he actually reads ' The beginning of the Gospel of the Son of
God,'—omitting the words ' JESUS CHRIST ': not, of course, as disallowing
them, but in order the more effectually to emphasize the Divine Sonship of
MESSIAH.

[2] Ἐγώ φησι (*sc.* ὁ Μάρκος) τὴν ἀρχὴν τοῦ Εὐαγγελίου ἀπὸ Ἰωάννου ποιήσομαι·
Εὐαγγελίου δὲ τοῦ υἱοῦ Θεοῦ, οὕτω γὰρ ἐν τοῖς προφήταις γέγραπται, ὅτι υἱός ἐστι
Θεοῦ . . . . δύνασαι δὲ τό, ὡς γέγραπται ἐν τοῖς προφήταις, συνάψαι τῷ, ἰδοὺ ἐγὼ
ἀποστέλλω τὸν ἄγγελόν μου· ἵνα τὴν ἀρχὴν ποιήσομαι τοῦ Εὐαγγελίου τοῦ υἱοῦ
Θεοῦ τὸ τοῖς προφήταις περὶ Ἰωάννου εἰρημένον. This is the first scholium in

It is time to close this discussion. That the Codexes which Origen habitually employed were of the same type as Cod. $\aleph$,—and that from them the words Ὑιοῦ τοῦ Θεοῦ were absent,—is undeniable. But that is the sum of the evidence for their omission. I have shewn that Serapion and Titus, Basil and Victorinus and Cyril of Jerusalem, do but reproduce the teaching of Origen : that Epiphanius delivers no testimony either way : while Irenaeus and Severianus bear emphatic witness to the genuineness of the clause in dispute. To these must be added Porphyry (A.D. 270)[1], Cyril of Alexandria[2], Victor of Antioch, ps.-Athanasius[3], and Photius[4], — with Ambrose[5], and Augustine[6] among the Latins. The clause is found besides in all the Versions, and in every known copy of the Gospels but three ; two of which are cursives. On what principle Tischendorf would uphold the authority of $\aleph$ and Origen against such a mass of evidence, has never been explained. In the meantime, the disappearance of the clause (Ὑιοῦ τοῦ Θεοῦ) from certain of the earliest copies of St. Mark's Gospel is only too easily accounted for. So obnoxious to certain precursors of the Gnostic sect was the fundamental doctrine which it embodies, that St. John (xx. 31) declares it to have been the very purpose of his Gospel to establish 'that Jesus is the Christ, the Son of God.' What more obvious than that the words at some very remote period should have been fraudulently removed from certain copies of the Gospel ?

the Catena as edited by Possinus,—p. 6. What follows is a well-known scholium of the same Catena, (the first in Cramer's ed.), which C. F. Matthaei (N. T. ii. 20) prints from six of his MSS. :—Ἰωάννην οὖν τὸν τελευταῖον τῶν προφητῶν ἀρχὴν εἶναι τοῦ Εὐαγγελίου φησὶν ὁ Μάρκος, ἐπιφέρων " ὡς γέγραπται ἐν τοῖς προφήταις· Ἰδοὺ κ.τ.λ."

[1] *Ap.* Hieron. vii. 17.   [2] vi. 330 *diserte.*   [3] ii. 413.
[4] A. D. 890.   De objectionibus Manichaeorum, *ap.* Galland. xiii. 667.
[5] i. 1529 d.   [6] Cons. 39.

APPENDIX V.

THE SCEPTICAL CHARACTER OF B AND ℵ.

THE sceptical character of the Vatican and Sinaitic MSS. affords a strong proof of the alliance between them and the Origenistic school. Instances found in these Codexes may be classed thus :—

Note 1. The following instances are professedly taken from the Gospels. Only a few are added from elsewhere.

Note 2. Other Uncials are also added, to indicate by specimens how far these two MSS. receive countenance or not from other sources, and also in part how far the same influence enter them.

I. Passages detracting from the Scriptural acknowledgement of the Divinity of our Lord :—

Υἱοῦ τοῦ Θεοῦ omitted—St. Mark i. 1 (ℵ*).
Ὁ Χριστὸς ὁ Υἱὸς . . . τοῦ ζῶντος omitted — St. John vi. 69 (ℵBC*DL).
Κύριε omitted—St. Mark ix. 24 (ℵABC*DL).
Τοῦ Κυρίου Ἰησοῦ omitted—St. Luke xxiv. 3 (D).
Θεοῦ changed into Κυρίου—Acts xx. 28 (AC*DES).
Omission of faith in CHRIST. εἰς ἐμέ—St. John vi. 47 (ℵBLΓ).
Slur on efficacy of prayer through CHRIST :
    Insert μέ—St. John xiv. 14 (ℵBEHUΓΔ).
      Transfer ἐν τῷ ὀνόματί μου—St. John xxi. 23 (ℵBC*LXVΔ).
Omission of εὐθέως in the cure—St. Mark vii. 35 (ℵBDLWᵈΔ)
        Cf. St. Mark ii. 12.

Judgement-seat of God instead of Christ — Rom. xiv. 10
(א*ABC*D &c.).

ʽO ὢν ἐν τῷ οὐρανῷ omitted—St. John iii. 13 (אBLΓᵇ).

Omission of Κύριε in penitent thief's prayer—St. Luke xxiii. 42
(אBC*DLM*).

,,   ,,   the Ascension in St. Luke. ἀνεφέρετο εἰς τὸν οὐρανόν—
St. Luke xxiv. 51 (א*D).

Insertion of οὐδὲ ὁ Υἱός from St. Mark xiii. 32 in St. Matt. xxiv.
36. Cf. Basil to Amphilochius, iii. 360-2 (Revi-
sion Revised, p. 210, note).

Omission of Θεός in reference to the creation of man—St. Mark
x. 6 (אBCIΔ). Cf. St. Matt. xii. 30 (BD).

,,   ,,   ἐπάνω πάντων ἐστίν—St. John iii. 31 (א*D).

,,   ,,   ὁ Υἱὸς μένει εἰς τὸν αἰῶνα— St. John viii. 35 (אXΓ).

,,   ,,   διελθὼν διὰ μέσον αὐτῶν, καὶ παρῆγεν οὕτως—St. John
viii. 59 (אBD).

τὸν Υἱὸν τοῦ ἀνθρώπου for τ. Υ. τ. Θεοῦ—St. John ix. 35 (אBD).

Κυρίου for Θεοῦ—2 Pet. i. 1 (א).

Omission of ὅτι ἐγὼ ὑπάγω πρὸς τὸν Πατέρα—St. John xvi. 6
(אBD).

,,   ,,   Κύριος—1 Cor. xv. 47 (א*BCD*EFG).

ʽΟς for Θς—1 Tim. iii. 16 (א, Revision Revised, pp. 431–43).

ʽΟ for ʽΟς—Col. ii. 10, making the Fulness of the Godhead the
head of all principality and power (BDEFG).

II. Generally sceptical tendency :—

N.B.—Omission is in itself sceptical.

Πνεῦμα Θεοῦ instead of τὸ Πνεῦμα τοῦ Θεοῦ—Matt. iii. 16 (אB).
Cf. Acts xvi. 7, τὸ Πνεῦμα Ἰησοῦ for τὸ Πνεῦμα—
(אABC²DE₂¹).

Γένεσις for γέννησις, slurring the Divine Birth — Matt. i. 18
(אBCPSZΔ).

Omission of the title of 'good' applied to our Lord—Matt.
xix. 16, 17 (אBDL).

,,   ,,   the necessity of our Lord to suffer. καὶ οὕτως
ἔδει—St. Luke xxiv. 46 (אBC*DL).

,,   ,,   last Twelve Verses of St. Mark (אB).

----

¹ E₂ of the Acts and Cath. Epp. (Laudianus) in the Bodleian Library at
Oxford, of the sixth century.

Omission of passages relating to Everlasting Punishment (closely Origenistic):

αἰωνίου ἁμαρτήματος for αἰων. κρίσεως—St. Mark iii. 29 (ℵBLΔ).

ἁμαρτίας (D)—ibid.

ὅπου ὁ σκώληξ αὐτῶν οὐ τελευτᾷ, καὶ τὸ πῦρ οὐ σβέννυται—St. Mark ix. 44, 46 (ℵBCLΔ).

„ „ the danger of rejecting our Lord — St. Matt. xxi. 44 (D).

„ „ καὶ πᾶσα θυσία ἁλὶ ἁλισθήσεται—St. Mark ix. 49 (ℵBLΔ).

„ „ the condemnation of Pharisaic treatment of widows—St. Matt. xxiii. 14 (ℵBDLZ).

„ „ καὶ τὸ βάπτισμα ὃ ἐγὼ βαπτίζομαι βαπτισθῆναι—St. Matt. xx. 22, 23 (ℵBDLZ).

„ „ αὐτῆς τὸν πρωτότοκον—St. Matt. i. 25 (ℵBZ).

„ „ the verse about prayer and fasting—St. Matt. xvii. 21 (ℵ*B).

„ „ the words giving authority to the Apostles to heal diseases—St. Mark iii. 15 (ℵBC*).

„ „ the forgiveness of sins to those who turn—St. Mark iv. 12 (ℵBCL).

„ „ condemnation of cities and mention of the Day of Judgement—St. Mark vi. 11 (ℵBCDLΔ).

„ „ fasting—St. Mark ix. 29 (ℵ*B).

„ „ taking up the Cross—St. Mark x. 21 (ℵBCDΔ).

„ „ the danger of riches—St. Mark x. 24 (ℵBΔ).

„ „ the danger of not forgiving others—St. Mark xi. 26 (ℵBLSΔ).

„ „ εὐλογημένη σὺ ἐν γυναιξίν—St. Luke i. 28 (ℵBL).

„ „ ἀλλ᾽ ἐπὶ παντὶ ῥήματι Θεοῦ—St. Luke iv. 4 (ℵBL).

„ „ ὁ διάβολος εἰς ὄρος ὑψηλόν—St. Luke iv. 5 (ℵBL).

„ „ ὕπαγε ὀπίσω μου, Σατανᾶ—St. Luke iv. 8 (ℵBDLΞ).

„ „ reference to Elijah's punishment, and the manner of spirit—St. Luke ix. 55, 56.

„ „ the saving effect of faith—St. Luke xvii. 19 (B).

„ „ the day of the Son of Man—St. Luke xvii. 24 (BD).

„ „ the descent of the Angel into Bethesda—St. John v. 3, 4 (ℵBC*D).

„ „ ἣν ἐγὼ δώσω—St. John vi. 51 (ℵBCLΔ).

U

III. Evincing a 'philosophical' obtuseness to tender passages:—

Omissions in the records of the Institution of the Holy Sacrament: thus—

φάγετε . . . τὸ . . . καινῆς—St. Mark xiv. 22–24 (אBCD).
καινῆς—St. Matt. xxvi. 27 (אB).
λάβετε, φάγετε . . . . κλώμενον—1 Cor. xi. 2–4 (אABC*).

Omission of Agony in the Garden and strengthening Angel—
St. Luke xxii. 43, 44 (ABRT, first corrector).

„   „   First Word from the Cross — St. Luke xxiii. 34 (אᵃBD*).

Mutilation of the LORD's Prayer—St. Luke xi. 2–4 : i.e.
Omission of ἡμῶν ὁ ἐν τοῖς οὐρανοῖς (אBL).

„   „   γενηθήτω τὸ θέλημά σου, ὡς ἐν οὐρανῷ, καὶ ἐπὶ τῆς γῆς (BL).

„   „.   ἀλλὰ ῥῦσαι ἡμᾶς ἀπὸ τοῦ πονηροῦ (א*BL).

Omission of εἰκῆ—Matt. v. 22 (אB).

„   :,   the verse telling of our LORD's coming to save what was lost—St. Matt. xviii. 11 (אBL*).

„   „   εὐλογεῖτε τοὺς καταρωμένους ὑμᾶς, καλῶς ποιεῖτε τοὺς μισοῦντας ὑμᾶς—St. Matt. v. 44 (אB).

:,   „   the prophecy of being numbered with the transgressors —St. Mark xv. 28 (אABC* ᵉᵗ³DX).

„   :,   ἐν τῷ φανερῷ—St. Matt. vi. 6 (אBDZ).

„   „   reference to the last cry—St. Mark xv. 39 (אBL).

„   „   striking on the face—St. Luke xxii. 64 (אBLMTΠ).

„   „   triple superscription (γράμμ. Ἑλλην. κ. Ῥωμ. κ. Ἑβραϊκ.)— St. Luke xxiii. 38 (BCL). So א* in St. John xix. 20–21.

„   „   καὶ ἀπὸ τοῦ μελισσίου κηρίου — St. Luke xxiv. 42 (אABDLΠ).

„   „   καὶ ἐζήτουν αὐτὸν ἀποκτεῖναι—St. John v. 15 (אBCDL).

λύσαντι for λούσαντι—Rev. i. 5 (אAC).

δικαιοσύνην for ἐλεημοσύνην—Matt. vi. 1 (א* ᵉᵗ ᵇ BD).

IV. Shewing attempts to classicize New Testament Greek.

These attempts have left their traces, conspicuous especially for omissions, all over B and א in a multiplicity of passages too numerous to quote. Their general character may be gathered in a perusal of Dr. Hort's Introduction, pp. 223–227, from which passage we may understand how these MSS. may have commended themselves at periods of general advancement in learning to eminent scholars like Origen and Dr. Hort. But unfortunately a Thucydidean compactness, condensed and well-pruned according to the fastidious taste of the study, is exactly that which does not in the long run take with people who are versed in the habits of ordinary life, or with scholars who have been exercised in many fields, as was shewn by the falling into disuse of Origen's critical manuscripts. The echoes of the fourth century have surely been heard in the nineteenth.

APPENDIX VI.

THE PESHITTO AND CURETONIAN.

[The Rev. C. H. WALLER, D.D., Principal of St. John's Hall, Highbury.]

A CAREFUL collation of the Curetonian Syriac with the Peshitto would I think leave no doubt on the mind of any one that the Curetonian as exhibited by Cureton himself is the later version. But in order to give full effect to the argument it would be necessary to shew the entire Curetonian fragment side by side with the corresponding portions of the Peshitto. Otherwise it is scarcely possible to realize (1) how entirely the one version is founded upon the other—(2) how manifestly the Curetonian is an attempt to improve upon the other; or (3) how the Curetonian presupposes and demands an acquaintance with the Gospels in general, or with views of Gospel history which belong to the Church rather than to the sacred text.

Even in those brief passages exhibited by Dr. Scrivener from both editions this can be made out. And it is capable of still further illustration from almost every page of Dr. Cureton's book.

To take the fragments exhibited by Dr. Scrivener first. (a) In St. Matt. xii. 1–4, where the Peshitto simply translates the Textus Receptus (not altered by our Revisers), saying that the disciples were hungry 'and began to pluck ears of corn and to eat,' the Curetonian amends thus:—'and the disciples were hungry and began to pluck ears of corn, and *break them in their hands*, and eat,' introducing (as it frequently does, e.g. St. Matt. iv. 11, 'for a season'; St. Matt.

iv. 21, 'laying his hand'; St. Matt. v. 12, 'your fathers';
St. Matt. v. 47, 'what thank have ye?') words borrowed
from St. Luke vi. 1.

But in the next verse of the passage, where the words
'on the Sabbath,' are absolutely required in order to make
the Pharisees' question intelligible to the first readers of
St. Matthew, 'Behold, thy disciples do what is not lawful
to do on the Sabbath' (Textus Receptus and Peshitto; not
altered by our Revisers), the Curetonian must needs draw
on the common knowledge of educated readers by exhibiting the question thus, 'Why are thy disciples doing what
is not lawful to do?' an abbreviated reading which leaves
us ignorant *what* the action objected to might be; whether
to pluck ears in another man's field, or to rub the grain
from them on the Sabbath day? On what possible ground
can such emendations as this have the preference of antiquity in their favour?

Again, the shewbread in ver. 4 of this passage is, not as
we have it in the Peshitto, 'the bread of the table of the
Lord,' ܠܚܡܐ ܕܦܬܘܪܗ ܕܡܪܝܐ, a simple phrase which every-
one can understand, but the Old Testament expression,
'face-bread,' ܠܚܡܐ ܐܦܝܐ, which exhibits the translator's
knowledge of the earlier Scriptures, as do his emendations
of the list of names in the first chapter of St. Matthew,
and, if I mistake not, his quotations also.

(*b*) Or, to turn to St. Mark xvi. 17–20 (the other passage
exhibited by Dr. Scrivener). Both the Peshitto and Curetonian shew their agreement, by the points in which they
differ from our received text. 'The Lord *Jesus* then, after
He had *commanded* His disciples, *was exalted* to heaven
and sat on the right hand of GOD'—is the Curetonian
phrase. The simpler Peshitto runs thus. '*Jesus* the Lord
then, after He had *spoken with them*, ascended to heaven,
and sat on the right hand of GOD.' Both alike introduce
the word 'Jesus' as do our Revisers: but the two slight

touches of improvement in the Curetonian are evident, and
belong to that aspect of the matter which finds expression
in the Creed, and in the obedience of the Church. Who
can doubt which phrase is the later of the two ? A similar
slight touch appears in the Curetonian addition to ver. 17
of 'them that believe *on Me*' instead of simply 'them that
believe.'

The following points I have myself observed in the
collation of a few chapters of St. Matthew from the two
versions. Their minuteness itself testifies to the *improved*
character of the Curetonian. In St. Matt. v. 32 we have been
accustomed to read, with our Text Received and Revised
and with all other authorities, 'Whosoever shall put away
his wife, except for the cause of *fornication.*' So reads the
Peshitto. But whence comes it that the Curetonian Syriac
substitutes here *adultery* for fornication, and thereby sanctions,—not the precept delivered by our Lord, but the
interpretation almost universally placed upon it ? How is
it possible to contend that here the Curetonian Syriac has
alone preserved the true reading? Yet either this must
be the case, or else we have a deliberate alteration of
a most distinct and precise kind, telling us, not what our
Lord said, but what He is commonly supposed to have
meant.

Not less curious is the addition in ver. 41, 'Whosoever
shall compel thee to go a mile, go with him two *others.*'
Our Lord said 'go with him twain,' as all Greek MSS.
except D bear witness. The Curetonian and D and some
Latin copies say practically 'go with him *three.*' Is this
again an original reading, or an improvement? It is no
accidental change.

But by far the most striking 'improvements' introduced
by the Curetonian MS. are to my mind, those which
attest the perpetual virginity of our Lord's Mother. The
alterations of this kind in the first chapter form a group

quite unique.   Beginning with ver. 18, we read as follows:—

In the Peshitto and our *Greek* Text without any variation.

Ver. 16. 'Jacob begat Joseph *the husband of Mary* of whom was born Jesus, who is called Messiah.'

ver. 18. 'Now the birth of Jesus Christ was on this wise (Peshitto, and Textus Receptus: Revised also, but with some uncertainty).'

ver. 19. 'Joseph *her husband* being a just man,' &c.

ver. 20. 'Fear not to take unto thee Mary *thy wife.*'

ver. 24. 'Joseph . . . did as the Angel of the Lord had bidden him, and took unto him *his wife.*'

ver. 25. 'And knew her not until she brought forth [her first-born] a son.'

In the Curetonian.

'Jacob begat Joseph *to whom was espoused* Mary *the virgin,* which bare Jesus *the Messiah.*'

'The birth of *the Messiah* was thus.'

ver. 19. '*Joseph,* because he was a righteous man,' &c. [there is no Greek or Latin authority with Cn. here].

. . . 'Mary *thine espoused*' (Cn. seems to be alone here).

. . . . . 'and took *Mary*' (Cn. seems alone in omitting 'his wife').

'And purely dwelt with her until she bare *the* son' (Cn. here is not alone except in inserting the article).

The absolute omission from the Curetonian Syriac of all mention of Joseph as Mary's *husband,* or of Mary as his *wife* is very remarkable.   The last verse of the chapter has suffered in other authorities by the loss of the word 'firstborn,' probably owing to a feeling of objection to the inference drawn from it by the Helvidians.   It seems to have been forgotten (1) that the fact of our Lord's being a 'firstborn' in the Levitical sense is proved by St. Luke

from the presentation in the temple (see Neh. x. 36); and
(2) that His being called a 'firstborn' in no way implies that
his mother had other children after him.   But putting this
entirely aside, the feeling in favour of Mary's perpetual
virginity on the mind of the translator of the Curetonian
Syriac was so strong as to draw him to *four distinct and
separate omissions*, in which he stands unsupported by any
authority, of the word ' husband ' in two places, and in two
others of the word ' wife.'

I do not see how any one can deny that here we have
emendations of the most deliberate and peculiar kind.
Nor is there any family of earlier readings which contains
them, or to which they can be referred.   The fact that the
Curetonian text has some readings in common with the
so-called *western* family of text (e.g. the transposition of
the beatitudes in Matt. v. 4, 5) is not sufficient to justify
us in accounting for such vagaries as this.   It is indeed
a 'Western' superstition which has exalted the Virgin
Mary into a sphere beyond the level of all that rejoice in
God her Saviour.   But the question here suggested is
whether this way of regarding the matter is truly *ancient*;
and whether the MS. of an ancient version which exhibits
such singular phenomena on its first page is worthy to be
set above the common version which is palpably its basis.
In the first sentence of the Preface Dr. Cureton states that
it was obtained from a Syrian Monastery *dedicated to
St. Mary Deipara*.   I cannot but wonder whether it never
occurred to him that the *cultus* of the Deipara, and the
taste which it indicates, may partly explain why a MS. of
a certain character and bias was ultimately domiciled there.
[See note at the end of this Chapter.]

Shall I be thought very disrespectful if I say that the
study which I have been able to devote to Dr. Cureton's
book has impressed me with a profound distrust of his

scholarship? 'She shall *bare* for thee a son,' says he on the
first page of his translation ;—which is not merely bald
and literal, but absolutely un-English in many places.

In Matt. vi. in the first verse we have *alms* and in the third and
fourth *righteousness*. An explanation.

In ver. 13 the Cn. has the *doxology*, but with *power omitted*, the
Peshitto *not*.

In ver. 17. Cn. *wash thy face* and *anoint thy head* instead of our
text.

In ver. 19. Cn. leaves out βρῶσις 'rust' and puts in 'where *falleth*
the moth.'

In x. 42. The *discipleship* instead of *disciple*.

In xi. 2. Of *Jesus* instead of *Christ*.

In xiii. 6. Parable of Sower, a *Targum*-like alteration.

ver. 13 a *most important Targum*.

ver. 33 a *wise woman took and hid in meal*.

xiv. 13 leaves out 'by ship,' and says 'on foot,' where the
Peshitto has 'on dry land,' an odd change, of an opposite kind to
some that I have mentioned.

In St. John iii. 6, Cn. has: 'That which is born of the flesh is
flesh, *because of flesh it is born ;* and that which is born of the
Spirit is spirit, *because God is a spirit, and of God it is born.'*
And in ver. 8: 'So is every one that is born *of water and* of the
Spirit.' This is a *Targum*-like expansion: possibly anti-Arian.
See Tischendorf's Gr. Test. *in loco*. All the above changes look
like deliberate emendations of the text.

[It is curious that the Lewis Codex and the Curetonian
both break off from the Traditional account of the Virgin-
birth, but in opposite directions. The Lewis Codex makes
Joseph our Lord's actual Father: the Curetonian treats the
question as described above. That there were two streams
of teaching on this subject, which specially characterized
the fifth century, is well known : the one exaggerating the
Nestorian division of the two Natures, the other tending in
a Eutychian direction. That *two fifth-century MSS. should
illustrate these deviations* is but natural ; and their survival
not a little remarkable.]

APPENDIX VII.

THE LAST TWELVE VERSES OF ST. MARK'S GOSPEL.

It would be a manifest defect, if a book upon Textual Criticism passing under the name of Dean Burgon were to go forth without some reference to the present state of the controversy on the subject, which first made him famous as a Textual critic.

His argument has been strengthened since he wrote in the following ways:—

1. It will be remembered that the omission of the verses has been rested mainly upon their being left out by B and ℵ, of which circumstance the error is mutely confessed in B by the occurrence of a blank space, amply sufficient to contain the verses, the column in question being the only vacant one in the whole manuscript. It has been generally taken for granted, that there is nothing in ℵ to denote any consciousness on the part of the scribe that something was omitted. But a closer examination of the facts will shew that the contrary is the truth. For—

i. The page of ℵ on which St. Mark ends is the *recto* of leaf 29, being the second of a pair of leaves (28 and 29), forming a single sheet (containing St. Mark xiv. 54–xvi. 8, St. Luke i. 1–56), which Tischendorf has shewn to have been written not by the scribe of the body of the New Testament in this MS., but by one of his colleagues who wrote part of the Old Testament and acted as *diorthota* or corrector of the New Testament—and who is further identified by the same great authority as the scribe of B. This person appears to have cancelled the sheet originally written by the scribe of א, and to have substituted for it the sheet as we now have it, written by himself. A correction so extensive and laborious can only have been made for the purpose of introducing some important textual change, too large to be effected by deletion, interlineation, or marginal note. Thus we are led not only to infer that the testimony of א is here not independent of that of B, but to suspect that this sheet may have been thus cancelled and rewritten in order to conform its contents to those of the corresponding part of B.

ii. This suspicion becomes definite, and almost rises to a certainty, when we look further into the contents of this sheet. Its second page (28 v°) exhibits four columns of St. Mark (xv. 16–xvi. 1); its third page (29 r°), the two last columns of St. Mark (xvi. 2–8) and the first two of St. Luke (i. 1–18). But the writing of these six columns of St. Mark is so spread out that they contain less matter than they ought; whereas the columns of St. Luke that follow contain the normal amount. It follows, therefore, that the change introduced by the *diorthota* must have been an extensive excision from St. Mark:—in other words, that these pages as originally written must have contained a portion of St. Mark of considerable length which has been omitted from the pages as they now stand. If these six columns of St. Mark were written as closely as the columns of St. Luke which follow, there would be room in them for the omitted twelve verses.—More particularly, the fifth column (the first of page 29 r°) is so arranged as to contain only about five-sixths of the normal quantity of matter, and the *diorthota* is thus enabled to carry over four lines to begin a new column, the sixth, by which artifice he manages to conclude St. Mark not with a blank column such as in B tells its own story, but with a column such as in this MS. is usual at the end of a book, exhibiting the closing words followed by an ' arabesque' pattern executed with the pen, and the subscription (the rest being left empty). But, by the very pains he has thus taken to conform this final column to the ordinary usage of the MS., his purpose of omission is betrayed even more conclusively, though less obviously, than by the blank column of B [1].

iii. A further observation is to be noted, which not only confirms the above, but serves to determine the place where the excision was made to have been at the very *end* of the Gospel. The last of the four lines of the sixth and last column of St. Mark (the second column of leaf 29 *r⁰*) contains only the five letters το γαρ ([ἐφοβοῦν]το γάρ), and has the rest of the space (more than half the width of the column) filled up with a minute and elaborate ornament executed with the pen in ink and vermilion, the like of which is nowhere else found in the MS., or in the New Testament part of B, such spaces being invariably left unfilled [2]. And not only so, but underneath, the usual ' arabesque' above the subscription, marking the conclusion of the text, has its horizontal arm extended all the way across the width of the column,—and not, as always elsewhere, but halfway or less [3]. It seems hardly possible to regard these carefully executed works of the pen of the *diorthota* otherwise than as precautions to guard against the possible restoration, by a subsequent reviser, of a portion of text deliberately omitted by him (the

[1] This observation is due to Dr. Salmon; see the Note appended to Lecture IX of his Historical Introduction to the New Testament (5th edition, p. 147).

[2] This fact was first pointed out by Dr. Gwynn in a memorandum communicated by him to Dr. Scrivener, who inserted it in his Plain Introduction to the Criticism of the New Testament (3rd edition, p. xii; cp. 4th edition, vol. I, p. 94), and I am indebted to the same source for this admirable amplification of part of that memorandum.

[3] A sufficient facsimile of the page in question (29 *r⁰*) is given by Dean Burgon in his Last Twelve Verses, reproduced from a photograph.

diorthota) from *the end* of the Gospel. They are evidence therefore that he knew of a conclusion to the Gospel which he designedly expunged, and endeavoured to make it difficult for any one else to reinsert.

We have, therefore, good reason to believe that the disputed Twelve Verses were not only in an exemplar known to the scribe of B, but also in the exemplar used by the scribe of ℵ; and that their omission (or, more properly, disappearance) from these two MSS. is due to one and the same person—the scribe, namely, who wrote B and who revised ℵ,—or rather, perhaps, to an editor by whose directions he acted.

2. Some early Patristic evidence has been added to the stores which the Dean collected by Dr. Taylor, Master of St. John's College, Cambridge. This evidence may be found in a book entitled 'The Witness of Hermas' to the Four Gospels, published in 1892, of which § 12 in the Second Part is devoted to 'The ending of St. Mark's Gospel,' and includes also quotations from Justin Martyr, and the Apology of Aristides. A fuller account is given in the Expositor of July 1893, and contains references to the following passages:—Irenaeus iii. 11. 6 (quoting xvi. 19); Justin Martyr, Trypho, § 138; Apol. i. 67; Trypho, § 85; Apol. i. 45; Barnabas, xv. 9; xvi. 7; Quarto-deciman Controversy (Polycarp)? and Clement of Rome, i. 42. The passages from Hermas are, 1. (xvi. 12–13) Sim. ii. 1, Vis. i. 1, iii. 1, iv. 1, and v. 4; 2. (xvi. 14) Sim. ix. 141 and 20. 4, Vis. iii. 8. 3, iii. 7. 6; 3. (xvi. 15–16) Vis. iii, Sim. ix. 16, 25; 4. (xvi. 17–18) Vis. iv, Mand. i, xii. 2. 2–3, Sim. ix. 1. 9, iii. 7, ix. 26, Mand. xii. 6. 2; 5. (xvi. 19-20) Vis. iii. 1. Some of the references are not apparent at first sight, but Dr. Taylor's discussions in both places should be read carefully.

3. In my own list given above, p. 109, of the writers who died before A.D. 400, I have added from my two

examinations of the Ante-Chrysostom Fathers to the list
in The Revision Revised, p. 421, the Clementines, four
references from the Apostolic Canons and Constitutions,
Cyril of Jerusalem, Gregory of Nyssa, the Apocryphal
Acts of the Apostles, and two references to the four of
St. Ambrose mentioned in 'The Last Twelve Verses,' p. 27.
To these Dr. Waller adds, Gospel of Peter, § 7 (πενθοῦντες
καὶ κλαίοντες), and § 12 (ἐκλαίομεν καὶ ἐλυπούμεθα), referring
to the ἅπαξ λεγόμενον, as regards the attitude of the Twelve
at the time, in xvi. 10.

4. On the other hand, the recently discovered Lewis
Codex, as is well known, omits the verses. The character
of that Codex, which has been explained above in the
sixth chapter of this work, makes any alliance with it
suspicious, and consequently it is of no real importance
that its testimony, unlike that of B and ℵ, is claimed to
be unswerving.

For that manuscript is disfigured by heretical blemishes
of the grossest nature, and the obliteration of it for the
purpose of covering the vellum with other writing was
attended with circumstances of considerable significance.

In the first chapter of St. Matthew, Joseph is treated
as the father of our Lord (vers. 16, 21, 24) as far as His
body was concerned, for as to His soul even according to
teaching of Gnostic origin He was treated as owing His
nature to the Holy Ghost (ver. 20). Accordingly, the
blessed Virgin is called in the second chapter of St. Luke
Joseph's 'wife,' μεμνηστευμένη being left with no equivalent [1]: and at His baptism, He is described as '*being as
He was called* the son of Joseph' (St. Luke iii. 23). According to the heretical tenet that our Lord was chosen
out of other men to be made the Son of God at the
baptism, we read afterwards, 'This is My Son, My chosen'

---

[1] On the contrary, in Tatian's Diatessaron γυναικί is left out and μεμνηστευμένη is translated. For the Curetonian, see above, p. 295.

(St. Luke ix. 35), 'the chosen of God' (St. John i. 34), 'Thou art My Son and My beloved' (St. Matt. iii. 17), 'This is My Son Who is beloved' (St. Mark ix. 7); and we are told of the Holy Ghost descending like a dove (St. Matt. iii. 16), that It '*abode*' upon Him.' Various smaller expressions are also found, but perhaps the most remarkable of those which have been left upon the manuscript occurs in St. Matt. xxvii. 50, 'And Jesus cried with a loud voice, and *His Spirit went up.*' After this, can we be surprised because the scribe took the opportunity of leaving out the Last Twelve Verses of St. Mark which contain the most detailed account of the Ascension in the Gospels, as well as the καὶ ἀνεφέρετο εἰς τὸν οὐρανόν of St. Luke?

Again, at the time when the manuscript was put out of use, and as is probable in the monastery of St. Catherine so early as the year 778 A. D. (Introduction by Mrs. Lewis, p. xv), the old volume was pulled to pieces, twenty-two leaves were cast away, the rest used in no regular order, and on one at least, as we are told, a knife was employed to eradicate the writing. Five of the missing leaves must have been blank, according to Mrs. Lewis: but the seventeen remaining leaves contained passages of supreme importance as being expressive of doctrine, like St. John i. 1–24, St. Luke i. 16–39, St. Mark i. 1–11, St. Matt. xxviii. 8–end, and others. Reading the results of this paragraph in connexion with those of the last, must we not conclude that this manuscript was used for a palimpsest, and submitted to unusual indignity in order to obliterate its bad record?

It will be seen therefore that a cause, which for unchallenged evidence rests solely upon such a witness, cannot be one that will commend itself to those who form their conclusions judicially. The genuineness of the verses, as part of the second Gospel, must, I hold, remain unshaken by such opposition.

5. An ingenious suggestion has been contributed by

Mr. F. C. Conybeare, the eminent Armenian scholar, founded upon an entry which he discovered in an Armenian MS. of the Gospels, dated A.D. 986, where 'Ariston Eritzou' is written in minioned uncials at the head of the twelve verses. Mr. Conybeare argues, in the Expositor for October, 1893, that 'Ariston Eritzou' is not the copyist himself, who signs himself Johannes, or an Armenian translator, Ariston or Aristion being no Armenian name. He then attempts to identify it with Aristion who is mentioned by Papias in a passage quoted by Eusebius (H. E. iii. 39) as a disciple of the Lord. Both the words 'Ariston Eritzou' are taken to be in the genitive, as 'Eritzou' certainly is, and to signify 'Of or by Aristion the presbyter,' this being the meaning of the latter word. The suggestion is criticized by Dr. Ad. Harnack in the Theologische Literaturzeitung, 795, where Dr. Harnack pronounces no opinion upon the soundness of it: but the impression left upon the mind after reading his article is that he is unable to accept it.

It is remarkable that the verses are found in no other Armenian MS. before 1100. Mr. Conybeare traces the version of the passage to an old Syrian Codex about the year 500, but he has not very strong grounds for his reasoning; and even then for such an important piece of information the leap to the sub-Apostolic age is a great one. But there is another serious difficulty in the interpretation of this fragmentary expression. Even granting the strong demands that we may construe over the expression of Papias, Ἀριστίων καὶ ὁ πρεσβύτερος Ἰωάννης, and take Aristion to have been meant as a presbyter, and that according to the parallel of Aristion in Eusebius' history having been transliterated in an Armenian version to Ariston, Aristion 'the disciple' may be the man mentioned here, there is a formidable difficulty presented by the word 'Aristŏn' as it is written in the place quoted. It ought at least to have had a long ō according to Dr. Harnack, and it is not in the genitive case as 'Eritzou' is. ,Altogether, the expression is so elliptical, and occurs with such isolated mystery in a retired district, and at such a distance of years from the event supposed to be chronicled, that the wonder is, not that a diligent and ingenious explorer should advocate a very curious idea that he has formed upon a very interesting piece of intelligence, but that other Critics should have been led to welcome it as a key to a long-considered problem. \Are we not forced to see in this incident an instance of a truth not unfrequently verified, that when people neglect a plain solution, they are induced to welcome another which does not include a tenth part of the evidence in its support?

Of course the real difficulty in the way of accepting these verses as the composition of St. Mark lies in the change of style found in them. That this change is not nearly so great as it may appear at first sight, any one may satisfy himself by studying Dean Burgon's analysis of the words given in the ninth chapter of his 'Last Twelve Verses of St. Mark.' But it has been the fashion in some quarters to confine ancient writers to a wondrously narrow form of style in each case, notwithstanding Horace's rough Satires and exquisitely polished Odes, and Cicero's Letters to his Friends and his Orations and Philosophical Treatises. Perhaps the recent flood of discoveries respecting early Literature may wash away some of the film from our sight. There seems to be no valid reason why St. Mark should not have written all the Gospel that goes by his name, only under altered circumstances. The true key seems to be, that at the end of verse 8 he lost the assistance of St. Peter. Before ἐφοβοῦντο γάρ, he wrote out St. Peter's story: after it, he filled in the end from his own acquired knowledge, and composed in summary. This very volume may supply a parallel. Sometimes I have transcribed Dean

X

Burgon's materials with only slight alteration, where necessary imitating as I was able his style. In other places, I have written solely as best I could.

I add two suggestions, not as being proved to be true, because indeed either is destructive of the other, but such that one or other may possibly represent the facts that actually occurred. To meet the charge of impossibility, it is enough to shew what is possible, though in the absence of direct evidence it may not be open to any one to advocate any narrative as being absolutely true.

I. Taking the story of Papias and Clement of Alexandria, as given by Eusebius (H. E. ii. 15), that St. Mark wrote his gospel at the request of Roman converts, and that St. Peter, as it seems, helped him in the writing, I should suggest that the pause made in ἐφοβοῦντο γάρ, so unlike the close of any composition, of any paragraph or chapter, and still less of the end of a book, that I can recollect, indicates a sudden interruption. What more likely than that St. Peter was apprehended at the time, perhaps at the very moment when the MS. reached that place, and was carried off to judgement and death? After all was over, and the opportunity of study returned, St. Mark would naturally write a conclusion. He would not alter a syllable that had fallen from St. Peter's lips. It would be the conclusion composed by one who had lost his literary illuminator, formal, brief, sententious, and comprehensive. The crucifixion of the leading Apostle would thus impress an everlasting mark upon the Gospel which was virtually his. Here the Master's tongue ceased : here the disciple took up his pen for himself.

II. If we follow the account of Irenaeus (Eus. H. E. v. 8) that St. Mark wrote his Gospel—and did not merely publish it—after St. Peter's death, Dr. Gwynn suggests to me that he used his notes made from St. Peter's dictation or composed with his help up to xvi. 8, leaving at the end what were exactly St. Peter's words. After that, he added from his own stores, and indited the conclusion as I have already described.

Whether either of these descriptions, or any other solution of the difficulty, really tallies with the actual event, I submit that it is clear that St. Mark may very well have written the twelve verses himself; and that there is no reason for resorting to Aristion, or to any other person for the authorship. I see that Mr. Conybeare expresses his indebtedness to Dean Burgon's monograph, and expresses his opinion that 'perhaps no one so well sums up the evidence for and against them' as he did (Expositor, viii. p. 241). I tender to him my thanks, and echo for myself all that he has said.

APPENDIX VIII.

NEW EDITIONS OF THE PESHITTO-SYRIAC AND THE HARKLEIAN-SYRIAC VERSIONS.

A BOOK representing Dean Burgon's labours in the province of Sacred Textual Criticism would be incomplete if notice were not taken in it of the influence exercised by him upon the production of editions of the two chief Syriac Versions.

Through his introduction of the Rev. G. H. Gwilliam, B.D. to the late Philip E. Pusey, a plan was formed for the joint production of an edition of the Peshitto New Testament by these two scholars. On the early and lamented death of Philip Pusey, which occurred in the following year, Mr. Gwilliam succeeded to his labours, being greatly helped by the Dean's encouragement. He has written on the Syriac Canons of the Gospels; and the nature of his work upon the Peshitto Gospels, now in the press, may be seen on consulting his article on 'The Materials for the Criticism of the Peshitto New Testament' in the third volume of Studia Biblica et Ecclesiastica, pp. 47–104, which indeed seems to be sufficient for the Prolegomena of his edition. A list of his chief authorities was also kindly contributed by him to my Scrivener, and they are enumerated there, vol. II. pp. 12–13. The importance of this work, carried on successively by two such accomplished Syriacists, may be seen from and will illustrate the sixth chapter of this work.

In connexion with the Dean, if not on his suggestion, the late Rev. Henry Deane, B.D., when Fellow of St. John's College, Oxford, began to collect materials for a new and critical edition of the Harkleian. His work was carried on during many years, when ill-health and failing eyesight put a stop to all efforts, and led to his early death—for on leaving New College, after having been Tutor there for five years, I examined him then a boy at the top of Winchester College. Mr. Deane has left the results of his work entered in an interleaved copy of Joseph White's ' Sacrorum Evangeliorum Versio Syriaca Philoxeniana '—named, as my readers will observe, from the translator Mar Xenaias or Philoxenus, not from Thomas of Harkel the subsequent editor. A list of the MSS. on which Mr. Deane based his readings was sent by him to me, and inserted in my Scrivener, vol. II. p. 29. Mr. Deane added (in a subsequent letter, dated April 16, 1894):—' My labours on the *Gospels* shew that the H[arkleian] text is much the same in all MSS. The Acts of the Apostles must be worked up for a future edition by some one who knows the work.' Since his lamented death, putting a stop to any edition by him, his widow has placed his collation just described in the Library of St. John's College, where by the permission of the Librarian it may be seen, and also used by any one who is recognized as continuing the valuable work of that accomplished member of the College. Is there no capable and learned man who will come forward for the purpose?

GENERAL INDEX.

A.

A or Alexandrian MS., 24, 31, 57, 76, 175, 201, 213 note 2.

א or Sinaitic MS., 2, 24, 31, 32, 49, 57, 174, 219, 235; six conjugate leaves, 52, 165, 233; value, B–א, 55, 68–9; history and character, 153, 160 &c., 233–5; sceptical character, App. V. 287.

Acacius, 2, 155; probably the scribe of B, 154.

Acta Philippi, 100–20.

Acta Pilati, 100–20.

Adamantius, copies of, 167. *See* Origen.

Alexander Alexandrinus, 100, 113, 119.

Alexandria, school of, 2, 122, 234.

Alexandrians and Egyptians, 113.

Alford, 171.

Ambrose, St., 101–20.

Ammonius, 11, 242.

Amphilochius, St., 101-20.

Anaphora Pilati, 112.

Antioch, early Church at, 123–4.

Antiquity, 29–31.

Aphraates, 103 – 14, 213 note 4; witnesses to Peshitto, 130.

Apocryphal Acts of the Gospels, 103–15, 132.

Apollonides, 10.

Apostolic Canons and Constitutions, 100, 103–15, 119.

Apostolic Fathers, 99, 118.

Archelaus, 100, 105–13, 119, 130.

Arius, 110, 111, 114, 121.

Armenian Version, 23, 49, 136.

Asclepiades, 10.

Athanasius, 100, 103–15, 119, 121, 148, 235 note 1, 244.

Athenagoras, 99, 103, 115, 119.

Augustine, St., on Old-Latin Texts, 140–3; canon of, 61 note, 198.

B.

B or Vatican MS., 2, 24, 31, 32, 49, 57, 174; number of omissions, 78; history and character, 153, 160 &c., 233-5; sceptical character of, App. V. 287; B and א, their value, 55, 68–89.

Barnabas, St., 104, 107.

Bartolocci, 157.

Basil, St., 97, 101, 1c7–15, 117, 197, 281–2.

Basilides, 3.

Bengel, 3.

Beratinus, Codex (Φ), 25, 26, 175.

Bethabara or Bethany, 88.

Beza, 3.

Bigg, Dr., 151.

Birch, 157.

Bobiensis (k), 137.

Bohairic Version, 23, 30, 49, 136, 149–50, and *passim*.

Brixianus (f), 137.

Burgon, Dean, Indexes of, Preface, 94; addition by, to Greek MSS., 21 note 2.

Burkitt, Mr. F. C., 129 note 1.

C.

C or Parisian MS., 24, 31, 51, 57, 76, 175.

Caesarea (Turris Stratonis), library of, 2, 152, 163–5, 225, 274. *See* B and א.

Caesarea, School of, 121, 152–8.

Caesarea Philippi, our Lord's stay at, 124.

Callixtus, 99, 120.

Candidus Arianus, 101, 113, 120.

Canon of the N. T., 10, 13–14, 161, 172; settlement of the Canon followed by that of the Text, 173.

Celsus, 107.

Chase, Dr. F. H., 144. 176 note.
Chrysostom, St., 31, 161, 197.
Ciasca, Agostino, 132.
Claromontanus (h), 137.
Clemens Alex., 58, 62, 99, 103–15, 117, 121, 148, 149, 150, 234, 241, 246.
Clemens Rom., 105.
Clementines, 99, 105, 109, 111, 119.
Colbertinus (c), 137.
Complutensian edition, 3.
Concilia Carthaginiensia, 100, 108, 119.
Concordia discors, 17, 81–8.
Conflation, 80–1, 206–7, 227–9.
Consent without Concert, 17.
Constans, 163 note 3.
Constantine I, 160, 163 note 3.
Constantinople, Councils of, 173.
Constantius II, 160, 161 note 1.
Context, 61–5.
Continuity, 58–61.
Conybeare, Mr. F. C., 304–5, 307.
Cook, Canon, 163 note 4, 227.
Corbeiensis I, II, (ff¹, ff²), 137.
Cornelius, 100, 119.
Corruption, pre-Evangelistic, 146.
Crawford, the Earl of, 129.
Critical copies, 36 note.
Curetonian Version, 31, 91; date of, 123–34; origin of text, 144 &c, 182 note 2; 218 note 11, and passim.
Curetonian and Peshitto, App. VI. 292.
Cursive MSS., 24, 51, 156–8, 196–223; in relation to later Uncials, 199–203; main body of, not a single copy, 223; copied in part from papyrus, 235; the first extant, 200.
Cyprian, St., 100, 103–15, 120.
Cyril of Alexandria, St., 31, 119, 247.
Cyril of Jerusalem, St., 101, 103–15, 282.

D.

D or Cod. Bezae, 24, 31, 51, 76, 126, 144, 175–95; sympathy with Old-Latin MSS., 56.
D and E, Codd. of St. Paul, 54, 231.
Δ, Cod. Sangallensis, in St. Mark, 204.
Damascus, Early Church at, 122–4.
Deane, the late Rev. H., and Harkleian, App. VIII. 309.
Decapolis, 123 note.
Delicate expressions rubbed off in the old Uncials, 190.

Diatessarons, formerly abounded 252
Didachè, 99, 103, 104.
Didymus, 101, 103–15, 119, 120.
Diez, Fried., 143 note.
Diodorus (Tarsus), 101, 120.
Diognetus, Epistle to, 99, 118.
Dionysius Alex., 100, 107, 110, 121, 148, 234.
Doctrine and the Text of N.T., connexion between, 173.

E.

E, Cod. of Gospels, 203.
E of Paul = D of Paul, 54, 231.
Edessa, 134.
Egyptian Versions, 31.
Elzevirs, 3.
Ephraem Syrus, St., 103, 107, 110, 112, 132, 243; witnesses to Peshitto, 130.
Epiphanius, St., 101, 103–15, 117, 120, 133, 243, 283–4.
Erasmus, 3, 15.
Esaias Abbas, 101, 104, 120.
Ethiopic Version, 23, 49, 51, 136.
Eumenes II, 155.
Eunomius, 101.
Eusebian Canons, 242.
Eusebius (Caesarea), 2, 30, 31, 100, 103–15, 121, 133, 152, 162; personally favoured the Traditional Text, 100, 121, 153; probably not the scribe of B, 154; latitudinarian, 154, 172; on St. Mark xvi., 55, 58, 109, 242.
Eusebius (Emesa), 107.
Eustathius, 100, 114, 120.
Euthalius (Sulci), 164 note 2.
Evagrius Ponticus, 100, 110, 120.
Evan., 102 = B, 54.

F.

F of St. Paul, like G, 56.
Fathers, 19, 23, 26, 50, 52; value of quotations by, 57–8, 97–8; early, witness of, 94–122; indexes to quotations in, by Dean Burgon, Pref., 94–5.
Faustinus, 101, 114, 120.
Ferrar group, 56, 114, 200, 235–6.
Firmicus Maternus, 100, 108, 119.

G.

G of St. Paul, like F, 56.
Genealogy, 229–37.
Genealogy, the, in St. Luke iii., 181–2.
Giles, Mr. H. A., 156 note.
Gothic Version, 23, 136.

Gregory, Dr. C. R., prolegomena, 160.

Gregory Naz., St., 101, 103–15, 117, 119, 197.

Gregory Nyss., St., 101, 103–15, 117, 120, 249 note, 260.

Gregory Thaumaturgus, St., 100, 110, 119, 130, 152.

Griesbach, 3, 117, 148.

Gwilliam, Rev. G. H., Pref.; in Studia Biblica, 128, 129 note 1, 241 note; editor of Peshitto, App. VIII. 308.

Gwynn, Rev. Dr., App. VII. 298–301, 306.

H.

H of St. Paul, 164.

Haddan, A. W., 174 note.

Harkleian Version, 49, 133–4; new ed., App VIII. 309.

Harnack, Dr., 304-5.

Harris, Mr. J. Rendel, 144 note 1, 176.

Hedybia, 244.

Hegesippus, 99, 111, 118.

Heracleon, 10, 99, 121, 148.

Hermophilus, 10.

Herodotus, 155.

Hesychius, 243.

Hilary, St. (Poictiers), 104–15, 117, 119, 169.

Hill, Rev. J. Hamlyn, 133.

Hippolytus, St., 99, 104–15, 117, 119.

Hort, Dr., 4, 7, 95, 158, 176, 251, 291, and passim; admissions of, 14; involuntary witness of, 90–4; inaccurate upon the early Fathers, 117, 121; fancies of, 129 note 2; B and ℵ written at Rome, 165; W.-Hort, 208 note 11; on the Traditional Text, 221-2, 236; on Genealogy, 230. See Conflation.

I.

Internal Evidence, 65–7, 214-5.

Interpolations, 81.

Irenaeus, St., 98, 99, 103-15, 117, 119, 284.

Isaias. See Esaias.

Itala, 143.

Ἰωάννης or Ἰωάνης, 87.

J.

Jacobites, 133.

Jacobus Nisibenus, 132.

Jerome, St., on Old-Latin Texts, 140–2, 244.

Jona and Jonah, 87.

Julius (Pope), 100, 120.

Julius Africanus, 100, 112, 121.

Justin Martyr, St., 30, 99, 103–15, 117, 119; ps. Justin, 108, 111.

Juvencus, 100, 105, 110, 120.

L.

L or Regius, 4, 30, 32, 204.

Lachmann, 4, 90, 158, 225.

Lactantius, 100, 120.

Laodicea, Council of, 172.

Last Twelve Verses, i.e. of St. Mark, 55, 102, 232, App. VII. 298.

Latin MSS., Old, 4, 30, 31, 49, 51, 64, 126; do not fall strictly into three classes, 136–9; Wiseman's theory of, false, 142; did not come from one stem, 135–46; influenced by Low-Latin dialects, 135–146; derived much from Syrian pre-Evangelistic corruption, 144-6.

Lectionaries, 22 and note.

Letters in Guardian, Dean Burgon's, 200 note 3.

Lewis Codex, 131-2, 134 note, 144, 302-3, and passim.

Libraries, destruction of, 174.

Library at Caesarea. See Caesarea.

Low-Latin MSS., 122. See Latin MSS.

Lucifer (Cagliari), 101, 103, 104, 114, 120.

M.

Macarius Alexandrinus, 100 note.

Macarius Magnes, 101, 106-12, 120.

Macarius Magnus or Aegyptius, 100, 104, 110, 115, 120.

Mai, Cardinal, editions of B, 75, 159.

Manuscripts, multitude of, 24-7, 19, 21 and note 2; six classes of, 22 note; kinds of, 24; value of, 53-6; in profane authors, 21 note 1. See Papyrus, Vellum, Uncial, Cursive.

Marcion, 10, 97, 110, 111, 112.

Mariam and Mary, 84-6.

Maries, the, in N. T., 84-6.

Mark, St. See Last Twelve Verses.

Maronite use of the Peshitto, 128.

Maunde Thompson, Sir E., Pref., 155-6, 158.

Melito, 131.

Menander, 10.

Methodius, 100, 106, 110, 117, 119, 131.

Mico, 137.

Migne's edition of the Fathers, 96.

Mill, 3.
Miller's Textual Guide, 3 note, 91 note.
Miller's Scrivener (Plain Introduction, ed. 4), *passim*.
Ministry, our Lord's, in the North and North-West, 123.
Monacensis (9), 137.
Monophysite use of the Peshitto, 128.
Monothelitism, condemned in 680 A.D., 173.

N.

Nemesius, 101, 120.
Neologian Text, 99, 103.
Nestorian use of Peshitto, 128.
Neutral Text (so-called), 4, 92.
Nicodemus, Gospel of, 107, 257.
Notes of Truth, seven, 29, 40-67.
Novatian, 100, 106, 114.

O.

Omissions, 81, 280-1, 291.
Optatus, 100, 108, 110, 120.
Origen, 2, 10, 31, 50, 51, 58, 100, 104-15, 117, 121, 122, 130, 162, 169, 242, 247, 255 note 6, 272, 280-1, 291; his great influence, 162; a Textual Critic, 149-54; founder of the Caesarean school, 152-3, 162-5; character, 152; fancies, 169 note 2; critical copies, 274-5.
Origenism, condemned in 553 A.D., 173.
Orthodox, the, 264.

P.

Φ. *See* Beratinus.
Pacianus, 100, 103, 120.
Palatinus (e), 137.
Pamphilus, 2, 100, 115, 121, 152, 163-4.
Paper, first made in China, 156 note.
Papias, 99, 109, 118.
Papyrus MSS., 24, 154-8, 163, 201; copying from, 2, 175, 235.
Parisian Codex. *See* C.
Paul, St., 145.
Peshitto Version, 31, 91, 123; antiquity of, 125-134, 210, 224: Peshitto and Curetonian, texts of, App. VI. 292.
Peter (Alexandria), 100, 121, 148.
Peter, Gospel of, 99, 107, 111, 119.
Peter, St., App. VII. 306.
Philastrius, 101. 103, 120.
Phillips, Cod., 129 note.

Philo (Carpasus or Carpasia), 101, 103, 104, 107, 110, 120.
Philoxenian. *See* Harkleian.
Polycarp, 103.
Pontianus, 99, 120.
Porphyry, 108.
Prior, Dr. Alexander, 156 note.
Pusey, P. E., Pref. and 129.

Q.

Q, Cod., 175.
Quaestiones ex Utroque Testamento, 101, 105-15, 120.

R.

R, Cod. of St. Luke (Cod. Nitriensis), 204 note.
Rabbūla, 133.
Recensions, phantom, 79, 91, 93, 121.
Rehdigeranus (l), 137.
Respectability. *See* Weight.
Revision Revised, the, 91, 102, *passim*.
Revisers, 208 note 11, 212, 245.
Romance languages, origin of, 143.
Rossanensian Codex. *See* Σ.
Rulotta, 157.

S.

Σ (Rossanensian), Cod., 25, 76, 175.
Sachau, Dr., 129 note.
Sahidic (Thebaic) Version, 23, 136.
Sangallensia Fragmenta (n), 137.
Sangermanensis I (g²), 137.
Scholz, 4.
Scrivener, Dr, Pref., 5, 32, 135, 227, 231, 233, 272.
Seniores apud Irenaeum, 99, 118.
Serapion, 100, 109, 119.
Sinaitic MS. *See* ℵ.
Slavonic Version, 136.
Stephen, Rob., 3.
Synodical Letter, 100, 119.
Synodus Antiochena, 100, 105, 113, 119, 130.
Synoptic problem, 146.
Syria, rapid spread of the Church in, 123-4.
Syriac Canons, 109, 254 note.
Syriac Sections, 291.
Syriac Versions, 49, 123-34.
'Syrian,' an audacious nick-name, 91-2.
Syrio-Low-Latin Text, 135-47, 225; intercommunication between Syria and Italy, 145-6.

T.

T, Cod., **204** note.
Tatian, 97, 103, 110.
Tatian's Diatessaron, 126, 132–4, 242, 302 note.
Taylor, Rev. Dr., 300.
Tertullian, 99, 104–15, 120.
Testament of Abraham, 99, 104, 119.
Tests of Truth, seven, 24, 40–67.
Textual Criticism, 1–5; importance of, Pref., 6 note.
Textus Receptus, origin of the name, 3; character of, 5, 15–16, 30; imperfect, 5.
Theodoret (Cyrrhus), 133, 134.
Theodorus Heracleensis, 100, 107, 114, 119.
Theodotus, 10, 113, 114.
Theognotus, 100, 121, 148.
Theophilus Antiochenus, 99, 120.
Theophylact, 49 note 1.
Tischendorf, 4, 5 note, 7, 9, 49 note, 98, 99, 136, 158, 160 note 2; curious reasoning, 169 and note 1, 225.
Titus of Bostra, 101, 104–15, 119.
Tradition, nature of, 196–9, 224.
Traditional Text, character of, 5, 196–9; founded upon the vast majority of authorities, 13; relation to the Canon, 13–14, 32, 172–3, 197; variously attested, 29, 40–7; dates back to the earliest time, 90–147; settled first, 173; finally, 173; mode of settlement, 198; continuity of, 224; history of, 236–7; incontrovertible as a fact, 236.

U.

Uncials, 24, 51.
Uncials, later, 196–223. *See* Cursives.

V.

Valentinians, 10, 30, 113.

Valentinus, 260.
Variety, 49–53.
Vatican MS. *See* B.
Vellum, 154–8, 174.
Vercellensis (a), 137.
Veronensis (b), 137.
Versions, 19, 22, 26, 50, 52; value of, 56.
Victor of Antioch, 284.
Victorinus (Afer), 101, 105, 108, 113, 114, 120.
Victorinus (Pettau), 101, 108, 109, 119.
Viennensium et Lugdunensium Epistola, 99, 118.
Vincentius, 109.
Vindobonensis (i), 137.
Vulgate, 30, 31, and *passim*.

W.

Waller, Rev. Dr. C. H., Pref., App. VI. 292–7, App. VII. 302.
Weight, 53–8, 77, 226.
Westcott, Bp. of Durham, 4; on the Canon, 92.
Westcott and Hort, 226, 232.
Western Text, 135–47. *See* Syrio-Low-Latin.
Wetstein, 3.
White, Rev. H. J., 139, 142.
Wiseman, Cardinal, 135, 143.
Woods, Rev. F. H., 130.
Wright, Dr. W., 129 note 2.

X.

Ξ, Cod. Zacynthius, 204
Ximenes, Cardinal, 3, 236.

Z.

Z, Cod. Dublinensis, 204 note 1.
Zeno, 101, 107, 114, 120.

INDEX II.

PASSAGES OF THE NEW TESTAMENT COMMENTED ON.

ST. MATTHEW :

PAGE

i. 2–16 . . . 180–2
16, 18, 19,
20, 24, 25 } · 295
18 . . 192–3, 288
25 . . { 103, 138,
{ 149, 289
ii. 23 177
iii. 16 288
iv. 11 293
13 177
17–22 . . . 211–3
21 293
v. 12 293
22 290
32, 41 . . . 294
44 . . { 103, 138,
{ 149, 290
47 293
vi. 1 290
6 290
13 . 104, 138, 149
13, 17, 19 . . 297
vii. 13–4 . 104, 138, 149
viii. 5–13 . . . 219–20
ix. 13 . 104, 138, 149
x. 8 51–2
42 297
xi. 2 297
2–3 . . . 63–4
27 . .105, 138, 149
xii. 1–4 292
30 288
xiii. 6, 13, 33 . . 297
36 . . . 34 n. 2
xiv. 13 297
19 168

ST. MATTHEW (cont.) :

PAGE

xv. 35 168
xvii. 21 . { 62–3, 105,
{ 138, 149,
{ 289
22 55
xviii. 11 . { 106, 138,
{ 149, 290
xix. 16–7 { 78, 106,
{ 138, 149,
{ 259, 288
xx. 22–3 209–11, 289
28 178
44 289
xxiii. 14 289
38 . 106, 138, 149
xxiv. 36 288
xxvi. 32 187
34 140
35 140
39 140
71 . . . 190–1
xxvii. 34 . . . 253–8
46 30
xxviii. 2 . 107, 138, 149
19 . { 108, 138,
{ 149, 213 n.

ST. MARK :

i. 1 { 166, 279–86,
{ 287
2 . 108, 138, 149
11 140
14–20 . . 211–13
28 176
45–ii. 1 . . 176

ST. MARK (cont.) :

PAGE

ii. 12 287
13 177
17 104
27–8 176
iii. 16 289
26 177–8
29 289
iv. 1 179–80
12 289
vi. 11 289
22 66
33 80
vii. 35 287
viii. 6 168
7 . . . . 82 n.
ix. 24 287
29 289
44–6 289
49 289
x. 6 288
17–8 . . . 259–78
23–4 . . . 213–14
24 289
38 209–11
xi. 26 289
xiii. 32 288
xiv. 22–4 290
28 187
72 187
xv. 23 253–4
28 290
39 . . . 80, 290
43 190
46 187
47–xvi. 7 . . . 184
xvi. 3, 4, 6 . . . 187

ST. MARK (cont.):	PAGE	
xvi. 7 187		
9-20 { 109, 138, 149, 288, 293, 298–307		
ST. LUKE:		
i. 26 187		
28 . { 109, 138, 149, 289		
41 187		
60 187		
64 . . . 176-7		
65, 70, 71 . { 174, 185		
ii. 2 . . . 188 n.		
14 . 110, 138, 149		
39 177		
iii. 23-38 . . 180-2		
iv. 4 289		
5 289		
8 289		
31 177		
37 176		
v. 1-11 . . 211-13		
3 186		
14-15 . . . 176		
27 177		
vi. 1 293		
10 176		
vii. 18 64		
35 177		
ix. 55-6 . . . 289		
x. 12 176		
25 140		
41-2 . 110, 138, 149		
xi. 2 177		
2-4 . 84, 290		
4 166		
xiv. 8-10 . . . 178		
22 191		
xvi. 9 . . . 215-6		
xvii. 2 . . . 194-5		
19 . . . 289		
24 289		
xviii. 14 . 189, 193-4		
18-19 . . 259-78		

ST. LUKE (cont.): — PAGE
xix. 25 189
27 178
37 65
42 . . . 217-9
xx. 42 . . . 220-1
xxi. 25 140
xxii. 43-4 { 110, 138, 149, 290
44 80
64 290
xxiii. 34 . { 111, 138, 149, 290
38 . { 111, 138, 150, 290
42 288
45 . 112, 13⁵, 150
xxiv. 3 287
13 66
40 . 112, 139, 150
41-3 . . 239-52
42 . { 112, 139, 150, 290
46 288
51 288
ST. JOHN:
i. 3-4 . 113, 139, 150
9 140
18 . { 113-4, 139, 150
27 . . . 166
28 . . 88, 166
43 87
iii. 6 297
13 { 114, 139, 150, 288
31 288
v. 3-4 . 80, 82, 289
15 290
vi. 47 . . . 287
51 289
69 287
viii. 35 288
38-9 . . 170-1
59 288
ix. 35 288
36 191

ST. JOHN (cont.): — PAGE
x. 14 . 115, 139, 150
xiv. 14 287
xvi. 6 288
xvii. 24 . 115, 139, 150
xix. 20-1 . . . 290
25 . . . 85 n. 3
29 . . . 253-4
xxi. 5-13 . . 241-4
23 287
25 . 115, 139, 150
ACTS:
xvi. 7 288
xx. 28 287
xxiv. 23 146
ROMANS:
xiv. 10 288
1 COR.:
xi. 2-4 290
xvi. 47 288
2 COR.:
iii. 3 65
GAL.:
iii. 1 . . . 166-7
EPH.:
i. 1 166
v. 20 . . . 227-8
COL.:
ii. 10 288
1 TIM.:
iii. 16 288
HEB.:
iv. 2 . . . 48-9
2 PET.:
i. 1 288
REV.:
i. 5 290

THE END.

Oxford

HORACE HART, PRINTER TO THE UNIVERSITY

BY THE LATE DEAN BURGON.

The Last Twelve Verses of the Gospel According to St. Mark,

VINDICATED AGAINST RECENT CRITICAL OBJECTORS AND ESTABLISHED.

Demy 8vo, 6s. 1871.

'Dean Burgon's brilliant monograph . . . has thrown a stream of light upon the controversy; nor does the joyous tone of his book misbecome one who is conscious of having maintained a cause which is precious to him. We may fairly say that his conclusions have in no essential point been shaken by the elaborate and very able counter-plea of Dr. Hort.'—DR. SCRIVENER.

Oxford and London: JAMES PARKER & Co.

The Revision Revised.

Three Articles reprinted from the *Quarterly Review.* To which is added a reply to BISHOP ELLICOTT'S PAMPHLET, including a vindication of the Traditional Reading of 1 Tim. iii. 16. Second Edition, Demy 8vo, 14s. 1883.

Lives of Twelve Good Men.

New Edition, Demy 8vo, with Portraits, 16s. 1891.

London: JOHN MURRAY, Albemarle Street.

EDITED BY THE REV. EDWARD MILLER.

A Plain Introduction to the Criticism of the New Testament,

FOR THE USE OF BIBLICAL STUDENTS.

By the late F. H. A. SCRIVENER, M.A., D.C.L., LL.D.

Fourth Edition, 2 vols., large 8vo, 32s. 1894.

*** Appendixes F and G, published subsequently and containing additional information, with corrections, may be had gratis of the Publisher or Editor by possessors of the earlier copies on transmission of postage.

London: GEORGE BELL & SONS, York Street, Covent Garden.

BY THE REV. EDWARD MILLER.

Two vols., Large Post 8vo, cloth, reduced price 15s. 1878.

The History and Doctrines of Irvingism,

OR OF THE SO-CALLED CATHOLIC AND APOSTOLIC CHURCH.

'Mr. Miller has brought to his work the rare qualities of unmistakable fairness and candour, a thoroughly philosophical mind, untiring patience in research, and a calm spirit of charity, which must go far to render his volumes pleasant and profitable reading to the philosophically-minded student of religious phenomena.'—*Church Review.*

'Mr. Miller has done his work very thoroughly indeed.'—*Guardian.*

'The theological learning, philosophical insight, and calm and steady patience in dealing with the adverse argument, are most admirable.'—*Literary Churchman.*

London: KEGAN PAUL, TRENCH, TRÜBNER & Co., Limited.

The Church in Relation to the State.

Post 8vo, reduced price 4s. 1880.

'To those who desire to understand the true position of the Church and State question . . . we would recommend an attentive perusal of the Rev. Edward Miller's able and thoughtful essay.'—*National Church.*

To be had of the Author.

A Guide to the Textual Criticism of the New Testament.

Crown 8vo, 4s. 1886.

'A vast amount of information, stated with admirable clearness and precision, and in a form quite intelligible even to those not previously familiar with the subject.'—*Saturday Review.*

London: GEORGE BELL & SONS, York Street, Covent Garden.

A Greek Testament Primer,

AN EASY GRAMMAR AND READING BOOK FOR THE USE OF STUDENTS BEGINNING GREEK.

Second Edition, Extra fcap. 8vo, price 3s. 6d. 1893.

'Mr. Miller has done his work with spirit, intelligence, and accuracy.'—*Expositor.*

Oxford: CLARENDON PRESS; London: HENRY FROWDE.

APPENDIX

Published by

THE BIBLE FOR TODAY PRESS
900 Park Avenue
Collingswood, New Jersey, U.S.A.

September 15, 1997

ISBN #1-56848-008-3

A Brief Summary of
The Traditional Text
of the Holy Gospels
Vindicated and Established

By Dean John William Burgon
Edited by Edward Miller
1896

Summarized by
Rev. D. A. Waite, Th.D., Ph.D.

the
**BIBLE
FOR
TODAY**

900 Park Avenue
Collingswood, NJ 08108
Phone: 609-854-4452

B.F.T. 2771-P

[NOTE: This booklet is taken from a message delivered on Thursday evening, August 10, 1997, at the 19th Annual Meeting of the DEAN BURGON SOCIETY. The meetings were held at the Calvary Baptist Church, Kingston, Tennessee. The printed copy has been adapted for the present purpose, though a few references to the occasion have been included. DAW]

TABLE OF CONTENTS

SECTION   **PAGES**

I   Introductory Remarks 1
   A. The Purpose of This Booklet 1
   B. The Dean Burgon Society's New Hardback Edition 2
   C. The Editorship of Rev. Edward Miller 2

II   Background and Principles 3
   A. Dean Burgon's Scholarly Legacy 3
   B. Dean Burgon's Position on The Preservation of God's Words 3
   C. Two Irreconcilable Schools of New Testament Textual Criticism 3

III   Dean Burgon's Seven Tests of Truth 4
   A. Introducing the Seven Tests of Truth 4
   B. Explaining the Seven Tests of Truth 4
      1. Antiquity as a Test of Truth 4
      2. Number as a Test of Truth 5
      3. Variety as a Test of Truth 5
      4. Respectability or Weight as a Test of Truth 6
      5. Continuity as a Test of Truth 6
      6. Context as a Test of Truth 6
      7. Internal Evidence as a Test of Truth 7

IV   The Superiority of the Traditional Text 8
   A. Various Statements on the Superiority of the Traditional Text 8
      1. The Traditional Text Was a 3 to 2 Favorite with Those
         Church Fathers Who Died Before to 400 A.D. 8
      2. The Traditional Text Was in Existence and Predominant
         from the Earliest Years of the Churches 8
      3. Why The Traditional Text Does not Now Have Many
         Older Manuscripts 9
      4. Why The Traditional Text Later Manuscripts are Better
         than the Older Ones Like "B" and "Aleph" 9
      5. The New Testament Is Unique in Attempts at
         Doctrinal Depravations 10
      6. The New Testament Was Doctrinally Corrupted by Early
         Heretics 10
      7. The Traditional Text Is Incomparably Superior to the
         Westcott and Hort Type of Text 10
      8. The Traditional Text Has an Unbroken Succession 11

V The Inferiority of the Westcott and Hort Text 12
   A. Introductory Words About The Westcott and Hort Text 12
   B. Various Statements on the Inferiority of the Westcott and

Hort Text 12
1. The Westcott and Hort (B and Aleph) Text Was Based Only
   on the "Crime" of Partial and Unrepresentative Evidence 12
2. Professor Hort Tampered with the Facts of History in order
   to Sustain the Westcott and Hort (B and Aleph) Text 12
3. The Westcott and Hort (B and Aleph) Text Is in Error
   Because it Favored the Error-ridden Old Uncials 13
4. The Westcott and Hort (B and Aleph) Text Used
   Ingenious Speculation Instead of Facts 13
5. The Westcott and Hort (B and Aleph) Text Dwindled Down
   in Numbers of Manuscripts by the End of the 4th Century 13
6. The Westcott and Hort (B and Aleph) Text Should not be
   Followed, but Rather We Should Follow the "Main Body
   of New Testament MSS" 14
7. The Westcott and Hort (B and Aleph) Text Rejected 995
   copies out of Every 1,000 as Being Untrustworthy 14
8. The Westcott and Hort (B and Aleph) Text Is Based Upon a
   Number of False Theories Rather than Facts 15
9. The Westcott and Hort (B and Aleph) Text Is Based Upon a
   "Very Little Handful of Manuscripts" Rather than on the
   "Vast Multitude of Copies" 15
10. The Westcott and Hort (B and Aleph) Text, Though
   on a "Pedestal," Is Nevertheless Very Corrupt 16
11. The Westcott and Hort (B and Aleph) Text Was Formed
   by a Simplistic, Easy Process 16
12. The Westcott and Hort (B and Aleph) Text Was the Result
   of Habitual "Depravation" and "Persistent Mutilation." 16
13. The Westcott and Hort (B and Aleph) Text Differs Within
   itself Internally 17
14. The Westcott and Hort (B and Aleph) Text Contains
   Fragments of Many Other Texts 17
15. The Westcott and Hort (B and Aleph) Text Constructed a
   Short Text from a Fuller One 17
16. The Westcott and Hort (B and Aleph) Text Is "Fabricated,"
   "Depraved," "Refuse," and "Untrustworthy 18
17. The Westcott and Hort (B and Aleph) Text Is Not the Oldest
   Witness to the New Testament, Because Much Older
   Evidence Exists" 18
18. The Westcott and Hort (B and Aleph) Text Is Proved to Be
   a Bad Witness 19
19. The Westcott and Hort (B and Aleph) Text Is the Only Text
   In Dean Burgon's Day that Omitted Mark 16:9-20 19
20. The Westcott and Hort (B and Aleph) Text Has Many

Omissions 19

21. The Westcott and Hort (B and Aleph) Text Contains
Semi-Arian Heresies in Them 20

22. The Westcott and Hort (B and Aleph) Text Sank in
Acceptance with the Churches as Arianism Sank into
Condemnation 20

23. The Westcott and Hort (B and Aleph) Text's Three
Reasons for Superiority Are all False 21

25. The Westcott and Hort (B and Aleph) Text Was Condemned
by the Generations that Followed 21

26. The Westcott and Hort (B and Aleph) Text Is from a Small,
Lost Family of Misguided Texts 21

27. The Westcott and Hort (B and Aleph) Text Has Many
Serious Defects 22

28. The Westcott and Hort (B and Aleph) Text Had Been Once
and for All Condemned By the Early Churches and the
Traditional Text Had Been Settled 22

INDEX 23

About the Author 26

Order Blank (p. 1) 27

Order Blank (p. 2) 29

A Brief Summary of The Traditional Text of the Holy Gospels
Vindicated and Established

BY DEAN JOHN WILLIAM BURGON
EDITED BY EDWARD MILLER
1896

Summarized by Rev. D. A. Waite, Th.D., Ph.D.
President of THE DEAN BURGON SOCIETY, and
Director of THE BIBLE FOR TODAY, INCORPORATED
900 Park Avenue, Collingswood, NJ 08108
Phone: 609-854-4452; FAX: 609-854-2464;
Orders: 1-800-JOHN 10:9; E-Mail: BFT@BibleForToday.org

I
Introductory Remarks

A. The Purpose of This Booklet.

As the title indicates, it is the purpose and intention of this booklet to summarize some of the teachings and main arguments contained in Dean Burgon's excellent book, *The Traditional Text of the Holy Gospels*. This material was first given on overhead transparencies to the Dean Burgon Society's 19th Annual Conference, meeting at the Calvary Baptist Church, Kingston, Tennessee, July, 1997. It is hoped that the reader will purchase and read *The Traditional Text* in its entirety. It is available as **B.F.T. #1159** for a GIFT of **$15.00** + **$4.00** for postage and handling. It is the new hardback edition published by the Dean Burgon Society.

There has been no attempt to give all of the arguments used in *The Traditional Text*. This "SUMMARY" has sought to set forth some of the more important themes and statements found in this well-written textbook on textual criticism. The reader of the entire book will find it to be a worthwhile document. It is hoped that some of the following quotations will whet the reader's appetite for more of the truths so skillfully propounded by Dean Burgon.

B. The Dean Burgon Society's New Hardback Edition.

In keeping with its desire to publish important materials **"IN DEFENSE OF TRADITIONAL BIBLE TEXTS,"** the Executive Committee of the Dean Burgon Society, in its meeting in July, 1997, voted to make hardback copies of *The Traditional Text* (with the original page numbers) available for the many who should be reading it.

C. The Editorship of Rev. Edward Miller.

Prior to his death in 1888, Dean Burgon was unable to finish this very important work that he had been preparing for over thirty years. His friend and associate, Rev. Edward Miller, a fellow Anglican minister, knowing of Dean Burgon's desire to put his work into print, assembled the Dean's exhaustive notes and documents for this book. In so doing, Rev. Miller supplemented various comments, where needed, to round out Dean Burgon's thoughts and topics . He was able to be faithful to Dean Burgon's views on this subject due to his longstanding personal friendship with the Dean. Throughout *The Traditional Text,* Rev. Miller made clear which parts were Dean Burgon's and which were his own. In order to simplify references to the text, I considered the book as having been authored by Dean Burgon in its entirety. I have usually given Dean Burgon credit for the words employed, even though in some instances I might be quoting Rev. Edward Miller's comments. Should there be any question about whose words are used, the reader is urged to consult the page references to ascertain the actual source.

II
Background and Principles

A. Dean Burgon's Scholarly Legacy.

Rev. Miller wrote of Dean Burgon's thorough New Testament scholarship:
"The death of Dean Burgon in 1888, . . . cut him off in the early part of a task for which he had made preparations during more than thirty years. . . he examined manuscripts widely, making many discoveries at home and in foreign libraries; collated some himself and got many collated by other scholars, encouraged new and critical editions of some of the chief Versions; and above all, he devised and superintended a collection of quotations from the New Testament as he found in the words of the Fathers and in other ecclesiastical writings, going far beyond ordinary indexes, which may be found in sixteen thick volumes amongst the treasures of the British Museum." [**Dean John William Burgon,** *The Traditional Text of the Holy Gospels Vindicated and Established,* pp. v-vi]

B. Dean Burgon's Position on The Preservation of God's Words.

Many people are saying today that God abandoned His Hebrew and Greek Words rather than preserving them. Dean Burgon disagreed. He wrote:
"There exists no reason for supposing that the Divine Agent, who in the first instance thus gave to mankind the Scriptures of Truth, straightway abdicated His office; took no further care of His work; abandoned those precious writings to their fate." [Dean Burgon, *The Traditional Text*, p. 11]

C. Two Irreconcilable Schools of New Testament Textual Criticism.

The two rival schools are those who defend the Traditional Text and those who defend the false Westcott and Hort Text. Dean Burgon wrote:
"Indeed there exist but two rival schools of Textual Criticism. And these are irreconcilably opposed. In the end, one of them will have to give way: and, *vae victis!* unconditional surrender will be its only resource. When one has been admitted to be the right, there can no place be found for the other. It will have to be dismissed from attention as a thing utterly, hopelessly in the wrong." [Dean Burgon, *The Traditional Text*, p. 18]

The battle lines are still drawn to this day as these comments are being written (1997). They will be drawn right on into the 21st Century. There can be no turning back from the Hebrew and Greek Texts that underlie the King James Bible and from the King James Bible itself in the English language. The other Hebrew and Greek texts of Westcott and Hort, and their modern counterparts, are in error and must never be accepted as the truth. They are, as Dean Burgon so aptly phrased it, "hopelessly in the wrong."

III
Dean Burgon's Seven Tests of Truth

A. Introducing the Seven Tests of Truth.

These are Dean Burgon's seven tests or notes of truth in determining proper readings in the Greek New Testament. He wrote:

"I proceed to offer for the reader's consideration seven Tests of Truth . . . where these seven tests are found to conspire, we may confidently assume that the evidence is worthy of all acceptance, and is to be implicitly followed. A reading should be attested then by the seven following

NOTES OF TRUTH
1. Antiquity, or Primitiveness;
2. Consent of Witnesses, or Number;
3. Variety of Evidence, or Catholicity;
4. Respectability of Witnesses, or Weight;
5. Continuity, or Unbroken Tradition;
6. Evidence of the Entire Passage, or Context;
7. Internal Considerations, or Reasonableness

[Dean Burgon, *The Traditional Text*, pp. 28-29]

B. Explaining the Seven Tests of Truth.

Here is a summary of some of the more important explanations of Dean Burgon's Seven Tests of Truth.

1. Antiquity as a Test of Truth.

Dean Burgon wrote:

"The more ancient testimony is probably the better testimony. That it is not by any means always so is a familiar fact. To quote the known dictum of a competent judge [Dr. F. H. A. Scrivener]: 'It is no less true to fact than paradoxical in sound that the worst corruptions to which the New Testament has ever been subjected, originated within a hundred years after it was composed; that Irenaeus and the African Fathers and the whole Western, with a portion of the Syriac Church, used far inferior manuscripts to those employed by Stunica, or Erasmus, or Stephen, thirteen centuries after, when moulding the Textus Receptus.' Therefore Antiquity alone affords no security that the manuscript in our hands is not infected with the corruption which sprang up largely in the first and second centuries."

[Dean Burgon, *The Traditional Text*, p. 40]

In other words, the African Fathers and Irenaeus used corrupt Greek texts. Even though they were early and therefore a part of "antiquity," they were corrupted through the actions of many heretics. Their WRITING MATERIAL was OLD, but their WORDS were filled with CONTEMPORANEOUS CORRUPTION. The manuscripts that Erasmus, or Stephens, or Stunica used, though they were YOUNGER, they were, nevertheless, founded upon the WORDS of the original text which were THE OLDEST POSSIBLE. This was possible because they had accurate copies. Their WRITING MATERIAL was YOUNGER, but their WORDS were OLDER and PURER.

2. Number as a Test of Truth.

Dean Burgon wrote:

"'Number' is the most ordinary ingredient of weight, and indeed in matters of human testimony, is an element which even cannot be cast away. Ask one of Her Majesty's Judges if it be not so. Ten witnesses (suppose) are called in to give evidence: of whom one resolutely contradicts what is solemnly deposed to by the other nine. Which of the two parties do we suppose the Judge will be inclined to believe?" [Dean Burgon, *The Traditional Text*, p. 43]

Obviously, in the foregoing set of circumstances, "Her Majesty's Judges" would believe the nine witnesses. We have, in our day, over 99% of the evidence of our manuscripts favoring the type of text that underlies our King James Bible. Some 5,210 of the 5,255 of our manuscripts favor the Traditional Text that underlies our King James Bible. Less than 1% of the manuscripts side with the false texts of Westcott and Hort and their modern counterparts, the Nestle-Aland and the United Bible Societies. The Westcott and Hort people despise this test of truth because the number of manuscripts on their side is so small.

3. Variety as a Test of Truth.

Dean Burgon wrote:

"Witnesses of different kinds; from different countries; speaking different tongues:--witnesses who can never have met and between whom it is incredible that there should exist collusion of any kind:--such witnesses deserve to be listened to most respectfully. Indeed, when witnesses of so varied a sort agree in large numbers, they must needs be accounted worthy of even implicit confidence." [Dean Burgon, *The Traditional Text*, p. 50]

This is what we have in our Traditional Text which underlies our King James Bible. We have variety. Dean Burgon wrote further on this test of truth as follows:

"It is precisely this consideration which constrains us to pay supreme attention to the combined testimony of the Uncials and of the whole body of the Cursive Copies. They are (a) dotted over at least 1000 years: (b) they evidently belong to so many divers countries,--Greece, Constantinople, Asia Minor, Palestine, Syria, Alexandria, and other parts of Africa, not to say Sicily, Southern Italy, Gaul, England, and Ireland: (c) they exhibit so many strange characteristics and peculiar sympathies: (d) they so clearly represent countless families of MSS., being in no single instance absolutely identical in their text, and certainly not being copies of any other Codex in existence,--that their unanimous decision I hold to be an absolutely irrefragable evidence of the Truth." [Dean Burgon, *The Traditional Text*, p. 50-51]

This is a tremendous testimony in favor of the Traditional Text! Twelve or more countries, and parts of the world, witness to this same kind of text without collusion, cooperation, or complicity of any kind. This is true "variety."

4. Respectability or Weight as a Test of Truth.

Dean Burgon wrote:
"In the first place, the witnesses in favour of any given reading should be respectable. 'Respectability' is of course a relative term; but its use and applicability in this department of Science will be generally understood and admitted by scholars, although they may not be altogether agreed as to the classification of their authorities." [Dean Burgon, *The Traditional Text*, p. 53]

Any witnesses, such as "B" (Vatican) and "Aleph" (Sinai), which disagree one with the other in over 3,000 substantial places in the Gospels alone would certainly **not** be respectable witnesses. Certainly such false witnesses cannot be "respectable" by objective standards.

5. Continuity as a Test of Truth.

Dean Burgon wrote:
"When therefore a reading is observed to leave traces of its existence and of its use all down the ages, it comes with an authority of a peculiarly commanding nature. And on the contrary, when a chasm of greater or less breadth of years yawns in the vast mass of evidence which is ready for employment, or when a tradition is found to have died out, upon such a fact alone suspicion or grave doubt, or rejection must inevitably ensue."
"Still more, when upon the admission of the Advocates of the opinions which we are opposing the chasm is no longer restricted but engulfs not less than fifteen centuries in its hungry abyss, or else then the transmission ceased after four centuries, it is evident that according to an essential Note of Truth, those opinions cannot fail to be self-destroyed as well as to labour under condemnation during more than three quarters of the accomplished life of Christendom." [Dean Burgon, *The Traditional Text*, p. 59]

The Textus Receptus has continuity right on down the line. There are at least thirty-seven tremendous historical links of continuity. [See *Defending the King James Bible* by Dr. D. A. Waite, pages 44-48] The "transmission" of the B and Aleph type of texts "ceased after four centuries" and the worship of these false texts did not resume for another "fifteen centuries." It is evident that B and Aleph, and their allies, were not continuous and therefore are worthy of "condemnation."

6. Context as a Test of Truth.

Dean Burgon wrote:
"A word,--a phrase,--a clause,--or even a sentence or a paragraph,--must have some relation to the rest of the entire passage which precedes or comes after it. Therefore it will often be necessary, in order to reach all the evidence that bears upon a disputed question, to examine both the meaning and the language living on both sides of the point in dispute." [Dean Burgon, *The Traditional Text*, p. 61]

This is an obvious and essential test of truth.

7. Internal Evidence as a Test of Truth.

Dean Burgon wrote:

"Accordingly, the true reading of passages must be ascertained, with very slight exception indeed, from the preponderating weight of external evidence, just according to its antiquity, to number, variety, relative value, continuousness, and with the help of the context. Internal considerations, unless in exceptional cases they are found in strong opposition to evident error, have only a subsidiary force." [Dean Burgon, *The Traditional Text*, p. 67]

Though this test of truth is less objective and more subjective, it is one of the essential elements to consider.

IV
The Superiority of the Traditional Text

A. Various Statements on the Superiority of the Traditional Text.

1. The Traditional Text Was a 3 to 2 Favorite with Those Church Fathers Who Died Before to 400 A.D.

Dean Burgon wrote:

"No one, I believe, has till now made a systematic examination of the quotations occurring in the writings of the Fathers who died before A.D. 400 and in public documents written prior to that date. . . . The testimony therefore of the [76] Early Fathers is emphatically according to the issue of numbers in favour of the Traditional Text, being about 3:2. But it is also necessary to inform the readers of this treatise, that here quality confirms quantity. A list will now be given of thirty important passages in which evidence is borne on both sides, and it will be seen that 530 testimonies are given in favour of the Traditional readings as against 170 on the other side. In other words, the Traditional Text beats its opponent in a general proportion to 3 to 1." [Dean Burgon, *The Traditional Text*, pp. 94, 101-102]

Some of the leading Westcott and Hort followers of today are very bold to say that the Traditional Text, or the Textus Receptus type of readings, did not exist prior to 400 A.D., and certainly not before the 6th Century A.D. Here you have statistical data on 76 Church Fathers who died prior to 400 A.D., showing, not only that the Textus Receptus readings **did** exist prior to 400 A.D., but that they were in the majority. This was not merely a simple majority of barely over 50%, but it was a majority of 60% to 40% over the Westcott and Hort false text. Dr. Jack Moorman's recent and careful research on this same subject revealed an even greater percentage--70% to 30% in favor of the Textus Receptus as opposed to B and Aleph. This can be found in his excellent book, *Early Church Fathers' Witness to the Antiquity of the Traditional Text*, pages 34-35. It is **B.F.T. #2136, 63 large pages @ $6.50+P&H.** Don't believe any of the Westcott and Hort/B and Aleph devotees if they tell you that the Traditional Text readings or the Traditional Text itself was not in existence before 400 A.D. This is one of the falsehoods which D.A. Carson and other Westcott and Horters have put in their books.

2. The Traditional Text Was in Existence and Predominant from the Earliest Years of the Churches.

Dean Burgon wrote:

"As far as the Fathers who died before 400 A.D. are concerned, the question may now be put and answered. Do they witness to the Traditional Text as existing from the first, or do they not? The results of the evidence, both as regards the quantity and the quality of the testimony, enable us to reply, not only that the Traditional Text was in existence, but that it was predominant, during the period under review. Let any one who disputes this conclusion make out for the Western Text, or the Alexandrian, or for the Text of B and Aleph, a case from the evidence of the Fathers which can equal or surpass that which has been now placed before the reader." [Dean Burgon, *The Traditional Text*, p. 116]

Dr. Dan Wallace, a professor at Dallas Theological Seminary, disagrees with Dean Burgon and Edward Miller on this point. He has written to the effect that we may have Byzantine or Traditional Text "readings," but not a Byzantine or Traditional "text." As Dr. David Otis Fuller used to say, "He is playing antics with semantics!" How can you have **readings** if you don't have a **text** from which those **readings** were derived?

---

3. Why The Traditional Text Does not Now Have Many Older Manuscripts.

Dean Burgon's editor, Rev. Edward Miller, when talking about B and Aleph, wrote:

"How is it that we possess no MSS. of the New Testament of any considerable size older than those, [that is, B and Aleph] or at least no other such MSS. as old as they are? Besides the disastrous results of the persecution of Diocletian, there is much force in the reply of Dean Burgon, that being generally recognized as bad MSS. they were left standing on the shelf in their handsome covers, whilst others which were more correct were being thumbed to pieces in constant use." [Dean Burgon, *The Traditional Text*, p. 154]

What is meant by "the disastrous results of the persecution of Diocletian"? This Roman Emperor burned both the Christians and their Bibles. What kind of Bible did these believers have in their hands when they were hunted down to be tortured and slain? They had Textus Receptus or Traditional Text kind of Bibles. These kinds of Greek manuscripts were the ones that were destroyed by the multiplied hundreds.

---

4. Why The Traditional Text Later Manuscripts are Better than the Older Ones Like "B" and "Aleph."

Dean Burgon wrote:

"Nay, it will be found, as I am bold enough to say, that in many instances a fourteenth-century copy of the Gospels may exhibit the truth of Scripture, while the fourth-century copy in all these instances proves to be the depository of a fabricated text." [Dean Burgon, *The Traditional Text*, p. 8]

This is precisely the case with B, Aleph, and the some 43 other Greek manuscripts that follow them. They were depraved texts which had been doctored by heretics and others who were false in their doctrines.

5. The New Testament Is Unique in Attempts at Doctrinal Depravations.

Dean Burgon wrote:

"In fact, until those who make the words of the New Testament their study are convinced that they move in a region like no other, where unique phenomena await them at every step, and where seventeen hundred and fifty years ago depraving causes unknown in every other department of learning were actively at work, progress cannot really be made in the present discussion." [Dean Burgon, *The Traditional Text*, p. 9]

Unlike secular documents, theological heretics purposely and maliciously perverted New Testament documents. B and Aleph, and the other so-called "Old Uncials" (Aleph, A, B, C, and D), are examples of such perversion. Since this is true, those early copies are not to be trusted. If the perversions took place within the first hundred years after the New Testament was composed, then those early copies, such as B and Aleph, were the ones on which the heretics operated. This is what Dr. Scrivener and Dean Burgon both believe.

6. The New Testament Was Doctrinally Corrupted by Early Heretics.

Dean Burgon wrote:

"And the Written Word in like manner, in the earliest age of all, was shamefully handled by mankind. Not only was it confused through human infirmity and misapprehension, but it became also the object of restless malice and unsparing assaults. Marcion, Valentinus, Basilides, Heracleon, Menander, Asclepiades, Theodotus, Hermophilus, Apollonides, and other heretics adapted the Gospels to their own ideas." [Dean Burgon, *The Traditional Text*, p. 10]

If these nine above-named heretics adapted the Gospels to their own ideas and they lived during the first few centuries of the church age, it is entirely possible that B and Aleph and their allies might have been samples of some of their depravations. B and Aleph both were from Egypt. According to Dr. Bruce Metzger,

"*Every deviant Christian sect was represented in Egypt during the second century.*" [Bruce Metzger, *Early Versions*, p. 101, quoted in Dr. Jack Moorman, *Early Manuscripts*, p. 40]

He then listed no less than **eleven** such "deviant Christian sects." Egypt abounded with theological heresies. It is not unreasonable to assume that some of such heresies were transferred over to the New Testament texts which the heretics had in their possession.

7. The Traditional Text Is Incomparably Superior to the Westcott and Hort Type of Text.

Dean Burgon wrote:

"Accordingly, the text of which we are now treating, which is that of the later Uncials and the Cursives combined, is incomparably superior under all the external Notes of Truth. It possesses in nearly all cases older attestation: there is no sort of question as to the greater number of witnesses that bear evidence to its claims: nor to their variety: and hardly ever to the explicit proof of their continuousness, which indeed is also generally--nay, universally--implied owing to the nature of the case: their weight is certified upon stronger grounds: and as a matter of fact, the context in nearly all instances testifies on their side. The course of doctrine pursued in the history of the Universal Church is immeasurably in their Favour." [Dean Burgon, *The Traditional Text*, pp. 206-207]

All of these attestations refer to the Traditional Text which underlies our King James Bible. This text matches virtually all the seven tests of truth.

8. The Traditional Text Has an Unbroken Succession.

Dean Burgon wrote:

"The history of the Traditional Text, on the contrary, goes step by step in unbroken succession regularly back to the earliest times. . . . Erasmus followed his few MSS. because he knew them to be good representatives of the mind of the Church which had been informed under the ceaseless and loving care of mediaeval transcribers: and the text of Erasmus printed at Basle agreed in but little variation with the text of the Complutensian editors published in Spain, for which Cardinal Ximenes procured MSS. at whatever cost he could. No one doubts the coincidence in all essential points of the printed text with the text of the Cursives." [Dean Burgon, *The Traditional Text*, p. 236]

Unbroken succession is necessary. Can you really trust a text that arose in about 350 A.D. and was not copied and re-copied for the next 1500 years? Inasmuch as Westcott and Hort raised this discarded text from the dead, why should we believe it is the true and original text of the New Testament? It was, in fact, a text rejected by the churches as being corrupted? Erasmus had a text which had but "little variation" with the text of the Complutensian Polyglot of Cardinal Ximenes, yet one used manuscripts from Basle and the other used manuscripts from Spain. Why did they have so little "variation"? It was because the cursives from which they were taken were identical in "all essential points." You could pick any of those Traditional Text cursives and you would find that they agree with each other in "all essential points." This is why both Ximenes and Erasmus were right on target with their agreement between themselves because they were both based on the same stream of the Traditional Text. The vast numbers of New Testament Greek manuscripts are like a river. Anywhere you might collect samples of the water, they would test out the same. So with the Traditional Text manuscripts.

V
The Inferiority of the Westcott and Hort Text

A. Introductory Words About The Westcott and Hort Text.

In this section, I have identified the "Westcott and Hort" type of Greek text with that of manuscripts B and Aleph, since these were the two major manuscripts from which Westcott and Hort derived their New Testament Greek text. This Greek text was first brought out in 1881 by Anglican Bishop Brooke Foss Westcott and Anglican Professor Fenton John Anthony Hort.

B. Various Statements on the Inferiority of the Westcott and Hort Text.

1. The Westcott and Hort (B and Aleph) Text Was Based Only on the "Crime" of Partial and Unrepresentative Evidence.

Dean Burgon wrote:

"To cast away at least nineteen-twentieths of the evidence on points and to draw conclusions from the petty remainder, seems to us to be necessarily not less even than a crime and a sin, and only by reason of the sacrilegious destructiveness exercised thereby upon Holy Writ, but also because such a method is inconsistent with conscientious exhaustiveness and logical method." [Dean Burgon, *The Traditional Text*, p. xii]

Westcott and Hort used only partial evidence and a very unrepresentative sample agreeing with less than 1% of the manuscript history. Ximenes and Erasmus, on the other hand, though also using partial evidence, had a representative sample agreeing with over 99% of the manuscript history.

2. Professor Hort Tampered with the Facts of History in order to Sustain the Westcott and Hort (B and Aleph) Text.

Dean Burgon wrote:

"Again, in order to prop up his contention, Dr. Hort is obliged to conjure up the shadows of two or three 'phantom revisions,' of which no recorded evidence exists. We must never forget that subjective theory or individual speculation are valueless, when they do not agree with facts, except as failures leading to some better system. But Dr. Hort, as soon as he found that he could not maintain his ground with history as it was, instead of taking back his theory and altering it to square with facts, tampered with historical facts in order to make them agree with his theory." [Dean Burgon, *The Traditional Text*, p. 93]

This is an inexcusable tampering with truth and historical facts. It is an example of what they call "historical revisionism." It was to be deprecated as much then as it should be today!

3. The Westcott and Hort (B and Aleph) Text Is in Error Because it Favored the Error-ridden Old Uncials.

Dean Burgon wrote:

"Now I submit that it is a sufficient condemnation of Codexes B/Aleph/C/D as a supreme court of judicature (1) That as a rule they are observed to be discordant in their judgements: (2) That when they thus differ among themselves it is generally demonstrable by an appeal to antiquity that the two principal judges B and Aleph have delivered a mistaken judgement: (3) That when these two differ one from the other, the supreme judge B is often in the wrong: and lastly (4) That it constantly happens that all four agree, and yet all four are in error." [Dean Burgon, *The Traditional Text*, pp. 36-37]

Not only are these four old uncials distorted and mistaken, but they contradict each other as well as the Traditional Text. Dean Burgon also said of these old uncials:

"No progress is possible in the department of 'Textual Criticism' until the superstition--for we are persuaded that it is nothing less--which at present prevails concerning certain of 'the old uncials' (as they are called) has been abandoned." [Dean Burgon, *The Traditional Text*, p. 68]

Unfortunately, our modern self-styled "textual critics" failed to heed this word of warning. Instead, they continue the "superstition."

4. The Westcott and Hort (B and Aleph) Text Used Ingenious Speculation Instead of Facts.

Dean Burgon wrote:

"We oppose facts to their speculation. They exalt B and Aleph and D because in their own opinion those copies are the best. They weave ingenious webs, and invent subtle theories, because their paradox of a few against the many requires ingenuity and subtlety for its support. . . . In contrast with this sojourn in cloudland, we are essentially of the earth though not earthy. We are nothing, if we are not grounded in facts: our appeal is to facts, our test lies in facts, so far as we can we build testimonies upon testimonies and pile facts on facts." [Dean Burgon, *The Traditional Text*, p. 238]

You have to be ingenious to convince people that 1% of the evidence is true and 99% of the evidence is false. Hort was a master at this. So is Satan! Dean Burgon did not deal in "cloudland," nor does his defense of the Traditional Text. Because of Westcott and Hort's "paradox" referred to by Dean Burgon, they have based their position purely on subtle theories and rank speculation.

5. The Westcott and Hort (B and Aleph) Text Dwindled Down in Numbers of Manuscripts by the End of the 4th Century.

Dean Burgon wrote:

"During the life of Eusebius, if not under his controlling care, the two oldest Uncial Manuscripts in existence as hitherto discovered, known as B and

Aleph, or the Vatican and Sinaitic, were executed in handsome form and exquisite caligraphy. But shortly after, about the middle of the fourth century--as both schools of Textual Critics agree--a text differing from that of B and Aleph advanced in general acceptance; and, increasing till the eighth century in the predominance won by the end of the fourth, became so prevalent in Christendom, that the small number of MSS. agreeing with B and Aleph forms no sort of comparison with the many which vary from those two." [Dean Burgon, *The Traditional Text*, p. 2]

By the fourth century, and certainly by the eighth century, those few manuscripts which agreed with B and Aleph were not in existence. What happened to them? On the other hand, the manuscripts which agreed with the Traditional Text and also agreed one with another, were in abundance. They were and are the true texts.

6. The Westcott and Hort (B and Aleph) Text Should not be Followed, but Rather We Should Follow the "Main Body of New Testament MSS."

Dean Burgon wrote:

"Are we for the genuine text of the New Testament to go to the Vatican and the Sinaitic MSS. and the few others which mainly agree with them, or are we to follow the main body of New Testament MSS., which by the end of the century in which those two were produced entered into possession of the field of contention, and have continued in occupation of it ever since?" [Dean Burgon, *The Traditional Text*, p. 3]

This is a good question. We should follow the main body of New Testament manuscripts which form the Traditional Text. They won the battle with B and Aleph and their associate manuscripts. The churches recognized that the Traditional Text was the true text and copied and re-copied this text into hundreds and hundreds of manuscripts. To have approximately 5,210 Traditional Text kind of manuscripts in the Greek Language alone plus 8,000 in Latin, confirms that Christians believed these to be the true Bibles. Would you copy a Bible you thought to be false? I would not, and I don't believe the Christian copyists would have either.

7. The Westcott and Hort (B and Aleph) Text Rejected 995 copies out of Every 1,000 as Being Untrustworthy.

Dean Burgon wrote:

"I am utterly disinclined to believe--as grossly improbable does it seem--that at the end of 1800 years, 995 copies out of every thousand suppose, will prove untrustworthy; and that the one, two, three, four or five which remain, whose contents were till yesterday as good as unknown, will be found to have retained the secret of what the Holy Spirit originally inspired. I am utterly unable to believe, in short, that God's promise has so entirely failed, that at the end of 1800 years much of the text of the Gospel had in point of fact to be picked up by a German critic out of a waste-paper basket in the convent of St. Catherine; and that the entire text had to be remodelled after the pattern set by a couple of copies which had remained in neglect during fifteen centuries, and had probably owed their survival to that neglect; whilst hundreds of others had been thumbed to pieces, and had bequeathed their witness to copies made from them." [Dean Burgon, *The Traditional Text*, p. 12]

This German critic mentioned was Tischendorf. The text found in the waste-paper basket was manuscript Aleph (Sinai). Recently retired 89-year-old Pastor Carl Drexler, of Runnemede, New Jersey, used to refer to such higher critics as Tischendorf by a descriptive term. He called them "the higher liar, critics." This, in too many instances, is correct. The disuse of B, Aleph and a few others explains why they were preserved instead of being "thumbed to pieces."

8. The Westcott and Hort (B and Aleph) Text Is Based Upon a Number of False Theories Rather than Facts.

Dean Burgon wrote:

". . . the testimony is not only that of all the ages, but of all the countries: and at the very least so strong a presumption will ensue on behalf of the Traditional Text, that a powerful case indeed must be constructed to upset it. It cannot be vanquished by theories grounded upon internal considerations--often only another name for personal tastes--, or for scholarly likes or dislikes, or upon fictitious recensions, or upon any arbitrary choice of favouring manuscripts, or upon a strained division of authorities into families or groups, or upon a warped application of the principle of genealogy." [Dean Burgon, *The Traditional Text*, p. 13]

Westcott and Hort's text is simply theoretical rather than factual. They did not come up with the "powerful case" needed to supplant the Traditional Text.

9. The Westcott and Hort (B and Aleph) Text Is Based Upon a "Very Little Handful of Manuscripts" Rather than on the "Vast Multitude of Copies."

Dean Burgon wrote:

"Does the truth of the Text of Scripture dwell with the vast multitude of copies, uncial and cursive, concerning which nothing is more remarkable than the marvellous agreement which subsists between them? Or is it rather to be supposed that the truth abides exclusively with a very little handful of manuscripts which at once differ from the great bulk of the witnesses, and--strange to say--also amongst themselves?"

"The advocates of the Traditional Text urge that the Consent without Concert of so many hundreds of copies, executed by different persons, at diverse times, in widely sundered regions of the Church, is a presumptive proof of their trustworthiness, which nothing can invalidate but [by] some sort of demonstration that they are untrustworthy guides after all." [Dean Burgon, *The Traditional Text*, pp. 16-17   ]

There is an amassing of a tremendous amount of evidence by Dean Burgon in his masterful defense of the Traditional Text and in his demolition of the B and Aleph and Westcott and Hort errors. He combines logic with facts.

10. The Westcott and Hort (B and Aleph) Text, Though on a "Pedestal," Is Nevertheless Very Corrupt.

Dean Burgon wrote:

"It will be found in the end that we have been guilty of no exaggeration in characterizing B, Aleph, and D at the outset, as three of the most corrupt copies in existence. Let not any one suppose that the age of these five MSS. [B, Aleph, A, C, and D] places them upon a pedestal higher than all others. They can be proved to be wrong time after time by evidence of an earlier period than that which they can boast." [Dean Burgon, *The Traditional Text*, p. 25]

Earlier versions and quotations of Church Fathers have proved B & Aleph and the Westcott and Hort text, therefore, to be corrupt and in error time and time again.

11. The Westcott and Hort (B and Aleph) Text Was Formed by a Simplistic, Easy Process.

Dean Burgon wrote:

"To abide by the verdict of the two, or five, or seven oldest Manuscripts, is at first sight plausible, and is the natural refuge of students who are either superficial, or who wish to make their task as easy and simple as possible." [Dean Burgon, *The Traditional Text*, p. 26]

With the system of Westcott and Hort, you don't have to do much thinking. If B is the best manuscript, then you just go along with B as Westcott and Hort did. If Aleph goes along with B then it has to be right. After they had decided manuscript B was the best, they made their "canons of textual criticism" to corroborate B in every instance. They say the shortest is the best because B is the shortest. They say the most difficult reading is the best because B is the most difficult. They say the one that explains the rest is the best because B explains the rest. It is like going on a treasure hunt, that you yourself have constructed. You know where the treasure is located, so you make up the clues to match the location of the treasure. That's an easy game to play.

12. The Westcott and Hort (B and Aleph) Text Was the Result of Habitual "Depravation" and "Persistent Mutilation."

Dean Burgon wrote:

"But when we study the New Testament by the light of such Codexes as B/Aleph/D/L, we find ourselves in an entirely new region of experience; confronted by phenomena not only unique but even portentous. The text has undergone apparently an habitual, if not systematic depravation; has been manipulated throughout in a wild way. . . . There are evidences of persistent mutilation, not only of words and clauses, but of entire sentences. The substitution of one expression for another, and the arbitrary transposition of words, are phenomena of such perpetual occurrence, that it becomes evident at last that what lies before us is not so much an ancient copy, as an ancient recension of the Sacred Text." [Dean Burgon, *The*

Traditional Text, p. 32]

B and Aleph are mutilated, depraved, and recension texts. That word recension comes from two Latin words, "Re" and "Sensio," to censure again, or to look over as an editor would do. It is amazing that thinking people still buy into this false Westcott and Hort textual theory.

13. The Westcott and Hort (B and Aleph) Text Differs Within itself Internally.

Dean Burgon wrote:

"The consent without concert of (suppose) 990 out of 1000 copies,--of every date from the fifth to the fourteenth century, and belonging to every region of ancient Christendom,--is a colossal fact not to be set aside by any amount of ingenuity. A predilection for two fourth-century manuscripts closely resembling one another, yet standing apart in every page so seriously that it is easier to find two consecutive verses in which they differ than two consecutive verses in which they entirely agree:--such a preference, I say, apart from abundant or even definitely clear proof that it is well founded, is surely not entitled to be accepted as conclusive." [Dean Burgon, *The Traditional Text*, p. 33-34]

990 out of 1000 copies from the 5th to the 14th centuries from every region of the world characterizes the Tradition Text. Why cling to the 4th Century B and Aleph which have internal differences on every page?

14. The Westcott and Hort (B and Aleph) Text Contains Fragments of Many Other Texts.

Dean Burgon wrote:

"Although for convenience we have hitherto spoken of Codexes B/Aleph/D/L as exhibiting a single text,--it is in reality not one text but fragments of many, which are to be met with in the little handful of authorities enumerated above. Their witness does not agree together. The Traditional Text, on the contrary, is unmistakably one." [Dean Burgon, *The Traditional Text*, p. 34]

Again, Dean Burgon repeats his charges of major disagreement between the texts of B, Aleph, and their followers. This shows that they are "fragments of many" other manuscripts rather than being unified. Not so with the Traditional Text which is "unmistakably one."

15. The Westcott and Hort (B and Aleph) Text Constructed a Short Text from a Fuller One.

Dean Burgon wrote:

"There is no difficulty in producing a short text by omission of words, or clauses, or verses, from a fuller text: but the fuller text could not have been produced from the shorter by any development which would be possible under the facts of the case." [Dean Burgon, *The Traditional Text*, p. 34]

The Westcott and Hort theory of taking their short text and making it into a longer

Textus Receptus is illogical. How can you begin with a short text and then, all of a sudden, make a long text where each verse and word of that longer text agrees with hundreds of other manuscripts at the same book, chapter, and verse? For example, how could all twelve verses of Mark 16 be constructed in the same order and with the same words in hundreds of copies if the ORIGINAL of Mark's Gospel did not contain them? On the other hand, it would be simple to take a full text, like the Textus Receptus or Traditional Text, and have B and Aleph's scribes cut out the last twelve verses of Mark's Gospel which, of course, they did.

16. The Westcott and Hort (B and Aleph) Text Is "Fabricated," "Depraved," "Refuse," and "Untrustworthy."

Dean Burgon wrote:

"Codexes B/Aleph/C/D are the several depositaries of a fabricated and depraved text: . . . [and] are probably indebted for their very preservation solely to the fact that they were anciently recognized as untrustworthy documents. Do men indeed find it impossible to realize the notion that there must have existed such things as refuse copies in the fourth, fifth, sixth, and seventh centuries as well as in the eighth, ninth, tenth, and eleventh? And that the Codexes which we call B/Aleph/C/D may possibly, if not as I hold probably, have been of that class? [Dean Burgon, *The Traditional Text*, p. 36]

What would you do with what you considered to be an untrustworthy document? Would you have it in your library? Would you give it to your children? If a New Testament document is untrustworthy, you would probably not touch it. This is why B and Aleph were in such good condition. They were not used by the Christians and the churches. They were rightly considered to be depraved copies.

17. The Westcott and Hort (B and Aleph) Text Is Not the Oldest Witness to the New Testament, Because Much Older Evidence Exists.

Dean Burgon wrote:

"But though there are in our hands as yet no older manuscripts [than B or Aleph], yet we have in the first place various Versions, viz., the Peshitto of the second century, the group of Latin Versions which begin from about the same time, the Boharic and the Thebaic of the third century, not to speak of the Gothic which was about contemporary with your friends the Vatican and Sinaitic MSS. Next, there are the numerous Fathers who quoted passages in the earliest ages, and thus witnessed to the MSS. which they used. . . . So that there is absolutely no reason to place these two MSS. upon a pedestal by themselves on the score of supreme antiquity. They are eclipsed in this respect by many other authorities older than they are." [Dean Burgon, *The Traditional Text*, p. 74]

Anyone who says "the oldest is the best," will have to say the Traditional Text is the best because the witnesses to it are older than B or Aleph which have been "eclipsed" by it.

18. The Westcott and Hort (B and Aleph) Text Is Proved to Be a Bad Witness.

Dean Burgon wrote:

". . . there is a continual conflict going on all through the Gospels between B and Aleph and a few adherents of theirs on the one side, and the bulk of the Authorities on the other, and the nature and weight of these two Codexes may be inferred from it. They will be found to have been proved over and over again to be bad witnesses, who were left to survive in their handsome dresses whilst attention was hardly ever accorded to any services of theirs." [Dean Burgon, *The Traditional Text*, p. 77]

My Jehovah Witness Bible is in perfect condition. It is on my shelf because I never use it. It is still in its handsome dress. This is why B and Aleph were so carefully preserved as well. They were not used by the churches, but were rejected as the counterfeits they are.

19. The Westcott and Hort (B and Aleph) Text Is the Only Text In Dean Burgon's Day that Omitted Mark 16:9-20.

Dean Burgon wrote:

"Copies much more numerous and much older than B and Aleph live in their surviving descendants. . . . No amplification of B and Aleph could by any process of natural development have issued in the last twelve verses of St. Mark. But it was easy enough for the scribe of B not to write, and the scribe of Aleph consciously and deliberately to omit, verses found in the copy before him, if it were determined that they should severally do so." [Dean Burgon, *The Traditional Text*, p. 78]

The scribes who copied B and Aleph in Mark 16 were probably told by their editors **not** to copy these verses. Aleph left a blank space large enough to contain Mark 16:9-20. This bears witness to the authenticity of these last twelve verses of Mark. At that place, manuscript B copied fewer letters per line than in the rest of the book, making it entirely possible that Mark 16:9-20 could fit in there in its rightful place. So even B and Aleph bear witness to Mark 16:9-20 in a sense, even though they both omit the 12 verses. These were the only two manuscripts in Dean Burgon's day that did not contain Mark 16:9-20. For the full documentation favoring the verses, see Dean Burgon's book, *The Last Twelve Verses of Mark* (**B.F.T. #1139, 400 pages, @ $15.00+P&H**). You can find the documentation in tabular form in my Summary of Dean Burgon's book. This is **B.F.T. #2506, 39 pages, @ $3.00+P&H**).

20. The Westcott and Hort (B and Aleph) Text Has Many Omissions.

Dean Burgon wrote:

"First then, Codex B is discovered not to contain in the Gospels alone 237 words, 452 clauses, 748 whole sentences, which the later copies are observed to exhibit in the same places and in the same words." [Dean

Burgon, *The Traditional Text*, p. 78]

Dr. Jack Moorman found that, because of these many omissions, the B and Aleph/ Westcott and Hort text is shorter than the Textus Receptus by 2,886 words. (See *Missing in Modern Versions*, **B.F.T. #1726, 84 pages, @ $8.00+P&H**).

---

21. The Westcott and Hort (B and Aleph) Text Contains Semi-Arian Heresies in Them.

Dean Burgon wrote:

"The fact is that B and Aleph were the products of the school of philosophy and teaching which found its vent in Semi-Arian or Homoean opinions. . . . In the first place, according to the verdict of all critics, the date of these two MSS. coincides with the period when Semi-Arianism or some other form of Arianism were in the ascendance in the East, and to all outward appearance swayed the Universal Church. In the last years of his rule, Constantine was under the domination of the Arianizing faction; and the reign of Constantius II over all the provinces in the Roman Empire that spoke Greek, during which encouragement was given to the great heretical schools of the time, completed the two central decades of the fourth century. It is a circumstance that cannot fail to give rise to suspicion that the Vatican and Sinaitic MSS. had their origin under a predominant influence of such evil fame. At the very least, careful investigation is necessary to see whether those copies were in fact free from that influence which has met with universal condemnation." [Dean Burgon, *The t*, pp. 160-161]

"Hom<u>oi</u>-ousia" is a Greek term that means "like" nature, but not the "same." "Hom<u>o</u>-ousia," on the other hand, means the "same" nature, not merely "like." The Lord Jesus Christ had the same nature with God the father and He was "Hom<u>o</u>-ousia." The Arians and the Semi-Arians said he was "Hom<u>oi</u>-ousia" or of like substance, but not exactly the full substance of Deity. These documents, because of their readings, represent Semi-Arian or "Hom<u>oi</u>-ousian" readings. The Westcott and Hort (B and Aleph) text, according to Dr. Jack Moorman, has 356 doctrinal passages which differ from the Textus Receptus. All of these 356 passages are in error in the B and Aleph manuscripts. On the other hand, all 356 passages are proper and doctrinally orthodox in the Textus Receptus.

---

22. The Westcott and Hort (B and Aleph) Text Sank in Acceptance with the Churches as Arianism Sank into Condemnation.

Dean Burgon wrote:

"Now as we proceed further we are struck with another most remarkable coincidence, which also as has been before noticed is admitted on all hands, viz.,. that the period of the emergence of the Orthodox School from oppression and the settlement in their favour of the great Nicene controversy was also the time when the text of B and Aleph sank into condemnation. The Orthodox side under St. Chrysostom and others became permanently supreme: so did also the Traditional Text." [Dean Burgon, *The Traditional Text*, p. 161]

When the churches got their doctrines straight, they got their Bible Texts straight. The result was that the early churches condemned the Westcott and Hort/B and Aleph text because of its propensities toward Arianism. They knew what was right and what was wrong so far as the true New Testament was. They knew that B and Aleph were wrong.

23. The Westcott and Hort (B and Aleph) Text's Three Reasons for Superiority Are all False.

Dean Burgon wrote:

"Of course, they have their reasons for dismissing nineteen-twentieths of the evidence at hand: but--this is the point--it rests with them to prove that such dismissal is lawful and right. What then are their arguments? Mainly three, viz. [1] the supposed greater antiquity of their favourite text, [2] the superiority which they claim for its character, and [3] the evidence that the Traditional Text was as they maintain formed by conflation from texts previously in existence." [Dean Burgon, *The Traditional Text*, p. 205]

Dean Burgon has proved that all three of these reasons are false. The Westcott and Hort or B and Aleph text (1) does not have "greater antiquity" than the Textus Receptus; (2) does not have superior character; and (3) has not proved "conflation" for the Textus Receptus. These three falsehoods are still being told in our day.

25. The Westcott and Hort (B and Aleph) Text Was Condemned by the Generations that Followed.

Dean Burgon wrote:

"B and Aleph . . . may be regarded as the founders, or at least as prominent members of a family, whose descendants were few, because they were generally condemned by the generations which came after them." [Dean Burgon, *The Traditional Text*, p. 233]

That is why there are so few New Testament Greek manuscripts that concur with B and Aleph, because they were condemned by the churches. Why do you think the English Revised Version of 1881 is no longer around? It is because it had been condemned by the churches that were using it. Why is the King James Bible of 1611 still around? Because it has been accepted and approved by the churches and Christians who use it.

26. The Westcott and Hort (B and Aleph) Text Is from a Small, Lost Family of Misguided Texts.

Dean Burgon wrote:

"But I suspect that in the little handful of authorities which have acquired such a notoriety in the annals of recent Textual Criticism, at the least of which stand Codexes B and Aleph, are to be recognized the characteristic features of a lost family of (once well known) second or third-century documents which owed their existence to the misguided zeal of some well-intentioned but utterly incompetent persons who devoted themselves to the task of correcting the Text of Scripture; but were entirely unfit for the

undertaking." [Dean Burgon, *The Traditional Text*, p. 234]
This is what we have in B and Aleph. We have "corrections" of the Words of God
in these mistaken and false manuscripts.

27. The Westcott and Hort (B and Aleph) Text Has Many Serious Defects.

Dean Burgon wrote:
"We have with us width and depth against the narrowness on their side.
They are conspicuously contracted in the fewness of the witnesses which
they deem worthy of credence. They are restricted as to the period of
history which alone they consider to deserve attention. They are confined
with regard to the countries from which their testimony comes. They would
supply Christians with a shortened text, and educate them under a cast-iron
system. We on the contrary champion the many against the few: we
welcome all witnesses and weigh all testimony: we uphold all the ages
against one or two, and all the countries against a narrow space." [Dean
Burgon, *The Traditional Text*, pp. 237-238]

B & Aleph have no continuity. They have one country, Egypt! The Traditional
Text/Textus Receptus was found in countries all over the then-known world. We
don't fear facts. We take all the manuscripts under consideration.

28. The Westcott and Hort (B and Aleph) Text Had Been Once and for All Condemned By the Early Churches and the Traditional Text Had Been Settled.

Dean Burgon wrote:
"In the Nature of the Divine Word, and the character of the Written Word,
were confirmed about the same time:--mainly, in the period when the
Nicene Creed was re-asserted at the Council of Constantinople in 381 A.D.;
for the Canon of Holy Scripture was fixed and the Orthodox Text gained a
supremacy over the Origenistic Text about the same time:--and finally, after
the Third Council of Constantinople in 680 A.D., at which the
acknowledgment of the Natures of the Son of Man was placed in a position
superior to all heresy; for it was then that the Traditional Test began in
nearly perfect form to be handed down with scarce any opposition to future
ages of the Church." [Dean Burgon, *The Traditional Text*, p. 173]

The Divine Word is the Lord Jesus Christ. It is important to see that when His
Person and Work were clarified, the true New Testament Greek text was also
clarified. Which text of the New Testament do you want? That of Origen with all
of its heresies and false doctrines contained therein? Or the Traditional Text which
has been attested as the true text from the very first of the Apostolic Age? This is
the question here. Praise God we have a text which we can defend and for which
we can stand. It is the text which underlies our King James Bible. It is a Superior
Text, it is a Traditional Text, and it is a text which God has been pleased to bless
down through the centuries.

INDEX

#1159 1
1,000 . . . . iv, 14
1% 5, 12, 13
1500 years 11
1611 21
1800 years 14
1881 . . . . 12, 21
1888 . . . . 2, 3
1896 . . . . i, 1
1997 . . . . ii, 1-3
19th Annual Meeting, DBS ii
3 to 2 TR favorite . . . . iii, 8
350 A.D. 11
356 20
356 doctrinal passages 20
381 A.D. 22
400 A.D. . . . . iii, 8
5,210 TR MSS 5, 14
5,255 Total MSS (1967) 5
60% to 40% TR favorite 8
680 A.D. 22
70% to 30% TR favorite 8
76 Church Fathers, 400AD 8
99% TR MSS 5, 12, 13
990 out of 1000 copies, TR . . . 17
About the Author (Dr. Waite) . . v
African Fathers 4
Aleph (Sinai) . . . iv-6, 8-10, 12-22
Alexandrian MSS 9
all essential points, 2 TR's 11
antics with semantics 9
antiquity . . . iii, 4, 7, 8, 13, 18, 21
Apollonides, a heretic 10
author (Dr. Waite) v
B (Vatican) i, iii-v, 1-6, 8-10, 12-22
Background . . . . iii, 3
Basle, Erasmus TR printed 11
BIBLE FOR TODAY . . . . ii, 1

blank space of Aleph 19
Boharic Version 18
British Museum 3
Burgon, Dean John W. . . i-iii, 1-22
Calvary Baptist Church, DBS ii, 1
Cardinal Ximenes, TR editor . . 11
Carson, Dr. D. A. 8
chasm of 1500 years (B/Aleph) . 6
Chrysostom 20
Church Fathers . . . . iii, 8, 16
cloudland, W/H theories 13
codex 5, 19
Codexes 13, 16-19, 21
collated, Dean Burgon 3
collusion, none between MSS 5, 6
Complutensian Polyglot 11
concert without consent . . . 15, 17
condemned, B/Aleph . . . v, 21, 22
consent without concert . . . 15, 17
Constantine 20
Constantinople 5, 22
context . . . . iii, 4, 6, 7, 11
continuity . . . . iii, 4, 6, 22
convent of St. Catherine 14
corruptions in B/Aleph 4
Cursives 10, 11
D. A. Waite . . . . i, 1, 6
Dallas Theological Seminary . . . 9
Dean Burgon . . . . ii, iii, 1-22
Dean Burgon Society . . . . . ii, 1, 2
Dean John William Burgon . . . i, 1
Dean's 2
Defending the King James Bible 6
depravations in B/Aleph . . . iii, 10
depraved text of B/Aleph 18
depraving causes 10
died out, B/Aleph kind of MSS . 6
different countries had TR 5

different tongues had TR 5

difficult reading said to be best . 16

Diocletian persecution 9

divers countries had TR 5

Divine Agent, the Holy Spirit . . . 3

Divine Word, the Lord Jesus . . . 22

Dr. Dan Wallace of DTS 9

Dr. David Otis Fuller 9

Dr. Jack Moorman books . . 10, 20

Dr. Frederick H. A. Scrivener . . 10

Drexler, Pastor Carl 15

Early Fathers 8

editor 9, 17

editorship .... iii, 2

Edward Miller, Rev. . i, iii, 1, 2, 9

English Revised Version 21

Erasmus 4, 11, 12

essential points, two TR's 11

Eusebius 13

fabricated text of W/H 9, 18

Fathers ...... iii, 3, 4, 8, 9, 16, 18

fifteen centuries 6, 15

foreign libraries, Burgon went . . 3

four centuries, B/Aleph ceased . . 6

fragments, B/Aleph .... iv, 17

Fuller, Dr. David Otis ... iv, 9, 17

genealogy, wrong theory 15

German critic found Aleph . 14, 15

Gospels ...... i, 1, 3, 6, 9, 10, 19

Gothic Version 18

handful of manuscripts, W/H . . 15

hardback edition .... iii, 1, 2

Her Majesty's Judges 5

heresy 22

heretics .... iii, 4, 9, 10

homoean, like nature 20

hundred years after N.T. 4, 10

hungry abyss, 1500 years 6

Inferiority of the Westcott
        and Hort text ... iii, 12

internal considerations ... 4, 7, 15

irreconcilably opposed, 2 sides . . 3

Jehovah Witness Bible, W/H . . 19

Judge 4, 5, 13

King James Bible 3, 5, 6, 11, 21, 22

Kingston, Tennessee, DBS . . . ii, 1

Latin Versions 18

manuscripts ..... iii, iv, 3-5, 9-22

Marcion, a heretic 10

Mark 16:9-20, genuine .... iv, 19

Miller, Rev. Edward . . i, iii, 1-3, 9

Moorman, Dr. Jack 10, 20

MSS 5, 9, 11, 14, 16, 18, 20

mutilation of B/Aleph ..... iv, 16

Natures of the Son of Man 22

Nicene Creed 22

nineteen-twentieths for TR . 12, 21

Note of Truth 6

notes of truth, seven 4, 11

number iii-5, 7, 11, 14, 15

omissions, B/Aleph ..... v, 19, 20

order blank for materials v

Origen, a heretic 22

orthodox side 20

Pastor Carl Drexler 15

pedestal, B/Aleph put on . . . 16, 18

persistent mutilation, B/Aleph . 16

preservation of Bible .... iii, 3, 18

preservation of God's Words   iii, 3

quotations from the New
            Testament 3

readings 4, 8, 9, 20

respectability .... iii, 4, 6

Rev. D. A. Waite .... i, 1

Rev. Edward Miller ...... iii, 2, 9

revisionism 12

rival schools, irreconcilable 3

scholarly legacy .... iii, 3

Scrivener, Dr. Frederich H. A. . 10

semi-arian heresy during B . . v, 20

seven tests of truth ..... iii, 4, 11

short text, B/Aleph .... iv, 17, 18

shortened text, B/Aleph 22

shortest not always the best 16

Sinai, Aleph MS 6, 15

Sinaitic, Aleph MS 14, 18, 20

sixteen thick volumes, quotations 3
sojourn in cloudland, W/H 13
Spain, Complutensian TR 11
St. Catherine's Convent, Sinai . 14
Stunica, used TR 4
Superiority of the
      Traditional Text . . . . iii, 8
superstition of B/Aleph 13
surrender, none possible 3
Syriac Church 4
tampered with the facts . . . . iv, 12
tests of truth, seven . . . . . iii, 4, 11
Textual Critics 14
Textus Receptus 4, 6, 8
      9, 18, 20-22
The Traditional Text . . . i, iii, 1-22
Thebaic Version 18
thirty years, Burgon labored . . 2, 3
thumbed to pieces, copies . . 9, 15
Tischendorf, German critic . . . 15
traditional text . . . . . i, iii, v, 1-22
transmission ceased
      after four centuries, B/Aleph 6
treasure hunt, know clues 16
unbroken succession, TR . . iii, 11
Uncials . . . . iv, 5, 10, 13
unconditional surrender needed . 3
Universal Church 11, 20
unrepresentative evidence . . iv, 12
Valentinus, a heretic 10
variety of TR iii-5, 7, 11
Vatican, "B" 6, 14, 18, 20
Versions 3, 10, 16, 18, 20
Waite, Dr. D. A. . . . . i, 1, 6
Wallace, Dr. Dan, DTS 9
waste-paper basket, Aleph . 14, 15
Westcott and
      Hort . . . iii-v, 3, 5, 8, 10-22
Western text 4, 9
witnesses . 4-6, 11, 15, 18, 19, 22
worst corruptions in 1st 100 yrs. 4
Ximenes, Cardinal, TR 11, 12

"B," Vatican MS . . . . iii, 9

About the Author

The author of this booklet, Dr. D. A. Waite, received a B.A. (Bachelor of Arts) in classical Greek and Latin from the University of Michigan in 1948, a Th.M. (Master of Theology), with high honors, in New Testament Greek Literature and Exegesis from Dallas Theological Seminary in 1952, an M.A. (Master of Arts) in Speech from Southern Methodist University in 1953, a Th.D. (Doctor of Theology), with honors, in Bible Exposition from Dallas Theological Seminary in 1955, and a Ph.D. in Speech from Purdue University in 1961.   He holds both New Jersey and Pennsylvania teacher certificates in Greek and Language Arts.

He has been a teacher in the areas of Greek, Hebrew, Bible, Speech, and English for over thirty-five years in nine schools, including one junior high, one senior high, three Bible institutes, two colleges, two universities, and one seminary. He served his country as a Navy Chaplain for five years on active duty; pastored two churches; was Chairman and Director of the Radio and Audio-Film Commission of the American Council of Christian Churches; since 1971, has been Founder, President, and Director of THE BIBLE FOR TODAY; since 1978, has been President of the DEAN BURGON SOCIETY; has produced over 700 other studies, booklets, cassettes, or VCR's on various topics; and is heard on both a five-minute daily and thirty-minute weekly radio program IN DEFENSE OF TRADITIONAL BIBLE TEXTS, presently on 25 stations. Dr. and Mrs. Waite have been married since 1948; they have four sons, one daughter, and, at present, eight grandchildren.

Order Blank (p.1)

Name:_____

Address:_____

City & State:_____Zip:_____

Credit Card #:_____Expires:_____

[ ] Enclosed is $_____. Send _____copy(ies) of *Summary of The Traditional Text* (36 pages) each for a GIFT of $3 +$2 P&H) Ask for quantity prices on this new book!

[ ] Send *The Revision Revised* by Dean Burgon ($25 + $4) A hardback book c. 640 pages in length. Due out 12/96.

[ ] Send *The Last 12 Verses of Mark* by Dean Burgon ($15+$4) A perfect bound paperback book c. 400 pages in length.

[ ] Send *The Traditional Text* by Dean Burgon ($15 + $4)

[ ] Send *The Causes of Corruption* by Dean Burgon ($14 + $4)

[ ] Send *Inspiration and Interpretation*, Dean Burgon ($25+$4)

[ ]Send *Contemporary Eng. Version Exposed*, DAW ($3+$2)

[ ] Send the "DBS Articles of Faith & Organization" (N.C.)

[ ] Send Brochure #1: "900 Titles Defending KJB/TR" (N.C.)

[ ] Send information on DBS pamphlets on KJB & TR (N.C.)

Send or Call Orders to:
THE BIBLE FOR TODAY
900 Park Ave., Collingswood, NJ 08108
Phone: 609-854-4452; FAX:--2464; Orders: 1-800 JOHN 10:9
E-Mail Orders: BFT@BibleForToday.org; Credit Cards OK

Order Blank (p.2)

Name:_____

Address:_____

City & State:_____Zip:_____

Credit Card #:_____Expires:_____

Other Books on the King James Bible

[ ] Send *Westcott & Hort's Greek Text & Theory Refuted by Burgon's Revision Revised--Summarized* by Dr. D. A. Waite ($3.00 + $3+$2 P&H)

[ ] Send *Defending the King James Bible* Dr.Waite ($12+$4)

[ ] Send *Guide to Textual Criticism* by Edward Miller ($7 + $4)

[ ] Send *Heresies of Westcott & Hort* by Dr. Waite ($3+$3)

[ ] Send *Westcott's Denial of Resurrection*, Dr. Waite ($4+$3)

[ ] Send *Four Reasons for Defending KJB*, Dr. Waite ($2+$3)

[ ] Send *Vindicating Mark 16:9-20* by Dr. Waite ($3 + $3)

[ ] Send *Dean Burgon's Confidence in KJB* Dr. Waite ($3+$3)

[ ] Send *Readability of A.V. (KJB)* by D. A. Waite, Jr. ($5 + $3)

[ ] Send *NIV InclusiveLanguage Exposed* by DAW ($4+$3)

Send or Call Orders to:
THE BIBLE FOR TODAY
900 Park Ave., Collingswood, NJ 08108
Phone: 609-854-4452; FAX:--2464; Orders: 1-800 JOHN 10:9
E-Mail Orders: BFT@BibleForToday.org; Credit Cards OK

Send Gift Subscriptions

All gifts to Dean Burgon Society are tax deductible!

THE DEAN BURGON SOCIETY

Box 354 - Collingswood, Now Jersey 08108, U.S.A.,
Phone; (609) 854-4452; FAX: (609) 854-2464

Membership Form

I have a copy of the "Articles of faith. Operation and Organization" of The Dean Burgon Society, Incorporated. After reading these "Articles," I wish to state, by my signature below. that I believe in and accept such "Articles." I understand that my "Membership" is for one year and that I must renew my "Membership" at that time in order to remain a "Member" in good standing 6f the Society.

[ ] I wish to become a member of The Dean Burgon Society for the first time.

[ ] I wish to renew my membership subscription which has expired as of: _____

SIGNED:_____

DATE:_____

I enclose: **Attention: The Dean Burgon Society**
                    Box 354 - Collingswood, Now Jersey 0810&

*Membership Donation ($7.00/year) $_____
*Life Membership Donation ($50.00) $_____
*Additional Donation To The Society $_____
                                TOTAL: $_____

.Please PRINT In CAPITAL LETTERS your name and address below:

NAME:_____

ADDRESS: _____

CITY:_____

STATE: _____   ZIP: _____

Although I am not a member of **The Dean Burgon Society**, I do wish to subscribe to the **Newsletter**, by making a gift of $3.50 to the Society.

NAME:_____

ADDRESS: _____

CITY:_____

STATE: _____   ZIP: _____

*1 understand that, included in my first **$3.50 gift** accompanying any donation or order regardless of the amount of the order or donation, is my year's subscription to **The Dean Burgon Society NEWSLETTER**.

Canada & All Foreign Subscriptions $7.00 Yearly

Order Blank (p.1)

Name:_____

Address:_____

City & State:_____Zip:_____

*Credit Card #:*_____*Expires:*_____

[ ] Send *The Traditional Text* by Dean Burgon ($16 + $4)
   A hardback book, 384 pages in length.

[ ] Send *The Revision Revised* by Dean Burgon ($25 + $4)
   A hardback book, 640 pages in length.

[ ] Send *The Last 12 Verses of Mark* by Dean Burgon ($15+$4)
   A perfect bound paperback book 400 pages in length.

[ ] Send *The Causes of Corruption* by Dean Burgon ($15 + $4)

[ ] Send *Inspiration and Interpretation*, Dean Burgon ($25+$4)

[ ] Send *Foes of the King James Bible Refuted* by DAW ($9
   +$4 P&H) A perfect bound book, 164 pages in length.

[ ] Send *Summary of Traditional Text* by Dr. Waite ($3 + $2)

[ ] Send *Summary of Causes of Corruption*, DAW ($3+2 P&H)

[ ]Send *Contemporary Eng. Version Exposed*, DAW ($3+$2)

[ ] Send the "DBS Articles of Faith & Organization" (N.C.)

[ ] Send Brochure #1: "900 Titles Defending KJB/TR" (N.C.)

Send or Call Orders to:
THE DEAN BURGON SOCIETY
Box 354, Collingswood, NJ 08108, U.S.A.
Phone: 609-854-4452; FAX:--2464; Orders: 1-800 JOHN 10:9
E-Mail Orders: DBSN@Juno.com. Credit Cards are OK.

Order Blank (p.2)

Name:_____

Address:_____

City & State:_____Zip:_____

Credit Card#:_____Expires:_____

Other Materials on the KJB & T.R.

[ ] Send *Defending the King James Bible* by Dr.Waite $12+$4
A hardback book, indexed with study questions.

[ ] Send *Westcott & Hort's Greek Text & Theory Refuted by Burgon's Revision Revised—Summarized* by Dr. D. A. Waite ($3.00 + $3 P&H)

[ ] Send *Guide to Textual Criticism* by Edward Miller ($7 + $4)

[ ] Send *Heresies of Westcott & Hort* by Dr. Waite ($3+$3)

[ ] Send *Westcott's Denial of Resurrection*, Dr. Waite ($4+$3)

[ ] Send *Four Reasons for Defending KJB* by DAW ($2+$3)

[ ] Send *Vindicating Mark 16:9-20* by Dr. Waite ($3 + $3)

[ ] Send *Dean Burgon's Confidence in KJB* by DAW ($3+$3)

[ ] Send *Readability of A.V. (KJB)* by D. A. Waite, Jr. ($5 + $3)

[ ] Send *NIV Inclusive Language Exposed* by DAW ($4+$3)

[ ] Send *23 Hours of KJB Seminar (4 videos)* by DAW ($50.00)

Send or Call Orders to:
THE DEAN BURGON SOCIETY
Box 354, Collingswood, NJ 08108, U.S.A.
Phone: 609-854-4452; FAX:--2464; Orders: 1-800 JOHN 10:9
E-Mail Orders: DBSN@Juno.com. Credit Cards are OK.

Order Blank (p.3)

Name:_____

Address:_____

City & State:_____Zip:_____

Credit Card#:_____Expires:_____

More Materials on the KJB &T.R.

[ ] Send *Scrtvener's Greek New Testament Underlying the King James Bible*, hardback, $14+$4 P&H

[ ] Send *Why Not the King James Bible?--An Answer to James White's KJVO Book* by Dr. K. D. DiVietro, $9+$4 P&H

[ ] Send *Forever Settled--Bible Documents & History Survey* by Dr. Jack Moorman, $21+$4 P&H

[ ] Send *Early Church Fathers & the A.V.--A Demonstration* by Dr. Jack Moorman, $6 + $4 P&H.

[ ] Send *When the KJB Departs from the So-Called "Majority Text"* by Dr. Jack Moorman, $16 + $4 P&H

[ ] Send *Missing in Modern Bibles--Nestle-Aland & NIV Errors* by Dr. Jack Moorman, $8 + $4 P&H

[ ] Send *The Doctrinal Heart of the Bible--Removed from Modern Versions* by Dr. Jack Moorman, VCR, $15 +$4 P&H

[ ] Send *Modern Bibles--The Dark* Secret by Dr. Jack Moorman, $3 + $2 P&H

[ ] Send *Early Manuscripts and the A.V.--A Closer* Look, by Dr. Jack Moorman, $15 + $4 P&H

Send or Call Orders to:
THE DEAN BURGON SOCIETY
Box 354, Collingswood, NJ 08108, U.S.A.
Phone: 609-854-4452; FAX:--2464; Orders: 1-800 JOHN 10:9
E-Mail Orders: DBSN@Juno.com. Credit Cards are OK.